Professing Sincerity

Susan B. Rosenbaum

Professing Sincerity

Modern Lyric Poetry, Commercial Culture, and the Crisis in Reading

University of Virginia Press
Charlottesville and London

University of Virginia Press
© 2007 by the Rector and Visitors of the University of Virginia
All rights reserved
Printed in the United States of America on acid-free paper

First published 2007

9 8 7 6 5 4 3 2 1

Library of Congress Cataloging-in-Publication Data

Rosenbaum, Susan B., 1968–
   Professing sincerity : modern lyric poetry, commercial culture, and the crisis in
reading / Susan B. Rosenbaum.
         p.   cm.
   Includes bibliographical references and index.
   ISBN-13: 978-0-8139-2610-0 (alk. paper)
   1. Sincerity in literature. 2. English poetry—18th century—History and
criticism. 3. English poetry—19th century—History and criticism.
4. Romanticism—England. 5. American poetry—20th century—History and
criticism. 6. Authors and readers. I. Title.
   PR575.S52R67 2007
   821'.609353—dc22

                                                               2006032724

Historicism contents itself with establishing a causal connection between various moments in history. But no fact that is a cause is for that very reason historical. It became historical posthumously, as it were, through events that may be separated from it by thousands of years. A historian who takes this as his point of departure stops telling the sequence of events like the beads of a rosary. Instead, he grasps the constellation which his own era has formed with a definite earlier one.

—Walter Benjamin, *Theses on the Philosophy of History*

Contents

Acknowledgments

This book has proven to be as much a geographical as a personal and intellectual journey, accompanying me from Ann Arbor to Virginia, Chicago, and Georgia, and benefiting in ways both small and large from the colleagues, friends, and loved ones who have made the journey both rewarding and pleasurable.

This project would not have come to fruition without the inspired teaching and guidance of my dissertation committee at the University of Michigan. Marlon Ross's great knowledge, critical acumen, and unstinting generosity as a mentor have sustained me at every turn; he exemplifies what the profession can be. Rei Terada's perceptive readings have always challenged me to extend my thinking, and her advice and friendship at some difficult moments in the writing of the book made all the difference. Marjorie Levinson's kinetic seminars resulted in the juxtapositions at the center of this book: her critical imagination, intellectual integrity, and great warmth continue to inspire me. Ross Chambers signed on to the dissertation from Australia, and for his generosity of spirit I am grateful: his incisive comments proved invaluable as I wrote the book. Thanks also to Geoff Eley, whose interdisciplinary seminar on modernity was for many of us a life-changing event.

I am indebted to Cathie Brettschneider, my editor at the University of Virginia Press, for her support of this project and her patience in seeing it through the revision process. I would also like to thank the two anonymous readers for the University of Virginia Press, whose insightful readings and astute suggestions pushed me to test my assumptions and clarify my argument in ways that have immeasurably strengthened the book.

Many friends and colleagues have contributed to the book by reading and commenting on chapter drafts, and by discussing the issues it raises. My graduate cohort from Michigan has provided unfailing friendship and support, as well as commentary on the book from its earliest to its latest stages: my heartfelt thanks to Jani Scandura, Eliza Richards, Elizabeth Allen, David Anthony, Erin Desmond, and Christine Cooper. My colleagues at Loyola University Chicago—David Chinitz, Chris Castiglia, Pamela Caughie, Joyce Wexler, Phoebe Stein-Davis, and Danielle Glassmeyer—provided feedback and intellectual support that I continue to appreciate. Colleagues at the University of Georgia have given generous feedback on the manuscript and book proposal: particular thanks to Adam Parkes, Tricia Lootens, Kris Boudreau, Roxanne Eberle, Andrew Cole, Jed Rasula, Doug Anderson, Anne Williams, Rachel Gabara, Aidan Wasley, Anne Mallory, and Sujata Iyengar. Suzanne Kaufman and Bill Sites provided wise counsel and wonderful friendship throughout the writing of the book. Thanks also to Brian Henry for sharing his vast knowledge of poetry, and to Romita Ray for her art historical wisdom. Seminars and panels at the Modernist Studies Association provided a fertile location for the exchange of ideas, and I am grateful to Marsha Bryant and Elizabeth Bergmann-Loizeaux for their feedback and help. Thanks also to Lanny Hammer for his advice on a draft of the introduction, and more generally for introducing me to the lifelong joy of reading Bishop. The Elizabeth Bishop Society has introduced me to many wonderful people; special thanks to Tom Travisano for his judicious advice and to Jonathan Ellis for his insightful suggestions on the introduction.

Students at Loyola University and the University of Georgia in my courses on confessional literature have helped me to form the ideas in this book: particular thanks to Melissa Crowe, Liz Beasley, Josh Schneiderman, Ann Fievet, Megan Leroy, Adam Hardigree, Scott Gilbertson, Julie Orlemanski, and Paul Killebrew. For their able research assistance I am grateful to Scott Reed and Melissa King.

I am grateful to a number of institutions that have provided fellowships for research and writing. A Mellon Foundation Dissertation Grant provided a year of support, and the Rackham Graduate School at the University of Michigan provided a semester's teaching release. At Loyola University Chicago I benefited from a semester's leave at the Gannon Center for Women and Leadership: my warm thanks to Carolyn Farrell and the Center's staff. I am grateful to the University of Georgia Center for the Humanities and Arts, which provided a semester's fellowship that helped in the final stages of this book. The University of Georgia Research Foundation has provided much-appreciated grants for travel and research.

Finally, my thanks to my family, whose love, help, and patience have made this journey possible: to all the Sopers (Skip, Dick, Les, Tony, Ariella, Emily); Susan Storch and in memory of Margot Honey; Karen and Ellen

Rosenbaum; Joel Rosenbaum and Connie Drysdale. To my mother, Nancy Honey Rosenbaum, a special thanks for her unquestioning support of these literary endeavors. My deepest gratitude to Steven Soper, the person whose love, help, and unfailing sense of humor have seen me through every day and every word of this book. And finally, to Natalie, whose first words have coincided with the final words of this book.

I am grateful to Special Collections at Vassar College Libraries for their permission to quote from unpublished materials by Elizabeth Bishop, Robert Lowell, Anne Sexton, and James Merrill. I have appreciated the expert help of Nancy MacKechnie, now retired, and Dean Rogers in Special Collections at Vassar, as well as the able assistance of Virginia Fox at Farrar, Straus & Giroux.

Reprinted by permission of Farrar, Straus & Giroux, LLC:

Excerpts from *The Collected Prose* by Elizabeth Bishop. © 1984 by Alice Helen Methfessel. Excerpts from *The Complete Poems, 1927–1979* by Elizabeth Bishop. © 1979, 1983 by Alice Helen Methfessel. Excerpts from *One Art: Letters* by Elizabeth Bishop, selected and edited by Robert Giroux. © 1994 by Alice Methfessel. Excerpts from *The Letters of Robert Lowell* by Robert Lowell. © 2005 by Harriet Lowell and Sheridan Lowell. Excerpts from "Notes for Poetry Reviews," "Gallery Note for Wesley Wehr," "True Confessions," marginal notes for "The Bees," and "Remarks on Translation" by Elizabeth Bishop. © 2007 by Alice Helen Methfessel. Reprinted by permission of Farrar, Straus & Giroux, LLC, on behalf of the Elizabeth Bishop Estate.

Excerpts from unpublished letters written by Robert Lowell to Elizabeth Bishop from the forthcoming volume *Letters between Elizabeth Bishop and Robert Lowell.* © 2007 by Harriet Lowell and Sheridan Lowell. Reprinted by permission of Farrar, Straus & Giroux, LLC, on behalf of the Robert Lowell Estate.

Excerpt from the unpublished letter of James Merrill to Elizabeth Bishop used with the permission of the Executors of the Estate of James Merrill, J. D. McClatchy and Stephen Yenser. © 2006.

Excerpts from *Lunch Poems,* © 1964 by Frank O'Hara, used by permission of City Lights Books. Excerpts from *The Collected Poems of Frank O'Hara,* © 1971 by Maureen Granville-Smith, Administratrix of the Estate of Frank O'Hara, used by permission of Alfred A. Knopf, a division of Random House, Inc.

Excerpt from the unpublished letter of Anne Sexton to Elizabeth Bishop reprinted by permission of SLL/Sterling Lord Literistic, Inc. © by Anne

Sexton. Excerpt from "The Play," from *The Awful Rowing Toward God* by Anne Sexton, © 1975 by Loring Conant Jr., Executor of the Estate of Anne Sexton, reprinted by permission of Houghton Mifflin Company.

Reprinted by permission of HarperCollins Publishers and Faber & Faber Ltd.: Excerpts from *Ariel,* © 1961, 1962, 1963, 1964, 1965, 1966 by Ted Hughes, foreword by Robert Lowell; *Crossing the Water,* © 1962 by Ted Hughes; *The Collected Poems of Sylvia Plath,* © 1960, 1965, 1971, 1981 by the Estate of Sylvia Plath; and editorial material © 1981 by Ted Hughes.

A portion of chapter 2 was published in an earlier version as "Frank O'Hara, Flaneur of New York," in *The Scene of My Selves: New Work on New York School Poets,* edited by Terence Diggory and Stephen Paul Miller (Orono, ME: National Poetry Foundation, 2001). An earlier version of chapter 5 appeared as "'A Thing Unknown, Without a Name': Anne Laetitia Barbauld and the Illegible Signature," in *Studies in Romanticism* 40.3 (Fall 2001): 369–99. Reprinted courtesy of the Trustees of Boston University. A section of chapter 6 is reprinted with permission from *Reading the Middle Generation Anew,* edited by Eric Haralson, published by the University of Iowa Press. I am grateful for the permission to reprint these materials.

Introduction

Western man has become a confessing animal. Whence a metamorphosis in literature: we have passed from a pleasure to be recounted and heard, centering on the heroic or marvelous narration of "trials" of bravery or sainthood, to a literature ordered according to the infinite task of extracting from the depths of oneself, in between the words, a truth which the very form of confession holds out like a shimmering mirage.

—Michel Foucault, *History of Sexuality*, vol. 1

I have displayed myself as I was, as vile and despicable when my behaviour was such, as good, generous, and noble when I was so. I have bared my secret soul as Thou thyself hast seen it, Eternal Being! So let the numberless legion of my fellow men gather round me, and hear my confessions. Let them groan at my depravities, and blush for my misdeeds. But let each one of them reveal his heart at the foot of Thy throne with equal sincerity, and may any man who dares, say "I was a better man than he."

—Jean-Jacques Rousseau, *Confessions*

Sincerity and Confessional Culture

Writers over the past two centuries have more than embraced Rousseau's challenge to reveal their hearts with equal sincerity. One has only to survey the popular media of the past decade to recognize that Rousseau's influence persists: we live in a confessional culture, surrounded by tell-all talk shows, Internet diaries, best-selling memoirs, and autobiographical

poems.[1] Regardless of the forum, these autobiographical practices rely on
the rhetoric of sincerity, the range of expressive conventions used to mark
the voice, figure, and experience of the first-person speaker as that of the
author, including claims to originality, spontaneity, authenticity, artless-
ness, and immediacy. Claims to sincerity in autobiographical texts make
the essentially moral promise that the author is who she says she is and that
she means what she says: in short, that she speaks openly and honestly. De-
spite the widespread fascination with private lives made public, however,
authorial claims to sincerity are as likely to inspire irony and skepticism as
trust; accusations of fictionalization, sensationalism, and "selling out" are
as rife as the memoirs that line bookstore shelves. "Sincerity" seems a naive
term in the age of "spin." As Lionel Trilling remarked in his 1972 study of
sincerity, "When we hear it, we are conscious of the anachronism which
touches it with quaintness. If we speak it, we are likely to do so with either
discomfort or irony" (*Sincerity and Authenticity*, 6).

But there is ample precedent for such skepticism. We might look to
American "confessional" poetry of the 1950s and '60s, and to the reception
of a poet such as Anne Sexton. Sexton dramatized autobiographical experi-
ence in her poetry, violating conventions of poetic decorum by addressing
taboo subjects such as abortion, menstruation, adultery, incest, and mental
illness. Revealing experience that was normally kept hidden abetted Sex-
ton's claim to the sincerity of her first-person lyrics, but also contributed to
her theatricality and showmanship: she was renowned for her glamour, as
displayed in her author's photos; for her dramatic readings as one of the
"best-paid poetry performers in America"; and for bridging poetry and pop
culture by singing her lyrics with a chamber rock band, "Anne Sexton and
Her Kind."[2] Sexton acknowledged the commercial aspects of poetic perfor-
mance, writing to Elizabeth Bishop that she felt like a "whore" on the uni-
versity reading circuit and that she regarded the reading as a strange "sort
of show—an act such as a comedian has."[3] She critically engaged the mean-
ing of this show in "The Play," asking her audience to consider the odd
transaction of watching her perform her everyday dramas in public:

> It is difficult for one woman
> to act out a whole play.
> the play is my life,
> my solo act
> . . . .
> It was a bad performance.
> That's because I'm the only actor
> and there are few humans whose lives

will make an interesting play.
Don't you agree?   (*Complete Poems*, 440–41)

Sexton's performances allowed her to cultivate literary celebrity but also to insist on her sincerity by challenging distinctions between good versus bad poetry, proper versus shameful conduct, public versus private drama.

No poet of the era has received a more divided reception: while Sexton's poetry has proven extremely popular, reaching an audience beyond poets and academics, it has also triggered outraged, virulent criticism, exemplified by Charles Gullans's review of *Live or Die* (1966).[4] Gullans equates the book with a psychiatric session, arguing, "It is painful, embarrassing, and irritating. The immediacy and terror of her problem are painful; the personal character of the confessional detail is embarrassing; and the tone of hysterical melodrama which pervades most of the writing is finally irritating. Either this is the poetry of a monstrous self-indulgence, in which case it is despicable; or it is documentation of a neurosis, in which case to pretend to speak of it as literature at all is simply silly" (in McClatchy, *Anne Sexton*, 131–32). Gullans suggests that Sexton's poems utterly lack artifice, in which case "they are not poems, they are documents of modern psychiatry"; or the poems lack sincerity, revealing shameful experience for self-indulgent ends. Either way, Gullans finds Sexton guilty of the "neo-Romantic stereotype" that "says that anyone who is sensitive and suffers is a poet" (131). Sexton's betrayal of "critical standards," Gullans implies, involves the use of private pain to appeal to her readers' voyeuristic interest. Gullans's perspective on confessional poetry, if extreme, was echoed by other critics of the period such as Anne Stevenson, who found Sylvia Plath's poetry a symptom of the "extremism, self-indulgence, [and] narcissism" of the "latter-day Romantics" (*Bitter Fame*, 79–81).

And yet the writers of the romantic era, although they popularized the cult of sincere self-expression, were often suspicious of it. Richard Hurd set the stage for this skepticism, commenting in 1765 that "sincerity, or a scrupulous regard to truth in all our conversation and behaviours, how specious so ever it may be in theory, is a thing impossible in practice" (*Moral and Political Dialogues*, 5). A compelling precursor to Sexton in this regard is Mary Darby Robinson, a popular poet and actress on the London stage in the late eighteenth century who became the mistress of the Prince of Wales and a figure of public scandal and intrigue, famously painted by Reynolds and satirized as a prostitute in cartoons by Gillray.[5] Aware of these conflicting public images, Robinson emphasized the sincerity of her self-portraits, as in "Stanzas to a Friend, Who Desired to Have my Portrait" (*Selected Poems*, 139–42). The occasion of the poem—the friend's desire for a painted portrait of the poet, with "looks eternally the same, and lips that never move"—suggests the ways in which Robinson's image had become subject to the vicissitudes of celebrity and public sentiment (Mellor, "Making an Exhibition," 22). Robinson asserts control by "painting" a portrait comprised of her "frank confession" (line 36). Pronouncing herself "no sinner, yet no saint" (line 108), Robinson promises that her conduct and demeanor convey her true intentions:

> My faults I own—my virtues know
> . . . .
> And Candour is my pride:
> I always speak what I believe;
> I know not if I can deceive;
> Because I never tried.   (lines 40, 45–48)

Despite such avowals of honesty, Robinson's poetry was trailed by skeptical accounts of her scandalous life. As one reviewer of her *Poetical Works* argued, "The private character of an author"—the question of whether the poems "proceed from the pen of vice or virtue"—must influence the reading of poetry. Reminding readers of the notorious person behind the poetic persona, the reviewer cites an ode that purports to "the genuine expression of feeling, but which affords in fact only that kind of unmeaning exaggeration and decorated inanity which are the miserable resources of a cold heart, a vitiated taste, and a defective genius" (in Robinson, *Selected Poems,* 388–90). Sincerity, it turns out, has long been read as duplicity, a rhetoric that harbors ulterior designs: as Oscar Wilde quipped ironically in *Dorian Gray,* "Being natural is simply a pose, and the most irritating pose I know."

This book examines a persistent conflict in Anglo-American literary culture: its simultaneous investment in and deep suspicion of the rhetoric of sincerity. Most critical studies have upheld an opposition between sincerity as a moral ideal of honest expression and the self-interested performances of a profit-driven society, an opposition nowhere more evident than in the history of lyric poetry. Sincerity has dominated both the reading and writing of Anglo-American poetry since the late eighteenth century, influencing the widespread understanding of the lyric poem as a site of private, individual expression, an aesthetic and moral refuge from the taint of commercial culture. In contrast, *Professing Sincerity* demonstrates that sincerity in the romantic and postromantic lyric in many ways was a product of commercial culture: poets who made a living from their writing sold the moral promise that their lyrics were sincere, and engaged this conflict in their work. On the one hand, through textual claims to sincerity, poets addressed

moral anxieties about the authenticity, autonomy, and transparency of lit-
erature written in and for a market. On the other hand, by performing their
"private" lives and feelings in public, poets marketed the self, cultivated
celebrity, and advanced professional careers. Professing sincerity was a
moral practice, but it was also good business. This book examines the vexed
history of this conflict, focusing on two moments—that of British roman-
tic and post-1945 American poetry—when anxieties about the commercial
nature of sincerity became prominent.

These moments reveal the contours of a long-standing culture of sensi-
bility (extending from roughly the mid-eighteenth century to the present)
in which the practice of writing for a literary marketplace generates a re-
current anxiety about whether authors can be trusted, resulting in a para-
doxical desire for and deep skepticism of sincerity's rhetorical forms. Sin-
cerity stands at the center of a persistent crisis in reading the lyric, a crisis
that stems from the blurring of the moral ideals and commercial practices
of authorship. How could readers distinguish "true" claims to sincerity
from calculated performances of honesty? The text written for profit might
masquerade as a sincere text written for moral ends, and how would the
reader know? Professional authorship, as it began to supplant patronage in
the late eighteenth century, brought these readerly anxieties to the fore. The
commercial mediation of texts, the increasing anonymity of market ex-
change, and the specter of self-interest all threatened to compromise the
ideal of a shared moral trust that could ground social relations and guaran-
tee the stability and readability of an author's identity, intentions, and val-
ues. To cite Wordsworth, what moral values would bind together a social
fabric "melted and reduced / To one identity by differences / that have no
law, no meaning, and no end?" (*Prelude*, 7.703–5). While claims to sincerity
in autobiographical writing promise access to the "real" author, such claims
"cannot be verified," as writers from St. Augustine to Paul de Man have
pointed out.[6] And poets, in turn, have often emphasized the fictive nature
of their textual doubles; Robert Lowell stated that he "tinker[ed] with fact"
so as to make the reader "believe he was getting the *real* Robert Lowell" (*In-
terviews and Memoirs,* 57), while Anne Sexton argued that to make the poem
"clear and dramatic" the poet can "even lie" about her life (*No Evil Star,* 75).
Built into the textual promise of sincerity was its opacity—the necessity
of artifice, fiction, and theatricality. Fueling the distrust of the rhetoric of
sincerity was its status *as a rhetoric.*

These doubts about the truthfulness of the rhetoric of sincerity were
epistemological. As the self became the locus for questions of origins and
origination, truth and truth telling, during the Renaissance, it also be-
came subject to new distrust: the rhetoric of sincerity sought to mediate

this distrust by promising a congruence between outer expression and inner feeling (Martin, "Inventing Sincerity," 1312). By the eighteenth century, concern about the self as a ground for truth claims came to center on the "origins and locations of feelings." Adela Pinch points out that writers tried to "claim their emotions as the guarantors of their individuality" but found feelings to be "autonomous entities that do not always belong to individuals but rather wander extravagantly from one person to another" (*Strange Fits*, 3). As my discussion of Robinson and Sexton suggests, anxieties about the "extravagant" nature of feeling were noticeably heightened around commercial culture and have tended to center on women, who entered the literary marketplace in large numbers in the late eighteenth century. The poetry of Wordsworth or Lowell, for instance, has been less likely to generate the kinds of responses Robinson and Sexton received. Thus, while the vast scholarship on the modern individual, subjectivity, and emotion attests to the variety of historical and theoretical perspectives one might use to elucidate issues of sincerity, this book emphasizes the importance of gender and commercial culture to epistemological concerns about self-expression.[7] The expansion of commercial culture in the eighteenth century engendered deep-seated moral anxieties about the marketing, sale, and circulation of "private" expression, anxieties that have intensified at particular moments since the eighteenth century but which have consistently articulated points of epistemological impasse: the entanglement of truth and fiction, sincerity and theatricality, moral conduct and commercial practices.

Indeed, the dynamic of reception that this book examines—extending from the romantics to the poststructuralists—reveals a persistent problem in how to read conventions of sincerity. Debates about how and why readers should connect or disconnect the biographical author and her textual speakers, the art and the life, have dominated readings of the lyric from the openly moral tenor of late-eighteenth- and nineteenth-century biographical criticism to current poststructuralist and ideological approaches. Skepticism about authorial claims to sincerity has consistently been matched by speculation about the relationship between author and textual speaker, a desire for sincerity enjoined to a pleasure in tracking where it hesitates: even Paul de Man's essays on Rousseau's *Confessions* have been read as encrypted confessions, an implicit commentary on de Man's own past "misdeeds."[8] Confession is historically a ritual for the production of individual truth in a religious context; that confession becomes a dominant frame for reading autobiographical literature in a modern and largely secular culture speaks to the deep desire for and skepticism of the author as a moral ground for truth claims.[9] This study demonstrates how a "confessional culture" influences habits of reading conventions of sincerity in the lyric, and, in turn, how poets respond to this climate of reception through their uses of the rhetoric of sincerity. I show that the readings of the romantic era that rely on a biographical author and poststructuralist readings that insist on the death of the author partake of—indeed, are overdetermined by—an uninterrogated, long-standing opposition between sincere expression and debased performance, and that both kinds of reading articulate deep-seated moral anxieties about literary commerce. Thus the figure of the author haunts the modern lyric, despite persistent and sophisticated efforts on the part of poets and recent critics not simply to connect the lyric to the biographical author but to evacuate it, de-privatize it, ironize it, de-lyricize it.

Rather than repeat the long-standing opposition between sincere expression and debased performance, I draw out poets' complex engagements with this very problem. Romantic and post-1945 poets were not only aware of the contradictions of selling sincerity, and of the consequent "crisis in reading," but grasped in this dilemma the potential for internal critique. Approaching romantic and postromantic lyric through its commercial endeavors, I find not a history of unwavering belief in the expression of a transparent, autonomous self, but poets' material and critical engagements with the difficulty or impossibility of this ideal.[10] Thus we can not assume that the use of the rhetoric of sincerity implies an oppositional stance toward or a moral critique of commercial culture. In short, poets were much more savvy about the merging of moral and commercial practices of authorship than has been recognized, and have long negotiated the fictive and commercial nature of their textual selves. What Foucault calls the "author function" is not simply an invention or psychologizing projection of naive or biographically obsessed readers who seek to unify, explain, and anchor the text,[11] but is a figure that has been complexly mobilized by poets to respond to the contradictions and pressures of writing professionally and to influence the commercial channels through which their poetic texts circulate.

For instance, Wordsworth responded to the risk that his autobiographical *Prelude* would be read as self-advertisement by treating it as an epitaph to a younger self, a textual strategy confirmed by his decision to postpone publication until after his death. In this way he positioned his future readers not as consumers but as elegiac mourners, guided in their acts of sincere remembrance by the figure of the poet himself. This textual act served to justify his efforts to extend the term of copyright, an effort commensurate with a moral practice of elegiac memory. In contrast, Sylvia Plath was less interested in serving as moral exemplar than in turning the tables on her readers. Revealing that the female poet must perform moral purity and economic disinterest to attain commercial success, Plath's first-person lyrics challenge her audience to consider their own role in drawing moral fault lines between sincerity and performance, poet and persona, lyric and commodity. In other words, this book shows that the lyric poem is not simply an idealizing refuge from or debased acquiescence to the problems of modern society, but is a stage on which the moral expectations of literary authorship have been variously performed, interrogated, and remade in concert with a commercializing literary world. This remaking is not only moral but formal in nature: in looking at sincere ideals in the context of the literary market, I suggest that the forms feelings take are shaped by anxieties about feeling taking a potentially commodified form. The desire for poetic value to inhere in the poet's personal conduct, or, conversely, in a poem's textual or aesthetic qualities distinct from the poet's biography, articulates a sincere ideal that is put under pressure in the modern lyric, with the lyric's dominant modes, forms, and conventions shaped by varied engagements with this pressure.

This book assumes sincerity's importance to Anglo-American poetry since the late eighteenth century, but it does not trace this history in linear fashion. Rather, I compare an early and late moment in a genealogy of what Lauren Berlant calls the "unfinished business of sentimentality" ("Poor Eliza," 644). Each section of the book explores how both a British romantic and a post-1945 American poet use a similar trope of sincerity to interrogate the supposed opposition between sincerity and theatricality, lyric and commercial culture. This method of historical constellation allows me to provide a detailed understanding of how commercial, professional, and aesthetic pressures converge to influence specific negotiations of conventions of sincerity. At both moments I study, the profession of letters undergoes vast change, and sincerity becomes a highly contested rhetoric among poets and their readers. Sincerity emerged as the dominant rhetoric of poetry in late-eighteenth-century England, as aristocratic patronage shifted to the patronage of a broader reading public, and changes in legal and literary understandings of property permitted writers to make a living by selling their work to booksellers. Following World War II, American poets experienced the ever-accelerating growth of what Elizabeth Bishop termed "Poetry as Big Business" (*One Art*, 201–2): the rise of the university as an institutional patron of poetry, the emergence of the publishing house as international corporation, and a culture of literary celebrity that at times rivaled the Hollywood star system. In contrast to their modernist precursors, many postwar poets explicitly embraced the rhetoric of sincerity as a means of claiming the lyric voice as their own (Tebbel, *Between Covers*, 421, 444–49). Juxtaposing romantic and postmodern poets while paying close attention to differences of historical context, I illuminate striking continuities both in the uses of conventions of sincerity and in the anxieties that plague their reception. My use of juxtaposition suggests the need for new practices of reading that can explain cultural as well as aesthetic reasons for the repeated emergence of the rhetoric of sincerity.

Thus, although literary influence is certainly at work (the postwar poets I study call themselves minor, belated, and postromantics),[12] influence is not at the center of this book. Studies that are solely literary in focus tend to reinforce an artificial distinction between the lyric and material conditions of authorship, perpetuating the embedded moral distinctions my study challenges, between sincerity and theatricality, aesthetics and markets, the poet and other kinds of professional writers. For instance, Deborah Forbes has recently described the role of sincerity in the romantic tradition, but does so in strictly aesthetic terms, reaffirming the long-standing moral opposition between lyric poetry and commercial culture.[13] Ignoring the role of commerce and the epistemological anxieties that it engenders, Forbes and others are unable to explain *why* sincerity is such a persistent and anxiously debated rhetoric of lyric from the late eighteenth century onward. Such studies are symptomatic of the very problem in reading conventions of sincerity that this book seeks to bring to light.

The organization of academic literary study around the literary period has exacerbated this problem, with literary history defined by a series of ruptures between successive periods and literary schools. In the case of both the romantic and the confessional poets, the oppositions are those of the authority of the self versus the authority of tradition, feeling versus reason, excess versus restraint, and so forth. Recent scholarship has sought to complicate this understanding of rupture and even the logic of the literary period, but has done so locally.[14] In focusing on confessional poetry as solely a mid- or late-twentieth-century American phenomenon,[15] we risk losing sight of the poetry's role in a longer tradition of sincerity; conversely, while romanticists see the need for scholars of later periods to address the implications of their work, the reverse is less often true, and we have often overlooked the extent to which modernist ideals define approaches to romantic-era literature. Scholarship on conventions of sincerity—whether in the late eighteenth, nineteenth, or twentieth centuries—could benefit from recognition of a shared problematic connected to the professionalization of literature and the commercialization of sentiment. This recognition can help us to place reactions against sentiment in historical perspective, not as a radical departure from the culture of sensibility but as part of the epistemological debates that characterize it. With this dialogue in mind, I necessarily build on scholarship not only in romantic and postmodern studies but also in Victorian and modernist studies, all of which contribute to a broader field that Julie Ellison usefully terms "sensibility studies" (*Cato's Tears*, 4).

In privileging sensibility, this book challenges the legacy of what Suzanne Clark calls "modernist anti-sentimentalism," joining recent scholarship that explores how twentieth-century literary culture extends and revises—rather than simply rejects—sentimental logics.[16] Work on the marketing of modernism contributes to this effort by arguing that modernist aesthetics are part of rather than an aberration from the commercial dynamics I explore here.[17] Avant-garde women writers such as Gertrude Stein and Mina Loy might be studied less for their rejection of sentiment than for their radical renegotiation of it, and work such as Sianne Ngai's on "Ugly Feelings" and Maggie Nelson's on women and the New York School chart this path.[18] Scholars working on a number of nineteenth-century writers have challenged the antisentimental bias and the ways in which it has occluded the complex role of sentiment, sincerity, and theatricality in Victorian literature and culture.[19]

Similarly, a variety of critics have shown that modernist poetics, even those predicated on resistance to autobiography and to biographical reading, remain deeply concerned with issues of sincerity. Pound and Eliot define the "impersonal" lyric against the expectation that the poet is the lyric speaker, associating nineteenth-century literature with a commercially inflected "sentimentality": the dramatic monologue, the mask, and Eliot's notion of impersonality position the poetic persona as a created thing distinct from the poet, suggesting that questions of sincerity pertain to the poem rather than to the poet. Robert Langbaum and Carol Christ have pointed out that this tendency is consistent with rather than a radical departure from the romantic and Victorian lyric, however, and Helen Vendler suggests that we can read modernist personae and polyvocality as forms of "disguised autobiography."[20] In their attempts to resist the conflation of poet and lyric speaker, many modernists refigure sincerity, associating it not with the person of the poet or with dramatic personae but with precisionist techniques of making the poem; Bonnie Costello (*Marianne Moore*) and others point out that sincerity remains a guiding moral concern in imagist and objectivist poetics, for poets such as Moore, Pound, Olson, and Bishop.[21] Work on the discourse of authenticity in Harlem Renaissance writing indicates the importance of the rhetoric of sincerity to African American modernism even while race necessarily complicates understandings of sincerity.[22] Modernists in the surrealist vein relocate sincerity to a new site of spontaneous expression—unconscious or automatic processes—while critiquing notions of the singular, coherent author. Today the first-person autobiographical lyric remains a popular form, but we also see the skeptical inheritances of modernism in experimental poetry (whether language-oriented or lyric) that explodes notions of speaker, voice, and author. That the first-person lyric has long been involved in a similar interrogation of voice and author is a less familiar but no less important insight.[23] Rather than rely on assumed distinctions between kinds or styles of lyric (autobiographical, personal, impersonal, dramatic), then, I emphasize the conflicts that inform the rhetorical choices of poets and their readers, arguing that stances regarding the "sincere" or "theatrical" possibilities of voice and speaker cannot be separated from—and become legible in—a culture riven by competing moral and commercial demands.[24]

In revealing a constellation of distinct historical moments, I seek to initiate new ways of thinking about this longer history. My goals are heuristic rather than comprehensive: this book aims to inspire readers to consider why Anglo-American literary culture simultaneously desires and distrusts the rhetoric of sincerity; to think about issues of sincerity with greater complexity, moving past the conventional moralizing opposition between sincerity and theatricality, lyric and commercial culture; and, finally, to reflect on how the professionalization of letters has shaped understandings of authorship, genre, and literary history.

Professing Sincerity: Literary Property and the Profession of Authorship

It is telling that the concept of sincerity, as it enters European culture, comes to mean the absence of artifice: sincerity is constituted by that which threatens it. And this threat, beginning in the sixteenth century, is consistently attributed to a theatricality of representation associated with acting, the theater, and, as Jean Christophe-Agnew has argued, with secular, market culture (*Worlds Apart*, 99–114). Most studies of the literature of sincerity suggest that during the Renaissance, sincerity becomes a moral category. Lionel Trilling notes that in its earliest uses in the sixteenth century, sincerity means "clean, or sound, or pure" and referred primarily to things rather than people (*Sincerity and Authenticity*, 12), but "it soon came to mean the absence of dissimulation or feigning or pretence" (13). The Puritans in particular opposed sincerity and the theater, resulting in what Jonas Barish calls "the anti-theatrical prejudice"; this moral bias against acting and the theater gained influence in the sixteenth and seventeenth centuries, but it persists into our own day.

Critics have long examined sincerity and theatricality in resolutely op-
positional terms, sounding variations on a persistent theme. On the one
hand, they have read the literature of sincerity as morally idealistic, anti-
theatrical, unmediated or unaware of mediation, naive about or transcen-
dent of consumer culture; on the other hand, they have read it as morally
bankrupt, theatrical, duplicitous, clichéd, melodramatic, utterly absorbed
into consumer culture. Historians have documented sincerity's role as a
moral ideal opposed to a theatricality associated with commercial culture,
especially in Puritan thought, while recent scholars have reconsidered the
role of theatricality in modern culture by challenging the antitheatrical prej-
udice.[25] While both literatures have historicized and contested the opposi-
tion between sincerity and theatricality, in studies of the lyric this oppo-
sition remains stubbornly in place.

This opposition is evident in the recent reception of lyric sincerity. Sin-
cerity had a brief heyday as a privileged theme of humanist criticism of the
1960s and early '70s, due in part to the renewed interest in romanticism ev-
idenced by feminist, confessional, beat, and black arts poetry, and the
emancipatory ideologies of the subject guiding political movements of the
era.[26] This scholarship tended to emphasize sincerity's moral transparency,
overlooking its fictive or theatrical elements. In contrast, in academic liter-
ary theory, sincerity has been regarded as a suspect, even failed, rhetoric
since modernism and certainly since the New Critics' introduction of the
"intentional fallacy," a trend that culminated in Barthes' 1968 "Death of
the Author." The poststructuralist turn to discourse, or what historians call
"the linguistic turn," rendered claims to sincerity suspect, challenging ref-
erences to an author "behind" the text, to a subjectivity prior to or outside
of language.[27] De Man's essays on Rousseau's *Confessions* exemplified this
turn, demonstrating that Rousseau's confessions were necessarily his "ex-
cuses."[28] Scholarship influenced by poststructuralism has been truly inno-
vative in opening up the study of sentiment to discourse, revealing feeling
to have ironic rather than transparent aims and effects, and emphasizing
the limits of readings that assume a transparent connection between bio-
graphical author and persona, feeling and selfhood.[29] Although recent schol-
arship has emphasized the discursive nature of sentiment and its implica-
tion in economic, nationalist, and imperialist practices, it has also tended to
repeat the moral opposition between sincerity and theatricality, poetry and
the marketplace, rather than seeing them as intimately connected.

In revealing and challenging the cultural practices that sustain this op-
position, my study joins—and puts into cross-period conversation—recent
work on the lyric by Judith Pascoe (*Romantic Theatricality*) and Deborah
Nelson (*Pursuing Privacy*). By showing that commercial culture combines

sincerity and performance, rendering them indistinguishable practices, I explain literary critics' persistent desire to oppose them: at stake is the moral autonomy of the "literary" profession itself. In awarding the lyric a privileged role as a site of this moral autonomy, critics have repressed, ignored, or vilified the modern lyric's engagements with commercial culture, and have thereby missed the generative tensions so central to its forms and history. On the one hand, we make the agency of sincere feeling impossible, exposing it as psychologism, moralism, naiveté, ideology, or mystification; on the other hand, in studying sentiment under the sign of poststructuralist irony, we risk making all emotion over into irony, losing sight of its often contradictory aims and effects, its moments of unabashed absorption in the marketplace, the professed desire for nondiscursive experience. This study shows that the lyric can simultaneously assert a desire for a nondiscursive ideal and undercut this ideal, can be both sincere and ironic, can pronounce the death and life of the author. In trying to talk about this complexity, I have continually run up against shortcomings in our critical vocabulary: I see this as a symptom of the need for a different kind of reading, one attuned to the tension between sincerity's moral promise and its implication in the theater of the market, a tension fundamental to the history of poetry as a professional endeavor.

This tension is evident in early definitions of "profession" and the related verb, "to profess." In its earliest uses, "to profess" meant "to take the vows of a religious order," and, similarly, "to declare openly, announce, affirm; to avow, acknowledge, confess." But a contradictory definition emerged alongside this usage with religious connotations: "To make profession of, to lay claim to (some quality, feeling, etc.); often implying insincerity, as 'to profess and not practice'; to make protestation of; to pretend to." The very act of professing, of avowing a private feeling in public, opened the verbal profession to the charge of insincerity. This anxiety would carry over into dual meanings of a "profession" as (1) "any calling or occupation by which a person habitually earns his living" (the professional is one who "make[s] profession of, or claim[s] to have knowledge of or skill in [some art or science]") and (2) "the declaration, promise, or vow made by one entering a religious order." While a promise or vow is central to both definitions, the aims of this promise are on the one hand moral and on the other hand economic: this schism would prove central to the livelihood of poetry. In the case of the poet, the act of professing in a moral sense and the work of the professional merge:[30] "the action or fact of professing" is "a business or profession that one publicly avows." Poetry as a profession by which one makes a living is shaped by a fundamental tension between its commercial investments and moral promise, and the rhetoric of sincerity as it came to

prominence in the late-eighteenth-century lyric emerged from and artic-
ulated this tension. Betraying the anxieties that riddle its usage, the word
"profession" alludes euphemistically not only to prostitution but also to the
theater. Thus it's no surprise that Mary Darby Robinson, poet, actress, and
mistress-courtesan, came to embody the late-eighteenth-century public's
ambivalence about professional writing.

Given the tensions that undergird poetry as a profession, does it even
make sense to call a poet a "professional"? After all, poets' livelihoods are
often only indirectly connected to the sale of actual poems. Thomas Haskell
asks this very question in an essay on professionalism: "On what grounds
can we lump together such diverse social types as poets and technicians,
professors and white-collar corporate managers, engineers and govern-
ment bureaucrats, lawyers, and chemists and treat them all as a single en-
tity with identifiable interests and a common destiny?" ("Professionalism
versus Capitalism," 183). Poetry indeed differs from the other professions
Haskell names, and this difference is what interests me here: the expecta-
tion of commercial disinterest exists in tension with the poet's economic in-
terests. Nowhere is the principle of what Bourdieu calls "loser wins," or the
economic world reversed, more evident than in poetry, and critics and po-
ets alike have often taken pride in poetry's status as an "impoverished" and,
as some would argue, marginalized genre (*Rules of Art*, 39, 114–15, 216).
Others have not. Langston Hughes punctures this moral ideal in his "Little
Lyric (Of Great Importance)": "I wish the rent / Was heaven sent" (*Selected
Poems*, 127); while Philip Larkin comments acerbically, "Lots of folk live on
their wits" but "No one actually starves" ("Toads," in *Collected Poems*, 89).
As Bourdieu's concept of the literary field helps us to see, lyric's investment
in an "economic world reversed" emerges from its engagement with that
economic world. Wordsworth asserted that the poet is the very opposite of
a professional type, that he is instead a man speaking to men. But this
moral conception of the poet emerged as poetry became a profession; as
Clifford Siskin argues, poetry was privileged in the understanding of "lit-
erature" as a distinct profession that emerged in the late eighteenth cen-
tury, because it signified "deeply imaginative writing," working to "em-
power" professionalism by naturalizing the discourse of professional
behavior (*Work of Writing*, 129, 132).

Most scholars locate the origins of professional authorship in the legal
and societal changes that permitted writers to make a living from the sale
of their work apart from patronage.[31] The general definition of a profession
as an occupation by which one makes a living obtains at both historical
moments I study, but the specific practices and understanding of "profes-

sional authorship" shifted.[32] More specifically, the understanding of a profession that most share today—a specialized occupation based on formal training and certification by educational bodies and associations—is a product of the great age of professionalization, the late nineteenth and early twentieth centuries.[33] While the legal changes in property law that permitted authors to make a living from the sale of their work occurred in the eighteenth century, organizations that began to address the concerns and needs of writers, and which formalized writers into a professional class, emerged in the nineteenth century; today, organizations such as PEN and the Society of Authors are an accepted part of the landscape, and certification of the writer as a professional is readily available through creative writing programs, which came to prominence after World War II.[34]

What joins the meaning of the literary professions at the two moments I study is an understanding of the literary text as a kind of property, and a focus on how poets use conventions of sincerity to respond to the poem as a form of property guides my discussion of early and late negotiations of authorship and professional careers. As Barthes and Foucault emphasize, the rise of the author as an organizing fiction for interpreting literary texts is closely aligned with the rise of a literary market and the treatment of the text as authorial property.[35] While this correlation is certainly true, the relationship itself is more complex: the assumption that the sincere lyric is the possession of an originating author is contradicted both by the history of textual property and by the commercial practices that accompany it, testifying less to the "birth" of the author through property than to his stillbirth, with the rhetoric of sincerity providing a lively commentary on the various misunions of economic constraints and moral ideals.

Changes in understandings of property are central to accounts of the rise of professional authorship. Historians of authorship posit a decline in aristocratic patronage and a shift to a nascent literary market controlled by booksellers in the late seventeenth and early eighteenth centuries. By the mid-eighteenth century in England, and by the 1820s in America, writers began to support themselves through the sale of their writing, and to regard themselves as literary professionals in the broad sense of making a living through the sale of their writing, with Daniel Defoe, Alexander Pope, and Samuel Johnson charting this professional path in England, and James Fenimore Cooper and Washington Irving doing so in America. Changing definitions of literary property in the legal system contributed to these changes in the economic status of the author: although the Statute of Anne (1710) permitted an early understanding of authors' rights in England, a clear legal understanding of copyright protection for authors did not come into being until 1774 in England and 1790 in America, permitting authors to secure profits from their works.[36] Although there is evidence that late-seventeenth- and early-eighteenth-century authors didn't see themselves as "rights-bearing proprietors in the modern sense," by the late eighteenth century a claim to a unique, recognizable name and identity began to prove crucial to the value of the literary work as a commodity in the marketplace.[37]

Subsequent developments in Anglo-American copyright law have deepened and extended the notion of literary property as an economic right of the copyholder, protected by statute for a specified duration.[38] While the treatment of literary works as economic commodities within copyright law helped authors to secure a livelihood, the treatment of literature as a form of property also required authors to accommodate the vocabulary and demands of the consumer market. The classic summary of this dilemma is that of Marx, alienation from the products of one's labor. Copyright law in some ways embodied this dilemma: as it developed in England and the United States, copyright was based on a limited term of statutory protection rather than on the Continental concept of "natural rights," in which the author was treated as the moral owner of the work.[39] In England and the United States, economic control of works was often ceded as soon as the booksellers bought the right of copy. Since the eighteenth century, different financial arrangements have ensued, including half profits and royalties, but to the present day, authors do not retain control of the work if they sell their copyright. Texts, once copyrighted, become formal representatives of, but not necessarily the property of, the author; even authors who retain copyright do not hold this property indefinitely.[40]

Until recently, histories of the rise of professional authorship have suggested that as aristocratic patronage declines and modern notions of literary property are established, the writer becomes increasingly autonomous and independent; this assumption corresponds to the association of the marketplace with classically liberal ideals. As my brief history of literary property suggests, however, the situation of the poet-professional has usually been—unless the poet is independently wealthy—one of dependence and constraint. It is the rare poet who has been able to support himself through proceeds from his poetry, and a comparison of late-eighteenth- and mid-twentieth-century poetic careers suggests that poetic patronage never disappears.[41] Rather, as traditional forms of aristocratic patronage wane, other forms of patronage appear, from the subscription practices of late-eighteenth-century England and America, to the white patronage of African American writers in the Harlem Renaissance, to the institutional and governmental forms of patronage of our own day.[42] In other words, the bonds of dependence that characterize literary patronage assume new forms, coexisting with a literary market: in considering uses of the rhetoric of sincerity as a mediation of conditions of authorship, one cannot draw hard-and-fast lines between a patronage system and a literary market. For instance, poets such as Jonson and Spenser employ sincerity conventions in dedications, prefaces, and their poetry to mitigate their dependence on patrons, and accusations of writerly insincerity were rife.[43]

Nevertheless, we can make some important distinctions between literary property and authorship practices under aristocratic patronage and in a literary market. As texts began to circulate not only among writers and their patrons or coteries but as commodities available for purchase through a bookseller, the connection between author and reader became less transparent. Raymond Williams points out that "production for the market involves the conception of the work of art as a commodity, and of the artist, however else he may define himself, as a particular kind of commodity producer" (*Sociology of Culture*, 44).[44] As aristocratic sources of patronage gave way to the institutions, practices, and forms of patronage that constitute the modern literary market, the bonds of dependence shifted: the writer who sought to sell and thus support herself through her writing became increasingly dependent not on a single benefactor or small coterie but on a reading public, or publics, and on standards of public taste. Not only might author and reader or patron never meet, but the means of textual circulation was often the purchase of the text. Market culture threatened to replace the "transparent" moral ties between members of a community with the "opaque" exchanges of the market.[45]

Situating uses of sincerity conventions alongside understandings of textual property and the commercial practices of professional writing helps to explain why romantic and postromantic poems have been so commonly figured and read as persons. With little or no contact between authors and readers, poems have been read as evidence of authorial conduct, and thus an author's negotiation of commercial practices inevitably influenced judgments of the poetry. The pervasive distrust that accompanied the rise of literature as a profession elicited both a desire for the author as a guarantor of the honesty of the text and a deep skepticism of this figure, such that first-person lyric speakers have often been read as figures of the author, regardless of (and often contrary to) the poet's intention. Thus decisions about the editing, advertisement, and circulation of poems or collections bear important consequences for the forms of sincerity expressed textually, in that they contribute to the reader's impressions of the work. For instance, choosing not to publish one's poems but to circulate them privately, to use a pseudonym rather than one's given name, to advertise one's work, to include a photograph or portrait frontispiece, or to read one's poems in public, convey subtle messages about the poet's views on conduct and commerce, contributing to the authorial persona constructed by the reader. The popularity of poetry readings—whether performed in a late-eighteenth-century salon, a nineteenth-century lecture hall, a 1950s art gallery, or a 1990s coffee shop—has contributed to the tendency to associate poet and poem.[46] More generally the publicity that surrounded the text privileged the lives and personalities of authors. Yet literary celebrity, as Mary Robinson experienced, could easily damage rather than enhance an author's reputation. In other words, the history of sincerity and professional authorship that I have discussed in broad terms is made material and specific through poets' varying negotiations of the lyric poem as a potential textual double and form of property that eludes individual control. As rhetorical strategies that seek to influence their readers, conventions of sincerity in these works not only bode forth or evacuate, animate or de-animate, the figure of the author in particular ways, but also anticipate and comment on their mode of circulation and the values likely to guide their reception.

Figuring Sincerity

The three sections of the book are organized around tropes of sincerity frequently used to establish the figure of the "sincere" poet in lyric since the late eighteenth century: the spontaneity of the urban walker, the authenticity of the elegiac mourner, and the accuracy of the miniaturist observer. Each section includes two chapters, one on a British romantic poet and the other on a post-1945 American poet who use the figure in question. Because I approach the production of sincerity as intimately connected not only to commercial practices but to readerly anxieties, I study how texts negotiate their readers, alongside the responses of historical readers. The sequence of sections brings into focus the intensity of the moral debates about the commercial nature of the rhetoric of sincerity, with the walker, mourner, and observer responding in turn to sincerity's commercial seductions, costs, and ethics. In the course of the book sincerity emerges as a shifting and contested rhetorical stage, with poets, their critics, and the literary profession itself equal participants in the ongoing drama.

The first section of the book explores the urban walk as a trope of spontaneity in William Wordsworth's *Prelude* and Frank O'Hara's *Lunch Poems*. Both poets use the trope of walking to engage the city's threats to the spontaneity of the poet's utterance, and to construct a utopian figure of sincere experience that accommodates this threat. The city—early-nineteenth-century London for Wordsworth and late-1950s to early-1960s New York for O'Hara—functions as a vast commercial stage, allowing each poet to dramatize the problem of the theatricality of representation, evident in urban spectacles and amusements, but most pressingly rendered by both poets through early and late practices of advertisement. Advertisement epitomized the commodification of the language of moral feeling, its subjection to the law of the market. In advertisement Wordsworth and O'Hara saw the threat of the poet as a professional "type" and the poem as a commodity-for-sale, capable, like the advertisement, of dissimulation and seduction. Both poets use the trope of the walk as a vehicle of spontaneous feeling that ideally participates in the economy of urban and literary advertisement while circumventing its flows; each poet generates feeling meant to exceed professional roles and the threat of self-commodification, either by transforming or reforming the theatrical potential of poetic language.

The moral anxiety that commercial behavior corrupts true sincerity has been consistently mapped onto debased feminine sexuality, and the prostitute (practitioner of the "oldest profession") surfaces as a figure for these anxieties in each section of the book. In section 1 she is a rival flaneur who prompts each poet to engage the sexual economy of urban walking. O'Hara's projection of an idealized, spontaneous desire onto a gay landscape located firmly within New York reveals how Wordsworth's location of desire in spontaneous habits of movement, thought, and memory allows him to evade the feminized seductions of London. However, Wordsworthian sincerity is not simply a foil for O'Hara's theatricality: O'Hara's poetry reveals how profoundly Wordsworth's performance of sincerity is shaped by his engagement with the commercial theater, while Wordsworth reveals that O'Hara—the consummate ironist and moral provocateur—is nevertheless deeply committed to a moral ideal of spontaneous feeling. Both poets use the walk as a figure of textual and sexual circulation: following the poet's walks, the reader receives instruction in how to interpret the city's seductions and, in turn, how to respond to the poem as a commodity. Connecting these practices of sincerity to each poet's historical reception reveals that while Wordsworthian sincerity grounds canonical and revisionary accounts of romanticism, O'Hara's embrace of the 1950s consumerist ethos and rejection of a Wordsworthian self constituted through memory and habit has influenced his reception as a minor poet, remembered more often for his personal celebrity than for his poems.

In section 2 (Charlotte Smith and Sylvia Plath) and section 3 (Anna Laetitia Barbauld and Elizabeth Bishop), I turn to professional authorship as experienced by women poets, whose relation to publishing and circulating their texts is quite differently gendered. To admit that one wrote for money was to risk the taint of immorality and insincerity associated with selling and living from one's earnings, a charge to which those disempowered in the literary field—writers of color, women writers, writers of the lower classes—have been particularly susceptible. Perceptions of a writer's authority influence determinations of authorial conduct and sincerity, and hence histories of unequal access to public power, the rights of citizenship, and economic property are an important part of the history I study. The marketplace created publication possibilities for writers who had been largely unable to reap the advantages of aristocratic patronage, and the late eighteenth century witnessed the growth of female authorship and the rise of the professional woman writer, able to support herself financially through her writing (Turner, *Living by the Pen*, 31–41). However, until the passage of the Married Women's Property Act (1882 in England, and between 1839 and 1895 in the United States, depending on the particular state), married female authors lacked the legal right to their literary profits, one of many hurdles faced by women entering the professions.

In that the entry of women into the literary professions challenged gendered and classed codes of conduct, women writers were particularly subject to readerly distrust and censure (Cross, *Common Writer*, 6). In section 2 the prostitute surfaces as a figure for the concern that women poets who perform sincerity "sell" themselves: the moral ideal of sincerity is at once upheld through recourse to feminine purity, while the morally contaminating, theatrical powers of the market are feminized and sexualized. In their lyric reflections on the connections between sincerity and commercial culture, women writers emerge less as belated respondents to the modern landscape than as architects of it, for, as Jennifer Wicke points out, "the culture of consumption is the culture of modernity" ("Joyce and Consumer Culture," 236).

Section 2 discusses Charlotte Smith and Sylvia Plath—two self-identified "poetesses"—as consummate actresses who expose and comment on their textual personae as dramatic creations born in the marketplace. For the female poet, sincerity was not so much a choice as an expectation: inevitably readers would scrutinize the work of women poets through the lens of gender, with the implicit expectation that "feminine" conduct is noncommercial conduct. I read the elegiac meditations of Smith and Plath as performances of sincerity compelled by gendered etiquettes of commercial exchange. Rather than avoid the language of advertisement and "type," both poets use conventions of sincerity to perform prescribed roles, to advertise their adherence to gendered and generic conduct, thereby disguising—however transparently—their desire to sell their work, and, and, even more taboo, their pleasure in doing so. In embracing the very aspects of authorship—such as marketing and selling their work— usually deemed alienating, Smith and Plath help us to move past the conventional opposition between critical agency and a feminized commercial culture, showing sincerity to be neither a form of naive moralism nor a cynical selling-out.

Smith and Plath entered the marketplace in mourning dress, selling their poetry by presenting their speakers not simply as mourners but as self-mourners, and even as beautiful corpses. Mourning, and elegy specifically, was a site of sincerity that the female writer of sensibility could access with propriety, its locus of inspiration ostensibly private and moral rather than public and professional. Yet the theatricality of elegiac rhetoric generated moral conflict as well as commercial success: what was real and what was performance? In both writers' work, representations of death reveal that the female poet's financial dependence on her audience necessitates her performance of sincerity, rendering the lyric's promise of an autonomous, authentic self an elusive ideal. Smith was legally barred from control of her earnings, while Plath struggled with the difficulty of making a living as a poet in the 1950s. The ideal of the sincere, self-possessing author was always already "dead" to these poets, and elegy served as a means not only of profiting from the sincere ideal but of critically engaging its gendered assumptions.

The "death of the author" names not only a problem of textual self-production for the female poet but a problem of commercial reception, both anticipated and actualized. While the walk figures an ideal circulation and reception of the poem in section 1, in section 2 that figure is the corpse, which must be carried, mourned, and gazed upon—exhibited, bought, and sold—by others. In sentimental culture the elegy ideally circulates sympathy and solidifies moral community, but Plath and earlier poetesses such as Smith replace sympathetic mourning with melancholia, challenging the values by which their poetic "corpses" will be received. While Smith seeks to inspire a leveling sympathy through the circulation of her self/poem as corpse, Plath repudiates a redemptive view of death and struggles to foreclose on what she views as the inevitable commodification of her work. This section treats issues of reception at length, showing the afterlife of textual melancholia and the re-production rather than progressive transcendence of writerly binds: critics of both poets' work seek to reaffirm the very distinctions the poets have questioned, between real experience and performance, poet and persona, economic and moral commerce.

As Smith and Plath make ostensibly "real" mourning the mainstay of their lyric, their efforts—complexly intertwined with their actual lives and deaths—fueled their celebrity. The poets I discuss in section 3, Anna Lae-titia Barbauld and Elizabeth Bishop, were quite critical of peers such as Smith and Plath for marketing their grief and cultivating a fame based on suffering. Although Barbauld and Bishop participated in the rituals of pro-fessional writing, both were concerned about its commercial taint and in-voked the concept of the amateur writer.[47] And yet it was difficult for pro-fessional writers to avoid the economy of celebrity: writers who depended on income from their work relied on the value of their names as signifiers in the marketplace. Literary conventions of sincerity in conjunction with copyright law helped establish the understanding of literary celebrity as property in the textually mediated self: through textual claims to sincerity, writers "authored" the self and became material beneficiaries—or poten-tially material victims—of their textual doubles.

Both Barbauld and Bishop sought to resist sincerity's ties to celebrity by developing a poetic practice centered on the ethical dimension of sincere rhetoric and the concealment or erasure of the figure of the author. They bring the figure of the poet into focus not as a body but as an observer, whose accurate description of minute visual detail submerges "personal-ity" and autobiographical expression to concern with a morally transparent use of language. By involving their readers in ethical observation, both poets tried to render their personal signature "illegible" and diminish the economic value of the name. For Barbauld the "illegible signature" was made quite literal in her uses of anonyms and pseudonyms; for Bishop her textual practice manifests itself in the slightness of her poetic production and her life on the literary margins in Key West and Brazil.

The miniature denotes not only a textual practice but a material one, a figure of circulation and reception: it can be held in the hand—as Bishop says "about the size of an old-style dollar bill"—and offers itself to a small, local audience, through the conceit of the gift rather than the commodity. A key thread in the fabric of the literature of sentiment, miniaturist poetry advertises itself as the product of feminine, domestic handicraft; in doing so, it appears to accept its "minor" status, its role as adornment, the themes of domestic life and moral virtues. While it is a literature defined by the limits of its formal and thematic reach, these limits also serve as the source of its power and critique: the miniature becomes the privileged unit of a literary and moral economy opposed to capitalist acquisitiveness, and to what each poet sees as its poetic counterpart, the expansive romantic self. By the end of this section we have come full circle—like Wordsworth, Bar-bauld deems theatricality a threat, and Bishop calls herself a "minor, fe-male Wordsworth"—but this section reveals the gendered implications of a Wordsworthian practice of sincerity. In the "minor" stance of these poets lies an ethical critique of a sentimental economy and its failure to change or influence political interests backed by economic power.

Boundaries of literary, moral, and generic decorum are as much at stake in readings of lyric sincerity as in the texts themselves: textual reception is part of the horizon of what defines the sincere text and author, a continuation of its performance or production.[48] A conclusion considers at greater length the ways in which current academic criticism is implicated in the "unfinished business of sentimentality." This chapter reveals that the academic literary profession's treatment of sincerity is profoundly shaped by struggles over its own professional aims and authority. Analyzing recent debates in the academy about "confessional criticism," I argue that these debates reveal anxieties about the commercialization of the profession, the critic's moral function, and generic boundaries, and that sincerity continues to serve as the stage on which these anxieties are performed and contained. By way of exploring why these anxieties have been mapped onto feminist criticism, I read Jane Tompkins's essay "Me and My Shadow" as a privileged touchstone in the confessional criticism debates, demonstrating that gender continues to serve as a key means of regulating the moral threat of literary commerce, in criticism as well as poetry.

Juxtaposing the romantic and postmodern moments asks us to reconsider some common narratives about this longer historical span: on the one hand, that it corresponds to a fall—of literature's critical capacities due to the increasing reach and "feminization" of commercial culture; and on the other hand, that it corresponds to a rise, the eighteenth-century emergence of women's poetry leading to its mid-twentieth-century feminist realization. Assumptions about sincerity and gender guide both narratives: a sincere ideal succumbs to the commodification of art and experience on the one hand; and on the other, sincere or "naked" forms of self-expression permit a stylistic and political breakthrough in women's post-1945 poetry.[49] Drawing attention to the ways in which post-1945 lyric and its readers restage romantic-era anxieties about the profession of moral feeling, I challenge understandings of postmodernity as an era marked by the loss or realization of a romantic ideal of autonomy, suggesting instead that the culture of sensibility is characterized by the repetition and restaging of persistent anxieties about the impossibility of a sincere ideal.[50] In asking readers to consider how commercial culture is historically implicated in the use and reception of the rhetoric of sincerity, *Professing Sincerity* invites a new understanding not only of romantic and post-1945 poetry but of the polarizing assumptions on which our narratives of modern literary tradition have been built. In this reading the lyric poem distills the contradictions of a confessional culture defined by a simultaneous desire for and deep skepticism of the public performance of private lives. To study genre in this way is to necessarily study the history of our cultural fictions, our ways of organizing knowledge, the "order of things," and our literary museums. To emphasize the artifice of such critical endeavors makes them no less effective, useful, or beautiful, but does suggest that they share something with the aesthetic forms they study: the "infinite task" of trying to extract "from the depths of oneself, in between the words, a truth which the very form of confession holds out like a shimmering mirage."

Part 1
The Poet in the Street
Walking and the Seductions of Sincerity

Lost in this mean world, jostled by the crowd, I am like a weary
man whose eye, looking backwards into the depths of years, sees
nothing but disillusion and bitterness, and before him nothing but a
tempest which contains nothing new, neither instruction nor gain.

—Charles Baudelaire, quoted in Walter Benjamin, *Illuminations*

How often in the overflowing streets
Have I gone forwards with the crowd, and said
Unto myself, "The face of every one
That passes by me is a mystery."
Thus have I looked, nor ceased to look, oppressed
By thoughts of what, and whither, when and how.

—William Wordsworth, *Prelude,* book 7

the shape of the toe as
                            it describes the pain
of the ball of the foot,
                         walking walking on
asphalt
       the strange embrace of the ankle's
lock
    on the pavement

—Frank O'Hara, "Walking"

*W*hen the figure of the poet takes center stage in the late-eighteenth-century lyric, he is often walking. The walk is virtually synonymous with the romantic lyric, a figure for its central preoccupations: for the autobiographical journey, for memory, for elegiac self-consciousness, for the relation of self to other.[1] We find the poet walking in the work of William Lisle Bowles, Charlotte Smith, Mary Robinson, Robert Southey, Samuel Taylor Coleridge, and William Wordsworth. And yet the figure of the poet has kept on walking, out of the eighteenth century, into the nineteenth and twentieth centuries, through pastoral locations in England and America but also through the streets of London, Dublin, Paris, New York, San Francisco, and farther afield. All of which begs the obvious question: why is the walk such an important and persistent trope of sincerity in romantic and postromantic poetry?

On the one hand, the walk is a utopian figure of sincere experience central to what Jerome McGann calls the romantic ideology: the walk poem embodies an ideal of spontaneous, unconstrained movement, feeling, and reflection, propelled by the poet's autonomous powers of locomotion rather than by any external authority. The walk would seem to be the perfect vehicle for what Wordsworth called the "spontaneous overflow of powerful feelings."[2] Demystifying this ideal, one might point to the ways in which the walk naturalizes the material conditions of poetic production, or seeks to resolve irreconcilable social and political conflicts at the level of language, nature, and imagination.[3] And yet, oddly enough, the walk poem often flirts with its own demystification, setting up a dialectic between the poet-walker and his external environment—"the strange embrace of the ankle's / lock / on the pavement"—that challenges and potentially undermines a spontaneous ideal. In the epigraphs above, we see that the pavement dictates the ankle's motion and that this friction causes "the pain / of the ball of the foot"; meanwhile the crowd jostles the walker-poet, and the sights of the city oppress and weary his eye. These sources of friction suggest that the walker's motion is not spontaneous but constrained, a struggle to move against resistance.

Nor is the urban nature of this resistance a coincidence. From the poetry of Wordsworth and Mary Robinson, to that of Whitman and Baudelaire in the nineteenth century, to the poetry of a succession of twentieth-century walkers—Wallace Stevens, W. C. Williams, Langston Hughes, Mina Loy, Charles Olson, and Frank O'Hara, among others—the city emerges as a stage on which to dramatize the conflict between a moral ideal of sincere expression and the obstructions that threaten it. To bring this conflict and its persistence into focus, the following chapters explore the urban walk in Wordsworth's *Prelude* and O'Hara's *Lunch Poems*. Both poets use the trope of walking to thematize the city's threats to the moral integrity of the poet, and to construct a figure of sincere experience that responds to this threat. In contrast to most scholarship on the romantic walk, I find that Wordsworth and O'Hara neither naively deny the material conditions of poetic production nor mystify or naturalize threats to the spontaneity of lyric expression. More specifically, both poets represent the city as a vast commercial stage set, whose theatrical street scenes, exhibitions, and popular entertainments entice the consumer, a seductive power addressed by both poets through early and late practices of advertisement. Figuring their walks against this backdrop explicitly challenges an understanding of sincerity as a nonperformative, untainted rhetoric.

Advertisement—the use of language and imagery to convey the merits of goods and to incite desire for them—conjoins the need to seduce the consumer to theatrical forms of representation capable of grabbing the consumer's attention. Some ads employed a language of sexual invitation, while others engaged in exaggeration and even outright fabrication. Professional writers, dependent on the patronage of a reading public, relied on publicity—reviews, notices, advertisements, and, in the twentieth century, lecture bureaus—to generate interest in their work: thus advertisement as the sign of professional self-interest posed a challenge to the moral aim of spontaneous, transparent lyric expression. Was generating interest in one's work a form of consumer seduction? Would the poet's use of the rhetoric of sincerity be read as an extended form of self-advertisement? In advertisement Wordsworth and O'Hara saw the threat of the poet perceived as a professional "type," desire reduced to a vocabulary of consumption, and poetry viewed as a good-for-sale, capable, like the advertisement, of dissimulation and seduction.

In the context of advertisement, the urban setting for the walk poem takes on a decidedly literary meaning: both early-nineteenth-century London and post–World War II New York served as the centers of professional literary culture for Wordsworth and O'Hara, respectively. Both poets, lacking the luxury of family fortune or consistent patronage, needed to participate in this economy in order to write. Wordsworth's income from poetry, particularly when he was younger, was paltry and sporadic. Sir George Beaumont became a patron of sorts, giving Wordsworth a deed of land in the Lakes and allowing him and his family to stay rent-free at the Beaumont house. In 1813, through his connection to Lord Lonsdale, Wordsworth received a salaried post as distributor of stamps, a post that he eventually passed on to his son. While Wordsworth managed to generate some income as a poet, O'Hara chose to support himself professionally through his job as a curator at the Museum of Modern Art and as an art critic, writing poetry on the side.[4] But side-stepping a professional literary economy would prove difficult.

As they represent the poet walking through the city, both poets stage the question of whether they can establish critical distance from commercial culture, given their need to engage commercial practices. Although I focus on an early and late instance of this conflict, it is so pervasive in the modern literature of walking that I call it the "flaneur's bind." Priscilla Ferguson locates the origins of flanerie in early-nineteenth-century Paris; the flaneur is a figure who walks through and observes the city, part of the crowd yet aloof from it.[5] His interests are primarily aesthetic, and his leisure is permitted by his wealth, which he signals through his lavish dress.[6] The brief fashion of walking not dogs but *turtles* exemplified the flaneur's resistance to the speed of "traffic, commodities, [and] thoughts" in the industrial city (Tester, *Flaneur,* 15). Many nineteenth-century French artists and intellectuals were attracted to flanerie because of its implicit criticism of bourgeois values, and used the flaneur as a figure for the modern artist. Charles Baudelaire, the emblematic nineteenth-century flaneur, equated the flaneur's detachment from the bustle of the city with resistance to industrial progress, a protest against the forces of consumption and mass production that threatened individual autonomy and originality.[7] In his words, the flaneur's passion is, "above all, the burning desire to create a personal form of originality, within the external limits of social conventions" (*Selected Writings,* 420). This is, in short, a desire to define a sincere ideal, while recognizing the need to do so within the very terms that threaten such an ideal.

In other words, the flaneur's protest was of necessity complicitous. While Baudelaire disdained the aristocracy, defining his dress as a symbol not of wealth but of "the aristocratic superiority of his spirit" (*Selected Writings,* 420), he nevertheless "expressed himself as a consumer" (Rosalind Williams, *Dream Worlds,* 118–20); his definition by commodities belied his

distance from bourgeois society.[8] This dependence on the very "social con-
ventions" one critiques is a problem endemic to flanerie, presenting it-
self not just to Baudelaire in mid-nineteenth-century Paris, but also to
Wordsworth in London at the turn of the century, and to O'Hara in 1950s
New York. How can the flaneur walk with the crowd and distinguish him-
self from it? More specifically, how can he distinguish himself from the
crowd if he must do so through the language of commodities, through his
clothing, profession, or leisure?

The poet-walker, more explicitly than any other figure of sincerity in
this book, engages the urban context and economy that contributed to the
habit of conflating the semiotic reading of social types with the textual
reading of authorial character. In an environment of pervasive distrust, po-
ems were read as textual stand-ins for the poet and were thus subject to
what I have called a "crisis in reading." How well did these textual stand-
ins correspond to the "real" author? And how could one know for sure, since
most readers would never meet the poet in person? This climate of dis-
trust finds its apt expression in representations of the city, where strangers
"read" other strangers on the street and interpret their gestures in com-
mercial exchanges. Readerly anxieties about discerning the author's mo-
tives influenced poets' anxieties about using conventions of sincerity, shap-
ing how they represented themselves walking in the urban theater. The
flaneur's bind, then, is a problem of writing inseparable from the semiotic
reading of persons and personifications.[9]

Through their negotiation of the bodiliness of walking, Wordsworth and
O'Hara engage the risks of writing about commercial culture as part of the
crowd, addressing the ways in which commercial culture can transform
people into theatrical types, and poems into advertisements. Both poets use
the movement of the walk to generate spontaneous feeling that circulates
in the economy of urban and literary advertisement while altering its flows.
Historically the seductive potentials and moral taint of self-advertisement
has been feminized and sexualized, symbolized by the figure of the prosti-
tute. This figure, and gender and sexuality more generally, proves crucial to
both poets' attempts not to deny but to transform or reform the theatrical
potential of poetic language. While critics of Wordsworth emphasize his
antitheatrical prejudice and his efforts to transcend the threat embodied by
the prostitute, what is striking and overlooked about Wordsworth is his use
of the urban walk, a discursive strategy that draws attention to the limits of
an embodied perspective. On the other hand, critics of O'Hara emphasize
his rejection of a "transcendent" perspective, citing his use of the walk
trope as crucial to an aesthetics of presence (Gilbert, *Walks in the World*, 18).

Yet readers neglect the idealizing, romantic understanding of sincerity that remains central to O'Hara's poetics, and how it depends on his use of irony.

By focusing on the walk as a form of lyric transportation rather than transcendence or presence, I illuminate its embodied engagement with commercial culture. Drawing on Certeau's understanding of a "rhetoric of walking," I explore the analogy between "linguistic and pedestrian enunciation," investigating how the walk as a textual strategy also functions—through its circulation and reception—as a material strategy through which to influence the social body (*Practice of Everyday Life*, 99). Both poets use the motion of the walk as a figure of textual circulation and reception: following the poet's walks, the reader receives instruction in how to interpret urban seductions and, in turn, how to animate the poem-commodity and the poet as a professional type. Tracing critics' readings of these walks reveals how textual and material practices of sincerity have influenced each poet's posthumous reception.

As we follow Wordsworth and O'Hara on their urban rambles, it's worth remembering that many poet-walkers might have assumed a starring role in this section: Whitman, who strolled the streets of New York in the nineteenth century, for instance, or Mina Loy, who recorded her walks along New York's Bowery in the 1940s. Juxtaposing an early and late flaneur challenges periodizing assumptions about the lyric poet's "autonomy," his distance from or immersion in commercial culture, a challenge we might extend to our readings of a host of flaneurs. While scholars of romantic poetry have denaturalized and critiqued the romantic ideology, the assumption remains that romantic poets are invested in this ideology, that through idealizations of nature, language, or imagination they claim to transcend the taint of commercial culture and the realities of literary production. In turn, the idealizations of the romantic era remain a touchstone for critics of late-twentieth-century culture, who suggest that the postmodern era of late capitalism blurs the distinction between the economic and cultural spheres, compromising the possibility of autonomy or critical distance. By juxtaposing Wordsworth and O'Hara in their use of the urban walk, I suggest that while the flaneur has traversed many different cities, altering his path, his speed, and his commercial habits, his bind persists.

Chapter 1
William Wordsworth

The Economy of Type

Following his first trip to London in 1788, Wordsworth visited every year from 1791 to 1797, and every few years thereafter. Yet his poetic corpus is marked by a surprising absence of poetry about the city.[1] Although addressed explicitly in only a handful of poems, London haunts Wordsworth's poetry of retirement: the city is present as a force that threatens his beliefs regarding nature, moral community, and the role of the poet. In the 1800 Preface to *Lyrical Ballads,* Wordsworth explicitly defines his duty as a poet in terms of this threat:

> For the human mind is capable of excitement without the application of gross and violent stimulants; and he must have a very faint perception of its beauty and dignity who does not know this, and who does not further know that one being is elevated above another in proportion as he possesses this capability. It has therefore appeared to me that to endeavour to produce or enlarge this capability is one of the best services in which, at any period, a Writer can be engaged; but this service, excellent at all times, is especially so at the present day. For a multitude of causes unknown to former times are now acting with a combined force to blunt the discriminating powers of the mind, and unfitting it for all voluntary exertion to reduce it to a state of almost savage torpor. The most effective of these causes are the great national events which are daily taking place, and the encreasing accumulation of men in cities, where the uniformity of their occupations produces a craving for extraordinary incident which the rapid communication of intelligence hourly gratifies. (*PLB,* 249–50)

Wordsworth locates "the magnitude of the general evil" in the accumulation of men in cities, and suggests that one of his central aims as a poet is to counteract the city's effects on "the discriminating powers of the mind." Specifically, he worries that the city has unfit the mind "for all voluntary exertion," which is essentially a concern about spontaneity. Wordsworth understood spontaneity not in the sense of an unpremeditated action, its primary connotation today, but as a form of voluntary action, learned habits of thought and feeling. Thus when Wordsworth writes that "all good poetry is the spontaneous overflow of powerful feelings," he adds that spontaneous feeling is "modified and directed by our thoughts"; the poet expresses "thoughts and feelings which, by his own choice, or from the structure of his own mind, arise in him without immediate external excitement" (*PLB*, 246, 256). The key to the spontaneous nature of feeling is that it arises internally, "without any external stimulus or constraint" (*PLB*, 246). In book 7 of *The Prelude*, the only such place in the Wordsworth canon, the poet walks through London as part of the crowd, thematizing that which impedes the "spontaneous overflow of powerful feelings."

Wordsworth presents the "general evil" of London as one of fallen or degraded representation, a moral debasement that he connects to theatricality.[2] He was only too aware that language is "a thing subject to endless fluctuations and arbitrary associations," that words did not always transparently correspond to things, but could be used to disguise and deceive.[3] In his third "Essay upon Epitaphs," he states: "Words are too awful an instrument for good and evil to be trifled with: they hold above all other external powers a dominion over thoughts. If words be not . . . an incarnation of the thought but only a clothing for it, then surely will they prove an ill gift; such a one as those poisoned vestments, read of in the stories of superstitious times, which had power to consume and to alienate from his right mind the victim who put them on. Language, if it do not uphold, and feed, and leave in quiet, like the power of gravitation or the air we breathe, is a counter-spirit, unremittingly and noiselessly at work to derange, to subvert, to lay waste, to vitiate, and to dissolve."[4] In likening language to air and gravity, forces necessary to the body's intrinsic processes, Wordsworth suggests a "natural" power of words, constituted by a necessary connection between word and thought. The image of incarnation underscores the moral necessity of this relation: words give thought tangible form. If words merely clothe thought, however, the connection between thoughts and words is arbitrary, and one outfit will do as well as the next. Words, like actors, may even cloak or deceive. Wordsworth encounters language as a counter-spirit in London: there, words do not incarnate thought, but become "only a clothing for it."

In book 7, Wordsworth recalls his time in London after completing his university degree in 1791: no longer a student, he "pitched [his] vagrant tent, / a casual dweller and at large, among / The unfenced regions of society" (lines 60–62).⁵ No longer a student and not yet recognized as a poet, he was himself "at large," and thus particularly attuned to the grand pageant of social and professional types that he encountered on his walks through London:

> Now homeward through the thickening hubbub, where
> See—among less distinguishable shapes—
> The Italian, with his frame of images
> Upon his head; with basket at his waist,
> The Jew; the stately and slow-moving Turk,
> With freight of slippers piled beneath his arm.
> Briefly, we find (if tired of random sights,
> And haply to that search our thoughts should turn)
> Among the crowd, conspicuous less or more
> As we proceed, all specimens of man
> Through all the coulours which the sun bestows,
> And every character of form and face:
> The Swede, the Russian; from the genial south,
> The Frenchman and the Spaniards; from remote
> America, the hunter Indian; Moors,
> Malays, Lascars, the Tartar and Chinese,
> And Negro ladies in white muslin gowns.   (lines 227–43)

Wordsworth orders the crowd by observing physiognomy and dress, distinguishing men and women by their racial heritage or nationality. He also identifies persons through their professions or economic roles; he distinguishes the Italian, the Jew, and the Turk in terms of the commodities they carry, presumably to market, and in an earlier passage he identifies the nurse, the bachelor, the military idler, and the dame (see lines 223–26). Wordsworth visually "reads" these individuals "with quick and curious eye" (line 581): the body and its clothing become a semiotic medium. While in some cases Wordsworth categorizes individuals, in other cases he is literally forced to read them; a person in "sailor's garb" lies "at length beside a range of written characters, with chalk inscribed" (lines 220–22); on stage, "Jack the Giant-Killer" wears black garb with the word "invisible" flaming forth upon his chest (lines 309–10); a blind beggar wears a "written paper, to explain / The story of the man, and who he was" (lines 614–15). The persons who bear these written messages are all supplicants, "inscribed" upon by an economic law that imprisons or enslaves them. The principle that guides this "language" of subjection is typology: visual appearance categorizes an individual as representative of a profession, class, gender, race, or nationality.

As types, these individuals are nameless. When the young Wordsworth first hears of London from a classmate, he is baffled by one problem, "how men lived / Even next-door neighbours, as we say, yet still / Strangers, and knowing not each other's names" (lines 118–20). "Type" is a "general form, structure, or character distinguishing a particular kind, group, or class of beings or objects" as well as "a person or thing that exhibits the character-istic qualities of a class"; type is both the general form or pattern and the particular person or object that exhibits this pattern.[6] The relation of the in-dividual to the type is that of the series, rather than that of part to whole. Thus, individuals of a type are copies, repetitions of a principle, replaceable parts. Wordsworth's concern with typology as the dominant "language" of London is a concern about the formation of moral community. His belief that language should "embody" thought indicates his anxiety about the power of language to mold the ties between citizens. A "natural" or transparent relation between word and thought—the sincere ideal—corre-sponds to a "natural" or transparent relation between individual and soci-ety; sincerity as an ideal of language use is grounded in a shared moral or-der, a social trust that anchors and permits the readability of an individual's identity, intentions, and values.

The language of type perverts community, removing what Wordsworth views as a natural relation between fellow beings and reducing reading to observation of surface distinctions. The sum of types, Wordsworth im-plies, is the aggregation or accumulation of distinctions. Indeed, many of the poet's descriptions of the crowd and street in book 7 take the form of detailed lists, which at once convey the overwhelming experience of read-ing the endless urban procession, but also enact the threat that book 7 merely proliferates these distinctions. Wordsworth says of the "blank con-fusion" of Bartholomew Fair that it is "a type not false / Of what the mighty city is itself" ("herself" in the 1850 *Prelude*) (lines 696–97). London typi-fies the problem of type:

> An undistinguishable world to men,
> The slaves unrespited of low pursuits,
> Living amid the same perpetual flow
> Of trivial objects, melted and reduced
> To one identity by differences
> That have no law, no meaning, and no end.   (lines 700–705)

Wordsworth views the relation between individuals in the crowd as meto-
nymic: they are connected only by reason of occupying the same ground at
the same time, rather than by a sense of common identity based on shared
moral beliefs, values, or sympathy. The urban crowd is ordered "by differ-
ences that have no law, no meaning, and no end": Wordsworth's inability to
distinguish between persons is ironically caused by overdistinction, by the
proliferation of distinctions guided solely by the economic logic and lan-
guage of the marketplace. Other eighteenth-century uses of "type" confirm
the connection between social types and economic types: "type" refers to a
"small rectangular block, usually of metal or wood, having on its upper
end a raised letter, figure, or other character, for use in printing," as well
as to this block's product, "a printed character or characters" (*OED*, def.
9a, 9c). In addition, "type" refers to "the figure on either side of a coin or
medal" (*OED*, def. 2b). Wordsworth's use of "melted and reduced" to de-
scribe "slaves" and "trivial objects" connotes the law of the coin, which gives
disparate objects "one identity" in the language of money. In the crowd the
poet witnesses the conflation of social type, coin type, and print type: the
capitalist economy renders Londoners into readable, reproducible, types.

In reading one another as types, Londoners conflate individuals with
their surface appearances, like so many objects for sale: "slaves" and "triv-
ial objects" become synonymous. As the poet walks the streets, faces appear
to blur into commodities for sale: "The comers and the goers face to face—
/ Face after face—the string of dazzling wares, / Shop after shop" (lines
156–58). This kind of reading is guided by the logic of advertisement, the
public description or presentation of goods with a view to promoting sales.
Wordsworth makes this conflation of man and commodity explicit when he
observes

> Stationed above the door like guardian saints,
> There, allegoric shapes, female or male,
> Or physiognomies of real men,
> Land-warriors, kings, or admirals of the sea,
> Boyle, Shakespear, Newton, or the attractive head
> of some quack doctor, famous in his day.   (lines 163–67)

Allegory, which works through a logic of moral typology, is degraded to
advertisement and the logic of economic type; these allegoric shapes may
look "like guardian saints," but they are used not to stand in for moral con-
cepts or values, but to advertise the wares inside the store. Wordsworth's
confrontation with the "physiognomies of real men" hanging above doors
as advertisements bodes forth the threat that his own claim to sincerity

will be read not as a moral, transparent use of language but as self-advertisement (Jacobus, *Romanticism,* 234). In that book 7 purports to present the physiognomy of the real poet walking, these advertisements serve as a disturbing mirror; one could easily imagine Wordsworth's allegoric shape next to that of "Shakespear."

The reading of type, which anticipates Georg Simmel's discussion of this urban phenomenon in the early twentieth century, was a discourse in circulation at the time Wordsworth observed types in London. While "reading" types, dress, or physiognomy was certainly a habit well before Wordsworth's era, the unprecedented urbanization and industrialization in the eighteenth century, accompanied by the influx of new populations and the emergence of new professions in the city, lent new valence to the discourse of physiognomy.[7] Lavater's *Essays on Physiognomy* were widely influential in late-eighteenth- and early-nineteenth-century Britain; he discussed the body, the gestures, and the gait as a *language* that reveals character, arguing that one should read man's outward appearance as "a manifestation" of "inner self."[8] Wordsworth, in contrast, suggests that such readings in London are tantamount to deception, given the absence of a "natural" connection between word and thought, clothing and body. If one reads with the expectation of sincerity, one may be duped. Consider these two passages from book 7:

> Advertisements of giant size, from high
> Press forward in all colours on the sight—
> These, bold in conscious merit—lower down,
> That, fronted with a most imposing word,
> Is peradventure one in masquerade.   (lines 211–14)

> . . . Folly, vice,
> Extravagance in gesture, mien and dress,
> And all the strife of singularity—
> Lies to the ear, and lies to every sense—
> Of these and of the living shapes they wear
> There is no end.   (lines 572–77)

Wordsworth likens an advertisement to a person in masquerade in that its language necessarily misrepresents, or disguises, its object in order to incite desire. To gain the attention of the passerby, the advertisement must exaggerate or "overdress" itself. Given the necessity of reading others in the city as types, Wordsworth fears that clothing, like words, could be used to disguise one's station, to further one's economic designs, to deceive others for false purposes.[9] When the bond between word and thought, or representation and a moral community, is broken, all of London becomes a stage, every passerby an actor or actress.[10] Hence, while the poet makes a point of describing his visits to the theaters of London (lines 400–457), the problem he sees in London is that its theatricality is not contained to the theater: theatricality is apparent not only in its "low" spectacles but also in "others titled higher," "the brawls of lawyers in their courts / Before the ermined judge, or that great stage / Where senators, tongue-favored men, perform" (lines 488, 490–92). Even the "holy church" becomes a stage for the preacher guided by the "crook of eloquence" (line 570).

Wordsworth's emphasis on the theatricality of London and the possibility of "misreading" one's fellow man or woman reveals his fear of a community unified not by moral commonality, but solely by competitive economic pursuit. London pits individuals against one another in "the strife of singularity"; throughout his walks, Wordsworth hears vendors, who "crack the voice in rivalship" (line 671). Engels's remarks on the crowds in the city streets (in *The Condition of the Working Class in England* in 1844) captures Wordsworth's nightmare: "The brutal indifference, the unfeeling isolation of each in his private interest becomes the more repellent and offensive, the more these individuals are crowded together, within a limited space. And, however much one may be aware that this isolation of the individual, this narrow self-seeking is the fundamental principle of our society everywhere, it is nowhere so shamelessly barefaced, so self-conscious as just here in the crowding of the great city. The dissolution of mankind into monads, of which each one has a separate principle, the world of atoms, is here carried out to its utmost extremes" (qtd. in Raymond Williams, *Country and City*, 216). City dwellers, pursuing their monadic interests, have neither the time nor the need to look beyond the surface of the crowd.

The Walker as Tourist

In short, Wordsworth suggests in book 7 that London alienates individuals from their "natural" capacity for "voluntary" or spontaneous thought and experience. In the 1800 Preface to *Lyrical Ballads,* he cites the "uniformity" of occupations in urban industrial culture as a key cause of the loss of voluntary exertion. While Wordsworth is not specific on this point, "uniformity" connotes the repetitiveness or mechanical nature of daily tasks, suggesting a limiting of experience that accompanies the increasing specialization and mechanization of industry in the late eighteenth century.[11] In repetitive work, the relation between moments is that of the series: the past moment is equivalent to the present moment because the worker's movements are the same, one moment and one day blending into the next. The worker performing a uniform task is forced to view time as a series of continuous presents, rather than as a narrative of growth from past to present. When Wordsworth describes Londoners' insatiable desire for news of "extraordinary incident" and for "gross and violent stimulants," he implies that the uniformity of work conditions the need for "shock," for momentary or instantaneous gratification; Benjamin would later write that "the Shock experience which the passer-by has in the crowd corresponds to what the worker 'experiences' at his machine" (*Illuminations,* 176; Arac, "Romanticism").

Individuals restrict their movements and thoughts to accommodate the pace and demands of urban life. Not only does London's economy promote atomization of the social body into types, then, but in eliciting desire for "gross and violent stimulants" it restricts "natural" or "voluntary" desire. As Marlon Ross points out, "Wordsworth finds in the city . . . [that] humankind is imprisoned by attempting to free itself from nature" (*Contours,* 77). Wordsworth sees spontaneous experience decay as nature is commodified, nature considered both in the sense of the pastoral landscape and in the sense of the human propensity for spontaneous thought, feeling, and movement as experienced in a nonurban setting. As man enslaves nature, so too does he lose the possibility to shape a community on common ground beyond that of economic rivalry.

Wordsworth makes the connection between the commodification of nature and the loss of spontaneous experience explicit when he views the spectacles of nature on display in London. Although he views these spectacles "at leisure," he suggests that, in London, even leisure provides no respite from the workplace and its strictures: in leisure, as at work, Londoners are "slaves unrespited of low pursuits" (line 701). In their shared commodification of nature, the spectacles of advertisement and shop windows blur into the exhibitions of the museum and fair. Wordsworth sees natural life that trade and travel have made accessible, "troops of wild beasts, birds and beasts / Of every nature from all climes convened" (lines 246–47); at St. Bartholomew's Fair, he sees "all moveables of wonder from all parts" (line 680). Similarly, he sees the panorama and the miniature, "mimic sights that ape / The absolute presence of reality / Expressing as in mirror sea and land, / And what earth is" (lines 248–51). Wordsworth objects to these spectacles not only because they are "imitations" but because they provide vicarious experience, taking away both the sensation of walking through nature as well as the need for such movement. The panoramic artist with "his greedy pencil" provides "a whole horizon on all sides," giving man "power / Like that of angels or commissioned spirits"; what is lost in gaining an omniscient perspective is the perspective one experiences walking through the landscape, in which nature unfolds in time, in relation to the moving body (lines 258–60). The "miniature of famous spots and things" (line 251) presents similar problems; the "mechanic artist" represents, by "scale exact," "every tree / Through all the landscape, tuft, stone, scratch minute, / And every cottage, lurking in the rocks— / All that the traveller sees when he is there" (lines 276–80). While bodily experience provides only a "partial" view of a landscape, the "whole" available only through the sequential unfolding of a temporal narrative, both the miniature and the panorama negate temporality, giving the spectator visual mastery over a landscape. This spatial knowledge is that of the exhibition, museum, and collection. As Susan Stewart points out, "The collection replaces history with classification, with order beyond the realm of temporality. . . . All time is made simultaneous or synchronous within the collection's world" (*On Longing*, 151).

Museums and popular exhibitions like the panorama and the miniature democratized tourism, permitting the masses access to otherwise unavailable sights. Tourism had long served as a form of collecting for the upper classes in the eighteenth century, a means of marking one's class, urbanity, and taste through access to place (Fabricant, "Literature of Domestic Tourism"). As Raymond Williams comments, "The picturesque journeys—and the topographical poems, journals, paintings and engravings which promoted and commemorated them—came from the profits of an improving agriculture and from trade. . . . Like the landscaped parks, where every device was employed to produce a natural effect, the wild regions of mountain and forest were for the most part objects of conspicuous aesthetic consumption: to have been to the named places, to exchange and compare the travelling and gazing experiences, was a form of fashionable society" (*Country and City*, 128). Wordsworth's poems and *Guide to the Lakes* were certainly part of this tradition, and risked, like the miniature and the panorama, rendering nature an object "of conspicuous aesthetic consumption," democratizing knowledge at the risk of diminishing the tourist experience to that of the eyes alone, to a purely superficial knowledge. But he implies that poems differ from visual imitations of nature, which pander to the lowest common denominator: they are "fondly made in plain / Confession of man's weakness and his loves" (*Prelude*, 7.254–55). In their concentrated appeal to vision, the spectacles of London negate the need for exertion: they "blunt the discriminating powers of the mind . . . reduc[ing] it to a state of almost savage torpor" (*PLB*, 246).

The ultimate expression of what may come of a nation unified by individuals "uniformly" enslaved by the market and the strife of singularity, is the mob. Throughout book 7, Wordsworth senses the mob's threat, even when there is "sky, stillness, moonshine, empty streets, and sounds / Unfrequent as in desarts" (lines 635–36). Since London is a vast stage set, and the poet cannot trust appearances, he fears such moments are "falsely catalogued: things that are, are not." He imagines "times when half the city shall break out / Full of one passion—vengeance, rage, or fear—/ To executions, to a street on fire, / Mobs, riots, or rejoicings" (lines 646–49). In this sense, the enslavement of the individual body that Wordsworth witnesses on a mundane level in the street and at spectacles throughout London is akin to the enslavement of the body politic. Persons driven only by self-fulfillment enjoin their desire to the economy, which thrives on the desire for the new, for instantaneous self-gratification, for "gross and violent stimulants." Theatricality, Wordsworth suggests, permits the expression of passions without discipline, and might easily flame into violence; while the specter of the French Revolution haunts book 7 (Friedman, "History," 132–34), Wordsworth's fear of the passions of the crowd is echoed throughout the nineteenth century and anticipates twentieth-century objections to fascist spectacle. Spontaneity, or the voluntary exertion of one's thoughts and feelings, is not simply a pastoral ideal generated by a poet who wishes to naively transcend or escape the theatricality of London, but might better be seen as an instance of "urban pastoral," a model of "natural" experience and identity generated by and for those *inside* the urban crowd, most subject to its risks.

The Flaneur's Bind

The conflict that Wordsworth dramatizes is that of the flaneur: how can one define the possibility for spontaneous desire, desire "arising or proceeding entirely from natural impulse, without any external stimulus or constraint," when, as Baudelaire puts it, one must do so from "within the external limits of social conventions"? How can one claim sincerity when surrounded by and dependent on theatrical modes of representation? Judith Pascoe has persuasively argued that "Wordsworth's walking was a kind of performance" and "that he was as reliant on theatrical modes of self-representation as his more overtly stagy contemporaries" (*Romantic Theatricality,* 190). Pascoe's reading of Wordsworth's pastoral poetry challenges the myth of the sincere rural dweller, helping us to see a "Wordsworth who is more cosmopolitan than rustic, more closely allied with theatricality than transparency" (186). In fact, what is striking about book 7 is that Wordsworth does not simply "neutralize" or "distance" his theatricality, as Pascoe suggests (192), but puts his theatricality on display: he dramatizes the walk as a "kind of performance," one that must be read in relation to the many kinds of theatrical display in London.

Wordsworth presents the flaneur's bind as a conflict between kinds of reading: can the poet find a way to read sincerely, or will he be forced to read the city as the tourist or shopper would, uncritically succumbing to the seductions of the largely visual iconography of consumer culture? In turn, this problem of reading thematizes a problem of writing: can the poet-walker resist reducing "reading" to visual typology, bodies and things to their visual surfaces, poetic language to self-advertisement? Finally, given the impossibility of proving his sincerity, can the poet teach the reader "sincere" habits of reading, influencing how both he and his words will be read?

This dilemma involved the professional poet's need to engage the literary marketplace and a fragmented reading public (of which Wordsworth's sense of the fragmentation of community in London gives some indication).[12] But Wordsworth saw this not only as an unwelcome necessity but as an opportunity to democratize poetry and its audience by presenting "a selection of the language really spoken by men" (*PLB*, 254). In making sincere feeling the criterion of poetry, he hoped to put it on an equal footing with prose: "Poetry sheds no tears 'such as angels weep,' but natural and human tears; she can boast of no celestial Ichor that distinguishes her vital juices from those of prose; the same human blood circulates through the veins of them both" (*PLB*, 254). Poetry, he told his readers, was a word of "very disputed meaning" (*LB*, 7): Wordsworth's attempts to broaden its meanings were quite radical at the time, and the *Lyrical Ballads* received both admiration and scathing criticism for this perceived violation.[13] His "experiments" (*LB*, 7) anticipate those of modernists such as Frank O'Hara, writing 150 years later.

While Wordsworth wanted to speak the "language of men" in his poetry, a democratic goal, in doing so he risked the collapse of his work into the language he criticized, a language that panders to the consumer's "savage torpor." How could he distinguish his poetic walks around rural locales from the vicarious tours offered to city dwellers by panoramas? Or from the texts that surrounded him in London, the newspapers, the "frantic novels, sickly and stupid German tragedies, and deluges of idle and extravagant stories in verse" (*PLB*, 249)? How could he claim the moral value of his poetry if "value" was to be determined by an audience whose taste had been shaped by such literature? Wordsworth put the challenge this way: "Every author, as far as he is great and at the same time *original,* has had the task of *creating* the taste by which he is to be enjoyed" (*ESP*, 408). To create the taste for his work, he needed to persuade readers of its value, and his numerous prefaces can be read as a series of advertisements; in fact, he termed the introduction to the 1798 *Lyrical Ballads* an "Advertisement" (*LB*, 7–8). In sum, how could Wordsworth both rely on the practices of commercial culture and distinguish his work from them?

Wordsworth's anxieties about the seductions of consumer culture emerge most forcefully in relation to the figure of the prostitute. The prostitute is a rival flaneur as she strolls the streets—she is Wordsworth's potential double, one who embodies his fears of how he and his words could be perceived by readers in the public domain.[14] The prostitute's body is a commodity for sale, her surface a literal advertisement; as Benjamin remarked, "In the prostitution of large cities the woman herself becomes a mass article" (qtd. in Buck-Morss, *Dialectics of Seeing*, 190). In selling her body, she mechanizes what Wordsworth views as her "natural" movements and desires; sex unchained from the narrative of reproduction becomes a *series* of continuous thrills, shocks, presents. Through her, urban male "consumers" fulfill their desire for momentary or instantaneous gratification, much as they turn to novels or newspapers or theatrical spectacles (Simpson, "Poor Susan," 605). When Wordsworth describes a prostitute in book 7, he states that

> . . . a barrier seemed at once
> Thrown in, that from humanity divorced
> The human form, splitting the race of man
> In twain, yet leaving the same outward shape.   (lines 424–27)

Walking through the streets, the prostitute embodies the theatrical split between words and things, movement and experience, that Wordsworth equates with the commodification of representation: as a visual type equivalent to advertisement, as a body (like print type) subject only to the market's law of reproduction, she is a human form "divorced" from her capacity for "natural" experience.

Wordsworth stages encounters with "types" in London that explicitly link the figure of the sincere poet to the prostitute, suggesting that the poet's "outward shape" might conceal a similar theatricality. He meets an "English ballad singer" in the street, presumably singing his wares for money. He also sees "files of ballads" that "dangle from dead walls" (line 209). In both cases, he confronts the poet as part of the marketplace, an identifiable professional type. In the much discussed "blind beggar" episode, in which Wordsworth encounters a beggar "wearing a written paper, to explain / The story of the man, and who he was," he fears that "in this la-bel was a type / Or emblem of the utmost that we know / Both of ourselves and of the universe" (lines 614–15, 618–20). Critics have ignored the reso-nance of the word "type" in exploring the limits of self-knowledge Words-worth records in this passage. Given the language of typology to which he responds throughout book 7, Wordsworth fears that in the city, with its ab-sence of moral community, he can only know or "read" others and himself through type. Although Wordsworth asserts that the poet speaks "not as a lawyer, a physician, a mariner, an astronomer or a natural philosopher, but as a Man," differing from other men not in kind, but in degree (*PLB,* 258, 261), in book 7 he addresses the fear that the poet cannot transcend distinc-tions of kind, that he too speaks as a type.

More specifically, in writing *The Prelude,* an autobiographical poem, Wordsworth risks the language of the advertisement, of selling himself and his moral experience as "poet," much as the prostitute sells her wares. Mary Jacobus calls *The Prelude* a "self-advertisement" (*Romanticism,* 234) and Clifford Siskin describes it as "the most extraordinary résumé in En-glish Literary history" (*Work of Writing,* 112). Siskin suggests that romantic poetry was central to the project of "constituting" the profession of litera-ture as "deeply imaginative writing" (132); thus Wordsworth's project in *The Prelude* is one not only of advertisement but of codifying the professional behavior of the poet: "This vita-like detailing of personal identity turns mat-uration into a preoccupation with occupation: in this case, how to become, behave like, and perform as a professional poet" (112). Wordsworth's deci-sion to withhold publication of *The Prelude* until after his death was an im-plicit acknowledgment that a long autobiographical poem could be read as an extended "résumé" or self-advertisement, an act of egotism.

Wordsworth engages this risk textually. Although his "solution" to the flaneur's bind is fraught with contradictions, his adherence throughout book 7 to an embodied perspective is significant. Not once does the figure of the poet leave the representational confines of the body in motion, or the threat of the urban theater. Even at Bartholomew's Fair, where the poet asks "for once" for the muse's help to escape the "press and danger of the crowd," he places himself on a "showman's platform" (lines 682–85). In the position of the showman, he remains visible to the crowd, and places himself within the economy of the fair. Compared to other poems in which Wordsworth clearly evades this threat, and to other representations of "walkers" in the city from about the same time, this perspective is striking. Deborah Epstein Nord records other "peripatetic" accounts of the city such as Pierce Egan's *Life in London* (1822), which offer a "camera obscura" view of the city, allow-ing urban observers to "maintain their own invisibility and invulnerability while absorbing—and even learning from—the 'shows' of the city" ("City as Theater," 171–73). It is precisely the reduction of the body to a pair of eyes, to a voyeuristic "camera obscura," that Wordsworth seeks to resist through his walk in book 7.

Most critics of book 7 have overlooked this fact, emphasizing how Wordsworth attempts to transcend the dangers of London by mapping onto the female body all that he fears: theatricality, the moral taint of consumption, sexuality unhinged from reproduction. Anne Mellor's response is indicative of this strain of criticism: she perceives the project of *The Prelude* as the construction of "a self that is unified, unique, enduring, capable of initiating activity, and above all aware of itself as a self," and argues that the self Wordsworth constructs "is not the higher—and potentially universal—self he dreamed of, but rather a specifically masculine self" (*Romanticism and Gender*, 145, 147). Wordsworth defines this masculine self through his rejection of the body: "To achieve coherence and endurance, this self or subjectivity must transcend the body and become pure mind. . . . It is crucial to see that the soul or self he constructs is bodiless. Despite Wordsworth's myriad sensory interactions with nature as child and man, his minute and detailed recollections of what he saw and heard and felt, his self remains curiously disembodied—we never hear whether he is hot or cold, whether he washes himself or defecates, whether he has sexual desires or intercourse." Mellor argues that Wordsworth conflates the body he rejects with a feminine "other," in the form of nature, his sister Dorothy, or the figure of the mother (149, 151). Similarly, Mary Jacobus argues that Wordsworth protects himself from his fall into representation in book 7 by conflating degraded representation with the prostitute, who stands in for the city and the consumer revolution; by figuring the prostitute as she who "splits" the race of man in twain, Wordsworth manages to maintain his wholeness, to defend the "fiction of a self that is not the subject of, or in, representation (and hence inevitably split)" (*Romanticism*, 214). That which threatens the "(masculine) single self" (222) is the body: "the gap or barrier created by Wordsworth's first sight of a prostitute effects a saving divorce between his soul and the body of representation" (223).

While I agree that Wordsworth seeks to evade dangers that he conflates with the feminine body, his body does not disappear; both critics assume that in "splitting" off the feminized body, Wordsworth preserves only the poetic "soul." As is particularly apparent in Mellor's case, this assumption results from our cultural expectations of what indicates or codes the presence of the "body" (dirt, defecation, sex, the feminine); because we equate the "bodily" with what Wordsworth represents as a threat, his body remains invisible. In choosing to dramatize the figure of the poet walking through

London, however, Wordsworth chooses to portray the poet's/poem's body as subject to the economy of "type," as the subject of or in representation, to use Jacobus's terms. The poet is the subject of the gaze as much as he gazes: both male and female bodies are subject in the London of book 7 to the equalizing gaze of the commodity form. Wordsworth uses the figure of the prostitute to represent the threat of degraded representation in book 7, not simply to avoid this threat but to bode forth the conflict that compels his negotiation of sincerity, so as to better teach a desired reading. To consider how Wordsworth uses the walk to respond to the theatricality of London, we need to keep in mind sincerity as a form of *embodied* masculine experience that Wordsworth expends so much effort to stage and preserve: after all, he wants to keep his reader "in the company of flesh and blood."

In London, Wordsworth realizes his body will be read as a text, a "type" like those around him; similarly, he sees that his poetry is necessarily part of the literary marketplace. The prostitute, as mirror flaneur, reveals to him one response to this predicament: she makes use of "typing" to position her body as a commodity for sale, profiting from the dominant social and economic vocabulary. In contrast, Wordsworth uses a poetry of sincerity to *reform* the language of type that impinges upon the body in the city. Since he must be read by strangers, both in the city crowd and through his poetry, Wordsworth uses his body/poem to teach a "resistant" reading. Through the representation of his walk in book 7, he demonstrates a practice of sincere experience, language, and community that offers an alternative to what he sees in London. Given his own theatricality, there are clear contradictions and limits to Wordsworth's response to the theatricality of London, but for the moment I will consider his attempt to constitute a community of "sincere" readers guided by principles other than type.

Wordsworth represents his experiences in London from a spatial and temporal remove, using the frame of remembrance to instruct the reader how to interpret his walks through London. Most notably, this remove locates him within a rural community (Grasmere), five years after beginning *The Prelude*, and two years after his most recent trip to London in 1802 (Gill, *Life*, 210, 233–38). Wordsworth frames even the act of "recollection in tranquillity" in the context of walking; he tells the reader that he recalls his walks through London while he walks in Grasmere. He begins book 7 by reflecting on the progress of his poetry, remarking how "slowly doth this work advance" (line 17). While the question of "progress" connotes pressures and expectations of what he should produce as a "poet," he immediately suggests that his work is subject only to "natural" rather than commercial pressures. While walking in the hills, he hears a "quire of redbreasts" announce the coming of winter, and is stirred to begin work anew.

By locating his inspiration to write in the changing of the seasons, Words-
worth suggests that he marks progress or change not through urban de-
mands but through natural cycles. His response to this change is akin to
that of the redbreasts: he says that he and they "in the hearing of bleak
winds / Will chaunt together" (lines 36–37). A similar feeling causes him
to begin composition:

> . . . my favorite grove—
> Now tossing its dark boughs in sun and wind—
> Spreads through me a commotion like its own,
> Something that fits me for the poet's task
> Which we will now resume with chearful hope.   (lines 50–54)

The movement of boughs in the wind fits the poet for his "task," rendering
poetic composition a spontaneous response to the natural forces that sur-
round him.

Wordsworth's walk through the fir grove implies the inherent tuning of
his body and voice to nature; he suggests that the walk is a literal as well as
metaphorical figure for the composition of his poetic narration. In fact,
Wordsworth composed much of his poetry while walking; Hazlitt reported
Coleridge's statement that "Wordsworth always wrote (if he could) walk-
ing up and down a straight gravel-walk, or in some spot where the conti-
nuity of his verse met with no collateral interruption" (qtd. in A. Bennett,
"Devious Feet," 147). Similarly, Dorothy described his process of walking
and composing thus: "Though the length of his walk be sometimes a quar-
ter or half of a mile, he is as fast bound within the chosen limits as if by
prison walls" (165). While we cannot know whether Wordsworth actually
composed book 7 within the fir grove, what is crucial about this opening is
that he figures himself thus, conflating walking and writing. Superim-
posed over the vision of a young Wordsworth walking in the London crowd
is the vision of an older Wordsworth walking in the fir grove; the danger of
his walk through London resurfaces in the fir grove as an obstacle of com-
position, the problem of reading the city becoming one of writing about
the city.

The risk of describing London, like the risk of walking through it, is the
risk that the poet will be seduced by fancy:

> . . . Shall I give way,
> Copying the impression of the memory—
> Though things remembered idly do half seem

> The work of fancy—shall I, as the mood
> Inclines me, here describe for pastime's sake,
> Some portion of that motley imagery. (lines 145–50)

Fancy is not "work," that is, transformative labor, but only the idle or uncritical copying of objects or sights. In the context of book 7, fancy is the language of imitation, the language of type, of differences without end: it results in the list or catalog, a form that, like the miniature or the panorama, copies objects or places but provides only visual, anatomical knowledge of them (Kramer, "Gender and Sexuality," 622). The risk of fancy is that it becomes indistinguishable from the spectacles it describes. Just as Wordsworth begins his sojourn in London "unbounded," at "leisure" ("yet undetermined to what plan of life / I should adhere," "At ease from all ambition personal" [lines 63–64, 69]), and thus susceptible to London's seductions, he is similarly "unbounded" as he begins to write about this experience.

Wordsworth seems to succumb to fancy, as evidenced by the visual lists or catalogs that comprise much of book 7. Just as he moved through London in the past, "With fancy on the stir from day to day," fancy stirs as he composes (lines 79–80). He signifies this potential seduction through his use of verb tense: at times, he is so absorbed by his memories of past sights that he switches into the present tense, erasing his temporal and spatial remove. For instance, he describes, in the present tense, "the look and aspect of the place— / The broad highway appearance, as it strikes / On strangers of all ages" (lines 154–56). The sights and sounds of the city enchant him:

> The wealth, the bustle and the eagerness,
> The glittering chariots with their pampered steeds,
> Stalls, barrows, porters, midway in the street
> The scavenger that begs with hat in hand
> The labouring hackney coaches. (lines 161–65)

Wordsworth signals his immersion in the urban tableau through the trope of the walk: "meanwhile the roar continues, till at length, / Escaped as from an enemy, we turn / Abruptly into some sequestered nook" (lines 184–86). In the 1850 *Prelude,* Wordsworth acknowledges that the memories of his walks in London threaten to turn into his seduction by its spectacles: "Genius of Burke! forgive the pen seduced / by specious wonders" (lines 512–13).

At intervals throughout book 7, Wordsworth reveals his struggle to resist the seductive grip of the past as he writes. For instance, he abruptly concludes his description of an urban prostitute with the exclamation, "I quit this painful theme, enough is said / To show what thoughts must often have been mine" (lines 437–38). He reminds his reader of time's passage and his implicit maturation when describing the attraction of London's spectacles, noting, "Life then was new / The senses easily pleased" (lines 440–41). Finally, Wordsworth presents images that "rise" to wrench him from his "wanderings" in the past to the present moment of composition, to his location in a rural space and community; such moments instruct the reader how to read and respond to Wordsworth's walks through and potential seduction by London, both as a young man and as the writer of *The Prelude*.[15]

Wordsworth addresses this potential seduction through the figure of Mary Robinson, the Maid of Buttermere, who was "nursed . . . / On the same mountains" as the young poet (lines 342–43). Mary was seduced by a bigamist, and in 1803 became the subject of a Sadler's Wells melodrama ("dramas of living men / And recent things yet warm with life" [lines 313–14]). Of course, the dramatic figuring of "living men" recalls Wordsworth's project in *The Prelude*. As he describes Mary's fall, an image of the unviolated Mary arises:

> These last words uttered, to my argument
> I was returning, when—with sundry forms
> Mingled, that in the way which I must tread
> Before me stand—thy image rose again,
> Mary of Buttermere! She lives in peace
> Upon the spot where she was born and reared;
> Without contamination does she live
> In quietness, without anxiety.   (lines 348–54)

The impediment that the memory of Mary Robinson presents to Wordsworth's walk is the potential of her "contamination" by the theatrical spectacles of London, and, in turn, Wordsworth's potential contamination by his representation of these seductions.

In fact, as Betsy Bolton argues, the figure of the notorious poet Mary Darby Robinson shadows the figure of Mary Robinson of Buttermere in book 7: Darby Robinson's *Lyrical Tales*, like Wordsworth's *Lyrical Ballads*, were published by Longman (Bolton, "Romancing the Stone"; Pascoe, *Romantic Theatricality*, 137). Not only did Robinson write poems about walking through London as what Pascoe calls a "spectacular flaneuse," but her association with the theater and promiscuous sexuality signified the threat of prostituting his art which Wordsworth engaged in book 7. More pointedly, the Maid of Buttermere's fall and Mary Darby Robinson's affairs connoted sexuality unhinged from reproduction within a family or moral community. What ostensibly distinguishes the two Marys—and Wordsworth from Darby Robinson—is that while the Maid of Buttermere is an "artless daughter of the hills," the very model of a sincerity that has been unwittingly corrupted, Darby Robinson is a professional actress who uses her art to seduce her audience. When Mary's image "rises" and stops the poet's walk, it pulls him back to his grove in the Lakes, enabling him to connect Mary's sincerity with her location in Buttermere, and to indicate that his location in Grasmere similarly spells a different habit of sincerity than that of Darby Robinson.[16]

While the process of composing book 7 tests Wordsworth's powers to resist fancy, this is a test completed at a distance: his location in a present removed spatially and temporally from London permits a walk ostensibly unencumbered by the city's physical dangers, a walk prompted by natural forces, that enables reflection, the tempering of the passions by thought, the exercise of voluntary powers. This frame of remembrance is consistent with his description of poetry as "the spontaneous overflow of powerful feelings: it takes its origin from emotion *recollected in tranquillity*" (*PLB*, 266; italics mine). And yet the question that book 7 raises is whether the power to control "fancy" is contingent upon a spatial and temporal remove, or whether Wordsworth (and the reader) could exercise such control in London. At the end of book 7, Wordsworth suggests that his habits of spontaneity are portable: he implies that the challenges of composition he meets as he walks in the fir grove are ultimately no different from those he met on his earlier walks through London:

> But though the picture weary out the eye,
> By nature an unmanageable sight,
> It is not wholly so to him who looks
> In steadiness, who hath among least things
> An under-sense of greatest, sees the parts
> As parts, but with a feeling of the whole.
> . . . .
> This did I feel in that vast receptacle.
> The spirit of Nature was upon me here,
> The soul of beauty and enduring life
> Was present as a habit, and diffused—
> Through meagre lines and colours, and the press
> Of self-destroying, transitory things—
> Composure and ennobling harmony.   (lines 708–41)

Although the urban "language" of type is equivalent to the visual spectacles of consumption that weary Wordsworth's "eye," it is the "habit" of viewing nature, a habit of *reading,* that permits him to see even in London "an under-sense of greatest." This habit of reading stems from the practices of moral community: Wordsworth is able to see through the "press / Of self-destroying, transitory things" because he has experienced, and retains the ideal of, a moral community in which individuals act from sympathy for their fellow man rather than from pure economic self-interest. While rural communities, due to their "simplicity and power," nurture this habit of reading, Wordsworth suggests that "education" and "early converse with the works of God" makes this reading practice possible "among all regions," even London (lines 716–21). His framing of his London walk by his Grasmere walk enacts such instruction: as he recollects nature's presence as "habit" in London, he instructs the urban reader how to follow in his footsteps.

Wordsworth does not transcend his body at the end of book 7, but rather defines a way in which to in*habit* it such that he, and his reader, can both participate in and yet retain critical distance from the language of type.[17] "Habit" is a practice not of vision but of memory, a repetition of a learned narrative that connects past to present; these "habits of mind" ideally become second nature, such that they can be obeyed "blindly and mechanically" (*PLB,* 247). For Wordsworth, habit generates a particular performance; as he walks through the fir grove, his movements mirror the "forms" and "language" of nature and align him with the habits of the moral community in Grasmere. The poet is "habitually impelled" to recreate such feelings "where he does not find them": the habit of remembering and thus re-creating this feeling ideally allows Wordsworth, and in turn his urban reader, to resist the "immediate external excitement" of London (*PLB,* 256). What is crucial to this habit of reading is not one's literal location in a pastoral setting (Grasmere), but the practice of "natural" or moral feeling, hence Wordsworth's statement that feeling in his poetry gives importance to the action and situation, and not vice versa (*PLB,* 248). Tellingly, he makes the same point about poetry and prose; while he argues that "there neither is nor can be any essential difference" between the genres, that "the same human blood circulates through the veins of both," he adds that the important distinction is between that of "true feeling" and the "vulgarity and meanness of ordinary life" (*PLB,* 253–54). Sincerity as the habit of "*true* feeling" becomes the very definition of the poetic profession, distinguishing poetry from prose, a theatrical from a genuine performance. And early reviewers of *The Prelude,* such as the critic for the *Gentleman's Magazine,* seemed to have learned the lesson of book 7 well: "All the life in his ballads, in his narrative poems, in his Excursion, is the reflex of his own being. The actors in his scenes are severe, aloof, stately, and uniform; grand in their isolation, dignified in their sorrows. They are not creatures of the market or the haven, of the senate or the forum."[18]

The tenuousness of the distinction between a theatrical and genuine performance is clear. Habit refers not only to "a settled disposition or tendency to act in a certain way, especially one acquired by frequent repetition of the same act until it is almost involuntary" but also to "the dress or attire characteristic of a particular rank, profession, function, etc.; especially the dress of a religious order" (*OED*). Wordsworth's habit reveals his profession, and reveals that it, too, is a kind of performance, despite the ideal of the poet as a figure who transcends the language of professional and economic type (*PLB*, 254). Recognizing that the poet and his writing are likely to be read through the language of type in the urban theater, Wordsworth chooses a "habit" that connotes the "dress of a religious order"—a moral performance of feeling—over the "poisoned vestments" of the prostitute.[19] The poet of book 7 teaches his reader that retaining spontaneous habits in the city is hard work: "Oppression under which even highest minds / Must labour, whence the strongest are not free" (lines 706–7). Spontaneity is the habitual, practiced movement of body, thought, and feeling to resist the seductions of consumer culture in London, and the poet is the professional who is best-trained in these actions.

The Walk, the Epitaph, and Wordsworth's Monumental Reception

This is clearly a contradictory, even complicitous, strategy: others have shown that Wordsworth's response to the figure of the prostitute is an anxious and phobic one, that he essentially splits the figure of the poet "in twain," displacing his necessary dealings with advertisement and the marketplace onto the prostitute so as to secure the moral basis of the poetic profession.[20] This argument has merit. But the distinction is less that of a debased theatricality versus an idealized sincerity than one between various possible performances of sincerity: in performing sincerity within the commercial theater, Wordsworth attempts to *reform* (rather than simply deny or repress) theatricality by charting a moral use and reading of literary property. By presenting his walks through London as "habits" of spontaneity, Wordsworth teaches his readers how to respond to its spectacles, and, in turn, how to read the sincere poem and poet as they circulate in the urban marketplace. The walk as embodied experience thus enacts the poet's desired relation to the poem as an embodied thing. Wordsworth cultivates his future reception by aligning the poet's name not with advertisement and what he saw as narrow self-interest but with the national monument and the perpetuity of moral values.

Wordsworth's cultivation of a future monumental reception was both a textual and a material strategy. As discussed above, his decision to postpone publication of *The Prelude* until after his death clearly stemmed from his anxieties that sincerity would be read as self-advertisement. He stated in a letter to Sir George Beaumont that it was "a thing unprecedented in Literary history that a man should talk so much about himself," and to Thomas Noon Talfourd he commented that "its publication has been prevented merely by the personal character of the subject."[21] However, Christopher Wordsworth indicated after Wordsworth's death in 1850 that *The Prelude* "was left ready for the Press by the Author," and that his "first duty here is to . . . prepare the posthumous Poem for publication."[22] Posthumous publication worked to ensure that readers would not see the poet's aims as self-interested, since he would not be present to benefit materially from publication. During his lifetime Wordsworth worked to establish the moral intent of *The Prelude,* assuring Sir George Beaumont that "it is not self-conceit, as you will know well, that has induced [me] to do this, but real humility." He justified "giving [his] own history to the world" by positioning *The Prelude* as preparatory to *The Recluse,* likening it to the "anti-chapel" to a "gothic church."[23] Following the publication of *The Prelude* in 1850, it was in the main read as a sincere text, suggesting the success of Wordsworth's efforts.[24]

Wordsworth's plans for posthumous publication of *The Prelude* were of a piece with his material efforts to secure copyright protection that would extend well beyond the life of the author. Mark Rose and others have described Wordsworth's repeated interventions on behalf of extending the duration of copyright. In contrast to the Continental model of *droit d'auteur* or "natural rights," in which the author was treated as the natural or moral owner of a work, copyright in England and America was based on a limited term of statutory protection. By 1814 in England, this term was "twenty-eight years after publication or the author's lifetime, whichever was longer" (M. Rose, *Authors and Owners,* 110). Wordsworth, Southey, and others preferred the Continental concept of natural rights; Wordsworth viewed "pecuniary emoluments" as "the natural Inheritance of the posterity of Authors" (qtd. in M. Rose 110). Thus Wordsworth worked assiduously on behalf of Thomas Noon Talfourd's parliamentary campaign to revise copyright by extending its term to sixty years past the author's lifetime, writing numerous letters and, in 1839, a petition to Parliament. The Copyright Act

of 1842 extended protection from twenty-eight to forty-two years from pub-
lication, or seven years past the author's death (M. Rose 111).

In suggesting that copyright is an author's natural moral right, Words-
worth looked to the future good of family and nation, rather than to the
material benefits an author might secure within his own lifetime. Words-
worth justified natural rights in terms of cultivating works that, in his
words, "are desirous of pleasing and instructing future generations" and
that would provide "for the benefit of his issue," his "family" and "descen-
dants" (Woodmansee, *Construction*, 5). In this vein, Susan Eilenberg has ar-
gued that Wordsworth's efforts to extend the term of copyright testified to
his interest in controlling his posthumous career: "What Wordsworth had
in mind as the proper tribute to the dead poet was a reform of copyright
laws: no monuments, just money. . . . Copyright is something due to the
memory of the dead, a symbolic refutation of the material facts it confirms,
and the money it brings a poet's heirs does the cause of literature more good
than all the sculpted marble in the world" (355). Wordsworth's efforts to ex-
ercise posthumous control over the material and moral legacy of *The Pre-
lude* for the posthumous benefit of family and nation work in concert with
the textual strategies of sincerity that I have discussed: what he specifically
hoped to elicit was a "sincere" reading that an understanding of the poem
as a form of literary property might guarantee rather than threaten.

Most important to the posthumous reading of sincerity that Wordsworth
cultivates in book 7 is the retrospective presentation of the poet's walk: the
frame of memory allows the reader to witness the poet looking back at a
younger self, with the help of ingrained habits of spontaneity. The first
public for the poem in 1850 would have read the voice of the poet with a
further temporal remove in mind, Wordsworth's recent death. Quite liter-
ally, then, they would have read *The Prelude* elegiacally, as a "posthumous
Poem." Autobiography would then ideally function less as advertisement
than as an epitaph for the dead poet, an epitaph written, as it turns out, by
an expert in the genre: "It may be said that a sepulchral monument is a trib-
ute to a man as a human being; and that an epitaph (in the ordinary mean-
ing attached to the word) includes this general feeling and something more;
and is a record to preserve the memory of the dead, as a tribute to his indi-
vidual worth, for a satisfaction to the sorrowing hearts of the survivors, and
for the common benefit of the living" (*EE1*, 327). Wordworth's description
of the aims of the epitaph captures what I have described as his moral and
financial motives for posthumous publication of *The Prelude*.[25] More gen-
erally, the "Essays Upon Epitaphs," written between 1809 and 1810, elabo-
rate the importance of sincerity to the poet's desired posthumous reception,

clarifying what the poet hoped would be buried and what remembered about an individual after his death.

Wordsworth states that one of his key aims in the essays is "chiefly to assist the reader in separating truth and sincerity from falsehood and affection" (*EE3*, 358). "A criterion of sincerity" is central to the writing and reception of epitaphs, Wordsworth argues, because "no faults have such a killing power as those which prove that [the poet] is not in earnest, that he is acting a part, has leisure for affectation, and feels that without it he could do nothing. This is one of the most odious of faults; because it shocks the moral sense: and is worse in a sepulchral inscription, precisely in the same degree as that mode of composition calls for sincerity more urgently than any other" (*EE2*, 345). A sepulchral monument must be sincere because, in preserving the memory of the dead, it influences the values of the living. Similarly, for Wordsworth the epitaph articulates an ideal of posthumous poetic reception. If we consider the "ideal" reading of *The Prelude* as an epitaph for the dead Wordsworth, then book 7 engages the poet's nightmare: a potential reading of the poem as self-advertisement. Through the framing of his walks through London in book 7, Wordsworth teaches his preferred reading of his performance of sincerity, attempting to supplant the theatricality of the advertisement with the stability, permanence, and transparency of the epitaph, thereby rendering his "personal" act of memory less self-interested than generic and monumental.

Epitaphs speak to man's common nature, and in this way provide the moral glue that may contain economic rivalship, "the strife of singularity": "For in no place are we so much disposed to dwell upon those points, of nature and condition, wherein all men resemble each other, as in the temple where the universal Father is worshipped, or by the side of the grave which gathers all human Beings to itself, and equalizes the lofty and the low. We suffer and we weep with the same heart; we love and are anxious for one another in one spirit; our hopes look to the same quarter; and the virtues by which we are all to be furthered and supported, as patience, meekness, good-will, justice, temperance, and temperate desires, are in an equal degree the concern of us all. Let an Epitaph, then, contain at least these acknowledgments to our common nature" (*EE1*, 334). Such monuments provide "a visible centre of a community of the living and the dead," a narrative of common feeling that can bind even Londoners into a moral community (330).[26] To this end, the epitaph "is exposed to all—to the wise and the most ignorant. . . . Its story and admonitions are brief, that the thoughtless, the busy, and indolent, may not be deterred, nor the impatient tired: the stooping old man cons the engraven record like a second horn-book;—the child is proud that he can read it;—and the stranger is introduced through its mediation to the company of a friend: it is concerning all, and for all" (334). To "concern all," the epitaph must subordinate "what was peculiar to the individual" to "what he had in common with the species" (*EE3*, 365).

To elicit a posthumous reading of the poet as a figure of sincerity, Wordsworth needed to entertain—and ideally circumvent—the possibility that *The Prelude* could be read as a self-serving performance. Wordsworth indirectly addresses this possibility in the "Essays upon Epitaphs." Epitaphs could be accused of insincerity, in that their idealizing rhetoric at best distorts and at worst misrepresents the lives of those they memorialize: the epitaphic poet looks at the character of the deceased not as "an anatomist, who dissects the internal frame of the mind" but "through a tender haze or a luminous mist, that spiritualises and beautifies" (*EE1*, 332–33). Asking "Where are all the bad people buried?" Wordsworth replies that he has considered "the anxieties, the perturbations, and, in many instances, the vices and rancourous dispositions, by which the hearts of those who lie under so smooth a surface and so fair an outside must have been agitated" (337–38). Wordsworth's solution is not to deny this conflict, but rather to justify what he sees as a proper reading of it, which amounts to a proper funeral ritual. In short, he asks his readers not to deny or evade but to actively "bury" the language of advertisement, associated in book 7 with dead letters, the prostitute, and the seductions of London.[27]

Rather than risk being read as a poet-prostitute—a "dead author" or debased personification—Wordsworth aspires to textual life through readings that reenact the poet's moral habit of sincerity. More specifically, animating the figure of the author—making the poet walk—is central to Wordsworth's attempt to influence his posthumous reception. As Susan Eilenberg emphasizes, Wordsworth's efforts to extend copyright ultimately aim "to secure a refuge from oblivion, a means to enable writing to transcend itself" ("Mortal Pages," 369). As readers engage Wordsworth's posthumous poem, they potentially animate the figure of the author as they read. Through the example of his walk, the poet from beyond the grave teaches a habit of reading sincerity/reading sincerely: the reader "walks" alongside the figure of the poet, reenacting the poet's temporal narrative involving memory, habit, and feeling.[28] As epitaph, the poem's "ideal" generic function is realized when readers enact the habit of sincere reading/walking that Wordsworth believed was essential to the maintenance of a moral community. By cultivating a sympathetic community of future walkers/readers, Wordsworth suggests that *The Prelude* can circulate indefinitely in the literary marketplace as that paradoxical entity, a moral commodity.

Wordsworth's positioning of *The Prelude* as epitaph has confirmed the reading of him as a poet of monumental stature. He had already achieved a monumental stature prior to his death; in 1843 Queen Victoria named him the poet laureate, the symbolic guardian of national values (Gill, *Life,* 383, 409). Marlon Ross and James Chandler have described how poets such as Wordsworth rendered themselves representative Romantics. Ross comments: "Wordsworth is a part of the period who can stand for a sense of the whole because of his power of representation. The author's representational mode of writing—his power to represent things through words—is continuously confused with his representative power—his ability to serve both as a figure for all other writers of the time and all that happens in the time, and as a standard against which all other writers of the time must be placed and judged" (Ross, "Breaking the Period," 126; Chandler, "Representative Men"). Wordsworth's representative power, I have suggested, is connected to his rhetorical demonstration of how to read conventions of sincerity in texts such as *The Prelude* and "Essays upon Epitaphs," and to his efforts to extend the term of copyright; rather than simply critique or denaturalize this ideal of reception, it's worth dwelling for a moment on its success. An anonymous critic for the *British Quarterly Review* in 1850 presciently stated that *The Prelude* "will stand, we believe, as a production *sui generis* in our literature, a memorial, executed by his own hands, egotistically perhaps, but still truly (and Wordsworth's very egotism is capable of a reverent interpretation) of the early life of a good and highly-gifted man."[29] Herbert Lindenberger suggests that *The Prelude* was initially received by Victorian readers as a memorial, not only to a man but to an earlier age whose concerns seemed dated; it would take twentieth-century readers to recognize *The Prelude*'s modernity. Indeed, post-1945 poets' explicit embrace of tropes of sincerity spurred a revitalization of interest in the theme of sincerity in literary criticism of the late 1950s and 1960s, with many critics connecting this trend to the influence of Wordsworth (*Wordsworth's Prelude,* 275–76). For instance, David Perkins argued in 1964 that "in describing the particular response of Wordsworth to the challenge of sincerity, one also suggests how the ideal of sincerity has influenced poetry throughout the last century and a half" (*Poetry of Sincerity,* 3).

Wordsworthian lyric sincerity has defined romanticism implicitly or explicitly since the nineteenth century: even recent readings guided by Jerome McGann's understanding of the romantic ideology presuppose a sincere ideal to be denaturalized. As Judith Pascoe states, "To Wordsworth can be traced the tendency to read romanticism as reflecting a solemn and constant subject status, and thus an inherently antitheatrical one" (*Romantic Theatricality,* 187). *The Prelude* has played an important role in fostering such readings, and, as I will argue in subsequent chapters, the representative power of Wordsworthian sincerity has profoundly shaped both the reading and the writing of conventions of sincerity in the Anglo-American lyric tradition. If generic traditions are themselves monuments brought into being and passed on through shared practices of reading, then looking afresh at the conflicts of reading that triggered the need for such monuments can help us to see the skeptical pressure underwriting Wordsworth's expressive rhetoric, and can in turn illuminate practices of sincerity overshadowed by the success of a Wordsworthian ideal. In other words, while it might be tempting to reverse the terms of book 7's reception, to read *The Prelude* as advertisement, such a reading would miss the very *tension over reading* that book 7 dramatizes: the effort to erect a monument to sincerity in theatrical terms and in a commercial age.

While Wordsworthian habits of spontaneity have influenced the perception of poetry's commercial disinterest, the commercial implications of this habit have been no less profound. To this day, the walking tour remains a popular way to experience Britain "authentically." Wordsworth played no small part in this trend. In using his walks through the Lake District to model an experience of moral reading and community, Wordsworth contributed to the popularity of this kind of tourist experience, one purportedly more genuine than the vicarious tours provided by panoramas, paintings, and poems.[30] He also helped to make the Lake District a popular tourist site, both by describing its virtues in his poetry, and by publishing a popular *Guide to the Lakes*. Despite Wordsworth's contradictory efforts to stop this tourist boon by opposing the building of a Kendal and Windermere Railway,[31] by 1847 trains "were steaming into the station," carrying crowds of walkers, there to try and spot the Poet Laureate walking along his famous paths (Gill, *Life*, 414). The train rendered visible, material, the traffic in commodities that book 7 staged and tried to contain: the dependence of the lakes on the city, the poetic walk on the tour, sincerity on theatricality, and nature on the commodity.

Chapter 2

Frank O'Hara

The Flaneur as Consumer

Frank O'Hara made his home in New York from 1951 until his death in 1966. The noise, heat, and smell of the city permeate his poetry: automobiles honk, sidewalks steam, traffic lights turn from red to green, neon bulbs flash in store windows, subways rumble below the street, skyscrapers loom. Nature in its conventional sense is conspicuously absent: "I have never clogged myself with the praises of pastoral life, nor with nostalgia for an innocent past of perverted acts in pastures. No. One need never leave the confines of NY to get all the greenery one wishes—I can't even enjoy a blade of grass unless I know there's a subway handy, or a record store or some other sign that people do not totally regret life. It is more important to affirm the least sincere; the clouds get enough attention as it is and even they continue to pass. Do they know what they're missing? Uh huh."[1] O'Hara mocks an older pastoral ideal, aligning it with nostalgia for a past-that-never-was, with the "naive" romantic values of innocence, sincerity, and depth. Instead, he celebrates a present of irony, surface, and the "least sincere," rejecting the desire to define a space distinct from the landscape of consumption. O'Hara would seem to inhabit the "poisoned vestments" that Wordsworth instructed his readers not to wear: and yet, I will suggest, O'Hara is not only deeply committed to a moral ideal of spontaneous feeling, but teaches his readers a new habit of reading, one that inverts a Wordsworthian moral universe so as to locate sincerity in the ephemeral, theatrical, and seductive potentials of the city.

While Wordsworth exemplifies an early instance of the flaneur's bind, O'Hara would reveal this bind to be no less pressing in the postwar era. As Fredric Jameson and others argue, the unprecedented consolidation and spread of capital after World War II compromised the possibility of "critical distance" (*Postmodernism*, 48). From this perspective, modernist alienation presupposed some separation of art and commerce, allowing artists to retain a model of identity based on notions of autonomy, depth, and privacy, while postwar culture absorbs such alienation, resulting in a celebration of surface and a "free-floating" euphoria (16, 28). In this history, the nineteenth-century flaneur's complicitous protest anticipates his late-twentieth-century downfall: his embrace of idleness, leisure, and extravagant consumption ushers in the consumerist ethos, the era of the shopping mall and the television shopping network.[2]

Along these lines, most critics, proceeding from the assumption that the sincere lyric must oppose the self-interested performances of commercial culture, feel that O'Hara's poetry of irony and surface lacks "moral seriousness" and "a political consciousness per se" (Elledge, "Lack of Gender," 228). And yet O'Hara's poetry challenges this assumption.[3] Guided by the belief that an oppositional stance toward commodity culture is not a prerequisite for sincerity, O'Hara uses consumer practices to redefine sincere feeling. As one of the foremost practitioners of the "camp" aesthetic, which proceeds from the "metaphor of life as theater," O'Hara's poetry reveals that the theatricality of commercial culture does not preclude sincerity.[4] O'Hara takes his position within the crowd as the grounds for a new poetics of sincerity generated by the relationship between poet, poem, and reader in a consumer culture.

In defining commercial culture as his "natural" element, O'Hara dispensed with modernist orthodoxy: he also worked inside the museum, a potent symbol of the institutionalization of modernism in the postwar era, often thought to mark the end of an autonomous avant-garde.[5] While romantic-era writers usually relied on some form of patronage, whether that of a wealthy patron or of subscription publishing, poets writing in the latter half of the twentieth century often depended on "institutional patronage," finding jobs or financial support through the museum, university, or federally funded arts organizations.[6] Creative writing programs marked a new stage in the professionalization of poetry and signified the university's prominence as an institutional home for poets and fiction writers; in 1951 O'Hara completed an MA in creative writing at the University of Michigan. Rather than pursue a career in the university or literary establishment after completing the MA, however, O'Hara chose to write poetry "on the side" while working at the Museum of Modern Art (MOMA) in New York. He began working at MOMA in 1951, first as a sales clerk, later as an assistant in the International Program, and finally, as a curator of painting and sculpture.[7]

O'Hara's career path represents that of many postwar poets in that he depended on an institution responsible for the professionalization of the arts. On the one hand, the museum allowed O'Hara to avoid the constraints of a conservative literary establishment and to pursue avant-garde experiment in a supportive community of visual artists; the museum provided a welcome shelter for those with progressive aesthetic and moral values, facilitating modernism's goal of "making it new." On the other hand, the museum was involved in the marketing of modernism, both at home and abroad, subsuming avant-gardism to the aims of stylistic and historical classification, public instruction, sales (particularly of design), and cold war propaganda (Staniszewski, *Power of Display*). O'Hara was an active member of the New York avant-garde, but he was equally involved in its institutionalization, through his work on exhibitions such as "The New American Painting" (1958–59) and through his contributions to the International Program, intended to maintain America's cultural status abroad during the cold war.[8] The museum's role as both shelter for and marketer of modernism defined O'Hara's conflicted position within it: he was a museum professional dedicated to the museum's policies, but he was also an experimental poet and friend of the painters whose avant-gardism—at least in theory—sought to elude the pressures of professionalization. O'Hara's desire for a spontaneous ideal stemmed from a dedication to "making it new," but he was simultaneously aware that in the postwar era such ideals were facilitated by the museum, a conundrum that Gertrude Stein put this way: "You can be a museum or you can be modern, but you can't be both."[9]

A further challenge to O'Hara's effort to articulate spontaneous desire was the widespread moral censure of homosexuality at mid-century.[10] New York was not small-town America, and O'Hara openly expressed his sexual identity at the museum and in avant-garde circles, but facing the general public was another matter (Gooch, *City Poet*, 197). Although homosexuality had become increasingly visible during World War II, the policing and harassment of gay men and women increased dramatically after the war: the risk of expressing gay identity in public was a risk of moral censure and persecution. The scapegoating of homosexuals was an important component of national ideology during the cold war (Chauncey, *Gay New York*, 360). The U.S. policy to contain communism on the international front was sustained on the home front in the 1950s through domestic ideology. The home served as a symbol of democratic ideals and as a buffer against political unrest; ideally, problems were to be resolved through the family rather than through public protest. Sexual norms enforced domestic ideology and in turn domestic consumerism; the government linked national strength to the containment of sex within marriage, and a family-centered culture prevailed, as exemplified by a huge increase in the birth and marriage rate (May, *Homeward Bound*, 3, 10, 11).

The federal government enforced these norms by defining homosexuals as a threat to national security (Chauncey 360) and by actively practicing and encouraging homophobia. Asserting that homosexuality made individuals morally weak and thus easy prey for communists, the Senate in 1950 issued a report discouraging the employment of homosexuals in government due to their weak "moral fiber" and potential for treason; meanwhile, the FBI made it a policy to investigate the sexual habits of suspicious persons (May 94–95; Chauncey 359). Elaine May writes that "gay baiting rivaled red baiting in its ferocity, destroying careers, encouraging harassment, creating stigmas, and forcing those who confessed their guilt to name others with whom they associated" (94–95). While gay culture in pre-Stonewall New York flourished in both public and private spaces around the city, the New York City police periodically enforced the national government's de facto policy, harassing homosexuals and closing bars to prevent the homosexual presence from becoming too overt.[11] Given this hostility, O'Hara's negotiation of the city as a gay man was a necessarily performative affair.

O'Hara's attempt to articulate a "personal form of originality" within the constraints of postwar culture assumes new meaning when we consider that these constraints, in terms of the sexual and moral economies guiding 1950s social life, took the shape of closets. Moreover, for O'Hara the moral and economic orders were coterminous, the values supporting economic production connected to reproduction and normative sexuality. Through the flaneur's relationship to the prostitute, a figure embodying the seductions and pleasures of consumer culture, O'Hara defined an alternative moral path. In this he followed in the footsteps of two earlier poet-flaneurs, Charles Baudelaire and Walt Whitman, who each wrote a poetry of the city that challenged common understandings of nature and morality, making possible an *urban* pastoral.[12] Rejecting the romantic view of nature "as ground, source and type of all possible Good and Beauty," Baudelaire argues in "Painter of Modern Life" that "Nature teaches us nothing, or practically nothing" (*Selected Writings*, 31). Nature, he suggests, is "none other than the voice of our own self-interest," while "Virtue, on the other hand, is artificial. . . . Good is always the product of some art" (32). Reversing the assumption that the theatricality of consumer culture taints man's "natural" moral capacities, Baudelaire reads "external finery as one of the signs of the primitive nobility of the human soul" (32) and fashion "as a symptom of the taste for the ideal . . . as a sublime deformation of Nature, or rather a permanent and repeated attempt at her reformation" (32–33). Whereas Wordsworth believed that the prostitute and the actress used theatricality for commercial gain—becoming the very type of professional insincerity—for Baudelaire they embody an ideal of "artificial nobility." Whitman too encompassed the prostitute within a "natural" order: in "To a Common Prostitute," he comments, "Be composed—be at ease with me—I am Walt Whitman, liberal and lusty as Nature, / Not till the sun excludes you do I exclude you, / Not till the waters refuse to glisten for you and the leaves to rustle for you, do my words refuse to glisten and rustle for you."[13]

Both poets thumbed their noses at the bourgeoisie by valorizing these fallen women, inverting received moral codes in ways that anticipated the modernist avant-garde. In doing so they shifted the understanding of the poetic profession: Baudelaire commented, "If in one aspect the actress is akin to the courtesan, in another she comes close to the poet. We must never forget that quite apart from natural, and even artificial, beauty, each human being bears the distinctive stamp of his trade, a characteristic which can be translated into physical ugliness, but also into a sort of 'professional' beauty" (36–37). Similarly, Whitman announced, "Lusts and wickedness are acceptable to me, / I walk with delinquents with passionate love, / I feel I am of them—I belong to those convicts and prostitutes myself, / And henceforth I will not deny them—for how can I deny myself?" (*LG*, 324–25).[14] Like these earlier flaneurs, O'Hara expands the understanding of "natural" moral behavior by appropriating the prostitute's transgressive sexuality, her theatricality, and her powers of consumer seduction; in Whitman in particular O'Hara found a model of homosexual desire as a utopian figure for an erotics of "sincere" circulation within commercial culture, and even for democracy itself.

By strategically connecting the language and economy of consumption to that of homosexual desire, O'Hara attempts to circumvent cold war ideals of national, moral, and sexual (re)production. Through his walk poetry, constitutive of his persona as a poet-flaneur, O'Hara seeks to actualize this desire within the urban landscape. In tracing O'Hara's strolls through the city, we trace how flanerie—through its immersion in the language and practices of consumption—continues to serve as a habit of sincerity in the late-twentieth-century city.

Lunch Poems

At the center of O'Hara's poetry is the figure of the poet himself: O'Hara, who loved Hollywood film, stars in the ongoing drama of his life. As he stated in the *New American Poetry*, "What is happening to me, allowing for lies and exaggerations which I try to avoid, goes into my poems" ("Statement for the New American Poetry," *CP* 500). O'Hara's reader follows the poet walking around the city, shopping, reading the paper, going to the movies, conversing in bars, cafés, and friends' apartments, visiting studios, galleries, and museums. In *Lunch Poems* (1964), the poet's visual and material consumption of the city serves as both occasion and metaphor for the collection. Several of the poems describe the walks O'Hara took during his lunch break from his job at the museum, as the blurb he wrote for the volume's back jacket indicates: "Often this poet, strolling through the noisy splintered glare of a Manhattan noon, has paused at a sample Olivetti to type up thirty or forty lines of ruminations, or pondering more deeply has withdrawn to a darkened ware- or firehouse to limn his computed misunderstandings of the eternal questions of life, co-existence and depth, while never forgetting to eat lunch his favorite meal."[15] "Lunch Poems" refers to these lunchtime walks, but more generally it refers to O'Hara's questioning of the relationship between consumption and poetry, surface and depth, as he explores the possibility of a sincere lyric immersed in urban consumer culture.

"A Step Away from Them" clarifies how O'Hara engages these concerns:

It's my lunch hour, so I go
for a walk among the hum-coloured
cabs. First, down the sidewalk
where laborers feed their dirty
glistening torsos sandwiches
and Coca-Cola, with yellow helmets
on. They protect them from falling
bricks, I guess. Then onto the
avenue where skirts are flipping
above heels and bow up over
grates. The sun is hot, but the
cabs stir the air. I look
at bargains in wristwatches. There
are cats playing in sawdust.
                                        On
to Times Square, where the sign
blows smoke over my head, and higher
the waterfall pours lightly. A
Negro stands in a doorway with a
toothpick, languorously agitating.
A blonde chorus girl clicks: he
smiles and rubs his chin. Everything
suddenly honks: it is 12:40 of
a Thursday.

> Neon in daylight is a
> great pleasure, as Edwin Denby would
> write, as are light bulbs in daylight.
> I stop for a cheeseburger at JULIET'S
> CORNER. Giulietta Masina, wife of
> Federico Fellini, *e bell' attrice.*
> And chocolate malted. A lady in
> foxes on such a day puts her poodle
> in a cab.
>   There are several Puerto
> Ricans on the avenue today, which
> makes it beautiful and warm. First
> Bunny died, then John Latouche,
> then Jackson Pollock. But is the
> earth as full as life was full, of them?
> And one has eaten and one walks,
> past the magazines with nudes
> and the posters for BULLFIGHT and
> the Manhattan Storage Warehouse,
> which they'll soon tear down. I
> used to think they had the Armory
> Show there.
>   A glass of papaya juice
> and back to work. My heart is in my
> pocket, it is *Poems* by Pierre Reverdy.
>
>   (*LP*, 18–19)

Upon a first reading, O'Hara's walk in "A Step Away from Them" appears to be no more than a spontaneous recording of what he happens to see while passing the lunch hour. O'Hara clearly takes visual, even erotic, pleasure in the surfaces he describes—he aestheticizes the bodies of the construction workers and the Puerto Ricans, describing them in terms of their glistening and warm surfaces. The excess or redundancy of the landscape affords him aesthetic pleasure: "neon in daylight," like the lady who wears furs despite the warm weather, indicates not need but a deliberate, even hedonistic, indulgence in consumption and display. Indeed, the parade of difference before his eyes constitutes an enjoyable spectacle, a spectacle in which O'Hara seems to un-self-reflexively participate as he eats lunch, "his favorite meal." Criticism of consumption appears to be the last thing on the poet's mind as he expresses both his visual and material appetites.

And yet, while he takes pleasure in the rituals of consumer culture,

O'Hara's observations reflect his awareness of the material constraints that impinge upon his life in postwar America. O'Hara describes these constraints as those of an economy structured temporally and visually. Stores, posters, neon signs, and brand names form a visual landscape of advertisements. The streets are busy and crowded with traffic because most employers have marked off the same time for lunch, making lunch an activity regulated by the workplace; the "synchronized" honking that O'Hara observes suggests that behind the apparent chaos of the street lies the structure of the workday. All over the United States, workers follow this schedule, participating in a national temporal economy.

The fact that the constraints of the lunch hour mark the limits of his walk, and the formal limits of his poem, indicates O'Hara's intent to thematize the constraints of this temporal economy, constraints that correspond narrowly to those of "institution art in post-war America," and more generally to the strictures of the American workplace (Lowney, "Post-Anti-Esthetic Poetics," 261). As E. P. Thompson observes, in modern industrial culture, "Time is now currency: it is not passed but spent" (*Customs in Common*, 395). A moral economy is embedded in this temporal economy: the Puritan ethic, particularly its "moral critique of idleness," is instrumental to conceptions of time as money in industrial capitalism (Thompson 391, 400). O'Hara's path through the city reflects the temporal discipline of the workforce; he stops to look at wristwatches, signifying the need to adjust his movements to his employer's schedule. Although O'Hara writes in free verse, enjambment conveys the tension between the poet's purposive motion and the external constraints that subtly direct his motion and train of thought. At first glance, many line breaks seem purely arbitrary: "JULIET'S / CORNER." But in this way the poem mimics the spontaneous shifts in thought and movement triggered by chance meetings with whatever arises in the poet's path; the word "corner" may come into view as the poet shifts his attention or direction, and through the line break the reader turns this corner with him. Although O'Hara may intend to walk toward Juliet's Corner for lunch, where he stops and what he chooses to eat seem incidental, as he indicates with his afterthought "and chocolate malted," forgetfully tacked on to the description of his meal. "Fast food" becomes a necessity; eating is a reflex, subordinated to the poet's agitated movement through the streets, itself a reflex of an economy that depends on this rush, on the equivalence between money and time.

What O'Hara eats for lunch is incidental because everything is for sale in this landscape: his choices are both infinite and constricted, the emphasis on buying overdetermining desire for any one product. Buying power is the overwhelming language of status and identity, as indicated by O'Hara's descriptions of the dress and movements of passersby. O'Hara's "reading" of these individuals as "types" reflects the recognition that "spatial and temporal practices are never neutral in social affairs. They always express some kind of class or other social content, and are more often than not the focus of intense social struggle. . . . Time and space both get defined through the organization of social practices fundamental to commodity production" (Harvey, *Condition,* 239). Much as Wordsworth reads the physiognomy of the crowd in the London streets, O'Hara singles out individuals in the crowd based on race, nationality, or profession, as well as the status or power accorded them in the economy. For instance, the wealthy woman wears furs not for warmth but to display her wealth, while her poodle functions as an accessory that indicates her leisure. The African American man O'Hara describes also seems to possess ample leisure, but he is "languorously agitating"; his agitation implies that his leisure is imposed rather than chosen, stemming from an economy influenced by racial discrimination. Gender and heterosexual desire also structure this economy: O'Hara passes magazines with nudes, and heads turn after the "blonde chorus girl" who clicks by, transforming the street into a grand stage where movement and costume record a complex social drama. O'Hara's description of the laborers testifies to the bodily segregation of the economy, with "unskilled" labor reduced to "glistening torsos." Through an ambiguous pronoun reference, O'Hara subtly compares these glistening torsos to bottles of Coca-Cola: do the laborers or the bottles of Coke have "yellow helmets / on" as protection from falling bricks? On O'Hara's shopping trip, glistening bodies blur into glistening commodities.

While he does not explicitly criticize an economy of type, O'Hara expresses a desire for some other means of self-determination when he reflects upon his friends who have recently died: "First / Bunny died, then John Latouche, / then Jackson Pollock." In listing their names he turns his attention away from his present-tense recording of the immediate environment to the past. This turn conveys his momentary dissatisfaction with the present ("and one has eaten and one walks"); his question ("But is the earth as full as life was full, of them?") juxtaposes a material and spiritual fullness, suggesting the emptiness he feels in a landscape that restricts the language of desire to "fulfilling" material appetites through a purchase. His reference in the next breath to the tearing down of the Manhattan Storage Warehouse, which he associates with the 1913 Armory show, a revolutionary event in the formation of the American avant-garde, signifies O'Hara's understanding of his cultural belatedness, his inability to believe that art can provide an autonomous critique of, or a language distinct from, postwar consumer culture.

While the economy of type overdetermines, or in Wordsworth's terms, "enslaves" desire, it presents O'Hara with an additional challenge given the pervasive homophobia of the Cold War era. The signs of this danger are subtly omnipresent in O'Hara's work.[16] In "Song," O'Hara clarifies the way in which the language of type conveys not only an economic order but a moral order that structures his interactions as a gay man in the city:

Is it dirty
does it look dirty
that's what you think of in the city

does it just seem dirty
that's what you think of in the city
you don't refuse to breathe do you

someone comes along with a very bad character
he seems attractive. is he really. yes. very
he's attractive as his character is bad. is it. yes

that's what you think of in the city
run your finger along your no-moss mind
that's not a thought that's soot

and you take a lot of dirt off someone
is the character less bad. no. it improves constantly.
you don't refuse to breathe do you   (*LP*, 26)

"In the city," the question of character is reduced to a question of visual surface. Judgments based on appearance are accepted as social norms, represented here by unnamed voices confirming the "badness" of some-one's character. "Dirt" connotes immorality, and given the postwar context, homosexuality. However, the refrain "you don't refuse to breathe do you" points out that the dominant culture, which defines "dirt," shares the air with those who supposedly contaminate it. O'Hara suggests that the city is contaminated not by homosexuality but by judgments based upon sur-face or type. Such judgments create "soot": rather than reveal character, they impose stereotypes, creating surfaces that distort rather then clarify. While character "improves constantly," just as people continue to breathe, typing renders people immobile, dead letters.

While the economy and language of type present a danger to O'Hara, the flip side of this danger is excitement and pleasure. Alice Parker argues

that the subtext to "Song" is one of "gay cruising or looking," the sugges-
tion that "what is bad or dirty is actually attractive and exciting" (85, 90).
Wordsworth conflates "dirt" and "immorality" with the unlicensed sexual-
ity of the prostitute and London, whereas O'Hara occupies the position of
"dirt," embodying what 1950s American society typed as sexually immoral
or degraded. In that O'Hara assumes the position that Wordsworth finds
threatening, O'Hara's reading of "type" necessarily diverges from Words-
worth's. The speaker, like the "you" he addresses, responds to surfaces
("he's attractive as his character is bad. is it. yes / that's what you think of in
the city"), but he is also able to "read" types theatrically, to consider "dirt" as
potentially attractive. For Wordsworth, the possibility that surfaces may
disguise intentions rendered theatricality a moral danger; for O'Hara, as he
commented in "Homosexuality: Self-Portrait with Masks," theater was a
way of life that could be "pierced by a glance," but which also promised art-
ful pleasure: "so I pull the shadows around me like a puff / and crinkle my
eyes as if at the most exquisite moment / of a very long opera, and then we
are off!" (*CP*, 181).

Thus, as he walks through New York on his lunch hour, O'Hara en-
counters the problem of type not simply as one of how to negotiate the com-
modification of the person, but as a problem of how to traverse the moral
order that structures the cityscape, limiting the expression of gay desire. He
represents this problem as one of how to remain *open* to experience and de-
sire, despite the necessity of self-protection, of remaining closed or clos-
eted. "F. (Missive & Walk) I. #53" presents this problem in terms of the walk:

> I'm getting tired of not wearing underwear
> and then again I like it
>   strolling along
> feeling the wind blow softly on my genitals
> though I also like them encased in something
> firm, almost tight, like a projectile   (*CP*, 420, lines 1–6)

Roger Gilbert remarks that in this poem O'Hara reflects upon his sexual
relationship to the world; is he to "remain passively open to the world's
caresses . . . or is he to assume a more aggressive yet more 'encased' stance
toward it, like a projectile?" (*Walks in the World*, 193). Later in the poem
O'Hara contrasts walking with riding on the bus: "when you / ride on a 5th
Avenue bus you hide on a 5th / Avenue bus I mean compared to you walk-
ing." The choice of encasement versus openness, like that of riding on the
bus versus walking, is one of hiding or protection versus exposure (Gilbert

193). This choice resonates in terms of the appearance O'Hara presents to the world as a gay man—the challenge of articulating gay desire in the landscape of consumption is also the challenge of remaining "open" despite the pressures to closet or contain his desire. In choosing to walk, O'Hara chooses a stance of openness toward the urban theater.

"The Scene of My Selves": Spontaneity and the Walk

In representing his acts of consumption in *Lunch Poems*, O'Hara stages the question of whether such actions negate a spontaneous ideal. By conflating poetry with eating, with the process of consuming the sights and sounds of the city, O'Hara risks, as he implies in "Spleen," mere regurgitation of what he has consumed: "I know so much / about things, I accept / so much, it's like / vomiting" (*CP*, 187). While he incorporates the stuff of consumer culture into his poetry—brand names ("Coke"), particular stores and commodities ("harmonicas, jujubes, aspirins"), celebrities (James Dean), pop culture (film, television), advertisements and newspaper headlines ("Lana Turner has collapsed!")—he resists rendering the poem simply another commodity and "Frank O'Hara" just another brand name. His emphasis upon openness and spontaneity in his walk poetry constitutes an effort to simultaneously participate in the flows of capital and to circumvent these flows, to materialize other potential sources of identity and desire.

As "A Step Away" demonstrates, O'Hara attempts to collapse the distinction between his lunchtime walks as experience and as trope, to render poetry the spontaneous observations and feelings of the moving body (Blasing, *American Poetry*, 161). While Wordsworth frames the representation of his walk in London *as* a representation that he creates from a spatial and temporal remove, O'Hara's present-tense rendition of his walk seeks to erase the distinction between composition and walking, to resist the distance created by memory ("emotion recollected in tranquillity"),that is, the abstraction of feeling from its fleeting incarnations into an exemplary condition. The ephemerality of feeling—its surprise appearances, its mutability, its ability to move from one person to the next, the difficulty of describing it precisely or of possessing it—serves in O'Hara's poetry as the guarantor of its spontaneity. O'Hara defends his inconsistencies of mood and feeling as the key to his spontaneity: "you can't plan on the heart, but / the better part of it, my poetry, is open" (*CP*, 231). Embracing the chance encounters and impediments that structure his walks, O'Hara suggests that writing poetry constitutes an active negotiation of the urban landscape, a collaboration that ideally includes his reader: "I am what people make of me—if they / can and when they will" (*CP*, 190).

O'Hara's method of composition underscores how seriously he desired to make poetry part of his experience of the city. While Gilbert suggests that O'Hara "absurdly literalizes the coincidence of experience and composition" (176–77) by stating on the *Lunch Poems* jacket that he would pause during his walk to type up his poems at a "sample Olivetti," O'Hara did not exaggerate as much as one might suppose. O'Hara wrote poems at the drop of a hat, and viewed the speed and spontaneity of composition as integral to his poetry. John Ashbery writes in his introduction to O'Hara's posthumous *Collected Poems,* "Dashing the poems off at odd moments—in his office at the Museum of Modern Art, in the street at lunchtime or even in a room full of people—he would then put them away in drawers and cartons and half forget them" (*CP*, vii). Kenneth Koch recalls: "One of the most startling things about Frank in the period when I first knew him was his ability to write a poem when other people were talking, or even to get up in the middle of a conversation, get his typewriter, and write a poem, sometimes participating in the conversation while doing so. This may sound affected when I describe it, but it wasn't so at all. The poems he wrote in this way were usually very good poems."[17] O'Hara relied on the typewriter as an instrument that would enable speed and spontaneity, referring to typing as "playing the typewriter."[18] Diane di Prima similarly remembers: "I would go over to Frank O'Hara's house pretty often. He used to keep a typewriter on the table in the kitchen, and he would type away, make poems all the time, when company was there and when it wasn't, when he was eating, all kind of times" (qtd. in *PP,* 115). Marjorie Perloff observes that O'Hara rarely revised more "than a phrase or two of a poem"; the poem was part of the moment and situation it recorded, and thus inviolable (*PP,* 117).

That O'Hara valued poetry as experience rather than as published product was also evident in his attitude toward publication; he was notoriously careless about marketing and even preserving his work. In general, O'Hara avoided poetry institutions such as the *New Yorker*—Donald Hall once rejected poems O'Hara sent to the *Paris Review,* which O'Hara took as "a great joke."[19] He published in small journals and small presses: Tibor de Nagy, Grove, Totem, and City Lights brought out the six volumes published during O'Hara's lifetime. The publication history of *Lunch Poems* exemplifies O'Hara's lackadaisical attitude toward publication. Lawrence Ferlinghetti met O'Hara at Larry River's studio in 1959; on hearing that O'Hara was writing poems on his lunch hour, he proposed that O'Hara prepare a book of lunch poems, which Ferlinghetti would publish through his City Lights Press (Gooch 440). Joe LeSueur recalls asking Frank every few months, "Have you decided what poems to send?" (*Digressions*, 274). It took O'Hara six years to gather the poems for this volume, and this process required the help of Donald Allen and Kenneth Koch, and nine letters to Lawrence Ferlinghetti (Gooch 440; LeSueur 275).

O'Hara's attitude toward writing and publication indicated his desire to preserve the spontaneity of the work; rather than define his writing as a profession, and his poems as products to be bought or sold, he defined poetry as an extension of everyday experience. *Lunch Poems* suggests that by conflating poetry with eating, with the process of consuming the sights and sounds of the city, O'Hara could materialize his immediate, voluntary thoughts and desires. Yet his understanding of poetry as sensory consumption was complicated by his awareness of its necessary absorption into and definition by an economy of production. This is the central conflict of his poetry, one that "Poetry" dramatizes:

> The only way to be quiet
> is to be quick, so I scare
> you clumsily, or surprise
> you with a stab. A praying
> mantis knows time more
> intimately than I and is
> more casual. Crickets use
> time for accompaniment to
> innocent fidgeting. A zebra
> races counterclockwise.
> All this I desire. To
> deepen you by my quickness
> and delight as if you
> were logical and proven,
> but still be quiet as if
> I were used to you; as if
> you would never leave me
> and were the inexorable
> product of my own time.   (*CP*, 49)

Like Marianne Moore's poem of the same name, O'Hara's poem explores whether poetry offers "after all, a place for the genuine."[20] O'Hara begins the poem with the goal of quietness, which he hopes he will gain through quickness. He wants to surprise "you," a you that may refer to the reader but also to the poem itself, through his speed. If he is quick enough, he will be able to surprise the poem, making it commensurate with experience itself. The animals he lists make use of time in a way that O'Hara desires: they are casual, innocent, unselfconscious. As he is only too aware, his consciousness about time marks his separation from the poem he writes. His use of "as if" signals the necessary turn writing takes as it transforms the "present" moment into trope. As he types a description of his experience, he transforms it into a written past, separating poet from text. Although O'Hara struggles against Wordsworthian memory, poems such as "In Memory of My Feelings" suggest that feelings and poems inevitably become subject to the past: "against my will / against my love / become art" (*CP,* 257). Similarly, the title "A Step Away from Them" refers to the necessity of this separation; to write about his walk is to distinguish the poem from the experience of walking and eating, to take a "step away" from purely spontaneous desire.

Although the typewriter enables the "quickness" O'Hara needs to convey spontaneous desire, this spontaneity is ultimately complicitous—it stems from the efficiency of the machine, a machine O'Hara samples in the Olivetti showroom during his lunch break, but which he also employs at work to type up memos and letters. His series of memo-poems, titled with variations on "F.Y.I." and typed at his desk at the museum, suggest how poetry enabled him to take a "step away" from the workday, but simultaneously indicate the convergence of poetry and professionalism.[21] The typewriter, as an icon of modernist "form meets function," enables speed by omitting the step of translating written language into print type. Yet as he types to capture spontaneous feeling, O'Hara quickens the translation of this feeling into a finished product—his book of *Lunch Poems*—ready for publication and consumption. "Playing" the typewriter, O'Hara packages himself in and as type. O'Hara's "step away" is rife with contradiction: it signals his failure to articulate a spontaneous desire distinct from the language of production and the postwar moral economy. Like Wordsworth, however, O'Hara stages the impediments to a sincere ideal to suggest that he can inhabit and transform, rather than simply critique, consumer culture. His walk poetry conveys this negotiation as a particular habit of movement and vision oriented to speed, surface, and the promises of the future.[22]

O'Hara resists romantic "depth" by alluding to the frame of memory that grounds a Wordsworthian sincerity, a distinction that he makes explicit in his poem "Post the Lake Poets Ballad." Responding to a friend's letter that

accuses him of "gorgeous self-pity," O'Hara replies that he thinks of him-
self as "a cheerful type who pretends to / be hurt to get a little depth into /
things that interest me," adding,

> I've even given that up
> lately with the stream of events
> going so fast and the movingly
> alternating with the amusingly   (*CP*, 336–37)

O'Hara defines his persona in terms not of depth but of speed and sur-
face—as he states in "Poetry," he desires to "deepen" through "quickness."
Confessing that he only "pretends to / be hurt," O'Hara suggests that re-
stricting sincerity to feelings of melancholy and loss while remaining
closed to artifice and amusement condemns poetry to dwell in an idealized
past. Marjorie Perloff observes that O'Hara borrowed the terms "push" and
"pull" from the abstract expressionist painters when referring to the sur-
face of his poems; he wrote that he wanted to "keep the surface of the poem
high and dry, not wet, reflective and self-conscious"—"wet" connoting the
tears of the romantics (*AA*, 175).

Pursuing this idea, we might say that O'Hara redeems surface while re-
sisting absorption by it through movement. "Interior (With Jane)" demon-
strates this negotiation:

> The eagerness of objects to
> be what we are afraid to do
>
> cannot help but move us   Is
> this willingness to be a motive
>
> in us what we reject?   The
> really stupid things, I mean
>
> a can of coffee, a $.35 ear
> ring, a handful of hair, what
>
> do these things do to us?   We
> come into the room, the windows
>
> are empty, the sun is weak
> and slippery on the ice   And a

> sob comes, simply because it is
> coldest of the things we know   (*CP*, 55)

These objects seem trivial, even "stupid," but as O'Hara states in the poem "Today," such things "do have meaning. They're strong as rocks" (*CP*, 15). O'Hara's inarticulate sob is a gesture on the one hand of unselfconsciousness, of absorption by things, a gesture that approaches the coldness of objects themselves. Conversely, his sob, and his poem, allow him to exceed absorption by objects. Although O'Hara expresses himself through consumption, through the objects that he purchases and collects, he rejects complete identification with them—they are more solid, more assertive, more final than he. His things do not symbolize or contain who he is, but refer metonymically to his use of them, pointing to a person who has shed them, moving onward in time, space, and feeling. The sob doesn't "express" or capture a self so much as allow the poem to be "moved" beyond objects: feeling makes use of and yet eludes the language of property and collection. In this way O'Hara makes possible an understanding of sincerity that incorporates accident and artifice, one that can give rise to conflicting feelings, multiple selves, and theatrical ruses, or, as he stated, "Grace / to be born and live as variously as possible" (*CP*, 256).

"To Move Is to Love"

Although O'Hara embraces the theatricality and artifice of consumer culture, he nevertheless articulates a moral ideal of sincerity: homosexuality serves as a utopian figure of a desire that can exceed moral and economic constraint, even while subject to it. Like Whitman, O'Hara saw an eroticized, sexually liberated "Mannahatta" as a model of the body politic, transforming the marginalization of homosexual desire into "a homocentric vision of unity and transcendent possibility against which [to] test an imperfect 'America.'"[23] Appropriating urban space through his walk poetry, O'Hara sought to realize this vision.

O'Hara's home is potentially any place in the city that enters his poetry; like the flaneur, for whom "it becomes an immense source of enjoyment to establish his dwelling in the throng, in the ebb and flow," O'Hara carries his home with him, a habit of vision rather than a collection of objects (Baudelaire, *Selected Writings*, 399). Crucially, the community that informs O'Hara's moral vision is present inside the city through which he walks: although he blended into the crowds in his walks around the city, he carried with him the knowledge of a "libidinal landscape" of bars, restaurants, apartments, parks, subways, and ship docks, a gay world invisible to the normative public (Gooch 197; Chauncey 23, 152). Baudelaire calls the flaneur "a prince enjoying his incognito wherever he goes"; he is able "to see the world, to be at the very centre of the world, and yet to be unseen of the world" (400). Walter Benjamin's description of the streets and arcades of Paris as a vast interior for the flaneur assumes particular significance for gay subcultures in the city. As Joseph Boone argues, "In much gay life, interiorized space becomes one vast street, a thoroughfare accommodating social, intimate, and anonymous interchanges impossible in the realm of the bourgeois home or its rarefied interior space" ("Queer Sites in Modernism," 262). The sexual topography of New York reflects this privatization of the public landscape, disclosing how gay men "appropriated public spaces not identified as gay," an act crucial to an understanding of O'Hara's walk poetry (Chauncey 23, 26).

At the time O'Hara was writing his walk poems in the late 1950s and early '60s, visual artists began appropriating various spaces around the city—art galleries, lofts, and backyards—for the ephemeral performances known as "happenings." Susan Sontag describes happenings as "animated paintings," a cross between painting and theater, and suggests that they developed out of the New York School's use of action painting (*Against Interpretation,* 268). In their use of collage, juxtaposition, shock, and found objects, the happenings also drew on the surrealist tradition; happenings were unified by artists' efforts to denaturalize their audiences' assumptions and habits, a goal often achieved by involving the audience in the proceedings (Sontag 265, 269; Gooch 418–19). Similarly, the European Situationist movement, headed by Guy Debord, attempted to critically transform everyday life in the city in the late 1950s and '60s; specifically, Debord wanted to subvert the society and economy of "the spectacle" through aesthetic practices that made use of urban public space.[24] A key practice of the Situationists was the *derivé,* or drift, wherein the walker charts a path through the city guided solely by leisure and desire rather than by work and purposefulness; Debord defined the derivé as an attempt to take consumption to its zenith (Sussman, *Passage,* 144, 127). In fact, one of Debord's accounts of a *derivé* resembles O'Hara's descriptions of his lunchtime walks: "Debord and Wolman continue to walk north along the beautiful and tragic rue d'Aubervilliers. They eat lunch on the way. . . . They follow the right bank of this canal heading north, making stops—sometimes long, sometimes brief—at various bars" (Sussman 139).

O'Hara's walk poems, like the *derivés* and happenings, render spatial practices central to his alternative vision of moral community. As Certeau remarks, if "a spatial order organizes an ensemble of possibilities . . . then the walker actualizes some of these possibilities. In that way, he makes them exist as well as emerge" (*Practice*, 98). Through his walk poems, O'Hara seeks to transform metaphoric appropriation of the city into material appropriation by circulating a vision of the city saturated with erotic desire, or as he put it, "a sexual bliss inscribe[d] upon the page of whatever energy I burn for art" (*CP*, 302). If speed is essential to O'Hara's redemption of surface (his efforts to "deepen through quickness"), stillness is essential to his efforts to saturate the urban landscape with desire:

> I really am a woodcarver
> and my words are love
> which willfully parades in
> its room, refusing to move   (*LP*, 13)

This paradoxical movement in stillness, what O'Hara calls "standing still and walking in New York," constitutes a journey that resists the values guiding the onward rush of progress (*CP*, 302). His "words are love," and as he states, "To move is to love" ("In Memory of My Feelings"): his walk poems allow him to enter the city's flows, but also to "stand still" by recording feeling and desire that symbolically slow down urban traffic, in a manner reminiscent of the nineteenth-century flaneur "walking" his turtle on a leash (Tester, *Flaneur*, 15). Pleasure—expressed through but not by leisure and consumption—serves as a key means by which O'Hara redefines social space in his poetry, slowing down the flow of an economy in which time equals money, and production reproduction.

   "Steps" (1961) illuminates how pleasure informs the "home" and persona O'Hara carves out of the public materials of the city through his poetry. The poem begins with an address to New York: "How funny you are today New York / like Ginger Rogers in *Swingtime* / and St. Bridget's steeple leaning a little to the left," followed by an address to his lover:

> here I have just jumped out of a bed full of V-days
> (I got tired of D-days) and blue you there still
> accepts me foolish and free
> all I want is a room up there
> and you in it   (*LP*, 52)

Throughout the poem O'Hara suggests that his vision of an offset New York stems from his feelings for his lover. He casts everything in the sun of his mood, stating that "even the traffic halt so thick is a way / for people to rub up against each other," and "even the stabbings are helping the population explosion / though in the wrong country." Similarly, O'Hara revels in the excesses of consumption:

> oh god it's wonderful
> to get out of bed
> and drink too much coffee
> and smoke too many cigarettes
> and love you so much.

As in "A Step Away," O'Hara reveals that the grounds of his actions are the cultural terms available, the terms of production and consumption. Yet in "Steps," O'Hara takes explicit pleasure in his acts of consumption, because he defines them in his own terms: crucially, time in the poem is marked not by his employer's restrictions, the constraints of the lunch hour, but by his leisure activities and by the pace of his reflections on his lover. Drinking and smoking too much do not limit the terms of desire but allow him to express it; he revels in excess, in enjoying that which he doesn't need ("not that we need liquor [we just like it]"). The visual and temporal narrative is bounded not by his lunch hour but by his reveries about various facets of the city that express his love ("the Pittsburgh Pirates shout because they won / and in a sense we're all winning / we're alive"). He takes pleasure in visual surfaces, in the reading and misreading of bodies and types, because of their erotic energy:

> everyone's taking their coat off
> so they can show a rib-cage to the rib-watchers
> and the park's full of dancers and their tights and shoes
> in little bags
> who are often mistaken for worker-outers at the WestSide Y
> why not

Although O'Hara embraces the status quo, is absorbed into the surfaces he describes and objects he consumes, these surfaces also reflect O'Hara's erotic pleasure; the city he portrays is filtered through his feelings. O'Hara incorporates the visual surfaces, brand names, and spectacles of the city into the home and community he defines through poetry, because he uses them in the service of gay desire: they mark the potential for, rather than absence of, love and moral community as he defines it.

In O'Hara's role as consumer, we see the convergence of advertisement and poetry, well before the dominance of pop art. For instance, the poem "Having a Coke with You" likens the experience of love to the effervescence of soda pop, and the reading of the poem to the drinking of a Coke (*CP*, 360). O'Hara contrasts drinking Coke with visiting modernist artwork in the museum to suggest that "making it new" stems from merging poetry and everyday life: "I would rather look at you than all the portraits in the world / . . . / and the fact that you move so beautifully more or less takes care of Futurism / just as at home I never think of the Nude Descending a Staircase" (*CP*, 360). One could argue, however, that the poem becomes an advertisement of sorts, selling its product—the "marvellous experience" of love—thereby contributing to the iconic status of Coke and, in turn, of "Frank O'Hara."

To accuse O'Hara of failing to provide an adequate critique of advertisement is to retain an ideal of lyric opposition that O'Hara saw as outmoded. As Terry Mulcaire points out in a discussion of Whitman, homosexual desire cannot be "extricated" from the "erotics of capitalism," conditions that in some sense produce it; however, like Whitman, O'Hara is less interested in providing a "critique of commodification" than a sense that "the power of mass industrial existence to commodify human bodies is matched by its power to humanize commodities" ("Publishing Intimacy," 494, 472). If erotic desire is subject to advertisement, the glistening bodies of construction workers inevitably transformed into bottles of Coke, then, conversely, Coke might provide a new metaphorics of human experience, and the "real thing" encompass a range of experiences that would have shocked the Coca-Cola company in the 1950s. O'Hara subtly normalizes homosexuality by appropriating a strategy of Coke ads: Coke sells its product as all-American by suggesting that people of all kinds come together by sharing the drinking of Coke. In leaving his "you" ambiguous, O'Hara renders the "marvellous experience" of love open to diverse definition.[25]

Excessive material and visual consumption indicates an accommodation to the language and economy of type, but also conveys a refusal to discipline one's body according to moral norms. In his embrace of consumption, O'Hara assumes a typically feminine role; Andrew Ross describes O'Hara as "a man on a shopping trip," arguing that he "mirrors or mimics the way in which a woman of means with a busy social schedule might have conducted herself as the fifties were drawing to a close."[26] Yet O'Hara uses this feminine role to nontraditional ends: through excessive consumption, O'Hara redeems surfaces and the full presence of things as an homage to gay eroticism, to bodies and physiques.

Indeed, in "On Rachmaninoff's Birthday," he literalizes excess as his penis, produced and reproduced ad infinitum:

> I am so glad that Larry Rivers made a
> statue of me
>
> and now I hear that my penis is on all
> the statues of all the young sculptors who've
> seen it
>
> instead of the Picasso no-penis shep-
> herd and its influence—for presence is
> better than absence, if you love excess.   (*CP*, 190)

This vision of excessive fertility is antiproductive, supporting not the logic of sexual difference and "birth" as origination, but the logic of same-sex desire and the copy. Similarly, in "Cornkind," O'Hara defines fertility as the experience and pleasure of orgasm rather than the production of children: "you are of me, that's what / and that's the meaning of fertility / hard and moist and moaning" (*LP*, 40–41). His poems—"unspent" money—are antiproductive and, in the dominant economy, "wasteful."

While the "blocks" to Wordsworth's walk help him to remember habits of pastoral re-production and to resist the seductive grasp of London's consumer pageant, O'Hara uses consumerist desire to block (re)production: his noon walks are efforts to follow a path defined by leisure and erotic pleasure, rather than by the rush of the workday. Thus "Pistachio Tree at Chateau Noir" presents O'Hara riding on a bus, dragging his feet to "slow down the damn bus" so "I can watch you smile longer"; he adds, "That's what the Spring is and the elbow of noon walks" (*LP*, 50; *CP*, 404). In "A Step Away," consider again what I initially described as O'Hara's pleasure in excess and aesthetic spectacle; we might now read this as O'Hara's willful saturation of the consumer landscape with erotic desire. The Manhattan Storage Warehouse appears in another O'Hara poem that suggests the homoerotic subtext to "A Step Away": "I suck off / every man in the Manhattan Storage & / Warehouse Co. Then, refreshed, again / to the streets! to the generous sun / and the vigorous heat of the city" (*Poems Retrieved*, 161). Reading, or rather misreading, the "types" and consumer icons he encounters by viewing them as potential objects of sexual desire allows O'Hara to use his role as consumer to alternative moral ends.

O'Hara indicates that different urban contexts and publics present varying degrees of resistance to his expression of spontaneous desire: for instance, in that "Steps" enables the expression of love for and identification with a lover rather than distinction from the crowd and the workplace, the trope of self-expression is one of steps toward rather than a step away, Ginger Rogers's dance steps rather than the rushed steps of the lunchtime crowd. Nevertheless, in all contexts he attempts to remain "open," to affirm the present moment, in all its contingencies.

Thus, in representing his movements through the city, O'Hara does not move inward like Wordsworth, to distinguish a "natural" or authentic performance from the theatricality of the urban landscape, but outward, conflating his body with the landscape in all its artifice.[27] In "Nocturne," the speaker blurs with the UN Building: "My eyes, like millions of / glassy squares, merely reflect" (*CP*, 225). Similarly, in "Grand Central," the speaker *is* the train station:

> The wheels are inside me thundering.
> They do not churn me, they are inside.
> They were not oiled, they burn
> with friction and out of my eyes
> comes smoke. Then the enormous bullets
> streak towards me with their black tracers
> and bury themselves deep in my muscles.
> They won't be taken out, I can still
> move. Now I am going to lie down
> like an expanse of marble floor
> covered with commuters and information   (*CP*, 168)

Although the imagery is of pain and war, O'Hara suggests that "one way of dominating the terminal" is to transform Grand Central from the economic nerve center of the city—the site through which the city literally extends its economic influence into the surrounding towns—into a site of sexual pleasure:

> During the noon-hour rush a friend
> of mine took a letter carrier across
> the catwalk underneath the dome
> . . . .
> He unzipped the messenger's trousers
> and relieved him of his missile, hands
> on the messenger's dirty buttocks,

the smoking muzzle in his soft blue mouth.
That is one way of dominating the terminal.

By relieving messengers of their mail, and guns of their bullets, sexuality in this poem derails and consumes the "vehicles" through which the dominant culture—the "Americans of American persuasion"—maintain their economic power and influence.

Though O'Hara puns wittily in "Grand Central" on trains, war, and sex, his discursive appropriations of the city amount to more than ironic commentary. The "accident" or "contingency" always potentially signifies danger and pain—as the speaker states at the end of "Grand Central," "It will be / my blood, I think, that dominates the trains." O'Hara's willingness to accept whatever may arise in his walks represents a willful emphasis upon the pleasures, rather than the costs, of its risks. In fact, O'Hara's understanding of sincerity as active and pleasurable self-definition amid varying publics is integral to his attempt to influence a diverse community of readers through his walk poetry, to involve his readers in the project of flanerie.

Walking and Textual/Sexual Circulation

O'Hara's views on the instructional nature of poetry—both in his essays and in the poetry itself—clarify how he hoped to influence a wider community through the circulation of his poetry. Where Wordsworth seeks to instruct the reader in a sincere habit of reading, O'Hara avoids following a route in his walks and poems that could be construed as prescribed, exemplary, or didactic, seeking to block, through pleasure, the conventional circulation of words, coins, and bodies. His views on tourism exemplify this attitude. In "Hotel Particulier," a poem about tourism and touring, O'Hara begins by describing how exciting it is not to be "learning Portuguese in Bilbao so you can go to Brazil," adding that, "I had a teacher one whole summer who never told me anything and it was wonderful" (*LP*, 39; *CP*, 359). He ends the poem with the question "Is this the hostel where the lazy and fun-loving start up the mountain?" If he chooses to walk up the mountain, to take a "tour," it is entirely for the sake of pleasure, not moral instruction.

Just as O'Hara dislikes poetry that instructs others how to see or feel, he refuses to exalt the consumption of poetry. In "Personism: A Manifesto" (1959), O'Hara parodies the manifesto genre, defining personism as a "movement which I recently founded and which nobody knows about."

He argues that people shouldn't have to listen to his ideas: "But how can you really care if anybody gets it, or gets what it means, or if it improves them. Improves them for what? For death? Why hurry them along? Too many poets act like a middle-aged mother trying to get her kids to eat too much cooked meat, and potatoes with drippings (tears). I don't give a damn whether they eat or not. Forced feeding leads to excessive thinness (effete). Nobody should experience anything they don't need to, if they don't need poetry bully for them, I like the movies too" (*CP*, 498). Consumerist choice supplants the manifesto's conventional didacticism, revolutionary rhetoric, and moral certainty. While O'Hara takes pleasure from poetry, others may not, and rather than prove the moral superiority of poetry over other cultural practices, O'Hara encourages his readers to follow their particular appetites.

This gesture is not equivalent to denying the importance of his work, nor to refusing to circulate it; rather, O'Hara circulated his work by invoking a practice that predates the literary marketplace, that of the literary coterie. He conceived of sincere poetry as a form of intimate conversation with an audience of particular artists, writers, gay friends, and lovers:

> One of its minimal aspects is to address itself to one person (other than the poet himself), thus evoking overtones of love without destroying love's life-giving vulgarity, and sustaining the poet's feelings towards the poem while preventing love from distracting him into feeling about the person. . . . It was founded by me after lunch with LeRoi Jones on August 27, 1959, a day in which I was in love with someone. . . . I went back to work and wrote a poem for this person. While I was writing it I was realizing that if I wanted to I could use the telephone instead of writing the poem, and so Personism was born. . . . It puts the poem squarely between the poet and the person, Lucky Pierre style, and the poem is correspondingly gratified. The poem is at last between two persons instead of two pages.   (*CP*, 499)

Like Whitman, O'Hara seeks to persuade readers of the sincerity of his poetry not only by embodying himself in the text but by presenting the text as a physical, even erotic, exchange between poet and reader: the poem is "correspondingly gratified."[28] O'Hara embedded many of his poems in literal letters and gave many as gifts; they often bear the signs of this exchange, if not in theme then in the naming of their recipient. It is a rare O'Hara poem that does not name friends, lovers, or particular social events in which he will be or has been involved. To a certain extent, naming distinguishes between those "in the know" and the general reader,[29]

and the fact that most of O'Hara's poetry, particularly his explicitly gay po-
etry, was only published posthumously suggests that O'Hara valued local
circulation.[30] On the other hand, while naming particular friends, places,
and events may exclude the general reader, this practice also cultivates
intimacy by positioning the general reader as the poet's confidante and
collaborator. O'Hara models his occasional lyrics and even his under-
standing of free verse on intimate conversation, espousing the value of
spontaneity and of writing as a social endeavor: while he chronicles his
conversations with particular friends, and quotes bits of conversation, he
often addresses an unspecified "you," which encompasses anyone who
might pick up the poem.[31] If Wordsworth's ideal posthumous reception
relies on the epitaph, O'Hara's spontaneous ideal relies on the eu-
phemistic invitation of the advertisement. By treating even his published
poems as a series of conversations, O'Hara sought to transform the poem
from a product in the mainstream marketplace to a relationship mobi-
lized through its "consumption" by the reader.[32]

The end of "A Step Away from Them" models this reception: the poet
states, "My heart is in my / pocket, it is Poems by Pierre Reverdy." Reverdy's
poems, worn on O'Hara's person, are positioned "squarely between the
poet and the person, Lucky Pierre style." The affinity O'Hara feels for Re-
verdy allows him to keep his "heart" in his pocket at work, rather than wear
his heart on his sleeve. This is a position both inside and outside of main-
stream culture, perfectly summed up in the word "pocket," an interior
space located on an external surface. O'Hara seeks to carve out a similar
pocket for his own work in the marketplace, as evidenced by the packag-
ing of the paperback *Lunch Poems*. One of City Lights Books' Pocket Poets
series, it is bite-sized and inexpensive, and is easily digested in one sitting.
Small enough to hide in one's pocket at work, it can circulate unobtrusively,
as "something / small and important and / unAmerican," "In a defiant land
/ of its own a real right thing" ("To the Poem," *CP*, 175). Masquerading as
just another commodity ("the real thing"), *Lunch Poems* invites consump-
tion by the reader so as to denaturalize the language of capital from within.
Like Wordsworth, O'Hara positions his reader as a flaneur who walks
alongside him, viewing the sights and sounds of the city, but in contrast to
Wordsworth, O'Hara refuses to offer moral instruction about how to read
or consume the city. Readers must make sense of the city-text themselves,
must consider the overlap and distinction between consumption and read-
ing: O'Hara's poetry demands an active negotiation of the city in all its flux,
noise, traffic, and complexity.[33] It is in this sense that O'Hara's poems
"walk": received, they elicit efforts to consider the forces that shape every-
day life in the postwar city as one "walks through" and reads it oneself. The

spontaneity and modernity of O'Hara's poetry resides in this intimate collaboration with a future reader-consumer.

While readers outside of O'Hara's coterie will miss particular meanings or resonances in his work due to the poetry's embeddedness in specific contexts, his utopian plea for individuals to practice a moral ideal of self-determination speaks across boundaries of history, race, class, and gender (see Boone, "Queer Sites," 250). "Ode: Salute to the French Negro Poets" expresses this democratic plea clearly:

> the beauty of America, neither cool jazz nor devoured Egyptian
>   heroes, lies in
> lives in the darkness I inhabit in the midst of sterile millions
>
> the only truth is face to face, the poem whose words become
>   your mouth
> and dying in black and white we fight for what we love, not are
>
> (CP, 305)

"Black and white" connotes both the lines of racial demarcation and the freeze-frame of photography: O'Hara suggests that we should struggle to redefine the static, visual categories of identity, of "type," which 1950s American culture reinforced in moral and economic terms. His words become our mouths when we do not simply consume the poem but make his ideals present and tactile, giving them voice and flesh.

What is surprising, given the conventional assumption of an opposition between lyric sincerity and commercial culture, and the tendency to view O'Hara's work as lacking "a political consciousness per se," is that the objects and language of consumption do not negate the moral energies of O'Hara's art (Elledge, "Lack of Gender," 228). Rather, O'Hara's poetry works within and through a landscape of consumption to elicit the expression of erotic desire, and the ideal of democratic self-determination more generally. O'Hara's habits are pleasure and humor rather than didacticism and political critique, but this style is itself a form of social and moral commentary, one that we overlook if we assume that conventions of sincerity must oppose consumer culture. His habits are those of the flaneur: they are the everyday habits of self-determination within the constraints of the workplaces, markets, and streets of capital cities.[34] In carving out a path amid the lunch-hour rush, in refusing to be jostled by the crowd, in keeping his heart in his pocket at work, O'Hara chose to walk with his eyes not on the bitterness of the past but on the potential pleasures of the future. Joe Brainard eloquently captures this attitude in his memoir of O'Hara: "I remember Frank O'Hara's walk. Light and sassy. With a slight twist and a slight bounce. With the top half of his body slightly thrust forward. Head back. It was a beautiful walk. Casual. Confident. 'I don't care.' And sometimes, 'I know you are looking'" (Berkson and LeSueur, *Homage*, 168).

Walking in the Secular City: O'Hara's Prosaic Reception

How did O'Hara's spontaneous aesthetic—one that embraced ephemeral feeling, transgressive sexuality, irony, and consumerist pleasure—shape his posthumous reception? If O'Hara inverts a Wordsworthian moral universe, what effect did the poet's walks in the secular city have on his readers? Comparing the posthumous publication of O'Hara's *Collected Poems* to Wordsworth's efforts to secure posthumous publication of *The Prelude* suggests that the differences in these poets' negotiations of sincerity took material as well as textual form, influencing the terms of their posthumous reception.

O'Hara's unexpected death at the age of forty forestalled any plans he might have had to secure posthumous publication of his work. Nevertheless, his emphasis on poetry as spontaneous experience resulted in a lackadaisical attitude toward preserving his work. As he stated in the *New American Poetry:* "I don't think of fame or posterity (as Keats so grandly and genuinely did)" (*SS*, 112). Although he published five slim volumes between 1952 and 1965, hundreds of manuscript poems remained uncollected. Diane di Prima comments, "The poems would get into everything and I would come over and go through, like, his dresser drawers. There would be poems in with the towels, and I'd say, 'Oh hey, I like this one,' and he'd say, 'OK, take it.' Very often it would be the only copy. My guess is that huge collected Frank O'Hara has only about one-third of his actual work" (qtd. in *PP*, 115). John Ashbery, in his introduction to O'Hara's *Collected Poems*, states that the task of tracking down manuscripts was not easy; "some survived only in letters," and others that "Frank's friends remembered having seen had simply disappeared" (*CP*, vii). It is thanks to O'Hara's friends that his work and memory were preserved, not only in *The Collected Poems* but also in *Homage to Frank O'Hara*, and in the Museum of Modern Art's 1967 tribute publication, *In Memory of My Feelings* (LeSueur, *Digressions*, 258, 303). O'Hara certainly anticipated the irony that his cultivation of a spontaneous poetic would secure his place in the modernist museum, but in contrast to Stein, he held out the hope that artwork in the museum could remain modern through its collaborations with future readers.[35]

O'Hara attracted attention from the poetry establishment only after his death in 1966: Alfred A. Knopf published *The Collected Poems* in 1971, which went on to win the National Book Award, and his reputation has since grown steadily. Although O'Hara's poetry is now a permanent exhibit in the American literary canon, his spontaneous practice has shaped his reception in telling ways. At their respective historical moments, both Wordsworth and O'Hara radically challenged an understanding of genre by defining poetry as the expression of sincere feeling. Wordsworth argued that "there neither is nor can be any essential difference" between poetry and prose (*PLB*, 253–54), but ultimately distinguished habits of "true feeling" from the "vulgarity and meanness of ordinary life." O'Hara took a step away from Wordsworth into the secular, prosaic city.

Some of O'Hara's early readers, guided by Wordsworthian habits of sincerity, did not follow O'Hara's turn into the secular city. Expecting sincere poems to be transparent utterances opposed to the theatricality of commercial culture, these readers found in the artifice and self-dramatization of O'Hara's poetry not a commentary on consumer culture but thinly veiled self-advertisement. Locating their judgments of the poetry in the poet's life and conduct, critics often deemed O'Hara "memorable less for his actual achievement than for his colorful life and his influence on others" (*MP*, 2). Some read the autobiographical component of O'Hara's work as a bid for celebrity. For instance, Pearl Bell in her review of *The Collected Poems* argued that O'Hara was less a poet than a "whimsically charming gadfly." Echoing some of Wordsworth's early readers, critics accused O'Hara's poetry of the meaninglessness they associated with commercial culture; they read his practice of naming as name-dropping and his present-tense rendition of experience as prosaic reporting, or what Wordsworth termed "fancy."[36]

These concerns subtly persist in current understandings of O'Hara's flanerie.[37] Recent critics use the concepts of "metonymy," "presence," and "immanence" to indicate how O'Hara's "I do this, I do that" poems resist metaphorical status, but sidestep the moral assumptions that guide this distinction. For instance, Roger Gilbert argues that it is "difficult to know on what grounds to praise 'A Step Away From Them'" because it pursues "the metonymic organization inherent in the walk as form to an extreme point," lacking the "metaphoric and thematic apparatus that traditionally unifies and justifies a poem" (179, 180). Guided by standards developed from his reading of Wordsworth's walk poetry, Gilbert argues that the difference between poetry and experience is that "while experience may repeat itself incessantly without losing its interest, a poem must be absolutely singular" (186). Wordsworth, he suggests, resolves this problem through his use of "spots of time," "moments of special intensity that organize the experience around them and give it meaning." In contrast, a poem such as "A Step Away from Them" ultimately "depends on its lack of self-consciousness regarding the illusion of immediacy that it creates" (185, 194, 196).

Guided by Wordsworthian habits, Gilbert reads metonymy as a factual record of detail, what Naomi Schor describes as "the shadow projected by the theological detail," a detail deserted by God (*Reading in Detail*, 61, 96, 147). Thus, O'Hara's walk poems appear to lack meaning beyond the poet's movement through the city. While his poetry eschews the "metaphoric and thematic apparatus that traditionally unifies and justifies a poem," I have argued that O'Hara's "openness" to chance, accident, and artifice reveals a sincere ideal: his moral resistance to any moral code that might usurp the various shapes and shades of desire. O'Hara's incorporation of "nonpoetic" subject matter—the stuff of consumer culture—signifies a rejection of the moral conventions used to determine what is and isn't "sincere" poetry. Allen Ginsberg commented astutely of O'Hara's sincere poetic that "any gesture he made was the poetic gesture because he was the poet, so therefore anything he did was poetry" (Berkson and LeSueur, *Homage*, 63). With sincere expression as the criterion for poetry, lines between poetry and nonpoetry, even between "good" and "bad" writing, blur: when asked about sincerity by the interviewer Edward Lucie-Smith, O'Hara said, "I really dislike dishonesty [more] than bad lines, in a certain way. Because I don't think there is such a thing as a bad line if it's true" (*SS*, 13).

In that O'Hara's spontaneous practice diverges from Wordsworth's, his poetry demands a different sort of reading, one attuned to the implications of his inversion of Wordsworth's moral universe. Marjorie Perloff, John Ashbery, and Kenneth Koch have all developed such a reading, and, tellingly, all praise *The Collected Poems*, the work that most other critics find sprawling and "uneven."[38] Ashbery defends this collection by arguing that O'Hara's career "stands as an unrevised work-in-progress; the fact that parts of it are now missing or unfinished is unimportant, except as an indicator of the temporal fluctuating quality that runs through his work and is one of its major innovations" (*CP*, vii). Kenneth Koch describes his reaction to reading *The Collected Poems* as "astonishment": "All those moments, all the momentary enthusiasms and despairs which I had been moved by when I first read them, when they were here altogether made something I had never imagined. It is not all one great poem, but something in some ways better: a collection of created moments that illuminate a whole life."[39] O'Hara's understanding of his poems as spontaneous utterances embedded in particular contexts asks that we read them not as self-contained pieces or "spots of time," but in relation to one another, as a dramatization of a life defined around the mutability of feeling and identity.

That many readers have resisted this reading is not surprising, given the pervasiveness of Wordsworthian habits of reading sincerity, and of O'Hara's resistance to didacticism. Reading these poets side-by-side in the context of commercial culture allows us to see Wordsworth's shadow reflected in the "million squares" of O'Hara's UN Building, and O'Hara's "heart" anticipated in Wordsworth's commitment to "powerful feelings." What is perhaps most striking is that despite writing 150 years apart, with different understandings of moral conduct, Wordsworth and O'Hara share an understanding of poetry as a habit of sincere feeling that not only accommodates the pressures of commercial culture but, in doing so, charts new paths for the lyric. Rather than take a "step away" from the threat of consumer culture, it's worth following these flaneurs into the midst of the crowd.

Part II

Modern Mourning

Elegiac Sentiment and the Costs of Sincerity

how dear the Muse's favours cost,
If those paint sorrows best—who feel it most.

—Charlotte Smith, Sonnet 1

Death is the dress she wears, her hat and collar.

—Sylvia Plath, "Widow"

Confess what you are smuggling: moods, states of grace, elegies.

—Italo Calvino, *Invisible Cities*

a lyric elixir of death
. . . .
sets
icicled canopy
for corpses of poesy

—Mina Loy, "Poe"

The moral anxiety that commercial behavior corrupts true sincerity has been consistently mapped onto femininity and debased sexuality, and as we saw in book 7 of *The Prelude*, the prostitute (practitioner of the "oldest profession") surfaces as a figure for these anxieties. The association of the prostitute and her sister in the theatrical arts, the actress, with the self-promotion of the literary professional posed a particular threat to women writers who sought to enter the literary marketplace.

Nevertheless, enter they did: as Virginia Woolf remarked, "Towards the end of the eighteenth century a change came about which, if I were rewriting history, I should describe more fully and think of greater importance than the Crusades or the Wars of the Roses. The middle-class woman began to write" (*Room of One's Own*, 65). In the last quarter of the eighteenth century the British public witnessed an unprecedented number of women poets in print, "a literary phenomenon without parallel in earlier history"; by the 1790s, British women writers dominated the novel, the theater, and poetry (Curran, "I Altered," 187–88). This would prove to be a transatlantic phenomenon, as evidenced by the central public role of American women writers in the nineteenth century (P. Bennett, *Public Sphere*). Woolf explained this phenomenon thus: it "was founded on the solid fact that women could make money by writing" (65). Women writers' success can be explained by a number of historical shifts, but chief among them are the growth of the literary marketplace, the rise of the literary professions, and an integrally related phenomenon, the culture of sensibility.

The history of the literary professions reveals an increasing record of women's participation, but also a persistent gendered anxiety about the commercialization of "private" sentiment. While women writers exercised an active public function in the culture of sensibility, their role was subject to moral expectations of white, middle-class conduct, including the ideal of femininity as a site of untainted "privacy." Professional women writers clearly violated this ideal, but it nevertheless exerted a powerful sway over their public discourse and its reception (Davidson and Hatcher, "Separate Spheres"). Given the prohibitions against middle-class women joining the professions or plying trades on their own, the woman writer who sought to publish and sell her work needed to carefully negotiate her public role and reputation. Disavowing commercial motives was one strategy used to avoid the taint of immoral conduct associated with selling and living from one's earnings.[1] This was especially necessary for the female poet, as the bias against writing for money had been attached to poetry with particular fervor. On the one hand, the moral ideal of poetry as a private, disinterested art matched ideals of untainted femininity, providing the woman poet with a particular claim to authority.[2] On the other hand, the woman poet was doubly taxed: facing idealizations of both gender and genre, she risked becoming poetry's abject other should literary commerce raise its threatening head. Thus for the female poet who sought to make a living from her writing, the rhetoric of sincerity was not a choice but an implicit expectation: her poetry was invariably conflated with her moral conduct and her person. Not only was the public performance of private lives essential to her success, but ideals of sincerity, privacy, and autonomy have consistently overdetermined readings of women's poetry.

The two writers I discuss in this section, Charlotte Smith (1749–1806) and Sylvia Plath (1932–63), exemplify both an early and a late use of sincerity as a negotiation of professional authorship, and an early and a late instance of what Anne Mellor and others have called the poetess tradition.[3] Although female poets of Smith's era were routinely called poetesses, it's perhaps surprising to learn that Plath pronounced herself in her journals "The Poetess of America" (*Unabridged Journals*, 360). This self-conscious identification should give us pause, for it indicates Plath's awareness of a rhetorical tradition connected with the figure of the female poet, and the ways in which this tradition speaks to gendered etiquettes of authorship in the twentieth as well as late eighteenth and nineteenth centuries. While the historical conditions of poetic authorship that Smith and Plath encountered were very different—Smith relied on the intimate relations of subscription publishing, aristocratic patronage, and male surrogates to negotiate her contracts with booksellers, while Plath marketed her poetry to the popular "ladies slicks," middle-brow literary magazines, and editors at British and American publishing houses, and negotiated a different kind of patronage, that of the university—their uses of sincerity conventions as response to and commentary on the conditions of professional authorship are strikingly resonant.

Both Smith and Plath attempted to make a living from their writing, and they viewed the publication and sale of their works as both an economic necessity and a desired opportunity. They also recognized the need to comply with feminine norms of conduct in order to succeed in the marketplace, and in this respect, their uses of sincerity conventions differ in both aim and effect from the strategies discussed in section 1. Wordsworth and O'Hara sought to distinguish their poetry from the language and economy of type by defining their walk poems as vehicles of spontaneous desire, a desire that could ideally enter into and circumvent the economy of urban advertisement. Their uses of sincerity conventions involve the generation of feeling meant to exceed imposed roles and the threat of self-commodification; thus they sought to transform (O'Hara) and reform (Wordsworth) the theatricality of self-representation, the gap between word and referent, into the engine of spontaneous feeling.

The gendered expectations guiding women's professional roles, both early and late, rendered claims to spontaneity a bit more problematic. Not coincidentally, the urban stroll of the flaneur has primarily served as a figure for male poetic production and circulation since the late eighteenth century,[4] suggesting that the woman writer's engagement with consumer culture and conventions of sincerity was differently gendered. Female "flaneuses"—from the romantic poet Mary Robinson to Virginia Woolf's Mrs. Dalloway to Mina Loy's Bowery pedestrian—have traversed urban space, but their walks tend to be a negotiation not just of shopping but of being shopped: immersion in the marketplace has spelled comparison to, not distinction from, the prostitute.[5] Emily Dickinson, who wrote "Publication— is the Auction / Of the Mind of Man—," responded to this dilemma by largely avoiding publication during her lifetime; instead she circulated poems by letter to a circle of friends and preserved them for posterity in sets and fascicles.[6] For writers such as Smith and Plath who wanted to sell their work, however, it was necessary to prove their compliance with feminine roles distinct from the marketplace. Rather than avoid what I call in section 1 the "language of type," Smith and Plath tend to use sincerity conventions to perform prescribed roles, thereby concealing—however imperfectly— their desire to sell their work and, even more taboo, the pleasure they gain from doing so.[7] Sincerity was by definition a theatrical rhetoric for the poetess; the need to profess sincerity implied its performative dimension, and therefore spelled the impossibility of a spontaneous lyric ideal.[8]

Thus, when the professional female poet takes center stage in the romantic and postromantic lyric, she is faced with a different conflict from that of the flaneur: the need to sell a particular performance of sincerity, while appearing to disdain theatricality and its commercial connotations. For the poetess sincerity was inseparable from commercial culture, and yet she needed to uphold the pretense of their opposition: her task was to "act naturally," to make her performance appear so natural as to be virtually invisible.[9] Literary and cultural precedent rendered the role of mourner one that the woman of sensibility could assume with propriety, and as the following chapters discuss at length, elegiac mourning came to be seen as one of the chief signifiers of poetic sincerity. Smith, Plath, and a host of other female poets—Mary Tighe, Letitia Landon, Felicia Hemans, the Poe circle, Edna St. Vincent Millay, Elinor Wylie, Mina Loy—chose to negotiate the literary marketplace in mourning dress, making elegiac occasions and elegiac sentiment the mainstay of their lyric. Dressed in melancholy garb, Smith and Plath emphasized that the inspiration to write poetry was essentially private rather than public and professional, that they were dedicated to artistic and moral ideals distinct from the marketplace. Presenting the poetess as a mourner, self-mourner, and even as a beautiful corpse, Smith and Plath claimed the authenticity of lyric feeling through its origin in death and mourning.

Although both Smith and Plath astutely exploited the theatrical and commercial dimensions of their art, the theatricality of sincere rhetoric yielded conflict as well as professional success: what was real and what was performance to the poetess?[10] Smith and Plath articulate this epistemological dilemma in different terms—Smith using the language of sensibility and Plath that of Freudian analysis—but both convey the impossibility of sincere self-representation, given the need to perform the role of melancholic muse. Held to the ideal of a transparent sincerity, Smith and Plath indicate that this moral ideal depends on a model of authorial origination and self-possession not available to the writer who must sell feeling and perform conventional roles.[11] The unattainability of this ideal made it a subject of critique, but it was no less desired: while Smith and Plath recognize the commercial nature of their performances of sincerity, they simultaneously profess a desire to grasp the "real," a nondiscursive ideal beyond performance. The theatricality of sincere rhetoric was for them a vexed, insoluble problem.

The "death of the author"—and poststructuralist critiques of authorship more generally—take on new meaning when read in the context of poetesses who perform the gap between author and persona as the repressed content of a literary culture deeply invested in the ideal of the sincere, self-possessing author.[12] The "death of the author" named not only a problem of textual self-production for the poetess but also a recurrent problem of reception. While the walk figures the ideal circulation of the poetic "body" in section I, the figure of poetic circulation in this section is the corpse, which must be carried, mourned, and buried, its locomotion contingent on the sympathy, and money, of others. Poe's famous statement that "the death . . . of a beautiful woman is, unquestionably, the most poetical topic in the world"[13] depicts the conflation of dead woman and poem as an ideal conduit for the circulation of moral feeling, but the poetess was well aware that the beautiful corpse could easily be unveiled as her debased double, the prostitute. Smith and Plath sought to influence the terms of their reception, but understood that their readers would ultimately legislate the distinction between the sincere and the theatrical. Melancholia is the affective symptom of this conflict: rather than use elegy to promote the health of the social body through mourning and the circulation of sympathy, both writers use their poetic "corpses" to simultaneously perform and expose the assumptions about self, feeling, and property that sustain elegy's redemptive, healing goals.[14]

The critical reception of both Smith and Plath has dramatically borne out the contradictions of their ambivalent dependence on readerly sympathy and moral evaluation.[15] Their readers have drawn and redrawn the line between the real and the performative, circling around the problem of how to connect (or disconnect) the poetry and the life, or, more pointedly, the poetry and the death. Recent critics have drawn attention to the problems of reception that plague mid-twentieth-century "confessional" poetry and the contemporary first-person lyric more generally, specifically the tendency to conflate the poet with her persona and to confuse evaluations of the art with moral judgments of the poet's life.[16] Juxtaposing Smith's and Plath's poetry and reception suggests that these problems are not new, but characterize responses to lyric poetry since at least the late eighteenth century. Despite both poets' attempts to interrogate the terms of their reception, gendered etiquettes of commercial culture continue to guide readings of their poetry.

In exploring death as a figure for the vexed connection between commercial economies and rhetorical conventions of self-representation in women's poetry, I pursue Celeste Schenck's sense that there is an "unsettling coherence of the female funeral aesthetic across centuries," which indicates "women poets have clearly enjoyed an elegiac mode of their own" ("Feminism and Deconstruction," 23). Juxtaposing an early and late occasion of poetess writing illuminates a shadowy map of modern lyric involving elegy, gender, and sincerity that haunts the canonical map, a "terra incognita beneath our very feet" (Curran, "I Altered," 189). That this map has remained unseen and uncharted is in part due to the period-bound emphasis of current literary scholarship, and the scholarship on elegy is an excellent example. The insight that elegy becomes a "mode" or sensibility that permeates other forms remains specific to work on romanticism, with little exploration of how this transformation influences the modern lyric.

Laura Quinney and Jahan Ramazani are the notable exceptions to this trend: both scholars connect elegiac themes and the discourse of melancholia and place them at the center of modern poetic history. Quinney's study of poetry from Wordsworth to Ashbery argues that "what romanticism bequeathed to Victorian poetry, and then, oddly enough, to modernism and postmodernism, is the psychology of unresolved disappointment" (*Poetics of Disappointment,* xiii). Quinney suggests that the "loss of the capacity for self-idealization" (11–12), central to poetic self-exploration since the romantic era, has affinities with the psychology of melancholia and depression, but it is also a literary and philosophical problem: "Disappointment attacks the aggrandized ontological status of the self in general" (12). Similarly, Ramazani argues that, even though "sometimes regarded as opposites, modern poetry and the elegy should be seen instead as inextricable" (*Poetry of Mourning,* 26–27). While poets prior to Swinburne write consolatory elegies, finding solace for the loss of the dead in "nature, in god, or in poetry itself," the modern elegy is melancholic, a form that articulates "not transcendence or redemption of loss but immersion in it" (4).

While both of these histories break new ground, the poetess remains a marginal figure. In drawing the boundaries of the modern elegy at the turn of the twentieth century, Ramazani diminishes the roots of elegiac displacement and of melancholia in the romantic period: he presents a shift from elegiac consolation to melancholic anticonsolation as a progressive narrative of gendered liberation that arrives at its culmination in the elegies of the post-1945 American poets Plath, Anne Sexton, and Adrienne Rich (*Poetry of Mourning,* 22, 295–97). Melissa Zeiger, following Ramazani's lead in her recent book on elegy, claims that "poetesses performed in a highly monitored and bounded elegiac space, establishing (but also confined to) a subordinate and largely ridiculed 'female consolatory tradition' of their own" and concludes, the "elegy has apparently remained a problematic and relatively uncompelling form for them" (*Beyond Consolation,* 62). Building on Quinney's insight, I suggest that romantic "consolation" and its relation to moral ideals is much more complex than has been acknowledged.[17] If Smith's use of the elegy helps us to clarify how elegiac sentiment and the problem of professing sincerity permeates "modern" work such as Plath's in which it has gone unnoticed, Plath's work helps us to see how earlier poetesses such as Charlotte Smith politicize the elegy in the context of gender, encoding a melancholic response to sympathetic community and its moral ideals. Elegy is indeed a "problematic form": it has served as the central and most compelling forum for exploring conflicts of female poetic authorship since the late eighteenth century.

Chapter 3
Charlotte Smith

"In a Robe of Darkest Grain": Elegiac Sensibility and the Performance of Sincerity

In "Nuns fret not" (1807), Wordsworth represents the constraints of the sonnet form as a room that is potentially a prison. To choose to write a sonnet, "one of the most highly determined formal structures in Western poetry and . . . probably the most familiar," is to enter a library lined with the works of previous sonnet writers, to submit oneself to the weight of tradition (Barbara Herrnstein Smith, *Poetic Closure,* 50). For a poet such as Wordsworth who asserted the authority of individual experience and feeling, such conventions would seem to counter a spontaneous ideal. Yet Wordsworth argues that liberty materializes only within and against such constraints:

> In truth the prison, unto which we doom
> ourselves, no prison is: and hence for me,
> In sundry moods, 'twas pastime to be bound
> Within the Sonnet's scanty plot of ground;
> Pleased if some Souls (for such there needs must be)
> Who have felt the weight of too much liberty,
> Should find brief solace there, as I have found.
>
> (Poetical Works, 199; lines 8–14)

Without the walls of a room to restrict one's movements, or the conventions of the sonnet's lines and the twist of its rhymes, personal liberty would remain abstract and immaterial, unfathomed and hence unvalued. In mastering the sonnet form, Wordsworth transforms inherited conventions—all that might seem to limit his power of spontaneous expression—into that which enables it. As Adela Pinch has argued, "Knowing one's feelings may always involve recognizing them through conventions or forms. . . . Feelings can either seem conventional themselves, or be seen as that which animates, or makes meaningful, conventions" (*Strange Fits,* 48). We might say that Wordsworth defines spontaneous feeling as the animation of inherited conventions or habits.

Prior to Wordsworth, the poet Charlotte Smith entered the sonnet's "narrow room," but she suggested that it was, potentially, a prison: for Smith, sonnet conventions signified a generic role for sincere feeling, a gendered cultural script that would prove difficult to animate or possess. Smith explicitly connected her lyric dispossession to her difficult material circumstances as a writer. William Cowper vividly conveyed her predicament when he wrote to William Hayley: "Poor Mrs. Smith—chained to her desk like a slave to his oar, with no other means of subsistence for herself and her numerous children" (Cowper, *Life and Letters,* 72). While Smith successfully transformed her "scanty plot of ground" into a means of supporting herself and her family with her literary proceeds, her poetry engages the costs of this endeavor. Smith conveys the sincerity of her experience and feelings not through the animation of convention but by theatrically suffering the impossibility of such an ideal. The need to perform a generic role rendered lyric self-possession out of reach, available only through sensibility of its absence.

Smith viewed the particular constraints of her life and career as inseparable from the ways in which England legally and ideologically restricted the rights of women, and throughout her career she referenced her personal experience of injustice to buttress her claims to suffering. Although born in 1749 into a wealthy family in Kensington, Smith's status in life changed when at age fifteen in 1765 she married Benjamin Smith, the son of Richard Smith, the director of the East India Company.[1] Benjamin Smith was a partner in his father's company, but largely spent his time and his father's money gambling and pursuing entertainment. The elder Mr. Smith did not trust his son, and in drawing up his will he appointed Charlotte, his son, and his wife joint executors in an effort to limit his son's power.

When Richard Smith died in 1776, however, the estate, valued at £36,000, could not be settled. The elder Mr. Smith's will was contradictory and confusing, and Benjamin, who wrested control of the estate from Charlotte and his mother, ignored his father's provisions for other members of the family, prompting lawsuits on the part of the slighted parties that remained unresolved until after Charlotte Smith's death. While the lawsuits continued, Charlotte and her children received no dividends from the estate. In 1784 the suing parties had Benjamin imprisoned at King's Bench for failure to preserve the value of the trust; instead of attempting to resolve the disputes, he had "squandered 16,000 pounds."[2] Charlotte spent seven months with her husband in King's Bench prison, and her career as a sonnet writer literally originated from this imprisonment; she succeeded in freeing her husband by earning the money to counter their debts through publication of the first edition of *Elegiac Sonnets*.

In 1787 Charlotte separated from her husband, a decision that left her and her children financially vulnerable. Since the couple were technically married, under British marriage law all of Charlotte's property, including her literary earnings, belonged to her husband, and he sometimes claimed them. Although her marriage agreement had provided her with three settlements, her trustees withheld them, because there was no provision for them in the case of a separation. While her nine children received some interest from the trust of the estate, the family lost more than they gained due to Charlotte Smith's endless trips to London to attempt to resolve their legal troubles.

Smith largely supported her family through the proceeds from her writing; she hoped to give her children the opportunities she felt they deserved considering her former station in life. Judith Stanton estimates that during Smith's most profitable years, 1788–98, she made between £200 and £400 a year in literary proceeds. She did not make enough money for her sons to receive a university education, and several joined the military; with her daughters she hoped for advantageous marriages. While she received some extra support from her patron, Lord Egremont, and her eldest sons eventually contributed some money to the family, Smith supported as many as eight of her children at any one time, and was often forced to beg for advances from her publishers and to spend on credit. Profit certainly became a motive inspiring Smith's literary endeavors, and she usually began a new work when she needed money.

Yet her dependence upon her literary income was dangerous to her public reputation—it signified not only impropriety but also her potential insincerity, the possibility that her motive for publication was simply to make money. Smith recognized that her readers would conflate her poetic persona with her moral conduct and person, and that she would thus need to use sincerity conventions to perform noncommercial feminine roles. While Smith expertly adapted her performance to readerly expectations,[3] the success of her poetic persona depended upon the willingness of her readers to believe that she was not playing a part for self-interested ends.

Drawing on the connection between elegiac sentiment and sincerity, Smith inaugurates the tradition of the poetess who enters the literary marketplace in mourning attire. As Karen Halttunen argues, "Within the sentimental cult of mourning, bereavement and sympathy were regarded as visible signs of a mourner's Christian piety, social benevolence, and sincere sensibility. Mourning, the natural human response to the greatest human affliction, was held sacred by sentimentalists as the purest, the most transparent, and thus the most genteel of all sentiments" (*Confidence Man*, 124). The dialogue about the dead and mourning assumed new importance in the eighteenth century as secular authority began to replace divine authority, and as political philosophers such as Adam Smith and David Hume sought to develop a secular theory of morals. By imagining the dead, or, in Adam Smith's words, by "our lodging . . . our own living souls, in their inanimated bodies, and thence conceiving what would be our emotions in this case," Smith hoped that his audience would look at the community of the living in a different light. The dead, in other words, could elicit a common sympathy that would ideally create moral consensus and mitigate economic conflict among the living.[4]

The importance of elegy in the literary realm mirrored that of mourning in the culture at large. As practiced by Thomas Gray at mid-century, the elegy was defined by sincerity, the poet's expressions of private grief and suffering serving to authenticate his motive in entering the literary marketplace: inducting the reader into a moral community founded on sympathy for the dead (Schor, *Bearing the Dead*, 50–51). Gray was instrumental in transforming the elegy from a metrically defined form applicable to a variety of subjects, to a "mode," or more specifically to a sensibility of loss expressed by the figure of the poet, usually located in a natural landscape. This sensibility permeated disparate forms such as the elegy, the sonnet, the ode, and the ballad.[5] As Schor argues, "The elegy becomes elegiac precisely when the public, moral significance of individual mourning becomes widely recognized" (21, 49). Gray's merging of elegy, melancholic sensibility, and sincerity proved an enabling influence for Charlotte Smith, who in the guise of a woman of sensibility could claim a public role with propriety. Given what Stuart Curran calls "the powerful shibboleth against the learned woman" ("I Altered," 195), the capacity to feel provided women with a prominent public role as the "moral guardians" of society, "preservers of the religious values of charity and compassion" (Todd, *Sensibility*, 18, 60; Ross, *Contours*, 192–93). The role of mourner was a natural vessel for these values, and it was a small step to espousing them in print (Hall, *White, Male*, 82–85; Hall and Davidoff, *Family Fortunes*, 149–92).

The implicit gendering of elegy abetted the woman poet's claims for propriety. Following Milton's painting of Melancholy in "Il Penseroso" as a "pensive Nun, devout and pure," dressed "in a robe of darkest grain," eighteenth-century poets and readers often feminized melancholy. Although many male poets summoned the melancholy muse as it came to encompass the artistic temperament, the traits associated with it were easily appropriated by women poets, and Milton's "pensive nun" provided a template for poetess performance.[6] While Gray's contemporary Collins and successors such as Goldsmith, Chatterton, and Burns wrote elegies and odes that invoked this sensibility, it was women poets, including Anna Seward, Helen Maria Williams, Anne Bannerman, Mary Robinson, and L.E.L., but chiefly Charlotte Smith, who developed and popularized the elegiac occasion and sensibility articulated by Gray.

Adorning the figure of the author in a "robe of darkest grain," Smith astutely manipulated elegiac conventions in order to market her work. Smith used elegy's connection to a sensibility of loss not only to elicit sympathy for society's victims but to decry her own particular losses, turning her vulnerability—financial and biographical—into the source of her public appeal. Thus Smith profited from the expectation that claims to sincerity corresponded to the author's biography. As Sarah Zimmerman argues, Smith sought to win the reader's sympathy by using the prefaces to her sonnets as "a serialized autobiographical narrative," presenting herself "as a woman wronged by a profligate husband and by a society that excuses his financial abandonment."[7] In various prefaces to the nine editions of the *Elegiac Sonnets,* Smith detailed the financial hardship she had endured due to the handling of her father-in-law's estate, and more specifically, due to particular lawyers who she felt had abused their power and the laws that served them. What might cost her in the public eye—her financial need, her transgression of feminine roles and proper conduct—she cloaked by portraying herself as a victim of other persons, emphasizing the moral debt she is owed. In this manner Smith sought to code the purchase of her works not as economic transactions, but as acts of moral sympathy on the part of her readers, who in buying her works ostensibly alleviated her suffering and promoted the well-being of Smith and her children (Labbé, "Selling One's Sorrows").

While Smith's claims to sincerity emphasized the moral nature of her literary commerce, the association of poet and poem also allowed her to generate interest in her personal drama.[8] To this end, Smith did not confess all. For instance, in the preface to the sixth edition of her sonnets, Smith alludes to circumstances that only her undisclosed "friend" knows and that she cannot reveal: "You know the circumstances under which I have now so long been labouring. . . . With these, however, as they are some of them of a domestic and painful nature, I will not trouble the Public now; but while they exist in all their force, that indulgent Public must accept all I am able to achieve—'Toujours des Chansons tristes!'"[9] By concealing "private" information, or rather by revealing just enough to tantalize her reader,

Smith invites her public to fill in the blanks by reading her other works and by discussing her plight: she discloses information in a manner meant to elicit both moral sympathy and voyeuristic interest.

In keeping with the "private" inspiration for her poetry, Smith distanced herself from professional ambition by indicating that her friends had pressed her to publish her work (Stanton, "Literary Business," 386–87). Smith concludes the preface to the sixth edition by affirming that she is "well aware that for a woman—'The Post of Honor is a Private Station'" (*Poems*, 6). This gesture toward privacy was highly conventional, a means of emphasizing that the inspiration to write poetry was essentially moral and familial rather than public and professional. More specifically, Smith sold her sonnets by representing the ultimate proof of the sincerity of her mournful sentiments: her desire for death, repeated in numerous sonnets. Smith states in the preface to the first edition of the sonnets that they have helped "be(guile)" some "very melancholy moments," yet in the sonnets suggests that the moments she spends writing lyric can little beguile her melancholy: the looming referent of the sonnets is the intractable nature of her woe, the only true escape, Death (*Poems,* 3). For the poetess, a desire for death became a conventional trope of sincerity because death connotes a state beyond representation and earthly experience, unshareable and hence supremely private; with her eyes cast toward the grave, how could one accuse the poetess of ulterior motives?

Smith abetted the autobiographical claims of the prefaces by presenting the sonnets as particular moments in her tragic life, often appending a footnote or specifying the date and location of composition in the title to emphasize that her poetic sentiments were a response to her "real woe" (Hunt Jr., "Wordsworth and Charlotte Smith," 88). To assure her readers of the biographical origin of the sonnets, Smith establishes the relation between lyric and personal experience as one of suffering. In her poems on "fancy," self-reflexive in the manner of Wordsworth's sonnets on the sonnet, Smith portrays fancy as a "false medium" that "shew'd the beauteous rather than the true," a fictive art that she strives to give up:

> May fancied pain and fancied pleasure fly,
> And I, as from me all thy dreams depart,
> Be to my wayward destiny subdued:
> Nor seek perfection with a poet's eye,
> Nor suffer anguish with a poet's heart!   (*Poems*, 44; lines 10–14)

In that fancy creates the illusion that the poetess can escape from her pain, Smith must turn to genuine suffering. However, she describes the necessity of real suffering through language that emphasizes the performative and figurative dimensions of her elegiac persona: she states that her lyric must "in darkest hues . . . dress / The spot where pale Experience hangs her head / O'er the sad grave of murder'd Happiness!" (lines 6–8; my ellipses). Her claims to artlessness are made artfully; as Adela Pinch notes, Smith advertises her artifice through practices of quotation, allusion, and stock conventions (*Strange Fits*, 66–68). While she often locates her sonnets in the context of her life, she just as often animates characters from literary tradition, or from her own novels, and draws attention to this fiction with titles such as "Supposed to have been written by Werter," or "Supposed to have been written in the Hebrides." In this way Smith claims "true" artistry: rendered in the face of nonpoetic exigencies, her skills testify to her irrepressible talents.

Smith emphasizes, however, that though her art "dresses" experience, this dress is no disguise; she does not wear Wordsworth's "poisoned vestments." For instance, "Reflections on some drawings of plants" contrasts art that mimics nature with the "portrait" of the poet's dead daughter imprinted on her "bleeding breast": "Grief . . . with too faithful art / Enshrines the image in thy Mother's heart" (*Poems*, 77–78; lines 13–14). The "true" art of suffering is not the result of choice or fancy but necessity—her body is not so much the willful originator of her daughter's portrait as the medium that is imprinted with it, the page rather than the press. Smith acknowledges that she deploys artifice, but assures the reader that her elegiac garb is not a costume she has chosen but one which circumstance has forced upon her, and thus one which corresponds to inner suffering. Thus, in her poem "Written for the benefit of a distressed player, detained at Brighthemstone for debt, November 1792," she comments: "Hard is his fate, whom evil stars have led / To seek in scenic art precarious bread," for "That eleemosynary bread he gains / Mingl[es]—with real distresses— mimic pains" (*Poems*, 100; lines 23–24, 27–28).[10] The actor's real distresses, his debt and poverty, inform his performance of "mimic pains," and thus the use of artifice should garner not condemnation but sympathy for the genuine feeling expressed through the role: "Smile on the generous act!— where means are given, / To aid the wretched is—to merit Heaven" (lines 70–71).

Although she espoused the values of sensibility in both her novels and her poems, Smith used her poetic persona to safeguard her reputation as a respectable woman. Her novels were more profitable than her poetry, despite the popularity of her sonnets.[11] But the fact that her novels provided the bulk of her income was a potential liability, given the prejudice against the earning woman, and against the connotations of the novel as a genre;

consumed largely by a middle-class reading public and authored by writers of varying class backgrounds, the novel was viewed as tied to consumer culture and the relaxation of morals in a way that poetry was not (Gallagher, *Nobody's Story*, xvii). Savvy of this generic distinction, Smith used her poetry to forge her persona as a mother driven to write from private suffering and cruel deprivation (Stanton, "Literary Business," 392). To remind the reader of her poetic persona, and that poetry was her "true" calling, Smith peoples her novels with characters who are poets, who as part of the narrative action recite elegiac sonnets. Similarly, she includes sonnets from her novels in editions of the poetry, implying that her novels are peopled with versions of the poet herself (Zimmerman, *Romanticism*, 66). In this way she shielded potential criticism of her use of the novel for economic ends.

Smith was wildly successful in her melancholy role. The first edition of *Elegiac Sonnets* appeared in 1784; by 1800 she had published the ninth edition, and one could not open a contemporary newspaper or periodical that did not contain sonnets, many penned by female poets (Curran, *Poetic Form*, 30). As an epigraph to the second volume of her sonnets, Smith quotes Petrarch's Sonnet 268: "Flee serenity and renewal; approach not, my song, where there be smiles or singing, no, only tears: it will not do for you to remain among happy people, disconsolate widow, clothed in black" (*Poems*, 1). Clothed in black, a "disconsolate widow," Smith seemed to have successfully negotiated the difficulties of professional authorship and the weight of the sonnet tradition (D. Robinson, "Reviving the Sonnet," 103; Raycroft, "Revising the Genealogy").

Death the Leveler

Smith was an astute marketer of her work and was deeply invested in its commercial success. Yet her melancholy garb yielded conflict as well as professional success, blurring the line between real experience and dramatic performance.[12] Smith's elegiac poetry explores the problem of how her dependence on and investment in the financial and social order—needing to profess sincerity, to sell her mourning as "real"—compromises a sincere ideal and the possibility of openly criticizing the persons and laws that constrained her. Smith negotiates this dilemma through her representation of her desire for death.

This professed desire is a theatrical convention, but it also authenticates her claim that she has suffered "real woe": in its dual nature, death is central to her negotiation of sincerity. As Elisabeth Bronfen argues, while death is read culturally as a trope, it simultaneously signifies "a failure of the tropic": "death remains outside clear categories. It is nowhere, because it is

only a gap, a cut, a transition between the living body and the corpse, a be-
fore . . . and an after . . . , an ungraspable point, lacking any empiric ob-
ject. . . . Death is the limit of language" (*Over Her Dead Body,* 54). Smith's
professed desire for death, while conventional and commercially driven, ex-
presses a desire for an ideal of "real" experience and expression that lies be-
yond performance. As a trope that signifies a "failure of the tropic," death
allows Smith simultaneously to turn in a flawless elegiac performance and
to expose its failure. In revealing death as a professional performance,
Smith anticipates the actress Sarah Bernhardt, who in 1884 arranged to be
photographed lying in a coffin feigning her own death. Bernhardt's widely
circulated photo suggests the connection between the professions of poet-
ess and actress, both involved in "kill[ing] off and animat[ing] multiple
selves" as a critical engagement with the gendered necessity of performing
authenticity (Scandura, "Deadly Professions," 21).

Although Gray's merging of elegy and melancholic sensibility provided
Smith with a respectable persona as a professional writer, Gray's work was
equally important to Smith because of its critical capacities, specifically his
use of death to express a leveling sympathy for the poor and powerless.
Gray's elegy and sonnet draw on a particular tradition of topographical
poetry codified by Milton's "L'Allegro" and "Il Penseroso" and used by the
Graveyard Poets Robert Blair and Edward Young.[13] Graveyard poetry is an
egalitarian, leveling poetry because anyone can feel or sympathize with the
lyric speaker, who lacks class identification; moreover, death levels the ma-
terial distinctions that figure so prominently on earth, promising egalitar-
ian treatment in the afterlife. Gray presents death as the great leveler in his
"Elegy Written in a Country Churchyard":

> The boast of heraldry, the pomp of power,
> And all that beauty, all that wealth e'er gave,
> Awaits alike the inevitable hour.
> The paths of glory lead but to the grave.   (lines 33–36)

The speaker meditates on the uncelebrated poor buried in the churchyard,
concluding with an epitaph commemorating a youth "to fortune and to
fame unknown": in this way Gray seeks to include the reader in an act of
sympathy toward the deserving but forgotten poor. While Gray uses death
to criticize distinctions based upon class, he does not urge tolerance of pres-
ent suffering in service of future immortality, like Blair and Young, but
sympathy in the present, a civil, secular end.

While Gray's "Sonnet on the Death of Mr. Richard West," which served
as "the motive force underlying the entire Romantic revival of the sonnet,"

is ostensibly a private lamentation for West, it too has leveling implications (Curran, *Poetic Form,* 30). Gray demonstrates the inconsolable melancholy characteristic of graveyard poetry, but he omits a Christian framework for his suffering; death may provide relief, not through the promise of Heaven but only because it will eliminate the poet's painful sensibility of loss. Gray's sonnet loosely followed the Elizabethan model, a "leveling" choice: in the latter half of the eighteenth century, a debate raged concerning the legitimate versus illegitimate sonnet, with the Elizabethan model decidedly "illegitimate," and the Petrarchan or Italian variety "legitimate."[14] The British sonnet tradition ceased following Milton's brief revival of the sonnet in the seventeenth century, largely because the Augustan poets deemed the sonnet nonclassical due to its association with the Elizabethans, whom they considered barbaric and unrefined (Curran 29). In choosing to revive the sonnet in accordance with the devalued Shakespearean model, Gray rejected adherence to dominant conventions, emphasizing the authority of his own sensibility.

The critical impetus of Smith's poetry stems not from her use of the sonnet but from her use of the elegiac sonnet: the tradition of elegy provided her work with its leveling implications. Smith acknowledged Gray's influence explicitly in the "Quotations, Notes, and Explanations" she included with her sonnets after the second edition (*Poems,* 81). Smith also follows Gray's example in her use of the "illegitimate" sonnet; she states in the preface to the first and second editions of her sonnets, "The little poems which are here called Sonnets, have, I believe, no very just claim to that title: but they consist of fourteen lines, and appear to me no improper vehicle for a single Sentiment. I am told, and I read it as the opinion of very good judges, that the legitimate Sonnet is ill calculated for our language" (*Poems,* 3). Smith at times departs from Gray and the graveyard tradition, however, by reflecting on the limits of sympathetic identification as a medium of social change. "The Dead Beggar," an elegy published in November 1792 and in the *Elegiac Sonnets* (1800), exemplifies this theme. A preface to the poem defines its occasion: "An elegy, addressed to a lady, who was affected at seeing the funeral of a nameless pauper, buried at the expence of the parish, in the church-yard at Brighthelmstone, in November 1792" (*Poems,* 96). Smith places us squarely in the occasion Gray delineated in his "Elegy," that of reflection upon the burial of the unnamed and unsung poor; however, it is not the poetess who is located in the country churchyard, but an anonymous "lady." Smith thus signals her distance from Gray's project: her subject is the sympathetic reader his "Elegy" addresses.

The lady's sympathy exemplifies the hypocrisy of the culture of sensibility:

Swells then thy feeling heart, and streams thine eye
O'er the deserted being, poor and old,
Whom cold, reluctant, Parish Charity
Consigns to mingle with his kindred mold?

Mournst thou, that here the time-worn sufferer ends
Those evil days still threatening woes to come;
Here, where the friendless feel no want of friends,
Where even the houseless wanderer finds an home?

What tho' no kindred croud in sable forth,
And sigh, or seem to sigh, around his bier;
Tho' o'er his coffin with the humid earth
No children drop the unavailing tear?   (*Poems,* 96, lines 1–12)

In contrast to Gray, who laments the unsung dead, Smith's mocking questions imply the insincerity of those who profess sympathy for the dead beggar. She balances the three opening stanzas with three concluding stanzas that instruct the lady to rejoice rather than grieve:

Rather rejoice that here his sorrows cease,
Whom sickness, age, and poverty oppress'd;
Where Death, the Leveler, restores to peace
The wretch who living knew not where to rest.

Rejoice, that tho' an outcast spurn'd by Fate,
Thro' penury's rugged path his race he ran;
In earth's cold bosom, equall'd with the great,
Death vindicates the insulted rights of Man.

Rejoice, that tho' severe his earthly doom,
And rude, and sown with thorns the way he trod,
Now, (where unfeeling Fortune cannot come)
He rests upon the mercies of his GOD.   (*Poems,* 97, lines 13–24)

Where Gray invoked the leveling power of death to seek his readers' sympathy, reminding them of the arbitrariness of class distinctions, Smith suggests that such sympathy changes nothing and vindicates no one—it merely preserves the status quo. The tears of the lady come too late; they have not saved the beggar, nor will they save others in his plight: sympathetic mourners only "seem to sigh" (line 10). As Smith herself was charged with feigning sorrow, we might read her celebration of "Death, the leveler" as emerging from her own situation, a means of engaging the limits on her ability to effect change due to her dependence on readerly sympathy.

By representing Death as a utopian state that she contrasts with British society, Smith suggests that the truly sympathetic reader should offer not tears over the beggar's death, but dedication to the cause of equality, to the "rights of man." Smith's readers did not miss the elegy's echoing of the ideals of the French Revolution, which were common parlance in 1792. Indeed, Smith was censured for making her sympathies with the revolution too explicit; death the leveler had assumed new connotations with the appearance of the guillotine. Smith's moral superiority as a woman of sensibility stemmed from her capacity to unite the nation, not to divide it by party sympathy. In a note to the "Elegy" published with the sonnets, Smith addressed this charge:

> I have been told that I have incurred blame for having used in this short composition, terms that have become obnoxious to certain persons. Such remarks are hardly worth notice; and it is very little my ambition to obtain the suffrage of those who suffer party prejudice to influence their taste; or of those who desire that because they have themselves done it, every one else should be willing to sell their best birth-rights, the liberty of thought, and of expressing thought, for the promise of a mess of pottage.
>
> It is surely not too much to say, that in a country like ours, where such immense sums are annually raised for the poor, there ought to be some regulation which should prevent any miserable deserted being from perishing through want, as too often happens to such objects as that on whose interment these stanzas were written.   (*Poems*, 96)

Smith sings the praises of the common good, blaming her accusers for the very crime with which they have charged her: that of party prejudice. Nevertheless, she struggles against the status quo; rather than leave the fate of the poor contingent upon the mercy of the individual reader, upon "cold, reluctant Charity," Smith emphasizes the need for a "regulation" or legal remedy to prevent deaths such as the beggar's. Influence gained through sympathetic channels was inevitably undercut by Smith's lack of legal and institutional power, her inability to turn feeling into action. If it is women's role to mourn and serve as vessels of sympathy, Smith suggests that women should use this role to press for the rights of the disenfranchised, including (implicitly) their own "liberty of thought." Thanks to Smith's prefaces, her readers would not miss the resonance of her own circumstances in the beggar's plight.

Smith makes this autobiographical resonance explicit in many of her sonnets, assuming the position of society's victims and imbuing the rhetoric of loss with personal and critical meaning. Thus, Smith's sonnets in which she anticipates the poetess's death subtly connect a leveling sympathy to her own desire for liberty of thought and action, as is evident in sonnet 44, "Written in the church-yard at Middleton in Sussex" (*Poems,* 42). Responding to the representation of the rural church graveyard as a location for the production of sympathetic community in Gray's "Elegy," an image Wordsworth would later make use of in his "Essays on Epitaphs," Smith emphasizes her isolation from this sympathetic community, indicting the society that has caused her loss and whose sympathy provides no compensation:

> Press'd by the Moon, mute arbitress of tides,
> While the loud equinox its power combines,
> The sea no more its swelling surge confines,
> But o'er the shrinking land sublimely rides.
> The wild blast, rising from the Western cave,
> Drives the huge billows from their heaving bed;
> Tears from their grassy tombs the village dead,
> And breaks the silent sabbath of the grave!
> With shells and sea-weed mingled, on the shore
> Lo! their bones whiten in the frequent wave;
> But vain to them the winds and waters rave;
> They hear the warring elements no more:
> While I am doom'd—by life's long storm opprest,
> To gaze with envy on their gloomy rest.

Smith assures her reader in a prose note that the location she describes is not fictional: "Middleton is a village on the margin of the sea, in Sussex, containing only two or three houses. There were formerly several acres of ground between its small church and the sea, which now, by its continual encroachments, approaches within a few feet of this half-ruined and humble edifice. The wall, which once surrounded the church-yard, is entirely swept away, many of the graves broken up, and the remains of bodies interred washed into the sea; whence human bones are found among the sand and shingles on the shore" (*Poems,* 42). While the sonnet dramatizes the sea's destruction, the prose description presents this destruction as a fact observable through its traces on the landscape: the observer in the prose passage writes from the perspective of a natural historian or tour guide who merely records nature's changes, while the observer in the sonnet is clearly subject to or "opprest" by the destruction she observes. By including the factual note, Smith anchors the sentiments she expresses in the sonnet to her life in Sussex. While Gray locates himself in an unnamed "country churchyard" that comes to represent England itself, Smith's gesture to her personal history ultimately suggests her exclusion from this cultural narrative.

Striking in both the lyric and prose versions is that the figure of the poetess appears in the landscape not through direct assertions of self but as the implicit observer of the phenomena she describes. In the prose note, Smith resists assertion of the authorial "I" through her use of the passive voice ("the wall . . . is entirely swept away"; "whence human bones are found"), giving agency to natural forces such as the sea and the bones rather than to the human observer. Similarly, although the sonnet's title indicates that Smith writes from within the churchyard, the reader learns of Smith's presence in the landscape only through her visual description, affirmed by the use of the imperative voice ("Lo! their bones whiten in the frequent wave"), which designates her occupation of the scene in terms of her contiguous surroundings. Tellingly, the "I" of the sonnet and note emerges in relation to a description of nature's destruction; Smith allies the lyric "I" with the whitened bones tossed and turned by the sea, conveying that she, too, is "opprest" by "life's long storm." When Smith uses the first-person voice in the sonnet's final couplet, it is not to define the self against this scene of natural destruction, but to state a desire to become like the dead, who lack consciousness of their misery.

Smith's isolation in this tempest alludes to her more general oppression by societal institutions, as detailed in her prefaces and notes. Whereas Wordsworth finds isolation in a natural setting conducive to imagining a sympathetic moral community, Smith sees in nature only her exile from a society that provides no remedy for her suffering. The authority of the church and community is powerless to withstand the destructive capacity of nature and history in what amounts to a profoundly secular vision. Smith conflates the bones sticking up "among the sand and shingles on the shore" with the nearby seashells, suggesting the contingency of human value and possession in a destructive natural world. Human efforts to resist this force are futile: man and his works are literally eroded, becoming fragments, ruins. Nature in this and other sonnets is an alien, unstable, often destructive force that offers no consolation for her losses.[15]

The only certainty that governs the landscape of the sonnets is that of future decay and destruction—it is a landscape filled with ruins and crumbling graves, in which nature destroys all traces of man's history. While "Man, and the works of man" are doomed to fall "to dark Forgetfulness," Smith locates truth in the permanence of natural change, in the "silent, slow, but ever active power / Of vegetative Life" (*Poems*, 299–303; lines 97–98, 90–91). Rejecting the production of value from man's transformations of the natural world, Smith instead locates value in nature's ebbs and wanes, motivated apart from any human commitments. Nature reflects the futility of man's illusions of possession: a child sees "the brilliant glow-worm, like a meteor, shine / On the turf-bank" and collects it; yet "with the morning shudders to behold / His lucid treasure, rayless as the dust!" (*Poems*, 51–52; lines 6–7, 12–13). The sonnet concludes, "So turn the world's bright joys to cold and blank disgust" (line 14).

The Landscape of Allegory

On the one hand, Smith's professed desire for death, repeated throughout her sonnet collection, is a highly conventional pose, serving to authenticate her grief and assure her readers that she lacks desire for earthly gain. On the other hand, these sentiments do not simply function as an acquiescence to elegiac convention or an admission of powerlessness. Rather, by repeating her desire for death, Smith signals her refusal to accept poetic or natural compensation for her loss. Smith's sonnets record destruction and suffering without the hope of progress or change (Schor, *Bearing the Dead*, 63–64); the sonnet sequence is not a progressive narrative of a poet's growth, like *The Prelude*, but rather the repetition or piling up of her losses, much like the "pile of debris" that the angel of history witnesses growing skyward in Walter Benjamin's famous description of Klee's "Angelus Novus" (*Illuminations*, 257–58). In negating the possibility of future change or movement in her sonnets, Smith upsets narratives of human progress and religious salvation, painting a landscape that resonates with Benjamin's understanding of the modern allegorical worldview: "Whereas in the symbol destruction is idealized and the transfigured face of nature is fleetingly revealed in the light of redemption, in allegory the observer is confronted with the *facies hippocratica* of history as a petrified, primordial landscape. Everything about history that, from the very beginning, has been untimely, sorrowful, unsuccessful, is expressed in a face—or rather in a death's head. . . . This is the heart of the allegorical way of seeing, of the baroque, secular explanation of history as the passion of the world; its importance resides solely in the stations of its decline" (*Origins*, 166). Rather than see in nature a reflection of God's order and man's divinely inspired destiny, allegorists from the sixteenth century onward see in nature only decay and transience: "It is fallen nature which bears the imprint of the progression of history" (180). Smith's evocation of a landscape of ruins registers history from the perspective of one excluded from England's political institutions and the privileges of its laws. The fragmentation and deanimation of Smith's first-person speaker provides a stark contrast to Wordsworth's efforts to animate the figure of the author.

By repeatedly asserting her longing for the utopian state of death and the freedom from suffering it will provide, the poet indicates that her need to perform a generic role precludes an ideal of sincere experience predicated on liberty of thought and action. Robert Burns serves for Smith as a potent symbol of the poet whose freedom was unjustly constrained. Smith writes that despite "daily pressure, rude, / Of labouring Poverty," Burns's "generous blood" was "fired with the love of freedom," which he finds only in the grave:

> Indignantly is fled
> Thy noble Spirit; and no longer moved
> By all the ills o'er which thine heart has bled,
> Associate worthy of the illustrious dead,
> Enjoys with them 'the Liberty it loved.'   (*Poems*, 71; lines 10–14)

By unhappily occupying a position of fixity—her generic role, her repeated longing for death—the poet subtly indicts the need to perform suffering: she suffers the need to suffer. By aligning her speakers with death and destruction, violent forces that transgress present limits and values, she challenges—in a coded manner—the moral authority of the institutions that have scripted her performance. Death functions as a "via negativa," a means of sensibly measuring an ideal of authorship through its absence or impossibility. In other words, through destruction and death Smith conveys the effects of immobility, suffering, and dispossession, but also reveals the possibility of future justice: surrounding the imprint upon her breast, like the white space surrounding a page of print, is an utopian ideal—in which social performance points to autonomy, suffering to release, oppression to freedom, loss to redemption.

"Written in the church-yard at Middleton" demonstrates this endeavor. While Smith describes the traces of nature's violence on the landscape in the prose version, in the sonnet she dramatically reenacts the scene of violence; in doing so she aligns herself with nature's destructive capacity. Smith signals her complicity in this violence at the beginning of the poem:

"Press'd by the Moon, mute arbitress of tides / . . . / The sea no more its swelling surge confines." The moon, feminized through the word "arbitress," presses the sea to swell and break its limits, though "mute." Although Smith claims at the end of the poem that she is "opprest," she has, like the moon, "press'd" the sea, an intentional pun (Schor, *Reading in Detail*, 66). Rather than defend tradition and religious values against a violent natural world, Smith presents a sea that breaks down all defenses: the wall of the churchyard, the confines of the grave and coffin, the orderly correspondence between marker and corpse, past traditions and present community.

The sonnet, in Schor's words, presents Smith's "alienation from a moral order based on the moral capital of the 'forefathers'" (69), and, in doing so, it reveals Smith's concern with cultural memory. Smith faced the likelihood that her name and verse would be forgotten, since she lacked access to channels of cultural preservation beyond her reader's sympathy. A poem titled "Elegy" also located in the Middleton Churchyard clarifies these concerns. In contrast to the Middleton sonnet, Smith writes in a note that the occasion of this poem is explicitly fictional (*Poems*, 80–83). An indigent young woman laments the death of her lover, whose father, "resenting his attachment," had sent him off to sea, where he drowned. Smith comments: "The father dying, a tomb is supposed to be erected to his memory in the church-yard mentioned in Sonnet the 44th. And while a tempest is gathering, the unfortunate young woman comes thither; and courting the same death as had robbed her of her lover, she awaits its violence, and is at length overwhelmed by the waves." In the elegy the drowned lover suffers the fate of erasure that Smith wishes to avoid. While the father's tomb relates "his name and wealth," the female speaker remarks of her lover:

. . . no tomb is placed for thee,
That may to strangers' eyes thy worth impart;
Thou hast no grave but in the stormy sea!
And no memorial but this breaking heart!   (lines 25–28)

Asking the sea to part and reveal her lover's "pale and mangled form," the speaker thinks she sees him, "dead, disfigured," but recognizes this vision as a "wild Illusion, born of frantic Pain"; emphasizing the inability of sensibility to effect a change in her material conditions, she states, "My tears, my anguish, my despaire are vain, / the insatiate ocean gives not up its dead" (lines 38, 49, 59–60). As in the Middleton sonnet, by aligning herself with the insatiate ocean, the female speaker vicariously wreaks vengeance on the patriarch and his tomb. Summoning "Despair, and Death, and Desolation," she watches the "embodied waters come," which "tear from its base the proud aggressor's tomb, / And bear the injured to eternal sleep!" (lines 64, 65, 67–68).

The sea in Smith's "Elegy" will not part to show the lovers' "pale and mangled form," but rather provides compensation for the speaker in the destruction of the father's tomb. At one level the elegy is a stock romance along the lines of *Romeo and Juliet*. But "pale and mangled forms" is also an apt description of Smith's elegies and elegiac sonnets, which seek—under the cover of leveling agents such as the sea, the ruinous power of time, and death—to expose the deforming power of Britain's "proud aggressor(s)." In materializing the "pale and mangled form" of the lover through the female speaker's sensibility of pain, Smith shades in the misuses of power that she cannot explicitly condemn. Like the "insatiate ocean," the speaker's refusal to give up the dead, which anticipates Freud's formulation of melancholia, permits Smith to express anger, but only because her speakers' bodies rather than those of her tormentors absorb its force. A "melancholic poetics" is the cost of both selling her poems and attempting to block the values of the culture in which they circulate.

The circumscription of her critique within the social order that gives rise to it exemplifies what Lauren Berlant calls "the female complaint," an "'aesthetic' witnessing of injury," and what Ross Chambers describes as the condition of a melancholic writing that foresees and anticipates its appropriation, yet nevertheless attempts to block or refuse it;[16] indeed, Smith's poetry suggests that the "female complaint" is inseparable from the melancholic's "plaint," and that melancholia is an affective response to an ideal of sincere authorship at once demanded and precluded by the literary marketplace. Rei Terada has argued that the recognition of the death or impossibility of a coherent, autonomous subject is what produces feeling: Smith's dramatization of this recognition suggests that melancholia is often the feeling generated (Terada, *Feeling in Theory*, 3, 24, 151). For Smith, the death of the author is not only textual but economic: the sale of sincere feeling entails a gendered performance that renders autonomy a fiction.

The "death of the author" also names a problem of reception that Smith tried to avert. Smith performs the role of mourner, but in adapting elegy to her own biographical circumstances, sought to influence the values by which she herself would be mourned. In this sense her melancholic texts function as figurative corpses that seek to transform elegy's "ideal" circuits of exchange—mourning and sympathetic identification—and its redemptive goals. By de-forming her elegiac lyrics, Smith criticizes the moral assumptions that support a sincere ideal, and attempts to re-form sympathy to leveling ends. More specifically, by circulating a leveling representation of death, Smith instructs her present and future readers how to read her text/corpse, and how to pass on her name: only future readings, she implies, might fulfill a sincere ideal.

Smith makes these instructions explicit in "The Emigrants" (*Poems*, 131–63). Written in 1793, "The Emigrants" treats the fate of French widows who emigrated to England during the Revolution; Smith clearly connects her personal troubles with the law to those of the exiled widows, who have similarly suffered at the hands of men whose "legaliz'd" greed Smith suggests prompted the Revolution in the first place (line 284). While not an elegy proper, one can read this poem as a sustained elegiac poem in the leveling tradition, in which Smith mourns the losses of the emigrants and, similarly, her own losses; throughout, Smith addresses a "Mourner," whom she tells to "cease these wailings: cease and learn" (bk. 1, line 74). The poem concludes with an account of how "the fearful specters of chicane and fraud" have pursued the poet's "faint steps" (bk. 2, lines 353, 358), an account that results in a vision of her death:

> Peace will at last be mine; for in the Grave
> Is Peace—and pass a few short years, perchance
> A few short months, and all the various pain
> I now endure shall be forgotten there,
> And no memorial shall remain of me,
> Save in your bosoms; while even your regret
> Shall lose its poignancy, as ye reflect
> What complicated woes that grave conceals!
> But, if the little praise, that may await
> The Mother's efforts, should provoke the spleen
> Of Priest or Levite; and they then arraign
> The dust that cannot hear them; be it yours
> To vindicate my humble fame; to say,
> That, not in selfish sufferings absorb'd,
> "I gave to misery all I had, my tears."
> And if, where regulated sanctity
> Pours her long orisons to heaven, my voice
> Was seldom heard, that yet my prayer was made
> To him who hears even silence.   (bk. 2, lines 372–90)

Smith suggests that her memory will only endure in and through her reader's hearts, or sympathy; like Gray's unnamed but deserving youth whom she quotes in line 386, she expects no memorial to preserve her name or fame. Tricia Lootens argues that this pose comes to characterize the poetess tradition: occupying the role of generic womanhood in a bid for canonization, the figure of the poetess is "shaped around vacancy" (*Lost Saints,* 73). Thus, "nineteenth-century women writers are canonized by a process that almost inevitably guarantees their downfall: from a long-term literary historical point of view, they are made secular saints and lost at the same time" (74).

Smith cannot press her luck in her attempt to influence her future reception; she privileges a verse "written not to be remembered," a verse based not on originality but on generic fixity, repetition, and loss (Ross, *Contours,* 158). Canonized verse and art have a superior claim to power and ostentation, she suggests, but not to "worth," an idea she articulates in "To the Fire-Fly of Jamaica, Seen in a Collection" (*Poems,* 204–7):

> Let vaunting OSTENTATION trust
> The pencil's art, or marble bust,
> While long neglected modest worth
> Unmark'd, unhonor'd, and unknown,
> Obtains at length a little earth,
> Where kindred merit weeps alone;
> Yet there, tho' VANITY no trophies rear,
> Is FRIENDSHIP'S long regret, and true AFFECTION'S tear!
>
> (lines 65–70)

Smith tries to influence her reader's feelings, to elicit a leveling sympathy that will inspire her readers to "vindicate" her "humble fame" and change the order of things, providing ghostly corpses and unmarked graves with a plot, a name, and a history. As she predicts in "To My Lyre," when she lies "silent in the tomb," "gentle minds will love my verse, / And Pity shall my strains rehearse, / And tell my name to distant ages" (*Poems,* 312; lines 46–48).

However, as Smith's prophetic line ("even your regret / shall lose its poignancy") from "The Emigrants" suggests, she anticipated the fickleness of a reception based upon sympathy for her "real woe"; once she died, her mourners might feel their sympathy was no longer necessary. Or worse, upon reflection of the "complicated woes that grave conceals," her readers might decide that Smith had exploited her suffering. Smith was only too aware of the costs of her melancholy garb.

The Limits of Sympathy: Smith's Critical Reception

Try as she did to morally justify the publication and sale of her work, Smith was vulnerable to the charge of acting the part of melancholic muse to make money. Moreover, Smith's financial dependence on her elegiac role limited the terms of her reformist efforts. Her solution to the impossibility of distinguishing the sincere lyric from commercial culture—selling the role of chaste, sincere mourner while critically exploring the leveling implications of the "death of the author"—was complicitous, as is borne out by the contradictions of her reception history. While Smith exposed the necessary overlap between the "real poet" and her performances, her readers have attempted to distinguish poet from persona, sincerity from theatricality, relying on moral assumptions about Smith's conduct as a writer for profit.[17]

Smith's sonnets received a largely sympathetic response while she was alive; many of her critics and readers defended the poetry on the basis of their belief in Smith's "real woe." Conversely, she faced charges of "querulous egotism," repetition, plagiarism, and irreligiosity, which implied the artifice and commercial origins of her elegiac sentiments; Anna Seward, for instance, called the sonnets "hackneyed scraps of dismality, with which her memory furnished her from our various poets. Never were poetical whipt syllabubs, in black glasses, so eagerly swallowed by the odd taste of the public."[18] Smith responded to such charges in many of her sonnets and prefaces; her handling of these accusations is instructive, revealing the limits of her elegiac role and of her influence over her readers.[19]

We see the strain of her attempt to walk the fine line between soliciting sales-via-sympathy and employing critical or reformist discourse most clearly in the prefaces to the works she published by subscription, in which buyers signed for a work that was yet to be published. Smith detested this form of payment, given her explicit dependence on specific readers; she stated that it rendered her "a kind of literary beggar" (Stanton, "Literary Business," 388) and identified herself as "one, herself made the object of subscription" (*Poems*, 71). A delay in the subscription edition of volume 2 of the sonnets prompted some of her readers to imply that she had cheated them. Her preface to volume 2 (May 15, 1797) is a lengthy and angry defense of her actions.

Having delayed publication of this subscription issue due to misfortunes including the death of her daughter and her own illness, Smith responds with indignation to those who suspected that she had collected their money with no plans to publish the promised edition. As in her previous subscription edition to the fifth edition of her sonnets, Smith tries to distance herself from a profit motive, reminding her readers that she "reluctantly yielded to the pressing instances of some of my friends; and accepted their offers to promote a subscription to another volume of Poems." She emphasizes that if she could have foreseen the misfortunes that caused the delay, she would not have agreed to the edition, and that she had made arrangements in the case of her death to reimburse her subscribers. After defending herself, she criticizes the readers who have suspected her of ill gain: "Surely, any who have entertained and expressed such an opinion of me, must either never have understood, or must have forgotten, what I was, what I am, or what I ought to be" (*Poems*, 7, 11, 8). Invoking her former class status, Smith reminds the reader that she depends upon the sales of her literary works through no fault or desire of her own, but due to her unfortunate circumstances.

In a manner reminiscent of her "Elegy," Smith then details the injuries she and her children have suffered at the hands of the "inhuman trustees" who have detained their property:

> The injuries I have so long suffered under are not mitigated; the aggressors are not removed: but however soon they may be disarmed of their power, any retribution in this world is impossible—they can neither give back to the maimed the possession of health, or restore the dead. The time they have occasioned me to pass in anxiety, in sorrow, in anguish, they cannot recall to me[.]—To my children they can make no amends, but they would not if they could; nor have I the poor consolation of knowing that I leave in the callous hearts of these persons, thorns to "goad and sting them," for they have conquered or outlived all sensibility of shame; they are alive neither to honesty, honour, or humanity. . . . [They] baffle me yet a little longer in my attempts to procure that restitution, that justice, which they dare not deny I am entitled to . . . perpetuating to the utmost of their power the distresses they have occasioned, and which their perseverance in iniquity has already put it out of the power of Heaven itself to remedy!   (*Poems*, 9)

She adds, they "embitter every hour of my life, and leave me no hope but in the oblivion of the grave" (*Poems*, 8–10).

Smith's frustration with her elegiac role is evident in this preface. Restricted to appeals to sympathy, dependent on the "honesty, honour, or humanity" of her readers and of her trustees, she is powerless to influence those with "callous hearts" who choose simply to ignore her feelings and pleas. Without the power to effect the resolution of the estate, or the financial independence to write without regard for her readers' judgments, Smith can only repeat the crimes against her, hoping to persuade her readers of the morality of her actions, and of the need for their sympathy. Her turn toward the grave is an angry declaration that emphasizes the crimes against her, but also speaks to her powerlessness to find a tactic beyond her elegiac role through which to press her case. To defend herself against charges of artifice, Smith can only supply more textual (un-verifiable) proof for the authenticity of her private struggles. She is as much trapped by the marketing strategy available to her as a woman of sensibility, that is, the repeated appeal to her readers' moral sympathy through demonstration of her elegiac sentiments, as she is by repetition as a form of critique—the insistence on her intractable melancholy and loss, and the coded allusions to those responsible. Repetition is a symptom of the conflict of using her elegiac role both to sell her poetry to a broad readership and to indict the system that requires her endless performances. Despite her attempts to guide readerly judgment of her conduct, during her lifetime Smith recognized that ultimately her readers held the power of judgment.

The moral nature of readerly judgment becomes particularly clear in the case of Smith's posthumous reception. Assessments of Smith's work after her death in 1806 depended largely on how critics interpreted her claims to sincerity, how they read the moral versus commercial valences of her work. Smith's revival and popularization of the sonnet, the central vehicle of women's poetry at this time, can be viewed as a testament to the success of her leveling project (Curran, *Poetic Form*, 30; D. Robinson, "Reviving the Sonnet," 99). Contemporary anthologizer Capel Lofft commented on female poets' contributions to the sonnet revival, stating that he chose the name *Laura, or An Anthology of Sonnets and Elegiac Quatuorzains* (1814) for his anthology because "many FEMALE POETS have grac'd this elegant Department of Poetry: many of whose beautiful Productions will be found in these Volumes" (1:ii). *Laura* contains more sonnets by Smith than any other poet (including Milton), except for Lofft himself.

Many of these poets use Smith's elegiac idiom, and several dedicated sonnets to Smith, making the sympathy she sought to elicit the occasion of their sonnets. Consider, for example, two elegiac sonnets mourning Smith's death included in the introduction to Capel Loftt's anthology. Mary Johnson's "To the Memory of Charlotte Smith" (1:238) begins with an invocation to Smith's muse to inspire her elegizers:

> SPIRIT of plaintive Tenderness! refine
> The breathings which to sound her Name aspire
> Her's who of Inspiration's Fount divine
> Most deeply quaff'd of BRITAIN'S female Choir!
> On the pale willow drooping o'er her Tomb,
> Still and unstrung suspended rests her lyre;
> The silence of the Grave its mournful doom,
> For no inferior hand can brace its Wire.   (lines 1–8)

Johnson responds to Smith's "To My Lyre," positioning Smith as the most inspired poet of a recognizable "female choir," with her "spirit of plaintive tenderness" continuing to inspire (literally, to breathe into) the songs of her successors. Moreover, Johnson follows Smith's instructions to pity her suffering and vindicate her name:

> Departed Poetess! the bitter Woe
> Which nipp'd thy hopes in Youth's expanding bloom,
> And ting'd thy soft effusions with its gloom,
> Shall sweetly to succeeding ages flow;
> And Rapture oft shall cry—Who would refuse
> To take thy sorrows could they give thy Muse?   (lines 9–14)

By commemorating Smith's sorrows, her successors will sweeten or transform her bitterness—her "bitter woe" will "sweetly to succeeding ages flow," as her continuing fame compensates for her suffering. Her elegizers too reap ample compensation as they occupy the poetic territory opened up by Smith: Johnson establishes her poetic authority through her elegiac tribute to Smith, an act of ventriloquism with "sweet" rewards.

Harriet Elizabeth Leathes's sonnet "On the Death of Mrs. Charlotte Smith" (1:250) indicates the influence of Smith's leveling agenda. Refusing to mourn Smith's death, Leathes has clearly understood Smith's message about the limits of sympathy, suggesting that in death Smith has finally found freedom from her woes. The octet opens with rhetorical questions reminiscent of Smith's questions in "The Dead Beggar":

> And can we mourn the stroke that snatch thee hence?
> And can we grieve that thou no more art here?
> No: —pious Hope shall check Affliction's tear:
> And upward pointing to the Realms of Light
> Shall bid us praise that glorious Providence
> Whose mercy, ever during, ever bright,
> Clos'd all thy sorrows, bade thy sufferings cease,
> And call'd thy Soul to Realms of harmony and Peace.   (lines 1–8)

Leathes's questions echo Smith's praise for death as a realm "of Harmony and Peace" in "The Dead Beggar" and in sonnets such as "To the Moon." That Leathes asks them at all indicates her desire to instruct her reader in a leveling sympathy for Smith, extending Smith's project while omitting reference to the specific injuries Smith endured.

As Smith anticipated, her fame was short-lived. Her poetry had all but disappeared a decade after her death, when the "real" figure was no longer present to authenticate it. By 1827, Alexander Dyce remarks in a short biography of Smith in *Specimens of British Poetesses* that Smith's sonnets were "once very popular"; similarly, Wordsworth, who met Smith prior to his first trip to France, wrote in 1833, "It seems a pity that the Poems of this genuine Singer should have gone out of sight" (qtd. in Hilbish, *Charlotte Smith*, 253). We might productively contrast Smith's posthumous reception with that of Emily Dickinson, who avoided publication and its attendant publicity during her lifetime but who secured an enduring posthumous fame.[20] While both Dickinson and Smith interrogate the claims of the first-person lyric, Dickinson did not tie her poetry to her "real woe" to publicize her verse, and the posthumous readings of her poetry do not challenge its enduring claims.[21]

The disappearance of Smith's work stemmed in part from a backlash against the literature of sensibility. By the last decade of the eighteenth century, the culture of sensibility was perceived as "anti-community, a progressing away from, not into, Humean social sympathy" (Todd, *Sensibility*, 136). The reaction against the literature of sensibility was motivated by fear of its leveling influence; by establishing feeling, rather than "achievement or breeding" as the basis of writerly authority, the literature of sensibility was wedded to democratic ideals and implicitly to the cause of the French Revolution. The initial reaction against sensibility was part of the counter-revolution that swept Britain following the nation's entrance into war with France in February of 1793: as Butler argues, "All the more innovatory styles of 1760–90 (including the "cult of tears") were to fall under suspicion for political reasons in an England at war with a revolutionary enemy" (*Romantics*, 36). While the reaction against the literature of sensibility stemmed from its appeal to the popular classes (34, 37), it was also a reaction against women readers and writers, who had gained influence through the commercial circulation of this literature, and who would clearly profit from reformation of existing institutions. The feminine culture of mourning became a particular target of criticism in nineteenth-century America: "Sentimentalists feared that the struggle for bourgeois gentility was poisoning even mourning with calculated self-interest and transforming mourning ritual into a masquerade of affected sensibility" (Halttunen, *Confidence Man*, 125).

This change in the fortunes of the literature of sensibility is apparent in the nineteenth-century criticism of Smith, which displays a lack of sympathy for her suffering, dismissing it as selfish and specious rather than communal and moral. Both Anna Laetitia Barbauld in her introduction to Smith's *The Old Manor House* in *The British Novelists* (1810) and

Julia Kavanagh in her *Collection of British Authors* (1863) comment on Smith's difficulties, but fault Smith for her handling of them. Barbauld commented, "The vexation attending these perplexities, together with the pecuniary embarrassments she was continually involved in, clouded the serenity of Mrs. Smith's mind, and gave to her writings that bitter and querulous tone of complaint which is discernible in so many of them" ("Mrs. Charlotte Smith," in *British Novelists,* ii). Similarly, Kavanagh blames Smith's reliance on her biography for her erasure from literary history: "There are lives that read like one long sorrow, and that leave little save sadness and disappointment behind them when they close in death. Such a life was that of Charlotte Smith, full of cares while it lasted, and, once it was over, doomed to fade away from memory. She had great talent . . . but the haste and facility with which she wrote, the gloom that overshadowed her life, robbed her of a durable literary fame" (91). Barbauld indicates that Smith has pressed the limits of the reader's sympathy: "Poets are apt to complain, and often take a pleasure in it; yet they should remember that the pleasure of their readers is only derived from the elegance and harmony with which they do it. . . . But for the language of complaint in plain prose, or the exasperations of personal resentment, he has seldom much sympathy" (v). Echoing Barbauld, Kavanagh censures Smith for her tone of complaint: "We miss a gentle, lenient, and kindly spirit in her writings. She could not forget her sufferings and her wrongs. . . . There is decidedly bad temper, a sin that can rarely be forgiven" (8). Both writers imply that Smith has exceeded the bounds of feminine decorum in her "tone of complaint," and name her "pecuniary embarrassments" as the cause; both judge the work on the basis of Smith's moral conduct.[22] In their reading of "the female complaint," Barbauld and Kavanagh overlook Smith's critical engagement with her economic circumstances, elegiac role, and reliance on readerly sympathy, suggesting that the moral failing is hers alone (vii).[23]

Smith's early-twentieth-century critics also see a moral failing, but they locate it in Smith's theatricality, a pose of sincerity that they suggest was commercially driven. James R. Foster states of Smith's suffering, "Certainly some of this is pose," while H. Carter Davidson writes in 1932 that Smith "sentimentalized her verse to the saturation point" (qtd. in Hilbish, *Charlotte Smith,* 255). The Viscount St. Cyres observed in 1903, "Having chosen to come forward as a Laureate of the Lachrymose, she thought herself bound in honour to live consistently up to her part, and treat whatever subject happened to engross her pen in terms of undiluted lachrymosity. She was not one, she proudly declared, to 'clothe affliction in a robe of flowers.' Nevertheless, she soon found out that her afflictions must be dressed up somehow, if they were to make any impression on the public; so she determined to attire them in a very Mourning Warehouse of funereal black. No other grief that sighed has worn so much crape and bombazine."[24] St. Cyres accuses Smith of hypocrisy, satirizing her refusal to "clothe affliction in a robe of flowers" as a commercially driven performance. While St. Cyres also blames the reading public, stating that "Mrs. Smith was the servant of the public, and her many-headed master called for a melancholy tune," he mocks the excessiveness of her response. These critics posthumously exhume the corpse as the prostitute in disguise; Smith's female critics were less likely to do so, given their own precarious status as authors, but rather wanted Smith to tow the generic line.

Smith's reception illustrates the cost of sincerity for the poet who conflates her writing and private self in a bid for publicness: what is often judged are the ways in which the figure of the poet meets or defies ideals of gendered and generic conduct. The polarities of Smith's reception—she is read as either sincere or theatrical, victim or manipulator, selfless or selfish, virtuous mourner (widow, nun, mother) or whore—suggests the precariousness of these ideals. Feminist scholars have in many ways reversed and revalued these polarities, republishing Smith's writings and revealing their importance. Her biography is now read with a sympathetic eye, in the context of her times, rather than occasioning judgment. In many ways current feminist critics are the future readers Smith hoped for: guided by an ethical mission, we tend to echo Smith's sense of herself as a victim of patriarchy. The risk is that the biography will take precedence over the work, providing an origin for Smith's sincerity while slighting the poetry's epistemological dilemmas. Sympathetic biographical readings often remain blind to the ways in which they judge tearful literature as minor literature: while scholars have claimed for Smith a central role in the revival of the sonnet, this is largely performed with an eye to claiming her as a "preromantic" whose voice influences subsequent developments in romantic poetry. Similarly, recent scholarship has attempted to reverse the antitheatrical prejudice that resulted in charges of feigning sorrow. In claiming the value and importance of Smith's theatricality, an anxiety about consumer culture persists, legible in the attempt to rescue all feeling as irony.[25]

Largely ignored in the Smith criticism is her role in transforming elegy. By emphasizing Smith's use of elegiac sentiment as simultaneously an anticonsolatory, leveling, and yet market-driven strategy, I have suggested that elegiac sensibility emerges from a particular sociohistorical bind, involving the tension between sincerity and theatricality, moral sympathy and economic commerce, poet and persona. If melancholia is a symptom of a conflict faced by writers disempowered in the literary field, Smith's poetry charts why: elegiac sentiment is a rhetoric of loss intimately connected to the female poet's professional role in the literary marketplace. In short, to materialize elegy's ghostly forms is not simply to shade in the existing map of romantic and postromantic poetry, but to place gender, the commodity, and the corpse at the very center of this map. These coordinates are starkly realized as we turn to an elegiac "poetess" who continues to provoke heated debate in our present historical moment, Sylvia Plath.

Chapter 4

Sylvia Plath

Writing Blocks and Melancholia

Sylvia Plath, though a disciplined and prolific writer, struggled with writing blocks; in December 1958, at the age of 26, she considered one of these blocks at length in her journal:

> Read Freud's "Mourning and Melancholia" this morning after Ted left for the library. An almost exact description of my feelings and reasons for suicide: a transferred murderous impulse from my mother onto myself: the "vampire" metaphor Freud uses, "draining the ego": that is exactly the feeling I have getting in the way of my writing: Mother's clutch. I mask my self-abasement (a transferred hate of her) and weave it with my own real dissatisfactions in myself until it becomes very difficult to distinguish what is really a bogus criticism from what is really a changeful liability. . . . RB.: You are trying to do two mutually incompatible things this year. 1) spite your mother. 2) write. To spite your mother, you don't write because you feel you have to give the stories to her, or that she will appropriate them. . . . So I can't write. And I hate her because my not writing plays into her hands and argues that she is right, I was foolish not to teach, or do something secure, when what I have renounced security for is nonexistent. My rejection-fear is bound up with the fear that this will mean my rejection by her, for not succeeding: perhaps that is why they are so terrible. . . . So my work is to have fun in my work and to FEEL THAT MY WORKS ARE MINE.[1]

Like many postwar American poets, Plath was interested in Freud and was herself in psychoanalysis, a process that prompted much self-analysis in her journals. The passage from Freud's "Mourning and Melancholia" to which Plath refers states, "The complex of melancholia behaves like an open wound, drawing to itself cathectic energy from all sides . . . and draining the ego until it is utterly depleted" (*Psychological Theory*, 174). Plath attributes this draining to a vampiric transaction, to her "mother's clutch," making explicit what Freud identifies as the ambivalence of the melancholic toward the lost love object. Freud explains that melancholia is caused by "a real injury or disappointment concerned with the loved person." Rather than transfer her attachments to a new object, as in normal mourning, the melancholic identifies the ego with the lost object: "Thus the shadow of the object fell upon the ego, so that the latter could henceforth be criticized by a special mental faculty like an object, like the forsaken object. In this way the loss of the object became transformed into a loss in the ego, and the conflict between the ego and the loved person transformed into a cleavage between the criticizing faculty of the ego and the ego as altered by the identification" (170). In Freud's understanding, melancholia stems from ambivalence and even anger toward the lost object, yet due to the subject's identification with the lost object, these feelings are expressed as self-reproaches. More specifically, melancholia arises "so as to avoid the necessity of openly expressing . . . hostility against the loved ones," but nevertheless serves as a form of aggression, of tormenting these loved ones (172). Plath read Freud's essay carefully, echoing his language in identifying her melancholia and her suicide attempt with a "murderous impulse" toward her mother that she directed at herself.[2]

Crucial to Freud's account of melancholia is that its sufferers respond to an environmental, rather than a fictional, cause: "Their complaints are really 'plaints' in the legal sense of the word" (169). In her journal, Plath suggests that her anger stems from a "plaint," the ways in which her mother seems to appropriate her work, using Plath's successes and accomplishments to bolster her own self-worth. Moreover, Plath sees her mother's love as contingent upon Plath's professional success; Plath states in the same journal entry that "approval, with Mother, has been equated for me with love. . . . I felt if I didn't write no body would accept me as a human being. Writing, then, was a substitute for myself: if you don't love me, love my writing & love me for my writing" (*J*, 448). And yet Plath sees no way to oppose her mother's use of her success. To spite her mother, she stops writing, yet to do so fuels her mother's perception that Plath should have chosen a more secure profession.

Plath identifies fear of her mother's rejection with a fear of rejection more generally: "Mother" stands in for all of the institutions that judge Plath on the basis of her writerly "success."[3] Foremost among these institutions was Smith College, Plath's alma mater, an institution that had rewarded Plath for her intellectual and creative achievements by showering her with prizes during her undergraduate years and by giving her a teaching position in 1957–58; in 1958, the year of the journal entry, Smith represented the academic security Plath had rejected in order to write poetry and fiction professionally (Hammer, "Plath's Lives," 66). In a similar position of power were the British and American literary establishments governing the journals, magazines, writing competitions, and publishing houses to which Plath sent her work, an establishment which if loosely defined nevertheless appeared as an impenetrable and all-powerful bloc to Plath, who weighed each response as newly signaling her absolute success or failure (*J*, 193). Plath's anger at her mother suggests frustration with a particular model of feminine behavior, one that emerges from a position of economic dependence and thus requires winning others' approval and meeting their moral standards, a model that Plath felt governed her conduct as a professional writer (see, for example, *J*, 421, 569). Juliana Schiesari argues that, in Freud's understanding, the melancholic's plaint is moral in character and that "Freud's moralizing conscience is consonant with the Law of the Father since the conscience or superego is derived from the culture that the parents stand for, which in the West means the patriarchal culture of the father" (*Gendering of Melancholia*, 53). But Plath's conflation of the "moralizing conscience" with the "Law of the Mother" suggests that the female writer's moral authority was both a role complexly inscribed within patriarchy and her ticket out of a position of economic dependence. Plath figures this dilemma in economic terms; to earn money through a performance of feminine moral authority was simultaneously to discharge a debt to her mother figures and to angrily suffer the costs.[4]

In her journals Plath repeatedly asserted a desire to define her "true" or "real" self through her works and her accomplishments, yet she also wanted economic success in the literary marketplace, a success contingent on meeting gendered ideals of professional conduct. Like Charlotte Smith, Plath identified lyric with a sincere ideal—a site of autonomous self-expression—but her writing would prove to be a troublesome double, one that continually eluded her efforts to possess it. This conflict explicitly propels much of her work; in her journals, letters, and poetry she connects this conflict to questions of property, thematizing the ways in which her writing would be commodified, received, and judged in terms of her conduct as a woman writer. Representing the impossibility of autonomy in the marketplace, Plath, like Smith, attempts to block the appropriation of her work through melancholia. An affective response to the cultural pressures and expectations Plath felt she must meet to succeed as a professional author, melancholia characterizes not just the particular "block" she describes in her journal, then, but also her negotiation of the literary marketplace more generally.[5]

Plath self-consciously enacts the ambivalent relation to the rhetoric of sincerity that characterizes the poetess tradition. Although female poets of the eighteenth and nineteenth centuries were routinely called poetesses, Plath's self-categorization in 1958 as "The Poetess of America" indicates her engagement with this lineage. This was certainly a complex inheritance, given the devaluation of the "sentimental" tradition by modernist writers such as Eliot and Pound. The passage is worth quoting in its entirety: "Arrogant, I think I have written lines which qualify me to be The Poetess of America (as Ted will be The Poet of England and her dominions). Who rivals? Well, in history—Sappho, Elizabeth Barrett Browning, Christina Rossetti, Amy Lowell, Emily Dickinson, Edna St. Vincent Millay—all dead. Now: Edith Sitwell & Marianne Moore, the ageing giantesses & poetic godmothers. Phyllis McGinley is out—light verse: she's sold herself. Rather: May Swenson, Isabella Gardner, & most close, Adrienne Cecile Rich—who will soon be eclipsed by these eight poems: I am eager, chafing, sure of my gift, wanting only to train & teach it—I'll count the magazines & money I break open by these best eight poems from now on. We'll see" (*J*, 360). Plath's desire to succeed not only in terms of literary merit but in terms of money and celebrity, and her acute sense of the fine line she would need to walk to achieve "dominion"—taking care not to "sell herself" like Phyllis McGinley—sound a familiar theme. Like earlier poetesses, Plath realized that she would need to espouse noncommercial ideals even while eyeing her rivals and waiting to "count the magazines & money."

Elegy would prove as important to Plath as it was to Smith. Although Plath labels none of her poems elegies, she writes both self-elegies and elegies for her father (Ramazani, *Poetry of Mourning,* 262). More specifically, Plath like Smith presents a series of first-person speakers who espouse elegiac sentiments and often a desire for death as a means of reflecting on the compromises the female poet must make to succeed in the literary marketplace. While Smith uses death to measure the female poet's financial dispossession, disempowerment, and suffering in British culture, Plath more explicitly dramatizes in her poetry the ways in which postwar literary culture extends the habits of the romantic tradition by requiring proof of the woman poet's sincerity through "true" experiences of elegiac suffering. Neither simply mouthpieces for the biographical poet nor dramatic personae lacking ties to the poet's life, Plath's speakers occupy the "edge" between these two possibilities, enacting the problem of epistemology central to the rhetoric of sincerity. In the tradition of Charlotte Smith, Mary Robinson, and L.E.L., but also of Byron and Baudelaire, Plath simultaneously performs and critiques claims to sincere feeling, drawing attention to sincerity as rhetorical performance and the poem as a stage. Nor does Plath position the audience as a silent or sympathetic witness: Plath questions her readers' investments in her elegiac performance and their role in sustaining the moral ideals by which her performance is judged.

Not only does Plath's work reveal that elegiac sentiment continues to be intertwined with the rhetoric of sincerity and the particular conflicts faced by the professional woman poet, but her history demonstrates quite dramatically how textual melancholia shapes the reception of her work. To study Plath is to take up the question of the elegiac nature of posthumous criticism, for Plath's suicide at age thirty overshadows the critical response to her work. While Charlotte Smith was largely forgotten after her death, the reverse is true of Plath: her death propelled her to bestsellerdom and generated a huge critical industry. For many readers Plath's suicide authenticates the melancholy sentiments of her verse. Recent scholarship has countered the more literal-minded biographical readings, particularly those that see Plath's poetry as evidence of her suicidal tendencies or psychological pathology, by emphasizing the artifice and theatricality of Plath's poetry as well as its public and political dimensions.[6] And yet, given the facts of Plath's biography, it is difficult to read her speakers' interest in death as solely generic or rhetorical, all pose. This dilemma—what is real, what is performance—not only engenders poetess poetry but propels its reception. As Jacqueline Rose astutely comments in her study of Plath's legacy, Plath seems to put "the whole enterprise of criticism . . . at risk" (*Haunting*, 15), an insight I connect to the melancholic strategies of her texts.

The "Cold Corpse": Marketing and the Problem of Self-Ownership

Plath's *Journals* provide ample evidence of her burning ambition, her careful plotting of how to market and where to publish her work, and her scrupulous recording of her rejections as well as her publications, prizes, and financial earnings. This concern is so prevalent that it cannot be suppressed, despite Ted Hughes's attempt in the foreword to the abridged *Journals* to persuade the reader that Plath's commercial instincts affected only her earlier writing and her prose, resulting in an artifice that she would shed in her movement toward a "real self" in her final volume of poetry, *Ariel*.[7] This distinction as Hughes defines it is one of commercial versus internal inspiration, the late versus the early writing, poetry versus prose, and implicitly British versus American culture. In suggesting that writing for profit is tantamount to artifice, Hughes invokes the ideal of the poet whose self-expression is spontaneous, sincere, and immune to economic pressures.

Plath's representation of the conflict engendered by a sincere ideal is quite different. Distinctions of poetry versus prose, art versus mass culture, and Britain versus the United States presented Plath not with the choice of a real versus false self, but merely with different personae, all of which required a performance of sincerity. In her poetry and journals, Plath represents the impossibility of self-ownership as a gap or division between her self and her writing. Rose describes this gap largely in Lacanian terms, as Plath's representation of how language enacts the loss and self-division involved in self-consciousness and, moreover, as Plath's awareness of the "contradictory, divided and incomplete nature of representation itself" (*Haunting*, 5, 31). While I agree with Rose, Plath was also a profoundly material thinker, and she consistently positions the gap between the author and her textual personae, the ways in which language defies a stable origin in the self, as a problem of epistemology connected to her immersion in consumer culture, a problem that materialized specifically through her encounters with the literary marketplace.

The necessity to "streamline" her work "for a particular market" to achieve commercial success embodied for Plath the ways in which the marketplace rendered self-possession elusive (*LH* 108). Gender shaped these generic expectations, and numerous critics have accounted for the ways in which expected feminine roles limited Plath's efforts at self-ownership. Scholars argue in the main that Plath's concern with self-division reflects the difficulty, even impossibility, of reconciling the role of poet with the roles of wife and mother.[8] Although greater numbers of women than ever before received college educations in the 1950s, by and large these women were expected upon graduation from college to become professional homemakers, an expectation fueled by the cold war. In her journals Plath devotes attention to a series of possible mates, to the expected role as wife and mother, and to the double standards of sexual behavior in 1950s America.[9] While it's clear that Plath faced the constraints of these roles, the conflict she emphasizes in her journals is less one of pursuing her poetry versus her duties as mother and wife, than one of pursuing a career as a poet versus pursuing a more lucrative career as a novelist, or pursuing a more financially stable profession altogether, such as that of an academic.[10] In Plath's understanding, if a woman were to pursue a career, she could only justify this choice by becoming a "perfect success" (*J*, 176). But the definition of "success" depended on one's vantage point, and in the 1950s context Plath encountered competing national understandings of success as an author. In "the pragmatic American world's cold eye," the "eye" Plath conflated with her "mother figures," success was financial; as Plath observed in her journals, "The Writer and Poet is excusable only if he is Successful. Makes Money" (*J*, 435, 438). But from another perspective, that exemplified by her English husband, Ted Hughes, professional literary success was contingent on pursuing the moral ideals of art distinct—at least on the surface—from commercial ambitions.

For Plath, this conflict between aesthetic and commercial success was sharply defined by distinctions of genre. In an essay she wrote for the BBC, "A Comparison" (1962), Plath fleshed out the commercial valences that distinguish poetry and prose.[11] The novel, she writes, is "relaxed and expansive, an open hand," and there is nothing that isn't relevant: "Old shoes can be used, doorknobs, air letters, flannel nightgowns, cathedrals, nail varnish . . . the whole much-loved, well-thumbed catalogue of the miscellaneous." Tellingly, this list includes "morals and money." The poem, in contrast, is "concentrated, a closed fist," and Plath comments: "I do not like to think of all the things, familiar, useful and worthy things, I have never put into a poem." The poem must transcend the mundane and contingent, transforming it into something symbolic or mythic. Plath clinches the generic distinction with a telling commercial metaphor: "I think of those round glass Victorian paperweights which I remember, yet can never find—a far cry from the plastic mass-productions which stud the toy counters in Woolworths. This sort of paperweight is a clear globe, self-complete, very pure, with a forest or village or family group within it. You turn it upside down, then back. It snows. Everything is changed in a minute. It will never be the same in there . . . So a poem takes place" (*Johnny Panic*, 62–64). If prose is akin to the Woolworth's paperweight, a "plastic mass-production," the poem, like the rare Victorian paperweight, should convey purity, self-completeness, perfection. Plath emphasizes the gendered connotations of this distinction, depicting the novelist as a "she" involved in all the domestic "junk of life"—"shuffling among the teacups, humming, arranging ashtrays or babies" with "all the time in the world," while she defines the poet by the "closed fist," by "precision and power," quickness and decisiveness. Implicitly, this is the masculine, public world of action and power, where minutes count and doors shut with "manic, unanswerable finality" (63). Indeed, Plath targeted much of the fiction she wrote for women's magazines and female readers. Describing a story she planned to send to *McCall's*, *Ladies' Home Journal*, *Good Housekeeping*, and *Woman's Day*, she states that "this is my best styled story and has enough seriousness, identity problems, fury, love etc. to be a winner" (*J*, 291). In contrast, the poetry market in the 1950s remained largely male-dominated, in terms of editors, judges, and published poets; Plath's journals refer to only a handful of female contemporaries, Adrienne Rich, Elizabeth Bishop, May Swenson, and Anne Sexton.

Plath's effort in "A Comparison" to distinguish poetry from prose in terms of their relation to consumer culture reveals that the "purity" of the poem is itself the style of a particular market, that of the literary magazines to which she sent her poetry (Rose, *Haunting*, 173). Indeed, Plath intently studied the style of *New Yorker* poems because she aspired to write poems of "The New Yorker sort" (*J*, 466), and succeeded in winning a first-reading contract with the magazine (Middlebrook, *Her Husband*, 118; *J*, 99). As much as she longed to find the rare Victorian paperweight, it too could be purchased, albeit in a more specialized store. Plath at times resists this conclusion, attempting to develop a motive for writing apart from publication and financial reward, in her words to "work without vision of world's judgment" (*J*, 519). She represents this effort as a movement "inward," as a search for purity, for a "real" self, for a way to break out of the "glassed-in cage" of her life (*J*, 484, 509). Yet she also recognizes the power of literary fashions and her desire to meet them: "To feel my work good and well-taken . . . corrupts my nunnish labor of work-for-itself-as-its-own-reward" (*J*, 484). As she concludes in 1957, "Write every story, not to publish, but to be a better writer—and ipso facto, closer to publishing" (*J*, 296). If Plath at times aspired to the moral ideal of "nunnish labor," she also aspired to live from the proceeds of her writing, and criticized the moral condemnation of popular writing (J. Rose, *Haunting*, 169–73); in her journals she commented on her efforts to craft a popular "true confessions" story: "It takes a good tight plot and a slick ease that are not picked up over night like a cheap whore" (*J*, 539–40). In the modern literary market Plath observed lyric and popular fiction, nun and whore, not as moral opposites but as generic styles capable of garnering different kinds of literary success, reputation on the one hand and financial compensation on the other.

That Plath embraced both genres and kinds of success was reflected by the fact that she did not define herself simply as a poet; she once wrote that "poetry is an evasion from the real job of writing prose" (*Johnny Panic*, 13). Usually, her self-representation as a poet or novelist was contingent upon her success. When Plath wrote "A Comparison," for instance, she was living in Britain with the publication of *The Colossus* to her credit, and had recently been billed by the *Listener* in Britain as a "famous poetess" (*LH*, 466); thus she identifies herself as a poet in the essay, beginning with: "How I envy the novelist!" And yet neither kind of success allowed her to achieve the sincere ideal articulated by Hughes. In both genres, and to both kinds of audiences, Plath realized that she would be received as a woman author, and her efforts at sincere self-presentation were necessarily mediated through generic expectations and her efforts to perform them "perfectly" to sell her work.[12]

Like Smith, Plath locates the unbridgeable gap between the biographical author and her textual personae in her material circumstances as a female writer. When Plath states in 1959, "I feel the weight on me. The old misery of money seeping away. A cold corpse between me and any work at all," she conveys how her attempt to attain financial success as a writer contributes to an affective gap between her self and her work, a gap figured as a corpse (*J*, 289–90). As she imagines it, the corpse literally blocks her writing, its bodiliness reminding her of the pressure to be a success, and of her failure to do so without compromise. In her poetry the corpse becomes her double, a "dead author," her body/text as packaged for, and seen through, the gaze of the marketplace and her various audiences. Plath locates the impossibility of a sincere ideal that could unite author and text in what Barthes calls the "epitome and culmination of capitalist ideology" (*Image-Music-Text*, 126), but rather than simply celebrate the death of this ideal as Barthes does, she also mourns its loss as at once textual and material, generic and gendered.

"The Blood Jet Is Poetry": Cutting the Ties of Sympathy

Plath placed herself in the lineage of the poetess soon after many of the leading modernist writers had "made it new" by rejecting what they perceived as the clichés of "sentimental" literature and of romanticism more generally. Eliot and Pound deemed lyric inwardness and personalism self-indulgent and feminine, and implied that such gestures were contaminated by the commercial contexts in which they circulated (Clark, *Sentimental Modernism*, 5–7). Prior to the publication of Ginsberg's *Howl* and Lowell's *Life Studies* in 1959, Eliot's influence remained central; in the late 1940s and '50s, Warren, Tate, and Ransom brought Eliot's ideas into the academy. As Kenneth Koch commented in "Seasons on Earth," "*The Waste Land* gave the time's most accurate data, / It seemed, and Eliot was the great dictator / of literature" (*Great Atlantic*, 310). The intentional and affective "fallacies" rendered the poet's biography and intentions and the reader's emotional response "illegitimate" grounds for reading and, implicitly, writing. Plath's challenge was to merge two seemingly incompatible traditions—that of Eliot's high modernism with expectations of gendered decorum, that is, the tradition of the poetess.

Thus, in her journals Plath emphasized that she wanted to write out of female experience, and yet she didn't want to be labeled a sentimental poet.

Although she began her career by writing sonnets in the early 1950s, an early sonnet, "Female Author," addresses the limiting, feminine connotations of the form:

> Prim, pink-breasted, feminine, she nurses
> Chocolate fancies in rose-papered rooms
> Where polished highboys whisper creaking curses
> And hothouse roses shed immoral blooms.
>
> The garnets on her fingers twinkle quick
> And blood reflects across the manuscript;
> She muses on the odor, sweet and sick,
> Of festering gardenias in a crypt.[13]

Edna St. Vincent Millay rather than Charlotte Smith was the sonneteer of the moment, but the generic performance that Plath associated with the sonnet had rendered the elegiac poetess a festering gardenia, stuck in a "crypt," able to engage blood and immoral blooms only in fancy. As Plath stated in her journals, "Until I make something tight and riding over the limits of sweet sestinas and sonnets, away from . . . the inevitable narrow bed, too small for a smashing act of love, until then, they can ignore me and make up pretty jokes" (*J*, 208; my ellipses). Plath would turn to free verse to signify her departure from conventions of "feminine" sentiment and sexual decorum. Thus in 1956 she proudly recounts to her mother Hughes's praise of her poems, as "strong and full and rich—not quailing and whining like Teasdale or simple lyrics like Millay; they are working, sweating, heaving poems" (*LH*, 244).[14] In 1958, referring to the second manuscript of poems she formed, she says that "of the 35 or so poems I've published in my career, I've rejected about 20 of these from my book manuscript as too romantic, sentimental and frivolous and immature. My main difficulty has been overcoming a clever, too brittle and glossy feminine tone, and I am gradually getting to speak 'straight out' and of real experience, not just in metaphorical conceits" (*LH*, 343).

Plath's effort to avoid the label of "sentimental" poet was complicated by gendered expectations of sincerity. Although Eliot could claim to reject the conflation of author and poetic speaker through an aesthetic of impersonality, Plath lacked this luxury, even as she emphasized her use of dramatic personae: she realized that her writing would be received as the work of a woman poet, and thus read in terms of her conduct and private life. That the sentimental tradition had been devalued by modernists writing in the teens and twenties made suffering and death no less an expectation of "authentic" female experience; indeed, given the association of sentiment with hackneyed women's writing, women writers faced increased pressure to prove that their intentions were commercially disinterested. Following in the footsteps of Mina Loy and H.D., Plath modernized the poetess, fashioning a poetic persona that accommodated a conventional emphasis on death, loss, and suffering by embracing the stoicism and violence prevalent in the writing of the male modernists.

The diction, form, and style of Smith's and Plath's poems are quite different, reflecting the aesthetic habits of their historical moments, but both were formal innovators, Smith merging elegy and sonnet, and Plath elegy and free verse. Indeed, Plath's evocations of an elegiac persona, landscape, and sensibility echo Smith's. We see this resonance in "Blackberrying," one of Plath's "New Yorker" poems (1961), in which she presents a first-person speaker similar to Smith's speaker in the Middleton Churchyard sonnet. Throughout the poem Plath conveys presence and movement not through direct assertion, but through the actions of objects upon her speaker. The poem begins with the speaker's erasure:

> Nobody in the lane, and nothing, nothing but blackberries,
> Blackberries on either side, though on the right mainly,
> A blackberry alley, going down in hooks, and a sea
> Somewhere at the end of it, heaving.   (*CP*, 168)

The blackberries, which one might expect to serve as a backdrop to the speaker, become the foreground. We are not sure that a speaker inhabits this landscape until the blackberries "squander" their blue-red juices on her fingers. Movement is conveyed through expressions of doubt ("I do not think the sea will appear at all") and through the agency of the landscape: "the berries and bushes end," "a last hook brings me." The speaker is passively propelled toward the sea; just as the blackberries "accommodate themselves to my milkbottle, flattening their sides," so the speaker accommodates the strictures of the pathway cut through the landscape. When she arrives at the sea, it is not she who observes it, but rather the "hills' northern face":

> A last hook brings me
> To the hills' northern face, and the face is orange rock
> That looks out on nothing, nothing but a great space
> Of white and pewter lights, and a din like silversmiths
> Beating and beating at an intractable metal.

As in Smith's landscapes, nature remains alien and destructive, mocking man's efforts to transform it into culture. There is no redemption through art: the "silversmiths / beating and beating at an intractable metal" alludes in ironic fashion to Keats's urn and to Yeats's Grecian goldsmiths. Just as Smith rejects "fancy" for "real woe," Plath suggests that her poetry offers a "real" confrontation with suffering rather than aesthetic escape or redemption. Free verse does not provide a release from Smith's sonnet-prison, then, but provides a different means of measuring the intractable nature of suffering.

What is striking about "Blackberrying" and other Plath poems is the absence of direct statements of feeling. Smith's churchyard sonnet ends with the speaker's profession of her desire for death; Plath's poem evokes a similar sentiment, but asks the reader to infer it from descriptions of the landscape. On the one hand, the landscape seems to elicit a desire to blend into it, to become a body lacking self-consciousness; thus the blackberries offer the poet a "blood sisterhood," a "honey-feast," a promise of sensual oblivion. On the other hand, the slap of the sea's "phantom laundry" and the "choughs in black, cacophonous flocks— / Bits of burnt paper wheeling in a blown sky" offer a more malevolent vision of nothingness. While Plath dramatizes a struggle about self-negation, she does so with deliberate stoicism, refusing to ask for the reader's sympathy. Taking up H.D.'s call "to find a new beauty / in some terrible / wind-tortured place" (*Selected Poems*, 7), Plath does not follow Smith's example of negating the lyric "I" to align it with a leveling death and destruction, but rather risks negation to show that her speaker can withstand the assault of destructive forces without flinching or "whining." Through stoic suffering the speaker becomes, like the landscape, resistant to pain: "an intractable metal." This persona is evident from Plath's first published volume, *The Colossus,* forward. Thus in "November Graveyard" (1956), for instance, Plath defines the "essential landscape" in opposition to that of the poetry of sentiment; the trees in this landscape "won't mourn, wear sackcloth, or turn / to elegiac dryads" (*CP*, 56).

Similarly, Plath seeks to cloak rather than emphasize the biographical component of her poetry. While recent scholars have reconstructed after Plath's death how the events of her life may have served as the occasion of her poetry, the poems themselves allude to such events only cryptically, and Plath avoids Smith's practice of autobiographical prefaces and notes that posit a biographical origin. If Plath teased her readers by including autobiographical clues, she also routinely undercut biographical readings. In fact, she commented in her journal that she tried to avoid "interiour she felts," what she called the "true-confessional" style (*J*, 155, 157). Her response to "confession" in poetry was influenced not only by modernist aesthetics but by the generic and commercial distinction she drew between sincerity in the lyric, on which she staked her reputation, and her "mercenary" goals in writing for *True Story* and similar magazines, in which confession often amounted to sexualized romance, "cheapness and slick love" (*J*, 275; Kunzel, "Pulp Fictions"). She commented in her journals, "I am now in the midst of writing the biggest 'True Confession' I have ever written, all for the remote possibility of gaignigh (that word the lady said is: gaining, as in weight) filthy lucer. a contest in True Story is in the offing, with all sorts of Big Money prizes. being a most mercenary individual, because mercenary can buy trips to europe, theaters, chop houses, and other Ill Famed whatnots, I am trying out for it. all you have to do, the blurb ways [*sic*], is write the story of your life or somebody else's life from the heart. . . . let me tell you, my supercilious attitude about the people who write Confessions has diminished" (*J*, 539–40). Writing the "story of your life . . . from the heart" involved the mastery of a commercial style closely aligned with the sentimental tradition.

Plath's objectification of pain and suffering in her poetry is in part a display of bravura, a refusal to be devalued as "sentimental." "Real" suffering is signified through stoicism, and Plath positions this experience of suffering as one born of violence. Thus in "Blackberrying" and in poems such as "Cut," "Kindness," "Contusion," and "Lady Lazarus," Plath suggests that, like the male modernists, the poetess can confront and withstand modern war and violence. Bravura involves walking the fine line between controlling one's performance and letting oneself spin out of control, or of having great control of letting oneself spin out of control, and this line (depicted as an "edge" or a "cut" in the poetry) is central to Plath's negotiation of the rhetoric of sincerity. Plath's professed desire for a "real self" beyond performance, even if only present in her poetry as a *via negativa*, coexists with her critique of sincerity as an idealized, ritualized performance, which is to say that it's a mistake to see her performances as entirely calculating or ironic: part of the "charge" of her poetry is that it's often impossible to tell what's performed and what's real. As the speaker states in "Lesbos," "It is all Hollywood, windowless" (*CP* 227), with no clear exit off the stage.[15] In this respect Plath anticipates contemporary female performance artists such as the singer Cat Power (Chan Marshall), whose "breakdowns" and displays of anxiety onstage have generated endless speculation about whether they are real or staged (Ratliff, "Performance Anxiety").

"Cut" not only explores the dilemma of distinguishing the real and the staged but also reveals the violence inherent to drawing such distinctions:

What a thrill—
My thumb instead of an onion.
The top quite gone
Except for a sort of a hinge

Of skin,
A flap like a hat,
Dead white.
Then that red plush.   (*CP*, 235)

The poem begins with a substitution: the first-person speaker has cut her "thumb instead of an onion." It's not clear whether this cut is accidental (a slip of the knife while chopping onions) or intentional, and this ambivalence about the origins and control of violence becomes the central concern of the poem. Does violence originate inside the speaker or is it imposed from or a response to external circumstances? And in a related vein, is a "real" cut the occasion of the poem or is it a figment of the poet's imagination? This epistemological uncertainty is conveyed by the word "cut," which can refer to the act of making an incision, to the incision itself, or to the slice of skin—"a flap like a hat"—that is created by the incision (as in a "cut of meat"). Right away the reader stands on shaky ground.

The speaker's "thrill" stems from this uncertain ground, the departure from the domestic routine. Rather than state how she feels about the cut, however, she objectifies it. The initial substitution of thumb for onion generates a string of metaphors on war and wounding that bleed rapidly into one another:

Little pilgrim,
The Indian's axed your scalp.
Your turkey wattle
Carpet rolls

Straight from the heart.
I step on it,
Clutching my bottle
Of pink fizz.

A celebration, this is.
Out of a gap
A million soldiers run,
Redcoats, every one.

Whose side are they on?
O my
Homunculus, I am ill.
I have taken a pill to kill

The thin
Papery feeling.
Saboteur,
Kamikaze man—

The stain on your
Gauze Ku Klux Klan
Babushka
Darkens and tarnishes and when

The balled
Pulp of your heart
Confronts its small
Mill of silence

How you jump—
Trepanned veteran,
Dirty girl,
Thumb stump.   (*CP*, 235–36)

The cut occasions not tears but stoicism, blood transformed into ink in the
form of a literary meditation on war and American history. It's a dazzling
performance of the dramatic potentials of free verse: Plath uses enjamb-
ment to dramatize the cutting of the line, and uses these cuts to evoke a cin-
ematic cutting from one image to the next.[16] Hence the break between lines
forms "a hinge / Of skin," simultaneously a cut and a point of connection.
Repetition of sound enacts a literal bleeding of one image into the next:
thus "hinge" becomes "skin," "pink fizz" becomes "a celebration, this is."
Plath's allusions to a "papery feeling," to the "balled / pulp" of the heart and
to a "mill" (slang for typewriter) indicate that at one level this "paper cut" is
a "celebration" of verbal dexterity.

   The speaker's bravura stems from her refusal to "gush" about suffering
in stereotypically feminine terms. Indeed one could read the poem as a
parody of sentimental poetry, or of "True Confessions" that require writ-
ing "straight from the heart." The speaker "step[s] on" the heart, turning
blood into "pink fizz." The parody works by literalizing tropes of romantic

interiority; the speaker literally looks at and describes her cut, but instead of "interior she felts" or "depth" we get more surface. In contrast to Smith, the speaker uses blood/ink to elicit admiration or repugnance rather than sympathetic identification. Plath depicts a similar act in the poem "Kindness"; while "Dame Kindness" neatens the speaker's house and seeks to cure all ills with sugar and tea (*CP*, 269–70), the speaker rejects this feminine gesture by emphasizing the inherent violence of the trope of writing from the heart: "The blood jet is poetry. / There is no stopping it" (*CP*, 269–70).

Plath's rejection of sympathy was not simply a liberating rejection of the constraints of a sentimental role, however, but the performance of the elegiac muse in a new guise. If "Cut" celebrates the transformation of the world of prosaic, feminine routine into poetry, it also provides a darker meditation on the costs of creating "authentic" poetry. The speaker's thumb, a "homunculus," connected to but distinct from her, can be read as a miniaturized double of the poet (a "Tom Thumb"). "Cut" in this sense is much like the poem "In Plaster," a more obvious "double" poem, in which the speaker considers her relationship to her plaster cast, which she describes as a "dead body" attached to her ("living with her was like living with my own coffin") (*CP*, 158–60). Doubles, like the "cold corpse" in Plath's *Journals,* function as self-conscious metaphors for the poet's textual personifications: the plaster cast is an empty double or "dead author." In this way Plath thematizes the epistemological dilemma central to the rhetoric of sincerity: is "Cut" action or incision; self or other; bodily wound or metaphor; biographical fact or fiction; an act of transcendence or of self-mutilation? We might read the series of metaphoric substitutions in "Cut" as the poet's staging of how to regard her thumb—and poem—as a double.

If at one level the "cut" appears metaphorical, at another the poem alludes to the cut's somatic origins ("I have taken a pill to kill the thin papery feeling"). In this way Plath suggests that a poetic claim to sincerity requires a display of "real" pain. While the speaker tries to align the thumb with an enemy who has betrayed her, naming it saboteur, kamikaze man, and KKK member, she cannot completely objectify or externalize it as the source of violence. The tone of the poem "darkens and tarnishes" as the speaker connects the beating of her heart to the bleeding thumb, the "cut" as source of play, fascination, and metaphor, to the cut as a bodily wound. Plath signals this shift by blurring distinctions between the speaker and her thumb, and between "I" and "you"; when she states, "The balled / Pulp of your heart / Confronts its small / mill of silence," it's not clear whose heart is referenced—the homunculus-thumb's, the poet's, or the poem's. Thus the ques-

tion she asks of the drops of blood, transformed into a "million soldiers"—
"Whose side are they on?"—is also asked of poet, poem, and reader.

The poem confronts us with the desire to define clear moral "sides" and
assign clear origins of violence, and one can read "Cut" as a meditation on
war, on the ease with which violence is aestheticized, distanced, and ex-
ternalized. Plath also toys with the possibility that her reader will interpret
the cut biographically, as a self-destructive act ("I am ill"), assigning it a
pathological cause. But in its epistemological slippages the poem under-
mines the urge to assign one origin or meaning to the cut. The poem si-
multaneously creates and subsumes distinctions: while it may seem to
draw clear sides, it ultimately shows their imbrication. Many of Plath's first-
person lyrics can be read simultaneously as poems with public, political
ramifications and as "private," biographically inflected reflections, as com-
plex demonstrations of how the lyric "I"—the conventional marker of pri-
vacy, autonomy, individuality—is, as Adorno argues, cut from the social
and political fabric ("Lyric and Society"). Plath's poetry evidences the vio-
lence and loss occasioned by these cuts and suffered to maintain an au-
tonomous ideal. Recent Plath scholars influenced by poststructuralism
have decried the tendency to confuse lyric poems with their authors, em-
phasizing the distinction between the biographical Plath and her textual
personae, joining scholars in nineteenth-century studies who emphasize
the need to ironize and de-privatize the reading of the poetess.[17] To read
the poem in purely biographical terms is to miss how the poet's thumb be-
comes her political "stump," its commentary on how identifying oneself as
an "American" catches one up in a national history of political, racialized,
and sexualized violence; to read the poem without reference to biography
or "real woe," however, is to miss its epistemological drama.

Plath emphasizes the audience's role in this drama, their involvement in
making epistemological "cuts" as they read the poem. The blurring of "I"
and "you" in the final stanza may refer to the poet's recognition (as many of
her biographically inclined critics have argued) that she is a "divided self,"
her own enemy, saboteur, kamikaze, a recognition that leads to the "jump"
and self-castigation at the end of the poem. On the other hand, as "I" be-
comes "you," the camera may pan back rather than inward: the speaker sees
the thumb and poem through the gaze of external judgment. This is the cel-
ebrated moment of romantic self-consciousness, of the "turn" from the
world leading to reconciliation with it; for Plath, however, this is the point
at which the poem is "cut" from her. Plath implies through the imagery of
shame the moral nature of external judgment: the "trepanned" veteran
suffers bodily shame or amputation, as do its analogues, the dirty girl and

thumb stump. "Dirty girl" connotes menstruation and unlicensed sexual activity, associating the female body with dirt and sin. The thumb, which lacks an extra phalange, is a "stump," an amputated limb. The guttural rhyme of "thumb stump" catches in the throat as if meaning itself has bled from the poem and all we are left with is amputated sound. The dexterous performance has become self-consciously clumsy, all thumbs, as the body—and the poem as a body beyond the control of the poet—insists on its presence.

The poem presents numerous possibilities about what has been diminished and demystified: the ideals of American liberty, mocked by its brutal history? The hope that poetry could transform a domestic incident into epic, could transcend the female body, turn poetess into soldier? The promise that the rhetoric of sincerity could unite poet and persona, literal and figurative cut, "make it real"? However we might understand the poem's ideals, the images of shame and amputation testify to their failure. But shame in the Rousseauian tradition of confession measures, as Diane Middlebrook puts it, "the whole culture's shame-making machinery" ("What Was Confessional Poetry?" 647). If the cost of self-representation as a coherent "I" is self-objectification, a violent cut between self and writing, then Plath suggests that the reader, the eye of moral judgment, also carries the knife. Finally, a cut can refer either to what's been excised from a work of art or to what's left after editing, as in the final "take" of a recording or film. Is "Cut," then, an amputee, or a perfected work? And for the poetess, subject to the eye of readerly judgment, is there a difference?

The Peanut-Crunching Crowd:
Audience in the Late Elegies

Scholars often discuss Plath's career in terms of a sea change, an explosive transformation that occurred in her last year of life. As conventionally narrated, this change is presented as an emergence marked by the shedding of restrictions (evident in Plath's first book of poetry, *The Colossus*)—whether of conventional form, limiting gender roles, or 1950s political paranoia—for a more autonomous or "naked" self that breaks taboos and asserts the authority of feminine experience (evident in the posthumously published *Ariel*). Plath herself presented the poetry she wrote in the last year of her life as a "breakthrough"; she stated, "I've been very excited by what I feel is the new breakthrough that came with, say, Robert Lowell's *Life Studies*. This intense breakthrough into very serious, very personal emotional experience, which I feel has been partly taboo" (qtd. in Alvarez, *Fiddle*, 199). Second-wave feminist criticism tended to conflate Plath's breakthrough with the achievement of a sincere ideal, overlooking the feminist implications of moral critiques of the autonomous self.[18] The narration of Plath's "break-through" ignores her continuing sense that to sell her work successfully, she had to style it, to negotiate generic conventions and audience expectations. While a stylistic change in Plath's late poetry certainly occurs, it does not involve gaining the selfhood that had eluded her: rather than resolve the bind of self-ownership in the literary marketplace, Plath displays its costs more explicitly, and angrily, to the reader.[19]

In late elegies such as "Lady Lazarus," "Fever 103," and "Edge," Plath addresses the hypocrisy of an audience and culture that espouses moral ideals about sincerity while harboring a voyeuristic interest in watching the poetess perform her stark drama between life and death. In an insightful reading of "Lady Lazarus," Jahan Ramazani argues that Plath exposes how she performs death so as to deconstruct it as a site of authenticity (*Poetry of Mourning*, 285):

> Dying
> Is an art, like everything else.
> I do it exceptionally well.
>
> I do it so it feels like hell.
> I do it so it feels real.
> I guess you could say I've a call.
> . . . .
> It's the theatrical
>
> Comeback in broad day
> To the same place, the same face, the same brute
> Amused shout:
>
> "A miracle!"
> That knocks me out.   (*CP*, 244–47)

Plath "criticizes the economic substructure and emotional pretensions of confessional poetry" (Ramazani 286). Thus, in lines such as "There is a charge / For the eyeing of my scars, there is a charge / For the hearing of my heart—/ It really goes," Plath reflects on "her own marketing of pain," the ways in which she is forced to commodify her "private" experience and feelings in order to sell her work. Ramazani concludes, "Her self-commod-ifying art requires her self-dismemberment" (287).

Read in the context of the poetess tradition, the critique made by this

poem is more pointed. With lines such as "The peanut-crunching crowd /
Shoves in to see / Them unwrap me hand and foot—/ The big strip tease,"
Plath emphasizes the sexual and economic nature of the audience's inter-
est in the "art of dying" as an art of confessional "truth." Plath's late elegies
position the dead female body—the ground of authenticity, privacy, and
truth in the culture of sensibility—as a sexual commodity to reveal that
elegiac literature authenticates its moral ideals through its opposition to a
feminized, sexualized commercial culture.[20] Thus in the late elegies Plath
exposes the dead virgin and prostitute as flip sides of the same coin as she
describes the ritualized death of the poetess as necessary to a "transcen-
dent," "authentic" work of art. "Fever 103" dramatizes this process of tran-
scendence:

> I think I am going up
> I think I may rise—
> The beads of hot metal fly, and I, love, I
>
> Am a pure acetylene
> Virgin
> Attended by roses,
>
> By kisses, by cherubim,
> By whatever these pink things mean.
> Not you, nor him
>
> Not him, nor him
> (My selves dissolving, old whore petticoats)—
> To Paradise.   (*CP*, 231–32)

As the poem moves down the page, the speaker provides a biting mockery
of what's necessary to "rise . . . / To Paradise": the poetess's moral purity and
commercial disinterest, her transformation into the Virgin as feminine
ideal. As the "I" rises, the descent down the page reveals the emptiness of
this feminine ideal, defined by what it is not ("Not you, nor him") and by
stock icons such as kisses, cherubim, and "pink things," which allude to the
early sonnet "Female Author." The sincere ideal is simply another feminine
costume, which requires the dissolving of its debased double, the speaker's
"old whore petticoats." In these elegies Plath thematizes the contradictions
of professional success as a poetess: the need to "sell" her compliance with
a sincere ideal through a "disinterested" performance of death. As Plath
comments in "Widow," "Death is the dress she wears, her hat and collar":

the role of "mourning," "that great, vacant estate," is enforced attire (*CP*, 164–65).

As the reception of Charlotte Smith indicates, the poetess who writes for money is inevitably unveiled as the whore in disguise: in doing the unveiling herself, Plath turns the tables on her readers. Plath positions the reader who watches "the big strip tease" of the female poet's death not as a sympathetic viewer, but as a voyeur at a freak show who pays to gets a sexualized "charge" from the eyeing of the female corpse. As Lady Lazarus comments acidly, "I turn and burn. / Do not think I underestimate your great concern." Plath suggests that the female elegy as embodiment of a sincere ideal is also a commercial transaction that feeds the basest desire for a voyeuristic experience of death. In Freud's understanding, the melancholic expresses anger and hostility by directing it at the self, but in Plath's late work these feelings are deflected outward to the reader as she challenges them to consider their complicity in sustaining the macabre performance.

By showing the hypocrisy of Lady Lazarus's audience, Plath suggests that the confessional lyric is "thoroughly imbued with relations of power" (Foucault, *History of Sexuality,* 60). Thus, in "Lady Lazarus," she presents the promise of liberation from a constraining power through self-expression—the belief that "confession frees, but power reduces one to silence; truth does not belong to the order of power, but shares an original affinity with freedom"—as false (Foucault 60). Plath introduced Lady Lazarus as "a woman who has the great and terrible gift of being reborn. The only trouble is, she has to die first. She is the Phoenix, the libertarian spirit, what you will" (*CP*, 294). The libertarian spirit—guided by the doctrine of the freedom of the will, as opposed to that of necessity—is an ideal that can only be enacted by the poetess for a price: "She has to die first." If "Lady Lazarus" alludes not only to Lazarus of the New Testament but to the American Jewish poetess Emma Lazarus (1849–87), who wrote "The New Colossus," the poem carved at the base of the Statue of Liberty, then the poem's commentary on the failed promise of a libertarian ideal becomes all the more acute.

Plath's treatment of the figure of audience forecloses on the redemptive possibilities of future readings. While Charlotte Smith attaches utopian potential to "death the leveler" in her work, opening up the possibility of redemptive posthumous readings, Plath's poetry utterly lacks this faith. Lady Lazarus can only "do it so it feels real": the necessity of performing and selling the real always negates its possibility. In measuring the impossibility of self-ownership, the late elegies emphasize the inevitability of the poetess/poem as subject to gendered social and economic codes. "Edge" displays this understanding of the reception of poetess writing:

> The woman is perfected.
> Her dead
>
> Body wears the smile of accomplishment,
> The illusion of a Greek necessity
>
> Flows in the scrolls of her toga.   (*CP*, 272–73)

The speaker contemplates a woman who has literally become Poe's ideal, a poem or artwork in the form of a beautiful female corpse. But more specifically Plath imagines the poetess/poem as it is posthumously received: the edge she engages is that of readerly reception. As Christina Britzolakis astutely points out, "The aesthetic and ideological closure represented by the image of the 'perfected' woman is more apparent than real. It is, after all, 'the illusion of a Greek necessity' which 'flows in the scrolls of her toga'" (*Theatre of Mourning*, 166). Mina Loy suggests in a similar poem, "Photo after Pogrom," that the ironic power of photographs of the dead is to cast an "unassumed / composure" over their faces, transforming even victims of violence to "utter beauty" (*Lost Lunar*, 122). Plath's speaker draws attention to the moral and epistemological problem of using death as ground for Poe's aesthetic ideal (Bronfen, *Dead Body*, 395–404): is the woman really perfected? The speaker in "Edge" lacks faith that a wider audience will consider the performance of sincerity or recognize the irony of conflating female death with aesthetic perfection. This theater of tragedy has only one figure of audience, the moon wearing her funereal blacks:

> The moon has nothing to be sad about,
> Staring from her hood of bone.
> She is used to this sort of thing.
> Her blacks crackle and drag.

The moon, conventional feminine symbol, is "used to this sort of thing": like the poetess, she carries out her ritual performance of mourning.

While Plath anticipates the failure of her desire to "feel that my works are mine," the anger of the melancholic would prove to have leveling implications. Lady Lazarus promises that she won't stay quietly buried, but will wreak vengeance through death:

> Beware
> Beware.
> Out of the ash

I rise with my red hair
And I eat men like air. (*CP*, 246–47)

Among the varied meanings of "Lady Lazarus" is that of a person who is considered a source of moral corruption or contagion. Plath's melancholic poetry raises from the dead the specter that writers from Adam Smith to Ted Hughes have tried to bury with their understanding of proper mourning: the specter of a contagious commercial culture, feminized and pathologized, which threatens the foundations of a patriarchal moral community. Plath got around but not past her writing block: she used the "cold corpse" lying between the writer and her work to hold up a mirror to the reader's critical gaze, revealing "sincerity" to be a problem of reception.

Mourning the Poetess: Reception, Confession, and the Plath Industry

Reception history has largely proven Plath right: the ways in which her work has been produced, circulated, and read after her suicide has borne out her ambivalence about mainstream commercial success. The association of Plath's suicide with the dilemmas of her poetic speakers has been overt, used to market her work after her death and to ground various kinds of scholarship, from the biographically informed to the psychologically pathologizing. Prior to her death, Plath had met with considerable critical success for a young writer starting out her career; in addition to publishing her poems and stories in numerous magazines, she had received favorable reviews in 1960 for her first book of poetry, *The Colossus,* and for her novel *The Bell Jar* in January 1963. She was making a name for herself in Britain, particularly as a poet; in 1961 and 1962 the BBC broadcast many of her readings of her poetry, and she reported to her mother that Alfred Alvarez, "the opinion-maker in poetry over here," told her that she was "the first woman poet he's taken seriously since Emily Dickinson" (*LH,* 476). Although she felt that she had made a great breakthrough with her new poems, some of which she recorded for the BBC in October 1962, the very poems that would cement her posthumous fame were rejected by all of the newspapers and magazines to which she sent them.

Plath's commercial success and literary celebrity is posthumous, beginning with the publication of *Ariel* in 1965 by Faber and Faber. A paperback edition followed in 1968; seven more reprints of the paperback edition appeared by 1981, totaling 152,000 paperback copies.[21] And these sales figures were for Britain alone. In the United States, Harper and Row (now HarperCollins) published *Ariel* in 1966 and a paperback version in 1968, with an excerpt from Robert Lowell's introduction printed on the front cover: "In these poems, written in the last months of her life, and often rushed out at the rate of two or three a day, Sylvia Plath becomes herself, becomes something imaginary, newly, wildly and subtly created." Plath would likely have appreciated the irony that the poems that engage the impossibility of "becoming a self" in commercial culture were marketed as the epitome of a sincere ideal, with the poet's death the seal of their authenticity. The success of *Ariel* was used to promote *The Bell Jar.* Although published in January 1963 by Heinemann in London under Plath's pseudonym Victoria Lucas, only a "token quantity" were printed (Tabor 14); Faber and Faber re-released the novel in 1966 under Plath's name, with a blurb from *Ariel* printed on the back cover. Harper and Row published an American edition in 1971 that included a biographical note on Plath's life by Lois Ames. Marketed as a thinly veiled autobiography, the novel quickly became a bestseller. Plath had achieved commercial success, and translations of her works brought her international celebrity (Homberger, "Uncollected Plath," 187–91). That Plath's life and work have inspired hundreds of scholarly assessments, numerous biographies, conferences, fictional renderings of her life, documentaries, film adaptations, and popular music lyrics indicates the extent to which her work has entered both literary and popular culture.

The posthumous nature of Plath's success has influenced readings of her use of the rhetoric of sincerity. While she has been pathologized and judged "self-indulgent" and "narcissistic," to my knowledge no critic has accused Plath of donning a "very Mourning Warehouse of funereal black" to sell her poems, as Viscount St. Cyres accused Charlotte Smith. In part this is due to the fact that Plath was not able to reap the commercial profits of *Ariel* and *The Bell Jar.* But it is also due to Plath's suicide, which overshadows readings of her work even by critics who argue for a strict separation between the life and the poetry. While I agree that Plath's first-person lyrics should not be read as transparent utterance, as a road map leading up to the suicide, to deny any connection between the poetry and the life (and for my purposes between the poetry and its investments in commercial culture) ignores the epistemological quandary it stages: what is real and what is performance? Plath's critics, whatever their allegiance, are haunted by this question.[22]

For the simple fact remains that anyone writing about Plath after her untimely death implicitly takes up the role of elegist. Ross Chambers argues that criticism that takes up melancholy texts is itself "deeply and intimately involved in the work of mourning and 'eternal protest' that is melancholy. . . . A critic cannot 'comment on' or 'interpret' a melancholy text without adopting a discursive practice that is itself melancholy" (*Writing*, 206). As elegists, Plath's critics respond to the ways in which a melancholic poetry anticipates its posthumous reception, finding themselves in the uncomfortable position of the peanut-crunching crowd in "Lady Lazarus." There is no position of innocence for the reader in her poetry. Thus it is not a coincidence that the charge of insincerity has been leveled at and by Plath's critics in regard to one another, rather than in regard to Plath herself: a recurrent plaint of her reception concerns the ways in which critics have used or profited from her death.

An early exchange between Alfred Alvarez and Ted Hughes illustrates this dynamic. Alvarez, the poetry critic for the *Observer* in the 1960s, was perhaps the person most instrumental to the growth of Plath's reputation, prior to but particularly after her death.[23] When Plath died, Alvarez published an obituary in the *Observer* that described her last poems in terms intended to create a stir; he stated that they signify "a totally new breakthrough in modern verse," establishing Plath "as the most gifted woman poet of our time." His subsequent memorials and reviews of Plath's posthumous works confirmed this evaluation. In 1971 Alvarez published the first half of a memoir of Plath in the *Observer;* the second half, at the request of Ted Hughes, was not published, but appeared later in a different venue.[24] Hughes's angry response to this memoir would set the stage for the ensuing debate about the literary critic's elegiac role.

Deflecting the charge of self-interest in their responses to Plath's death, both Alvarez and Hughes claim the role of proper mourning and, not surprisingly, write their elegiac works in the first-person voice, professing their sincerity. Yet each enacts, using the language of Plath's late elegies, the very oppositions that troubled Plath. The passage from Alvarez's memoir that most upset Hughes concerned Plath's inquest: "Earlier that morning I had gone with Ted to the undertaker's in Mornington Crescent. The coffin was at the far end of a bare, draped room. She lay stiffly, a ludicrous ruff at her neck. Only her face showed. It was gray and slightly transparent, like wax. I had never before seen a dead person and I hardly recognized her; her features seemed too thin and sharp. The room smelled of apples, faint, sweet but somehow unclean, as though the apples were beginning to rot. I was glad to get into the cold and noise of the dingy streets. It seemed impossible that she was dead" ("Memoir," 212–13). Plath's death authenticated the kinds of struggles that Alvarez felt should define poetry—she became for Alvarez not the "poet as a sacrificial victim," but poetry itself as "the quick of experience"—a quick rendered most dramatically "on the edge of disintegration and breakdown."[25] Thus he reads her poem "Edge," written soon before she committed suicide, as "specifically about the act she was about to perform" (209) and explains her suicide as life imitating art, "a last desperate attempt to exorcise the death she had summoned up in her poems" (210). In the inquest passage Alvarez takes up the position of the speaker in "Edge," but his description provides an ironic counterpoint to the poem, emphasizing what it "really" means to go over the edge. Plath's corpse is not the woman "perfected," the woman transformed into a classical statue or work of art, but the woman as flesh and blood, a difference he conveys by describing the superficial features of the corpse—its color and stiffness, the sharpness of the facial features, the ludicrous ruff. The odor bleeding "from the sweet, deep throats of the night flower" in "Edge" becomes the smell of apples, "faint, sweet but somehow unclean, as though the apples were beginning to rot," connoting Eve, the fallen woman. Alvarez implies that the fall he records is Plath's: she has mistakenly bitten the apple of "real" knowledge due to her textual preoccupation with death. While Plath indicts Lady Lazarus's audience for sustaining the big strip tease of death, Alvarez locates the sin—and blame—in Plath ("somehow unclean") both to uphold his ideals of "extremist" poetry and to position himself as mourner rather than peanut-cruncher. Recording Plath's bodily death in documentary detail authenticates the "truth" of his elegiac memoir (J. Rose, *Haunting*, 22–23).

Hughes, however, read this passage as evidence of Alvarez's role as ringmaster for the "big strip tease": "Sylvia now goes through the detailed, point-by-point death of a public sacrifice. . . . Now there actually is a body. The cries drew the crowd, but they came not to hear more cries—they came to see the body. Now they have it—they can smell its hair and its death. You present in the flesh what the death cries were working up to. The public isn't really interested in death cries unless they guarantee a dead body, a slow painful death, with as many signals as possible of what it is feeling like. And you present that, the thing the public really wants and needs—the absolutely convincing finalised official visible gruelling death." Directing Lady Lazarus's accusations against Alvarez, Hughes blames him for selling tickets to the Plath spectacle, of using a "bit of blood / Or a piece of . . . hair or clothes" to provide a voyeuristic experience of death for a "sensation-watching and half-hysterical congregation." In referring to Plath's "private killing of herself," Hughes implies that Alvarez has undressed Plath in public, forcing her to confess what "should" remain private. He adds, "Only one thing could go further: that she reappear and go through the whole thing again, correcting all errors of report, on TV" (qtd. in Malcolm, *Silent Woman*, 127–28). This statement is oddly reminiscent of Plath's journals: "I feel like Lazarus: that story has such a fascination. Being dead, I rose up again, and even resort to the mere sensation value of being suicidal, of getting so close, of coming out of the grave with the scars and the marring mark on my cheek" (*J*, 199). Yet while Plath reflects on her "self-commodifying art," Hughes blames Alvarez for this act, and thus tries to distinguish the poetess from the whore, mourning from commercial culture, elegist from peanut-cruncher, private death from public confession.

In the course of their lengthy exchange, Alvarez defended his moral role as critic, arguing that his "Memoir" was not sensationalist but was written as a "tribute to Sylvia." He reminds Hughes of how he has furthered both poets' careers, for no other end than the sake of poetry itself: "I have taken a lot of trouble to get both your poetry and Sylvia's read with understanding and a proper respect. I have done so not because you are friends of mine but because I think you the most gifted poets of your generation. Sylvia knew this, and knew I understood in some way what she was trying to do. To imagine now that I am simply cashing in on her death or making a glib intellectual point is a complete distortion of everything I have written, both here and before" (qtd. in Malcolm 125, 126). Alvarez invokes the aesthetic ideals of the poetic profession to defend his elegiac role, in particular his aim to make and pass on Plath's name.[26] Although his reading of Plath's suicide as proof of the authenticity of her poetry has been amply critiqued, and his sensationalist motives questioned, Alvarez's complex role helped Plath's work achieve her desired goal, literary *and* commercial success.

By directing Lady Lazarus's vengeance at Alvarez and other Plath critics, Hughes sidestepped Plath's commercial investments in her elegiac art and his own potential profit from it as her literary heir. Hughes predicted that Alvarez's memoir would generate a voyeuristic critical industry centered on Plath: "Between her writings and your article is a whole new world of hypothesis. And the commercial and career needs for articles and theses and class material will make sure that world gets overpopulated, and your facts get turned into literary historic monuments." Hughes argued that Plath's critics feed off of the living under the guise of mourning the dead, writing to Jacqueline Rose that "critics established the right to say whatever they pleased about the dead. It is an absolute power, and the corruption that comes with it, very often, is an atrophy of the moral imagination. They move onto the living because they can no longer feel the difference between the living and the dead" (qtd. in Malcolm 128, 142, 47).[27] Putting self-interest ahead of the feelings of Plath's family or of the moral good of the broader public, Plath's critics, Hughes argues, forsake the "moral imagination" central to elegiac literature since Adam Smith.

It's not surprising, then, that Hughes would embrace the rhetoric of sincerity—essential to elegiac literature, as Wordsworth emphasized—in *Birthday Letters,* an elegiac cycle of poems based on the lives of both Plath and Hughes, published shortly before Hughes's death. Indeed, Sarah Churchwell has suggested that we read *Birthday Letters* as Hughes's effort to assert his "private" version of Plath's life and work as the truth, versus the version offered by the "peanut-crunching crowd."[28] Ironically, he does so in a public forum—using a logic of what Churchwell calls the "open secret" ("Secrets and Lies," 139)—acknowledging, perhaps, the necessity of entering the fray; the book, a bestseller, has fanned the flames of the interest in Plath and Hughes (Middlebrook, *Her Husband,* 283). And yet Hughes's claim to the moral role of elegist has been met with the charge that he profited from the proceeds of Plath's works as her literary heir and executor despite the intestate state of her affairs and the ambiguous status of their marriage.[29] Hughes defended his financial gains from the Plath estate in an essay titled "Publishing Sylvia Plath" (1971), claiming the rights of the living over those of the dead.[30] On the other hand, Janet Malcolm describes Hughes's negotiations in 1970 to publish *The Bell Jar* in the United States while it was still saleable; in that the packaging of *The Bell Jar* in the United States drew on Plath's suicide, Hughes stood to profit from the publicizing of the very act he had asked Alvarez to keep private. Malcolm—in her own first-person account of Hughes and Plath—confesses that she viewed this act of Hughes with "coldness" (40), adding that the Hugheses "have compromised their claim to being alive by their financial gains from the dead poet's literary remains" (51). In Plath's reception her suicide inevitably leads to moral questions about her "literary remains": while we tend to think hers is a unique case, I've suggested that the "death of the author" is the subtext not just of the elegiac tradition but of modern, commercial culture.

Lady Lazarus, in implicating her readers in her melancholic performance, triggered a chain of confessional finger-pointing that continues to propel the Plath reception. In eliding the connection between the elegy and commercial culture, the figure of the martyred poetess and the prostitute, sincerity and performance, textual corpse and literary property, Plath's readers continue to deflect this charge. Whether we position Plath's speakers as biographically motivated or as fictive, dramatic creations, we tend to overlook Plath's staging of and commentary on this epistemological conflict and thus the ways in which our own readings assign blame, make cuts, define origins. My own reading privileges a commercial origin to challenge the ways in which gender and sexuality continue to sustain the opposition between sincerity and a feminized, debased theatricality in women's poetry. To overlook this particular origin is to miss a "terra incognita beneath our very feet" (Curran, "I Altered," 129).

Part III
The Illegible Signature
Miniaturist Description and the Ethics of Sincerity

Topography displays no favorites: North's as near as West.
More delicate than the historian's are the map-maker's colors.

> —Elizabeth Bishop, "The Map"

Thus geography, civil geography, would be seen to grow out of
history; and the mere view of the map would suggest the political
state of the world at any period.

> —Anna Laetitia Barbauld, Letter 3, *On the Uses of History*

There are no miniatures in nature; the miniature is a cultural
product, the product of an eye performing certain operations,
manipulating, and attending in certain ways, to the physical world.

> —Susan Stewart, *On Longing*

*E*lizabeth Bishop (1911–79) wrote to Marianne Moore in 1940 that "I have that continuous uncomfortable feeling of 'things' in the head, like icebergs or rocks or awkwardly placed pieces of furniture. It's as if all the nouns were there but the verbs are lacking. . . . And I can't help having the theory that if they are joggled around hard enough and long enough some kind of electricity will occur, just by friction, that will arrange everything."[1] Similarly, in a drafted poem ("Letter to Two Friends") written in Brazil for Moore and Robert Lowell, Bishop complained that the poem she was working on had dissolved into prepositions, "ins and aboves and upons."[2] Several lines later she pleads, "Cal, please cable a verb!"

While she can hover around the "things" in her head, the verbs that would bind these objects together—through a narrative involving action, time, and historical causation—remain elusive. Which preposition to choose, or how to "arrange everything," is more than a passing complaint by Bishop: it is a problem of power and spatial perspective that she thematizes in her poetry. Like Bishop, the poet Anna Laetitia Barbauld (1743–1825) was fascinated by objects and their spatial relationships. While Barbauld and Bishop claim in much of their poetry the sincerity of the first-person voice, both are concerned less with expressions of feeling and autobiographical experience than with accurate descriptions of objects, less with time than with space, less with history than with geography. As her "Letter" above suggests, Barbauld would agree with Bishop that "more delicate than the historian's are the map-maker's colors." The figure of the sincere poet materializes in their work as she is mediated by and absorbed into minute descriptions of objects and their spatial relations: the poetic persona is that of miniaturist observer and mapmaker.

These poetries enact what I call the "illegible signature," a practice of sincerity based on concealment of the poet's "personality" and resistance to the ways in which conventions of sincerity support the property value of the name. Long before the rise of a commercial market for literature, authors had traded in reputation, the name serving as a signifier of the author's moral character, the quality of their craftsmanship, their association with a particular patron, and so forth. But due to legal changes in understandings of literary property in the eighteenth century, and specifically to the development of the author's property rights, the name came to signify an author's unique, individual style, as manifested by his texts and protected by law. Regardless of who owned the right of copy (usually booksellers), texts came to be seen as property in and of the author's person.[3] The poetry of sincerity fleshed out this relationship, with authors often choosing to circulate textual versions of themselves. However—as the previous chapters have demonstrated—the moral ideal of the poem as the unique property of a private self was often an empty one.

Similarly, the name as guarantor of the moral reputation of an author could easily take on a life of its own in the marketplace, becoming a brand name, a personification of the author, a source of public notoriety, gossip, and intrigue. When Charlotte Smith presented her "real woe" in serial editions of her sonnets, she reassured her readers of the authenticity of her feelings, but also spurred sales by rendering her private travails an eighteenth-century soap opera. Plath published *The Bell Jar* under the pseudonym Victoria Lucas, but her suicide catapulted her to marquée status, making her an icon often compared to James Dean and Marilyn Monroe; the posthumous editions of the novel, published under her own name, advertised the relationship between "fiction" and the events of Plath's life. Facilitating this interest in the author's person was the proliferation of new media and technology, permitting, for instance, the late-eighteenth- and early-nineteenth-century practice of including a portrait frontispiece of the author, and its late-twentieth-century variant, the glossy author's photo. In the modern literary market, one could not easily disentangle the rhetoric of sincerity from the culture of literary celebrity.

To claim sincerity in one's lyric poetry was to risk becoming a literary personality, and Barbauld and Bishop deplored the cultivation of celebrity by their peers. Barbauld took Charlotte Smith to task for ceaselessly detailing her private woe, while Bishop disparaged the "confessional" style of suffering as popularized by Plath, Lowell, and Sexton. Both Barbauld and Bishop suggested that by dramatizing ostensibly "real" mourning, poets such as Smith and Plath profited from the spectacle of private suffering. By the mid-nineteenth century, "celebrity" had begun to connote inauthenticity, a vulgarized notoriety that was specifically associated with the taint of consumer culture and its modes of publicity.[4] Although Barbauld and Bishop were well-published writers, and Bishop, especially later in her career, was dependent on the income from her writing and teaching, both poets attempted to insulate themselves from the commercial aspects of the writing profession, preferring the guise of "amateur" to that of "professional." Like Wordsworth, then, Barbauld and Bishop regarded commercial culture as a potentially contaminating force, its theatrical modes of self-presentation a threat to sincerity. Bishop even called herself a "minor, female Wordsworth," but in these two adjectives we can chart a world of difference, a practice of sincerity critical of capitalist acquisitiveness and its poetic counterpart, the expansive romantic self.

To this end, each poet invents a miniaturist aesthetic. The miniature, defined by an emphasis on the accurate observation of minute detail, submerges individual "personality" and autobiographical expression to concern with an ethics of language use. Shifting the focus of lyric from dramatic self-expression to the discursive frames through which representation accrues meaning and power, Barbauld and Bishop resisted cultivating their own celebrity by drawing attention to the interests of self-representation, involving their readers in problems of scale and perspective. How to connect "in and above and upon" becomes an ethical dilemma in their poetry, spatial perspective implying an act of ethical placement: of self in relation to other, citizen in relation to nation, human in relation to nature, fiction in relation to fact. As Barbauld pointed out, "The mere view of the map would suggest the political state of the world at any period." In mapping the minutiae of the physical world, these poets sketched in the interests of the eye/I as it placed and was placed: epistemology, they suggest, presumes an ethics.

Indeed, the following chapters suggest that a miniaturist poetry provides an ethical critique of property at the level of self and nation. Barbauld and Bishop connected the exploitation of personal suffering in poetry to the pursuit of property in the name, and conflated the self-dramatizing practices of romantic authorship with forms of commercial expansion, accumulation, and exploitation. They observed the acquisitive drive not only in the literary market but in foreign wars, in colonial and postcolonial commerce, and in the national museums in which spoils of war and conquest were displayed. By way of contrast, they value the delicate, the slight, the invisible, the anonymous, and the dispossessed, taking up subjects, forms of writing, and modes of poetic circulation antithetical to capitalist expansion and accumulation. While Smith and Plath decried the gendered economic privileges sustaining a sincere ideal, Barbauld and Bishop found in the woman poet's marginal position an ethical vantage point. Their negotiation of literary property was shaped by their status as woman poets, but also by their varied experiences on the political and cultural margins: Barbauld was a Unitarian dissenter at a time of particular intolerance, and Bishop's penchant for the geographical margins (she lived first in Key West, and from 1952 to 1967 as an expatriate in Brazil) was influenced by her closeted homosexuality.

That both writers were actively engaged with the culture and literature of sensibility has been largely overlooked, however, due to their emphasis on descriptions of the object world rather than on expressions of private feeling. Barbauld wrote and published her work from the 1770s to the turn of the century, alongside the first-generation romantics, but has been read as part of an eighteenth-century neoclassical tradition. Bishop, too, has been positioned outside of a sentimental tradition; she began publishing in the 1930s, when the classicism espoused by modernists such as Pound and Eliot had gained sway at the expense of a romantic expression derided as excessive, clichéd, and sentimental.[5] Although Bishop's poetry registers the influence of Pound and the objectivists in its concern with visual accuracy, Bishop's critics assume that the irony and restraint of her poetry distances it from the "problems" of sentiment attributed to nineteenth-century women's poetry. This reading of Bishop is guided by what Suzanne Clark calls modernist antisentimentalism, a bias pervasive in Bishop scholarship. We might say that Barbauld suffers from the reverse bias, romantic anticlassicism.[6] If critics of romantic-era poetry are subject to what Jerome McGann calls the "romantic ideology," then critics of modernist poetry are subject to what we might in turn call the "modernist ideology," the poetry's claim to "make it new" resulting in critics' exaggerated claims for its break from a sentimental past. More pointedly, the poetry of these two writers reveals the problems with the habitual opposition of irony and sincere sentiment, used to periodize and categorize literature beginning with the romantic poets.[7]

Positioning both Barbauld and Bishop as part of the culture of sensibility allows us to see that their poetry engages long-standing debates about the role and efficacy of representations of suffering, debates that are fundamental to sentimental culture and to poetry in the romantic tradition, debates that did not begin with Wordsworth and end with modernism. While Barbauld and Bishop were certainly critical of the marketing of sentiment, they were also aware of their own implication in a sentimental economy, qualifying any clear opposition between their practices of sincerity and commercial culture. Rather than read their strategies of self-representation as removing their poetry from the problems of private sentiment and its circulation, the following chapters demonstrate that a miniaturist aesthetic emerges from and is subject to these very problems.[8] In juxtaposing Barbauld's and Bishop's uses of the miniature, then, we can look afresh at the complexities of feeling as it circulates in a marketplace.

Miniaturist poetry presents itself as the product of feminine, domestic handicraft, appearing to accept its "minor" or ancillary role.[9] While the culture of sensibility permitted late-eighteenth- and nineteenth-century British and American women writers to venture into print within the limits of feminine decorum, they typically avoided writing poems of overt political import, or subsumed such themes to their domestic or maternal duties. Professionally, as long as the female poet did not publicly disavow her minor status—as long as she appeared to accept the conflation of feminine writing with an instructional (morally didactic) or leisurely (occasional) activity—she could write and publish with propriety. Imaginatively, women poets faced an economy of poetic inspiration segregated by gender; "fancy" was aligned with traits and themes coded as feminine, and served as the muse of much late-eighteenth-century female poetry.[10] In contrast to the shaping spirit or transformative power of the imagination, fancy as a mental faculty was widely defined by its "inability" to transcend or transform the visual, the material, the contingent or particular; thus fancy was characterized by the accumulation or collection of miniaturist detail, by its status as a derivative craft, and by the logic of the copy versus that of the original.[11] While the use of the miniature was widespread in the literature of sentiment as practiced by writers of both genders, miniaturist themes and styles resonated with the limits of women's roles.

Inseparable from the tradition of sentimental women's poetry was the reception of the woman poet as an accomplished miniaturist; the label of "miniaturist" to this day retains the mark of condescension, of damning with faint praise, when applied to the work of women poets. If current readers tend to position Barbauld and Bishop outside of a sentimental tradition, their contemporaries perceived them as all too sentimental, and they each struggled against the categorization of their work as feminine, fanciful, and minor. In using the miniature, both risked simply reinforcing the limits of feminine roles, and some critics have argued that their social criticism is limited by their investment in middle-class norms of feminine conduct. But their uses of the miniature amount to a deliberate effort to oppose the common reading of the miniature as minor literature: by drawing attention to spatial relations and perspective they seek to expose the barriers to sympathy, providing an ethical critique of a sentimental economy and its failure to change or influence political interests backed by economic power.

The miniature is a figure that draws attention to its materiality: it can be "held in the hand," and offers itself to an intimate audience, as a gift rather than a commodity. While Wordsworth and O'Hara present the poet as walker, and Smith and Plath figure the poet as mourner and beautiful corpse, it is telling that both Barbauld and Bishop resist conflating the poem with the body of the poet. Rather, the poet is figured as an anonymous observer, a pair of eyes, and the poem circulates as an unusual map, a description meant to unsettle received coordinates. Sincerity resides not in the author's person but in an emphasis on accurate, honest craftsmanship: the body figured is that of writing itself, what Roland Barthes describes as "that neutral, composite, oblique space where our subject slips away, the negative where all identity is lost, starting with the very identity of the body writing" (*Image-Music-Text*, 125). For Barbauld the "illegible signature" was literalized in her textual practice of obscuring her name by using anonyms and pseudonyms; for Bishop her textual practice manifests itself materially in the slightness of her poetic production and in her attention to handicraft. Finally, by seeking to circulate their tiny "maps" as gifts rather than commodities, both poets attempt to carve out an intimate public contained within but resistant to the acquisitive logics of the marketplace.

Chapter 5

Anna Laetitia Barbauld

"A thing unknown, without a name"

Although she was a well-known and highly respected writer of poetry, children's literature, civil sermons, and critical prose, Anna Laetitia Barbauld (born Aikin, 1743–1825) was reluctant to view herself as a professional author. Most crucially, Barbauld did not depend on her writing for a livelihood, and she emphasized the social and moral concerns shaping her forays into print. Her notion of poetic labor was forged not only in the culture of sensibility but in the culture of religious dissent. The Aikins were active members of the nonconformist community located in Lancashire county; Barbauld's father, John Aikin, served as a tutor in divinity at Warrington Academy, and Barbauld was informally educated in this environment. In 1774 Anna Laetitia Aikin married Rochemont Barbauld, a graduate of Warrington and a dissenting minister. One of the most famous academies of its kind, Warrington served as an important center of dissenting thought in the late eighteenth century (Rodgers, *Georgian Chronicle*, 33–63). Joseph Priestley taught at Warrington from 1761 until 1767, and became close friends with the Aikins.

Barbauld's acquaintance with Priestley and his works purportedly inspired her to write her first poems.[1] Her initial readership was the dissenting community in which she lived; Barbauld circulated her poetry in manuscript to friends and to the students and tutors at Warrington. Through these channels, her fame spread, but Barbauld shunned publicity. In *A Legacy for Young Ladies,* she emphasized that women's role is "to be a wife, a mother, a mistress of a family. The knowledge belonging to these duties is your professional knowledge, the want of which nothing will excuse." Literary knowledge could be a "duty" for men, but for women it was to be used for "the purposes of adorning and improving the mind, of refining the sentiments, and supplying proper stores for conversation."[2] Accounts of Barbauld's literary career suggest that she had to be persuaded to publish her works at all. She published her first poems anonymously in 1772, in a volume of songs edited by her brother John, and in a volume of hymns edited by a tutor at Warrington, William Enfield. In response to "many demands," Barbauld prepared her first solo volume, *Poems,* which was published by Joseph Johnson in 1773 and printed by the Eyres Press in Warrington. *Poems* went through three editions that year, reaching a fifth edition by 1776 and a sixth by 1792; an American edition was printed in 1820. Following *Poems,* Barbauld published *Epistle to William Wilberforce* (1791) and *Eighteen Hundred and Eleven* (1812) with Joseph Johnson, and placed some additional poetry in magazines and anthologies.[3]

While Barbauld produced works in many genres, her total production as a poet was slight; much of her poetry remained unpublished until after her death.[4] Even following the success of *Poems,* printed under her name, she continued to circulate work by manuscript, often preferring to send poems to friends rather than publish them. Similarly, anonymity was not simply a cloak Barbauld wore prior to securing a measure of literary fame, as was the norm with many women writers (Jacobs, "Anonymous Signatures," 620); throughout the course of her career, Barbauld chose to publish some of her poetry anonymously, to sign some poems "A Lady," or to use the initials A.L.B. or A.B. The poetic persona she cultivated was one of privacy, modesty, and restraint.

Such claims to privacy by eighteenth-century women writers were highly conventional, serving to display compliance with gendered codes of public decorum. Barbauld was certainly influenced by these codes, and scholars have tended to view her as conservative in her acceptance of imposed gender roles and the doctrine of separate spheres. For instance, Carol Shiner Wilson notes the lack of conflict in Barbauld's poetry "between the needle of domesticity and the pen of artistic desire found in many women writers."[5] But recent work is beginning to suggest that representing her poetic labor as an extension of her private, domestic role did not simply signal Barbauld's acquiescence with gendered limits; it formed a complicated, albeit complicitous, critique of the political and economic systems that shaped her experience as a woman writer and religious dissenter.[6] Crucial to this revision is an understanding of how Barbauld's poetry was produced and circulated, knowledge that the scrupulous edition of Barbauld's poetry by McCarthy and Kraft has supplied.

Barbauld develops a lyric aesthetic based on the miniature object so as to textually and materially define a circulation distinct from the dominant, commercially controlled circuits of exchange. The miniaturist poem presents itself not as a commodity but as a handmade gift, one that seems to accept its "minor" status, its role as adornment, the themes of domestic life and moral virtues. While it is a literature defined by the limits of its thematic and formal reach, these limits also serve as the source of its power and critique: Barbauld positions her miniaturist poetry as the privileged unit of a representational and political economy opposed to capitalist expansion, and to what she saw as its poetic counterpart, romantic egotism. In using a miniaturist aesthetic, Barbauld promotes a model of poetic sincerity based not on autobiographical detail but on anonymity and the concealment of the personal. Although she wrote and published alongside the first-generation romantics, Barbauld—due to her use of Augustan diction and emphasis on the object world rather than on expressions of private feeling—has been seen as an anachronistic throwback to eighteenth-century neoclassical writers. An exploration of Barbauld's miniaturist aesthetic reveals that she was actively immersed in the cultural world of romanticism and that her poetry charts an influential if little-recognized response to the marketing of poetic sincerity and the culture of literary celebrity.

Anonymity and Literary Property

Barbauld reflects on the limits and possibilities of the miniature as a model for female authorship in an early unpublished poem, "An Inventory of the Furniture in Dr. Priestley's Study."[7] This poem considers the scene of poetic production from an unnamed or anonymous narrator's perspective, placing perspective itself in question. What renders Barbauld's poem a miniaturist study is its concern with spatial perspective rather than temporal narration: titled an "inventory," it advertises itself as the work of fancy versus imagination, as nothing more than the accumulation of visual, minute detail (see Alpers, *Art of Describing*, xxi, 83, 106). In overt theme and purpose the poem is domestic, its work comparable to the mental survey someone such as Priestley's wife or maid might perform as she glances in the study to check that everything is in its proper place.

Although an inventory would appear to have little political import, the narrator's description of Priestley's furniture belies this expectation. Priestley was one of the most well-known republican dissenters of the late eighteenth century. By describing the objects in his study, the narrator draws an implicit portrait of the man and his intellectual and political engagements, investing neutral objects with political meaning. Indeed, at stake in this poem about furniture is the relationship between possessions and their owners, property and authorship. The poem begins with a contrast between landed property and intellectual capital:

> A map of every country known,
> With not a foot of land his own.
> A list of folks that kicked a dust
> On this poor globe, from Ptol. the First;
> He hopes,—indeed it is but fair,—
> Some day to get a corner there.   (*Poems*, 38–39; lines 1–6)

The narrator alludes to works that Priestley has authored—*The New Chart of History* (1769) and *The Chart of Biography* (1765)—and implies that these books are the only form of property available to him. Priestley's lack of material property, and the unlikelihood that his name will pass into posterity, connotes the history of unequal treatment, specifically the deprivation of civil and political liberties, experienced by dissenters under British law.[8] This situation resonates doubly for Barbauld, who suffered exclusions not only as a dissenter but as a woman (Ross, "Configurations," 93).

Yet language, the narrator shows, is a medium able to subvert the exigencies of material circumstance:

> A group of all the British kings,
> Fair emblem! on a packthread swings
> The fathers, ranged in goodly row,
> A decent, venerable show,
> Writ a great while ago, they tell us,
> And many an inch o'ertop their fellows.
> . . . .
> The meek-robed lawyers, all in white;
> Pure as the lamb,—at least, to sight.   (lines 7–16)

While the classics of religion and law lining Priestley's shelves indicate that he is a faithful English citizen, the narrator implies that appearances deceive, through her description of the spatial arrangement of these works. The fact that the British kings are "swinging on a packthread" connotes an image of the kings hanging by their necks, an "emblem" not of justice and order but of the glorious revolution and Priestley's republican politics (*Poems*, 247). Similarly, by stating that the works of the church fathers make a "venerable show," and that the lawyers appear "pure as the lamb,—at least to sight," the narrator reveals the limits of the visible. In this manner she suggests that her project of visual description belies its manifest appearance, that the meaning of the inventory can be discerned not simply in the objects she catalogues, but in what she implies. More specifically, meaning accrues in her use and arrangement of Priestley's objects in the poem. The portrait of Priestley emerges through what remains invisible without the paintbrush of language: the history and use of his objects. Barbauld subscribes to the ideal that language itself, in its doubleness, its ability to refer to both what is visible and what is invisible, to ground itself empirically and to evade the exigencies of the material world, might elude the treatment of written texts as forms of property.

The narrator develops an apt metaphor for language as a propertyless medium—electricity—as she inventories the tools of science that Priestley employs in his study:

A shelf of bottles, jar and phial
By which the rogues he can defy all,—
All filled with lightning keen and genuine,
And many a little imp he'll pen you in;
Which, like le Sage's sprite, let out,
Among the neighbours makes a rout;
Brings down the lightning on their houses,
And kills their geese, and frights their spouses.
A rare thermometer, by which
He settles, to the nicest pitch,
The just degrees of heat, to raise
Sermons, or politics, or plays.   (lines 17–28)

Priestley wrote *History of Electricity* in 1767; the "phial" or Leyden jar was used to store electricity, which when discharged "made a spark like lightning" (*Poems*, 247). The narrator draws a parallel between writing and lightning through the use of a pun, that classic figure of doubleness: punning on the word "pen," she refers both to the electrical "imps" Priestley pens or cages in the jars and phials, and to the verbal "imps" he creates in his treatises. Like electricity, language is invisible until it is released from its "pen" and circulated; only at this point can it achieve contact, creating tangible sparks. Additionally, the allusion to "Le Sage's sprite" would resonate with a contemporary audience; it refers to *Le Diable Boiteux* by René Le Sage, in which "a student releases from a phial in a laboratory a spirit named Asmodeus, who creates a furor among the neighbors by lifting the roofs from

their houses and revealing their private lives" (*Poems,* 248). The narrator im-
plies that Priestley's muse, like Le Sage's sprite, aims to strike discord. On the
other hand, Priestley was immersed in a violent social conflict, a conflict that
would eventually result in personal domestic havoc, the burning of his study
and laboratory in the Birmingham riots of 1791.[9]

Through her alliance with the doubleness of language, the narrator
distinguishes herself from Priestley, criticizing his incendiary form of writ-
ing. Although dissenters are "unfairly" barred from property, power, and
civil liberties, the narrator presents Priestley's response to this, his agitation
for reform, as no different in kind from the oppression he seeks to counter.
His desire for a "corner" of the map renders his political "commerce" as
corrupt as that of his enemies:

> Papers and books, a strange mixed olio,
> From shilling touch to pompous folio,
> Answer, remark, reply, rejoinder,
> Fresh from the mint, all stamped and coined here;
> Like new-made glass, set by to cool,
> Before it bears the workman's tool
> A blotted proof-sheet, wet from Bowling.
> —"How can a man his anger hold in?"—
> Forgotten rimes, and college themes,
> Worm-eaten plans, and embryo schemes; —
> A mass of heterogeneous matter,
> A chaos dark, nor land nor water   (lines 29–40)

Comparing the varieties of polemical treatises in Priestley's study ("answer,
remark, reply, rejoinder") to freshly minted coins, the narrator points out
the connections between financial and political commerce. In using such
treatises, Priestley subjects his politics to the logic of the marketplace, to the
competition, one-upmanship, and desire for property and power that fuels
the proliferation of texts and commodities. More pointedly, the narrator
suggests that Priestley is not simply a victim of the marketplace, but that
the kind of polemical rhetoric he deploys drives the proliferation of print;
the marketplace thrives on political division and strife, the distinctions be-
tween the "shilling touch" and "pompous folio," and between their authors.
The image of the blotted proof-sheet, spoiled by excess ink, implies—by its
ambiguity or doubleness of reference—Priestley's culpability in this sys-
tem. On one hand, the question "How can a man his anger hold in?" could
allude to Priestley's righteous anger at the printer, who is guilty of a mis-

take; Priestley is thus the victim, the purity of his motives "blotted" by the market. On the other hand, the cause for the excess ink may lie with Priestley, the printer producing in the blurred proof-sheet an accurate representation of the dissenter's angry polemics; when they are subsumed by anger, individual words and meanings lose distinction. From this perspective, Priestley's politics are smudged or corrupted by his method.

The imagery of violence and chaos resonates with what seems to be a subtext for the entire poem, Pope's *Dunciad*, his satire on the "dulness" and maliciousness of hack writers. Consider Pope's rendition of the goddess of dulness overlooking her works:

> Here she beholds the Chaos dark and deep,
> Where nameless somethings in their causes sleep,
> 'Till genial Jacob, or a warm Third-day
> Call forth each mass, a poem or a play.
> How Hints, like spawn, scarce quick in embryo lie,
> How new-born Nonsense first is taught to cry,
> Maggots half-form'd, in rhyme exactly meet,
> And learn to crawl upon poetic feet.[10]

In Pope's vision of chaos, the literary market causes the proliferation of dullness; Martinus Scriblerus, Pope's editorial mouthpiece, tells us in his preface, "Paper also became so cheap, and printers so numerous, that a deluge of authors cover'd the land" (344). What results is reproduction run amok, with "Genial Jacob" (Jacob Tonson, a leading publisher) calling forth births before their time, producing deformities in a parody of divine procreation.[11] Similarly, in Barbauld's poem, the narrator presents an image of hideous birth and deformity:

> New books, like new-born infants, stand,
> Waiting the printer's clothing hand; —
> Others a motley ragged brood,
> Their limbs unfashioned all, and rude,
> Like Cadmus' half-formed men appear;
> One rears a helm, one lifts a spear,
> And feet were lopped and fingers torn
> Before their fellow limbs were born;
> A leg began to kick and sprawl
> Before the head was seen at all,
> Which quiet as a mushroom lay

Till crumbling hillocks gave it way;
And all, like controversial writing,
Were born with teeth and sprung up fighting.   (lines 41–54)

The reproduction of these texts involves both the author and the market, the newborns awaiting the "printer's clothing hand." Like Pope's "half-form'd maggots," these men/texts were born/printed too soon, their deformities indicative of what happens to political writing that conforms to the logic of the marketplace. The result is war without purpose or resolution, violence that breeds further violence. The narrator alludes to "Cadmus' half-formed men," an episode from Ovid's *Metamorphoses,* to flesh out this connection; Cadmus plants the teeth of a dragon, which are born "feet first, as armed men, who slay one another" (*Poems,* 248). Through the grotesque image of half-birthed bodies violently attacking one another before they can even see one another, the narrator conveys what happens when men/texts are governed, not by their "head" or reason, but by passion. Clear "sides" are lacking in such battle, as are winners and losers: all become tools of a stronger force, the marketplace that feeds off their passion, turning severed limbs into so many coins.

The inventory thus leaves the domestic scene and enters the arena of politics and economy, blurring the distinction between Priestley's professional domain and the domestic domain of the narrator.[12] Priestley's study emerges as a landscape of failed warfare. Personification renders what was implicit—the narrator's perspective on Priestley—explicit;[13] Priestley himself takes shape, through his implication in his texts, as one of Cadmus's half-formed warriors. Revealing the deformities of Priestley's writings through personification, Barbauld valorizes by contrast a form of literary production opposed to the person as target of competition and attack (Ross, "Configurations," 104–5). In using language as a weapon, Priestley achieved public notoriety and a certain amount of celebrity; his name thus became a kind of property in the marketplace, an allegorical signifier or personification of the man. In contrast, it is significant that Barbauld does not name herself in the poem, resisting the assertion of an authorial "I" except through the mediation of Priestley's property. By resisting the creation of property in her name, Barbauld signals that she does not use language as a weapon, nor as a source of celebrity or professional profit. Rather, her labor to make the implicit explicit suggests that she draws on the power of language as an ownerless medium—a shared, common currency—to make manifest the hidden interests and deformities of power. Her inventory radiates outward from furniture to suggest its embeddedness in questions of property, politics, and commerce, revealing that the interiority of the self,

like the bourgeois interior she inventories, is supported by political and eco-
nomic interests.

In this respect, Barbauld's critique of Priestley resembles her criticisms
of Coleridge, Southey, and female writers of sensibility such as Charlotte
Smith, who chose to follow the melancholic muse, and aligns her with
More, Wollstonecraft, and Austen in preferring "sense to sensibility."[14] In
general, Barbauld portrays these poets' tendencies toward isolation and
melancholy as self-indulgent, and their displays of emotion, like Priestley's
displays of anger, as excessive. The charge of self-indulgence was tied to
Barbauld's sense that in dwelling on private suffering, these poets over-
looked or ignored others' feelings and perspectives. Moreover, private suf-
fering fed the cause of celebrity in the marketplace; Barbauld implies that
these poets exploited and even marketed private emotion. Thus Barbauld
urges Coleridge (whom she met in 1797) to chase away "each spleen-fed
fog." Melancholy had "pampered" him "with most unsubstantial food," ren-
dering him indolent; she warns him to remain "on noble aims intent," to
seek "fair exertion, for bright fame sustained" (*Poems*, 132–33; lines 30, 36,
40). Fame was a noble goal only if sought "for friends, for country" (line 41).
While Barbauld shares with the poets of sensibility the delights of isolation
and nature, she stresses that she seeks out these retreats not to dwell on her
private pain, but to articulate divine presence:

> If friendless, in a vale of tears I stray,
> Where briars wound, and thorns perplex my way,
>
> . . . .
>
> In every leaf that trembles to the breeze
> I hear the voice of GOD among the trees;
> With thee in shady solitudes I walk.   (*Poems*, 5; lines 49–50, 61–63)

Barbauld transforms her exclusion from holding property, her position
on the margins of circuits of political and economic exchange, into a moral
advantage. A literary production involving slightness and anonymity signi-
fies her distance from motives of profit, property, and celebrity. Nameless-
ness connotes a form of self-representation dedicated to ideals distinct
from the marketplace, as is evident in the closing lines of "Inventory," in
which Barbauld imagines the poem's reception:

> "But what is this," I hear you cry,
> "Which saucily provokes my eye?"—
> A thing unknown, without a name,
> Born of the air and doomed to flame.   (lines 55–58)

These lines could refer to the reception of the poem as a "nameless" piece of trash to be thrown into the fireplace. Indeed, according to the logic of competition and celebrity, Barbauld's nameless poem would be "doomed to flame." Yet Barbauld's refusal to name "you" or "I" creates other possibilities. The "thing unknown, without a name" could just as easily refer to one of the political pamphlets lining the study; "namelessness" might connote, as it does in Pope's lines ("Here she beholds the Chaos dark and deep, / Where nameless somethings in their causes sleep"), not anonymous texts but texts churned out for the market, lacking distinction even when named.

In this manner Barbauld unsettles the significance of the name as a marker of property in the self. Another poem about Priestley, "To Dr. Priestley. Dec. 29, 1792," written soon after the passage of the Royal Proclamation Against Seditious Writings and Publications (May 1792) and the Birmingham riots, evidences Barbauld's attempts to redefine the value of the name. She asks of Priestley: "Burns not thy cheek indignant, when thy name, / On which delighted science lov'd to dwell, / Becomes the bandied theme of hooting crowds?" (*Poems,* 125; lines 5–7). Priestley's name, due to his outspoken criticism of the church and his immersion in political pamphlet wars, oversignifies, as a political marker of republican dissent and as a target of "the slander of a passing age." His name is reduced to common currency, his works to "nameless somethings," "doomed to flame." Yet Barbauld argues that his name is owed a "debt of fame," which she assures him will be paid, "when thy name, to freedom's join'd, / Shall meet the thanks of a regenerate land" (lines 20–21). Barbauld's poem works to change the valence of his name, to begin paying off that debt. Redefining the significance of the name, then, is connected to the goals of dissent, allied at this moment to the ideals of the French revolution, which also spurred acts of renaming—of the republic and its calendar.[15] Given the seditious writings act, Barbauld did not publish "To Dr. Priestley," but circulated it privately to Priestley's supporters; however, as she noted in a letter to her son, "some of the ministers . . . got hold of & would print (it)."[16] The poem appeared in the *Morning Chronicle* on January 8, 1793, unsigned.

Anonymity in this instance served as protection against political censorship and persecution, but this was not always Barbauld's motive in concealing her name; it is significant that she published both the *Epistle to Wilberforce* in 1791 and *Eighteen Hundred and Eleven* under her own name, even though both treated political affairs. Moreover, given Barbauld's thematization of naming in her poetry and prose, and her resistance to representing herself in her poetry, we can infer that concealment of her signature was also connected to her negotiation of literary commerce.

Name Disguise and the Rhetoric of Sincerity

Conventions of name concealment—including anonyms, pseudonyms, initials, anagrams, and numerous variations on these practices—were ubiquitous in British newspapers, periodicals, and volumes of prose and poetry during the romantic period. Conventions of name disguise accompany the emergence of the newspaper and periodical in the seventeenth century, and this tradition continues until the latter half of the nineteenth century (Hiller, "Identification," 124; Shevelow, *Print Culture,* 71–72). In many eighteenth-century periodicals, such as the *Tatler* (Isaac Bickerstaff), the *Spectator* (Mr. Spectator), the *Gentleman's Magazine* (Sylvanus Urban), and the *Lady's Magazine* (Mrs. Stanhope), the editor assumed a name and persona that was used to unify the periodical (Shevelow 71). Regular feature writers as well as correspondents to newspapers and periodicals often employed assumed names. The Nichols File of the *Gentleman's Magazine* best exemplifies how widespread this practice was: this file contains a complete record of the magazine from 1731 to 1863, with over 13,000 attributions of authorship filled in by the Nichols family; this figure does not include the enormous number of articles that remain unidentified (Kuist, *Nichols File,* vii, 18–20). Mary Hiller estimates that between 1824 and 1900, 75 percent of articles published in monthlies and quarterlies were signed with anonyms or pseudonyms (124). Southey, Shelley, Byron, Mary Robinson, Jane Austen, Anna Seward, and Coleridge all used name disguises at some point in their careers, indicating the centrality of this practice.

The practice of name concealment began to decrease in the late 1850s and early 1860s. Although the *London Review* was founded in 1809 on the principle of signed articles, it failed after four issues (Hiller 124). *Macmillan's Magazine* began to use signatures in 1859, and new periodicals established in the 1860s and early '70s explicitly defined their editorial policy around the value of the signature (Hiller 126; Mays, "Disease of Reading," 168; Shattock, *Politics,* 16). Established periodicals soon followed suit. The periodical the *Nineteenth Century,* established in 1877, printed the names of its celebrated writers on its front cover, indicating the ascendancy of the signature (Hiller 126).

With this shift from name concealment to signature, name concealment became a matter of historical interest;[17] dictionaries of anonyms, pseudonyms, and fictitious names began to appear in which scholars described this practice in its various forms, and revealed and catalogued the "true identities" of eighteenth- and nineteenth-century authors. The first of these dictionaries was published in 1868 by Olphar Hamst, Esq.

(an anagram for Ralph Thomas), *Handbook of Fictitious Names* (London, 1868); John Edward Haynes followed suit in 1882 with *Pseudonyms of Authors, Including Anonyms and Initialisms* (New York, 1882), as did Samuel Halkett and John Laing, in the 1880s, with *Dictionary of Anonymous and Pseudonymous English Literature.*[18]

The revelation of "true" authorship in these dictionaries was not a new practice, but was rather a formalization of the guesswork, gossip, and sharing of knowledge that had always accompanied uses of name disguise in the public media. Penetrating authors' disguises had become a game of sorts, and their assumed names riddles to be solved (Kuist, *Nichols File*, 15, 19; Ezell, "Reading Pseudonyms," 14); discussion of the identity of authors was a constant theme in eighteenth- and nineteenth-century correspondence (Shattock 16, Hiller 125). As it turns out, assumed names were often "open secrets" within certain circles of readers (Shattock 15, Hiller 142, Ezell 18). Authors were identified by their distinctive style or subject matter. Also, authors sometimes revealed their identity to friends, or provided clues to their coterie through their choice of name disguise (Ezell 18, 21). As Samuel Halkett stated in the preface to his dictionary, "Varying degrees of concealment can be traced, ranging from a pseudonym which offers a complete disguise to one which hides nothing at all. An author may desire to remain unknown to the general public only, and may therefore adopt a pseudonym which is transparent to his friends" (xii). For instance, while some authors completely obscured their names, using a series of asterisks and stars to mark their "signature," others simply used their initials or a variation thereof. Many authors used more than one assumed name; Richard Gough (1735–1809), who was the principal reviewer for the *Gentleman's Magazine* during the 1780s and '90s, used almost a hundred different signatures (*Nichols Files,* 10).

This brief history begs the obvious question: why were these practices of name disguise so pervasive, and why were they replaced by the explicit use of the signature in the late nineteenth century? An adequate answer would have to account for the great variety of contexts in which assumed names were used in the eighteenth and nineteenth centuries, clearly an enormous project. By way of beginning to approach this question, I turn to a repeated concern of the literature about assumed names: defenses of name concealment and defenses of uses of the signature both relied on the rhetoric of sincerity. Periodicals that defended name disguise argued that it permitted sincere expression without fear of reprisal, while critics of name disguise argued that only when authors had to append their signatures and assume public responsibility for their statements, would they write honestly and ethically (Hiller 125, Shattock 16).

Logically, name disguise and textual claims to sincerity would seem to be at odds, but in fact they are integrally connected. Judith Pascoe makes a similar argument; in comparing Mary Robinson's use of multiple pseudonyms with Wordsworth's stable authorial voice, she argues that Wordsworth no less than Robinson "struck a pose, but his was that of the sincere rural dweller" (*Romantic Theatricality,* 178, 242). Recent scholars have persuasively connected the theatricality of self-representation to authors' negotiations of their reputations in the literary marketplace;[19] conversely, we might view the rhetoric of sincerity as emerging to mediate both the author's increasing dependence on the value of their "name" in the literary marketplace and changing conditions of literary property.

Following Pope's lawsuit against Curll in 1741, the Statute of Anne was used to provide an early form of copyright protection. The name as sign of a distinct style and authorial origin marked the text as a particular kind of creation, one that now had value as property protected by law.[20] Given readerly anxieties about transparency of motive, name-concealment conventions played a vital role in the production of authorial sincerity: the assumed name was the garb that clothed the poem as a printed commodity, and helped guide the public in translating the poetic text into the figure of the "sincere" poet. Barbauld is not a theatrical poet in the manner of a Byron, Mary Robinson, or Charles Baudelaire, who assume and take off numerous disguises to expose and critique the theatricality of sincerity itself, drawing attention to the role of the reader and market in producing the values by which the poet's performance is judged. However, Barbauld was certainly aware of the theatricality or "doubleness" of language, that language could be used to disguise identity and to deceive others as much as to illuminate or expose. Barbauld lectures children on this very topic in "A Lecture on the Use of Words," stating that lying is wrong and that they must strive to use language accurately; imprecision itself is a fault, for "it hurts our sincerity" (*Legacy for Young Ladies,* 13). Like Wordsworth in his "Essays upon Epitaphs," Barbauld's textual strategy is to define and teach a morally transparent use of language, a language resistant to its own potential for theatricality or "doubleness." Her twist on the "autobiographical" poem "On a Lady's Writing" demonstrates this endeavor:

Her even lines her steady temper show;
Neat as her dress, and polish'd as her brow;
Strong as her judgment, easy as her air;
Correct though free, and regular though fair:
And these same graces o'er pen preside
That form her manners and her footsteps guide.   (*Poems,* 70)

Barbauld stresses the transparency of writing, the correspondence between a lady's moral conduct and her signature. Just as her dress and appearance convey her inner graces, so does the regular iambic pentameter and rhyme of her "even lines." The poem rests its claim to bode forth its author through its formal decorum. Rather than expressing sincerity in personal terms, Barbauld objectifies the signature, divesting it of particularity such that it comes to stand for all ladies, and perhaps for the common practice of signing a poem as "a lady." As in her "Inventory" poem, by resisting the assertion of subjectivity within the poem, Barbauld aligns herself with language itself, with the crisp, clear signature. In this act we see two meanings of "the generic" (literary type and nameless brand or product) coincide.

By blurring or obfuscating the particulars of her identity within her texts, a practice often corroborated by concealment of the name attached to the poem, Barbauld employs what we might call the "illegible signature." While Charlotte Smith sought to connect her poetic persona to her "real" suffering, which she described in the prefaces to her poems so as to garner readerly sympathy and a measure of celebrity, Barbauld claims the sincerity of the lyric voice but resists readerly efforts to read her poems for clues to her life, for details that might identify her as a recognizable personality. Although the illegible signature may seem to render Barbauld an abstract or generic "type," her self-presentation in her poetry serves to assure her readers that her goal is to cleanse language of deception and ground it in morality, to make the invisible visible. This is to say that the "illegibility" of her signature was planned; her signature was supposed to be read, or legible, in certain ways but not in others. Rather than stating in her work, "I am speaking sincerely and these experiences are real," Barbauld suggests that true sincerity must be inferred, that it is inconsistent with such proclamations.

Publishing poetry anonymously or by partially concealing her name with initials did not function simply as an erasure of self, but rather confirmed Barbauld's textual self-presentation. We can surmise that to readers Barbauld knew, or to readers familiar with Barbauld's work and style, her authorship of poems printed anonymously was an open secret. Although she participated in writerly commerce, Barbauld worked to articulate a "private" publicness, contingent on being recognized by a coterie of dissenting readers while remaining anonymous within the larger reading public. Hence name disguise served not only as a form of feminine decorum or as protection against persecution, but also as a model for a kind of "sincere" authorship opposed to the conflation of naming and property, to the culture of celebrity. Ironically, the illegible signature—by sectioning off a realm of "privacy" that the reader cannot penetrate—guarantees the sincerity (or what Barbauld refers to as the visual and moral transparency) of language.

Sincerity and Accurate Language:
The Poem as Miniature Object and Map

Thus we can conclude that the illegible signature within Barbauld's poetry is connected to how Barbauld viewed literary property, influencing how she published and circulated her work. In short, she devised strategies, both textual and material, for defining a poetic circulation distinct from, though often contained within, dominant circuits of exchange. This strategy helps to explain a central formal and thematic pattern in her poetry, related to the method she employs in "Inventory": the presentation of the poem as a small object and the poet as its implicit observer, absorbed into the act of looking. More specifically, Barbauld presents many of her poems as inscribed on or placed alongside a domestic object, toy, or piece of furniture. This body of work includes "Inscription for an Ice-House," "Inscribed on a Pair of Screens," "Lines placed over a chimney-piece," "Lines with a Wedding Present," "Lines written in a young lady's Album of different-coloured Paper," "Verses written in the leaves of an ivory Pocket-Book, presented to Master T(urner)," "Verses written on the Back of an old Visitation Copy of the Arms of Dr. Priestley's Family, with Proposals for a new Escutcheon," "Written on a Marble," "To a Lady, with some Painted Flowers," "To the Miss Websters, with Dr. Aikin's 'Wish,' which they expressed a Desire to have a Copy of," and so forth. While the verse epistle was a common poetic form, Barbauld's variation on it—the poem not simply as letter but as small object or gift—asks us to evaluate this pattern in the context of her criticisms of literary property.

Certain object poems, such as "Written on a Marble," employ the trope of inscription, while other poems were literally inscribed on or in the objects mentioned. For example, consider the production of "Verses written in the Leaves of an ivory pocket-book." William Turner writes that Barbauld visited his family, and "at the close of her visit, she presented to the writer of this paper, then a little boy between seven and eight years old, an ivory memorandum book, on the leaves of which, after she was gone, were found written the following lines" (*Poems*, 235). Similarly, several poems, such as "Lines with a Wedding Present," accompanied the gifts they name. Even poems not thematically presented as domestic objects or gifts were often treated as such. For instance, the story behind "The Mouse's Petition" is that Priestley found the poem waiting for him one morning, twisted among the wires of the cage housing a mouse he was planning to use for his experiments on gases (*Poems*, 244). One wonders whether Barbauld left "Inventory" for Priestley to find on the desk in his study.

In inscribing and circulating these poems as miniature objects, Barbauld establishes an economy of exchange based not on the commodity-for-sale, but on the gift (Rzepka, *Sacramental Commodities*, 17, 25). As Amanda Vickery argues, "Home-made gifts were usually offered by women and were seen as time, labour and affection made concrete."[21] In this manner Barbauld defines her poetic labor as the consolidation of private, moral community, exploiting the association of women's writing with feminine handicrafts to distinguish her works from those sold for profit.[22] The emblem of private community was the home, and she presents several of her object poems as inscriptions on furniture or appliances in the home. For instance, "Lines placed over a Chimney-Piece" bless the fireplace and the home's spiritual warmth: "Love and Joy, and friendly mirth, / Shall bless this roof, these walls, this hearth" (*Poems*, 98; lines 13–14). These lines are meant to be part of the chimney they celebrate and bless. In the case of the object poems she chose not to publish, Barbauld's handwriting testified that her labor was of the hand—personal and artisanal rather than public and commercial. But the logic remained the same in the case of the object poems she did print and publish: the trope of inscription on a gift evokes the labor of handwriting and the originary context of creation, resisting the status of the poem as a printed copy sold to an unnamed public. Thus Barbauld sought to transform exchange value to use value, resisting the alienation of her labor and the absorption of moral interests within economic commerce by positioning her reader as recipient of a gift.

In many of these object poems Barbauld attempts to do more than establish a mode of circulation opposed to purely economic commerce; several poems criticize the connection between representation, property, and the economy of empire. In this sense Barbauld's gifts are instructional, seeking to elicit resistance as much as affective ties. "Written on a Marble," an unpublished poem likely composed while the Barbaulds were teaching at the Palgrave School, uses the miniature object to juxtapose schoolboy scuffles and wars over empire:

> The world's something bigger,
>   But just of this figure
> And speckled with mountains and seas;
> Your heroes are overgrown schoolboys
> Who scuffle for empires and toys,
> And kick the poor ball as they please.
> Now Caesar, now Pompey, gives law;

And Pharsalia's plain,
Though heaped with the slain,
Was only a game at *taw*.   (*Poems,* 103)

Although the poem is not literally written on a marble, by using the trope of inscription Barbauld makes a visual analogy between the small poem and its object, implying that her poem as material object is akin to the marble. Thus the poem is embedded in the second analogy at work, that between a game of taw and nations fighting over empire; though bigger, the world is "just of this figure"—"figure" referring both to the marble and to the poem's figural representation of it. Barbauld's use of the "figure" of the marble serves to undercut and deflate the claims of size and power. Miniaturizing power—showing it to be motivated by schoolboy greed and competition—exposes the small, petty ambitions that underlie battles such as Pharsalia's plain. As in "Inventory," Barbauld's arrangement and juxtaposition of objects makes the invisible visible, drawing connections that would be otherwise obscured due to differences of scale and (presumed) importance.

The connection between games at taw and wars for empire is more than figural, Barbauld implies. Toys were materially connected to empire; in the eighteenth century "children had become a trade, a field of commercial enterprise for the sharp-eyed entrepreneur" (Plumb, "New World," 310). John Brewer observes that "in 1730 there were no specialized toyshops of any kind, whereas by 1789 toyshops everywhere abounded, and by 1820 the trade in toys, as in children's literature, had become very large indeed" (*Consumption,* 310). Not only did Britain's commercial growth and overseas trade influence the creation of new markets in "luxury" items such as children's toys, but the toys themselves often reflected national interests in growth and progress. For instance, popular toys often replicated, in miniature, machines such as printing presses and camera obscuras; also popular were toy soldiers and forts, and dolls' houses, toys that taught gender roles and also influenced attitudes toward the defense and value of property.

Barbauld, as an educator and writer of children's literature, actively contributed to this expanding market in children's education, welfare, and entertainment. But if children's toys often confirmed dominant values about property, Barbauld as educator sought to undo this link, to expose and denaturalize the connections between national interests and common objects. Thus, though "Written on a Marble" is on the one hand addressed to the adult reader potentially implicated in the engines of war and empire, it was more likely addressed to an impressionable audience whose conduct was Barbauld's responsibility: the boys she educated at the Palgrave school.

Similarly, in "The Baby-House," she presents the poem as a lesson given to a young girl, Agatha, about her toy's wider social and material significance. Barbauld reveals the economic system that the sale of dollhouses implicitly supports; she warns Agatha, "think not . . . you own / That toy, a Baby-House, alone" (*Poems,* 19–20; lines 177–78). Barbauld then proceeds to supply examples of the real houses these baby-houses invoke:

> The peasant faints beneath his load,
> Nor tastes the grain his hands have sowed,
> While scarce a nation's wealth avails
> To raise thy Baby-house, Versailles.
> And Baby-houses oft appear
> On British ground, of prince or peer;
> Awhile their stately heads they raise,
> The' admiring traveller stops to gaze;
> He looks again—where are they now?
> Gone to the hammer or the plough;
> Then trees, the pride of ages, fall,
> And naked stands the pictured wall;
> And treasured coins from distant lands
> Must feel the touch of sordid hands;
> And gems, of classic stores the boast,
> Fall to the cry of—Who bids most?   (lines 37–52)

In supplying this context, Barbauld implicates the dollhouse in a system of class and national interests that sustains itself at the expense of nature ("trees, the pride of ages"), peasants, and unseen peoples from "distant lands." The "admiring traveller," like the innocent child playing with her toy, is unknowingly complicit in supporting this system of class interests. In other words, by juxtaposing baby-houses with "something bigger, but just of this figure," Barbauld reveals that the idle games of children are connected to the "touch of sordid hands," the game of capital ("who bids most"). Barbauld's critique of property was certainly influenced by her gender; in her poems on the marble and dollhouse, she reveals how everyday objects, through their implication in a wider system of commercial and national interests, support conventional gender roles. Joanna Baillie, a friend and protegée of Barbauld, also explores the connections between gender roles and commerce in her two object poems ("Lines to a Teapot" and "Lines to a Parrot"), which similarly supply the histories of these objects as they move through circuits of exchange supporting empire and patriarchy

(Baillie, *Fugitive Verses*, 153–67; Henderson, "Passion and Fashion," 199). Although Barbauld's "gifts" are themselves implicated in commercial culture, contributing to the penchant for collecting toys and other items, she attempts to reveal and resist the ways in which collections consolidate and aggrandize unspoken interests.

Drawing "lines to" objects is a useful characterization of Barbauld's project; rather than simply describe objects, she maps what is implicit, the lines that radiate outward from objects to their use and meaning in commerce and politics. In a lecture to young ladies on the uses of history and geography, Barbauld clarifies the relationship between visual, spatial mapping and the representation of politics and power. Geography, she argues, is one of the "eyes of History," and thus the study of maps reveals more than meets the eye:

> Thus geography, civil geography, would be seen to grow out of history; and the mere view of the map would suggest the political state of the world at any period.
>
> It would be a pleasing speculation to see how the arbitrary divisions of kingdoms and provinces vary and become obsolete, and large towns flourish and fall again into ruins; while the great natural features, the mountains, rivers, and seas remain unchanged, by whatever names we please to call them, whatever empire incloses them within its temporary boundaries.[23]

When one joins history to geography, the lines on maps appear as "temporary boundaries" that reflect the interests of empire and the state of politics; similarly, the names of "mountains, rivers, and seas" appear as "arbitrary" designations, symbols used to signify an ownership and control of land that is fleeting. From Barbauld's perspective, the claims to possession put forth by names and lines on maps are undermined by the fact of historical change (the rise and fall of regimes), and by the permanence of the "natural features" of the earth; human history is subsumed by the frame of natural history.

Barbauld's thoughts on geography clarify her use of mapping and description in her poetry; her poetic miniatures, in supplying the history and contexts of geography (or the invisible frames supporting the visual, spatial world and its objects), seek to "unname" things, to resist the language, economy, and politics of property as practiced in late-eighteenth-century England. The miniaturist text—that which explicitly presents itself as a slight, fanciful, visually detailed description—is thus peculiarly qualified to sketch in the forces that spatialize and miniaturize it, that seek to limit its size and value. In Barbauld's hands, a map of the miniature becomes a history of the gigantic.

Juxtaposition and the Work of Translation

Barbauld's use of the trope of vision, her emphasis on accurate description, encodes a moral politics. Accuracy is the cornerstone of a miniaturist representation supposedly limited to the accumulation of minute visual detail, yet which strays from this task to reveal "circumstance" as the unspoken or hidden interests of power. Through her absorption into seeing and the objects she describes, or what I have called the "illegible signature," Barbauld turns language outward, focusing on how language mediates objects, perspective, and power. While the poet is the "seer" in these poems, sincerity functions not as evidence of the poet's autobiographical experience, nor as testament to her visionary power, but as an index of her ethical use of representation. Sincerity in Barbauld's writings refers to the use of language with attention to its power to speak for or represent others' interests, and, conversely, the power to misrepresent and exploit others' suffering.

Barbauld clarifies the ethical aspects of sincerity in the tracts she wrote in the early 1790s for appointed fasts, *Sins of Government, Sins of the Nation* (1793) and *Reasons for National Penitence* (1794).[24] The tracts define their occasion as a communal reflection on sin, but they merge religious and political conduct; as Barbauld states in *National Penitence*, "If we have committed any sins as a nation, we are called upon to confess them with sincere and unfeigned penitence. . . . We must resolve to turn from our evil conduct; and we must listen to a lesson of instruction, under the pressure of affliction. Unless we do this, the confession of our crimes will resemble the timid and superstitious devotion of savages" (v). In asking for sincere confessions, Barbauld locates individual responsibility for national political conduct at the level of responsibility for language. She articulates a political economy of representation in which everyday language use contributes to the system of representative government. Simply put, individuals express political citizenship not through the exercise of the vote but by using language sincerely, a moral practice open to all persons. Misrepresentation is thus an act of political violence, for it infringes on the political rights of others: "If you slander a good man, you are answerable for all the violence of which that slander may be the remote cause; if you raise undue prejudices against any particular class or description of citizens, and they suffer through the bad passions your misrepresentations have worked up against them, you are answerable for the injury, though you have not wielded the bludgeon or applied the firebrand" (*Sins of Government*, 409). As political citizens, individuals must take responsibility for hypocrisy regarding national political conduct: "For we can not surely exclaim with sincerity, that we are fighting to restore order and authority to a country, if treasons and rebellions have been the fruit of our intrigues, and if anarchy and dissention have formed a part of our policy. We have looked 'like the innocent flower,' but we have really been 'the serpent under it,' if we have displayed, by this perverse and inconsistent conduct, our zeal for the blessings of peaceful and regular government" (*National Penitence*, xi).

More trenchantly, in both tracts Barbauld argues that insincere representation is used to justify national economic interests, regardless of who is oppressed or killed in their pursuit. For instance, she describes the ways in which the language of religion, the "blessing of God," countenances war and imperialism: "We have calmly voted slaughter and merchandized destruction—so much blood and tears for so many rupees, or dollars, or ingots. Our wars have been wars of cool calculating interest, as free from hatred as from love of mankind" (*Sins of Government*, 401). Barbauld asks that individuals rewrite such prayers in "plain language," stripped of hypocrisy: "God of love . . . we beseech thee to assist us in the work of slaughter. Whatever mischief we do, we shall do it in thy name; we hope, therefore, thou wilt protect us in it" (403–4). What Barbauld calls for in the use of sincere representation is an act of translation: "We should, therefore, do well to translate this word war into language more intelligible to us. When we pay our army and our navy estimates, let us set down—so much for killing, so much for maiming, so much for making widows and orphans, so much for bringing famine upon a district, so much for corrupting citizens and subjects into spies and traitors, so much for ruining industrious tradesmen and making bankrupts . . . so much for letting loose the daemons of fury rapine and lust within the fold of cultivated society, and giving to the brutal ferocity of the most ferocious, its full scope and range of invention" (401). Translation involves denaturalizing a word such as "war," translating its exchange value to use value, economic profits to human costs, coins into maimed bodies. It is the process Barbauld tries to elicit from readers of her object poems when she juxtaposes a decontextualized object with its history in economic and political affairs.

Translation works not through sympathetic identification, but through the juxtaposition of scale and perspective. Barbauld was well aware of the limits of sympathetic identification; the failure of sympathy to produce political change is the occasion of *Epistle to Wilberforce*, in which Barbauld comments: "The Preacher, Poet, Senator in vain / Has rattled in her sight the Negro's Chain," for Britain "knows and she persists—Still Afric bleeds, / Uncheck'd, the human traffic still proceeds" (*Poems*, 114–18; lines 3–4, 15–16). Emotional rhetoric is powerless against the desire for profit: "All, from conflicting ranks, of power possest, / To rouse, to melt, or to inform the breast. / Where seasoned tools of avarice prevail, / A Nation's eloquence, combined, must fail" (lines 23–26). Barbauld also thematizes the limits of her own power to effect change. In "On Education," she points out these limits, arguing that "a fast, or a sermon, are prescriptions of very little efficacy" compared to the power of circumstance (*Works*, 1:320).

Rather than ask for identification with the oppressed, Barbauld employs a literature of limits, one that exposes the gaps in and barriers to sympathetic identification, and the labor required to oppose "circumstance" and achieve shifts in power. The political labor she describes is by definition difficult and painstaking: "We want principles, not to figure in a book of ethics, or to delight us with 'grand and swelling sentiments'; but principles by which we may act and by which we may suffer. Principles of benevolence, to dispose us to real sacrifices; political principles, of practical utility; principles of religion, to comfort and support us under all the trying vicissitudes we see around us. . . . Principles, such as I have been recommending, are not the work of a day" (*Sins of Government*, 411–12).

While sermons were well suited to inspiring this labor, I want to conclude by suggesting that Barbauld's miniaturist poetry was also involved in the ethical project of translation and sincere language-use, but went about its task in a different manner. Rather than preach, her poetry instructs readers by stimulating their imagination and reasoning abilities. Play and pleasure are central to Barbauld's educational method and political aims, and this helps to explain the curious mixture of lightness and gravity in her poetry (Armstrong, "Caterpillar on the Skin," 28). Barbauld in fact wrote many "puzzle" and "riddle" poems, so as to help children sharpen their skills of reason and imagination.[25] She argues that "finding out riddles is the same kind of exercise to the mind which running and leaping and wrestling in sport are to the body. They are of no use in themselves,—they are not work but play; but they prepare the body, and make it alert and active for any thing it may be called to perform in labour or war. So does the finding of riddles, if they are good especially, give quickness of thought, and a facility of turning about a problem every way, and viewing it in every possible light" (*Legacy*, 15). Her object poems are also puzzles of a sort; juxtapositions of scale ask the reader to consider spatial and societal relationships, and to interrogate their own "frame" or perspective. Barbauld asks readers to leave their shoes not to stand in those of another, as in sympathetic identification, but momentarily to take the position of the mapmaker, who looks down upon the world so as to ask how and why the map changes.

Barbauld articulates the importance and curious weight of her delicate labor at the end of "Washing Day," a poem in which she compares the labor of writing to the female work of washing:

> At intervals my mother's voice was heard,
> Urging dispatch; briskly the work went on,
> All hands employed to wash, to rinse, to wring,
> To fold, and starch, and clap, and iron, and plait.
> Then would I sit me down, and ponder much
> Why washings were. Sometimes thro' hollow bole
> Of pipe amused we blew, and sent aloft
> The floating bubbles, little dreaming then
> To see, Mongolfier, thy silken ball
> Ride buoyant thro' the clouds—so near approach
> The sports of children and the toils of men.
> Earth, air, and sky, and ocean, hath its bubbles,
> And verse is one of them—this most of all.
>
> (*Poems*, 133–35; lines 74–86)

As Marlon Ross argues, "The disparity between the child's leisure, the capacity to sit and ponder, and the women's endless hard work . . . is akin to Wordsworth's sense that the hard work of building a nation is at odds with the idle pursuit of poetry. But whereas Wordsworth attempts to recuperate poeticizing as hard work . . . Barbauld is satisfied to let the disparity stand" (*Contours*, 228). Even more pointedly, Barbauld implies that the hard work of nation building is achieved through the idle pursuit of poetry. The juxtapositions in the poem—between the child's play and the women's work, between the child's bubble and Barbauld's verse, between the verse bubble and Montgolfier's balloon—ask the reader to make connections, to "ponder" how these disparate activities are mutually implicated, just as they are asked to ponder how a toy marble is implicated in the struggle for empire. Barbauld's "labor," thematized in the poem ("then would I sit me down, and ponder much"), is to inspire this work of imagination. And it is ultimately her labor that connects the disparate activities in the poem: her verse bubble is connected to Montgolfier's balloon, the sports of children to the toils of men, in that both are the product of the flights of leisured imagination, of the power of the mind to make unexpected connections. Indeed, Elizabeth

Kraft points out that Barbauld was likely to have known the popular story of an orphan girl whose act of blowing bubbles was purported to have inspired Montgolfier's balloon.[26] Although Barbauld's verse bubble is shaped by the limits of her domestic role, she shows that this bubble allows her to venture out of the domestic domain and to participate in and shape, however invisibly (that is, through the nameless, propertyless medium of language), "the toils of men."

Language—in the form of published poems—is not propertyless, however, and the "bubble" also connotes "financial ruin, impractical plans, silly chimeras" (Kraft 36), alluding to the realities of property with which the dissenters were all too familiar. Nor could Barbauld avoid the reality of a culture of celebrity and the kinds of attacks on the poet's name and person that she decried. Southey was behind the *Quarterly* review of *Eighteen Hundred and Eleven,* a review so vicious that Barbauld did not publish again (Rodgers, *Georgian Chronicle,* 140–42). Coleridge ridiculed Barbauld in his lectures on Shakespeare in 1808, while Wordsworth wrote that Barbauld "was spoiled as a poetess by being a dissenter," though Crabb Robinson reported that Wordsworth thought her the "first of our literary women" (Rodgers 148–49). Charles Lamb damned the "cursed Barbauld crew" in a letter to Coleridge, arguing that Barbauld's children's literature had replaced poetry with science (qtd. in McGillis, "Great Writer").

Nevertheless, Barbauld attempted to transform disenfranchisement, both gendered and religious, into a virtue: the exigencies of names and property, her writing suggests, might be overcome by historical forces greater than human claims to possession. In this sense, like Montgolfier's balloon, Barbauld's verse bubble surveys the landscape from a superior vantage point, the mapmaker's perspective.[27] By exposing the lines drawn from the tiny bubble to the balloon, from washing to nation building, Barbauld not only sees the map but also sees backward and forward into history, sees that the names and boundaries distinguishing the sports of children from the toils of men are a product of circumstance that can change. As Elizabeth Bishop states in "The Map," "More delicate than the historians' are the map-makers' colors" (*CP* 3). While Wordsworth sought to ground his name and copyright in the stability and permanence of the epitaph, it is the delicacy of the mapmaker that permits Barbauld's confidence, that as a miniaturist who makes visible the vicissitudes of history, property, and empire, her bubble of breath can perhaps escape the weight of circumstance: "It is impossible to contemplate without a sentiment of reverence and enthusiasm, these venerable writings which have survived the wreck of empires; and, what is more, of languages; which have received the awful stamp of immortality, and are crowned with the applause of so many successive ages.

It is wonderful that words should live so much longer than marble temples; —words, which at first are only uttered breath; and, when afterwards enshrined and fixed in a visible form by the admirable invention of writing, committed to such frail and perishable materials: yet the light paper bark floats down the stream of time, and lives through the storms which have sunk so many stronger built vessels" ("On the Classics," in *Legacy*, 31).

Chapter 6
Elizabeth Bishop

A Manifesto of the Miniature

In March 1967 Elizabeth Bishop wrote a "Gallery Note" for her friend and former poetry student, the painter Wesley Wehr.[1] In treating Mr. Wehr's miniature paintings, the "Gallery Note" proclaims the value of the miniature more generally: "It is a great relief to see a *small* work of art these days. The Chinese unrolled their precious scroll-paintings to show their friends, bit by bit; the Persians passed their miniatures about from hand to hand; many of Klee's or Bissier's paintings are hand-size. Why shouldn't we, so generally addicted to the gigantic, at last have some small works of art, some *short* poems, *short* pieces of music (Mr. Wehr was originally a composer and I think I detect the influence of Webern on his painting), some intimate, low-voiced, and delicate things in our mostly huge and roaring, glaring world? But in spite of their size, no one could say that these pictures are 'small-scale.'" Like Wesley Wehr, Bishop painted miniature watercolors, as small as three inches square but most commonly between five and ten inches, small enough to be passed "from hand to hand" (see Bishop, *Exchanging Hats*). Bishop did not consider herself a professional painter, however, making no effort to exhibit or sell her work. Rather, her paintings served a private, social function; she gave many to friends as gifts for their homes, often including their name and the occasion on the painting itself. Like Barbauld's inscription poems, Bishop's miniature paintings ideally circulated as gifts rather than commodities, consolidating affective ties rather than participating in economic commerce.

Titling the essay "Note" implies that it is merely a brief observation, ancillary to Wehr's paintings; however, like Wehr's miniatures, the note is small but not "small-scale." In that the note foregrounds its diminutive status and aims, and unpublished, only reached an intimate audience, we might read it as a statement of Bishop's poetics, one that opposes the "huge and roaring" statement. Bishop's "Note" indicates values central to her poetry as well as her painting, a fact that "Poem," her oft-discussed ars poetica, makes clear. "Poem" takes as its subject a "little painting," "about the size of an old-style dollar bill," a painting that "has never earned any money in its life" but is "useless and free." The painting is "handed along collaterally" from generation to generation in Bishop's family, a "minor family relic."[2] The little painting cannot supplant the dollar bill as the dominant unit of exchange and value, nor can the familial economy erase the reality of a national economy, but by requiring a shift in scale to that of the hand, both painting and "Poem" invite a shift in—and reflection on—perspective.

The hand—signifying artisanal techniques and the local, intimate circulation of art—is central to Bishop's miniaturist practice. She weaves the image of the hand throughout "Poem" and "Gallery Note," emphasizing that miniatures can be held in the hand; the Chinese, she notes, unrolled their paintings to show their friends, and the Persians "passed their miniatures about from hand to hand." Her preferred method of writing was by hand, as her drafts and notebooks filled with her tiny crabbed handwriting attest. Susan Stewart observes, "Whereas industrial labor is marked by the prevalence of repetition over skill and part over whole, the miniature object represents an antithetical mode of production: production by the hand, a production that is unique and authentic" (*On Longing*, 68). Bishop would confront this ideal under pressure, for in the age of mechanical production the miniature object also represents the mass-produced commodity, the scaled-down version of the museum original available for purchase in the gift shop. In an age of gigantism that conflates size and quantity with quality, Bishop used a miniaturist art to make room for the labor of the hand, and for circulation by the hand.

The hand signifies a social, collaborative understanding of the value of poetry: like Barbauld, Bishop resists viewing the poem as a form of private property that upholds the market value of the author's name. The "Gallery Note," like Barbauld's "Inventory," questions the relationship between naming and property through mapping and description. Wehr is not a transparent stand-in for Bishop, for she carefully describes his particular paintings and work habits; however, Bishop's subjective predilections and values emerge through her perceptions of his objects. Her method is one of visual encounter that, given the demands of the miniature object, immediately becomes a reflection on perspective and its relation to subjectivity:

I have seen Mr. Wehr open his battered brief brief-case (with the broken zipper) at a table in a crowded, steamy coffee-shop, and deal out his latest paintings, carefully encased in plastic until they are framed, like a set of magic playing cards. The people at his table would fall silent and stare at these small, beautiful pictures, far off into space and coolness: the coldness of the Pacific Northwest in the winter, its different coldness in the summer. So much space, so much air, such distances and lonelinesses, on those flat little cards. One could almost make out the moon behind the clouds, but not quite; the snow had worn off the low hills, almost showing last year's withered grasses; the white line of surf was visible but quiet, almost a mile away. Then Mr. Wehr would whisk all that space, silence, peace and privacy back into his brief-case again. He once remarked that he would like to be able to carry a whole exhibition in his pockets.

As Mr. Wehr unfolds his tiny paintings, he pulls the observers from the crowded, noisy coffee shop into a vast, silent, lonely landscape. Bishop registers her surprise at this effect when she states, "So much space, so much air, such distances and lonelinesses, on those flat little cards." While the size and flatness of the cards would seem to oppose a sense of space and vastness, Bishop reveals that in fact the dimensions of the miniature enable the observer to experience this change in perspective. The miniature asks the viewer to enter its world, to adjust her sense of scale to its own. To do so, she must imaginatively reduce her body as a point of reference in the landscape, and in this way space expands before her eyes; thus Bishop describes the white line of surf in Wehr's painting as visible "almost a mile away."

But the capacity of Wehr's miniatures to convey the vastness of the external world stems not simply from their miniaturization of scale but from Wehr's handling of nature: "Mr. Wehr works at night, I was told, while a cat rolls crayons about on the floor. But the observation of nature is always perfectly accurate; the beaches, the moonlight nights, look exactly like this. Some pictures may remind one of agates, the form called, I think, 'fortification agate.' Mr. Wehr is also a collector of agates, of all kinds of stones, pebbles, semi-precious jewels, fossilized clams with opals adhering to them, bits of amber, shells, examples of hand-writing, illegible signatures—all those things that are small but occasionally capable of overwhelming with a chilling sensation of time and space." Wehr's method is one of visual accuracy, verified by Bishop: "The beaches, the moonlight nights, look exactly like this." So accurate are Wehr's renditions of the landscape that his paintings even resemble tiny fragments of the earth's shell, agates. Bishop comments that the various natural objects Wehr collects share the capacity to overwhelm the viewer "with a chilling sensation of time and space" despite their small size, a sensation identical to that elicited by his paintings.

This language of the natural world overwhelming the viewer alludes to the experience of the sublime. While readers of Wordsworth are more likely to associate the sublime with an experience of vastness rather than minuteness, Edmund Burke in fact argued that "as the great extreme of dimension is sublime, so the last extreme of littleness is in some measure sublime likewise"; in the same manner that we are overwhelmed by vastness, we "become amazed and confounded at the wonders of minuteness" (*Philosophical Enquiry*, 66–67). For Bishop the sublimity of nature—its capacity to overwhelm the boundaries of the self—is most powerful not when the natural object is vast but when it is small, when it appears that the observer can control or possess the natural object, hold it in her hand. This belief in the human ability to possess nature—through collection and through language—is precisely what the poetic miniature refutes. Bishop can hold Wehr's miniatures in her hand, just as she can hold agates, and yet these bits of the world, because of their scale and fragility, refer to the power and vastness of space and time distinct from any human commitments. Suddenly, rather than holding an agate, a piece of the world that has been named and quantified, Bishop is unnamed by it, experiencing herself as a minuscule object in an unpeopled world. The miniature estranges the observer from that which she thinks she possesses, permitting the world its strangeness, rendering human history but one facet of natural history.

Bishop as the writerly persona in the "Gallery Note" comes into focus solely as an accurate observer of Wehr's tiny art and artifacts ("I have seen . . ."), solely through this process of miniaturization, of being reduced and dispossessed in relation to the "vast and ancient world." Like Barbauld in Priestley's study, Bishop does not name herself, resisting the assertion of subjectivity except through her mediation of Wehr's collection. Bishop erases or obscures information, coded as private, by which one might place and type, motivate and intentionalize, the author. In this way her "signature" in the "Gallery Note," like the illegible signatures in Wehr's collection, resists a language of possession, the creation of property in the name. The interest of the signature for Wehr is precisely its illegibility, and herein lies the connection between handwriting and the other bits of the world he collects; like the opals adhering to the fossilized clamshells, the pattern of the illegible signature testifies to the historical exigencies of a particular life, exigencies at once evident and mysterious. In her refusal to distinguish between the types of objects in Wehr's collection, Bishop implies that illegible signatures are fossils, traces of life no different from "bits of amber."

Similarly, in her own use of the illegible signature, Bishop presents the "Gallery Note" as part of the odd collection of minute things that constitute a world too infinite to be counted or collected. Like Bishop's "Sandpiper," the miniaturist is a "student of Blake," but rather than see the world contained in a grain of sand, she sees "the millions of grains are black, white, tan, and gray, / mixed with quartz grains, rose and amethyst" (*CP*, 131).

Wehr's and Bishop's miniaturist aesthetic is one of collection, but not collection in the sense of the possession and categorization of the object world as in the museum. As Bishop points out, Wehr would ideally like to carry an exhibition in his pockets, the resting place of the hand. The image of the pocket resonates with the final lines of O'Hara's "A Step Away from Them": "A glass of papaya juice / and back to work. My heart is in my / pocket, it is Poems by Pierre Reverdy." In desiring to carry an exhibition inside his pockets, Wehr, like O'Hara, presents alternatives to the institutional contexts of art, choosing to circulate and create meaning locally, in a "pocket" carved from the bustling public world. Wehr has "framed" his paintings not in glass but in plastic, "like a set of magic playing cards." The "magic" his miniature cards inspire is the work of juxtaposition that Bishop performs in the "Gallery Note": the juxtaposition of the miniature and the vast, self and universe, possession and dispossession. Bishop's description of this dialectic enacts what she seeks to elicit from the reader in her poems: a challenge to the "huge and roaring, glaring world," a society "addicted to the gigantic" and guided by the acquisitive impulse, the desire to expand and conquer. Indeed, the display of Wehr's cards disrupts the noisy commerce of the coffee shop; the viewers "fall silent," the crowd and noise transformed into "space, silence, peace, and privacy." While this journey as Bishop describes it is a solitary one, its function is social. Circulation of the "flat little cards"—and of Bishop's flat little poems—ideally transforms them from commodities, objects to be possessed or consumed, to experiences that spur reflection on self, scale, and possession.

Bishop and Confessional Poetry: Sincerity and the Poet's Ethical Role

Bishop's poetic persona was shaped by her critique of the poetry of sincerity as practiced by many of her "confessional" contemporaries. Given the standard view that postwar American confessional lyric involves a first-person narrator, revelation of private or painful subject matter, and use of free verse that originates in the authority of lived experience rather than in adherence to lyric convention, scholars have not usually deemed Bishop a confessional poet. Not only did Bishop proclaim her dislike of the confessional style, but her "reticence," or reluctance to address "private" subject matter, combined with her use of traditional metrical forms, has influenced this view. Bishop scholars tend to follow Bishop's resistance to confession, and often discuss her work in isolation, or in relation to modernists such as Moore and Stevens.[3] Yet as Thomas Travisano has argued, Bishop's use of sincerity shares much with the postwar poets usually labeled confessional; in fact, Robert Lowell cited Bishop as the key influence upon the confessional style he adopted in *Life Studies* (1959), deemed the seminal work of the confessional school (Travisano, *Midcentury Quartet*, 36–39; Lowell, *Collected Prose*, 227). An emphasis on the rhetoric of sincerity allows us to chart Bishop's engagements with the conventions of the romantic lyric, beyond distinctions of school or group affiliation.

Bishop's criticisms of confession were shaped by her experience of gendered limits in the production and reception of poetry. Like Barbauld, Bishop faced the expectation that a feminine poetry was a miniaturist poetry, a poetry of visual detail addressing fanciful, domestic, minor subjects. And her poetry, particularly early in her career, was often received in this manner. For instance, in his 1947 review of her first book, *North and South*, Lowell approached her work in terms of her gender, stating that outside of Marianne Moore, Bishop's poems "Roosters" and "The Fish" were "the best poems . . . written by a woman in this century."[4] He observed that "on the surface, her poems are observations—surpassingly accurate, witty, and well arranged, but nothing more": rather than exploring the depths she plumbs through surfaces, his review emphasizes the quirky femininity of her surface presentation. More specifically, Lowell connected Bishop's gender to fancy and the miniature; he praises the "splendor and minuteness of her descriptions," and states of Moore and Bishop that "both poets use an elaborate descriptive technique, love exotic objects, are moral, genteel, witty, and withdrawn." Bishop thanked Lowell for the review, but added that "it seems to me you spoke out my worst fears as well as some of my ambitions."[5] Bishop's fear of being dismissed rather than valued as a miniaturist recurred throughout her career; in 1951 she wrote Lowell that "on reading over what I've got on hand I find I'm really a minor female Wordsworth," and similarly, from Brazil in 1960, she wrote that "I worry a great deal about what to do with all this accumulation of exotic or picturesque or charming detail, and I don't want to become a poet who can only write about South America."[6] At various points in her career, her sense of herself as a miniaturist prompted her to diminish the value of her work, as if anticipating the public's criticisms; for instance, when she was awarded the Pulitzer Prize in 1956, she wrote to Lowell, "It should have gone to Randall, for some of his war poems."[7] Connected to Bishop's anxiety that she was perceived as writing "frivolous" poetry was her concern that she did not produce poetry quickly enough, that the "slightness" of her material output implied a correspondent slightness of poetic worth. Her fear that she wrote too slowly was a recurrent concern throughout her life, an anxiety often aggravated by her publishers and fellow poets.[8]

Although she called herself a "minor female Wordsworth," Bishop expressed ambivalence about this role. On the one hand, she sought to oppose the assumption that a miniaturist poetry is of lesser poetic value, an assumption connected to its historical status as a feminine, sentimental poetry. She resented being labeled a woman poet, because of the way in which this label was used to diminish her work. For instance, she stated in an interview with George Starbuck, "Most of my writing life I've been lucky about reviews. But at the very end they often say 'The best poetry by a woman in this decade, or year, or month.' Well, what's that worth? You know?" Throughout her career Bishop opposed any separation of art by gender, refusing to include her work in women's anthologies, a decision she said "came from feminist principles, perhaps stronger than I was aware of."[9] From this perspective, Bishop's claim to be a "minor female Wordsworth" challenges the assumptions that undergird the reception of Wordsworth's (major, male) poetry. On the other hand, her sense that a more conventionally public poetry—a poetry such as Jarrell's that addresses war—should have received the Pulitzer Prize undercuts her claim that the miniature is anything but "small-scale," seeming to confirm the distinction of poetic persona, subject matter, and value along gendered lines.

Bishop suggested that her own miniaturist preoccupations stem from the historical confinement of women to the domestic sphere. In a 1965 letter to Ilse Barker, Bishop complained that men, with the exception of artists, do not observe the world around them; she added: "They're always having ideas & theories, and not noticing the detail at hand. . . . I have a small theory of my own about this—that women have been confined, mostly—and in confinement details count.—They have to see the baby's ear; sewing makes you look closely.—They've had to do so much appeasing they do feel moods quickly, etc."[10] While Bishop recognizes that attention to detail may have originated in women's domestic role, she does not use the miniature to uphold this role; in fact, she deplored what she felt to be the translation of social confinement in the domestic sphere into a correspondent confinement of women's poetry, commenting, "Women's experiences are much more limited, but that does not really matter—there is Emily Dickinson, as one always says."[11] In her unpublished "Notes for Poetry Reviews," written in July 1970, Bishop considered this topic at length, exploring the confluence of gender and subject matter in the poetry of Denise Levertov and Mona Van Duyn.[12] Van Duyn's poetry prompted her to write, "I am sick of 'domesticity'—men don't constantly write about shaving, having to go to work, whatever it is men do all day long—they go out and take walks, mostly, in their poems, and I wish women would, too," a thought she explored at greater length in a later draft: "Men seem to write poems taking walks. . . . A wild generalisation, but English male poets take walks in the country, in the daytime, and Americans take walks in the cities, at night. Both nationalities write poems talking in bars. Women, unfortunately, seem to stay at home a lot, to write theirs. There is no reason why the home, house, apartment, or furnished room, can't produce good poems, but almost all women poets seem to fall occasionally into the 'Order is a lovely thing' Anna-Hemspotad (*sic*)-Branch category, and one wishes they wouldn't. Sylvia Plath avoided this by when (*sic*) she wrote about babies, ovens, etc.—but sometimes one extreme is almost as bad as the other." Bishop objects to women who comply with expectations of feminine decorum, the "order is a lovely thing" persona, or what she calls elsewhere in the draft the "Happy Housewife tone." She makes a similar criticism of Anne Sexton and other women writers whom she feels attempt to prove their authority by signaling their social class.[13] But she doesn't entirely approve of Plath's solution, which is to expose the costs of conventional feminine roles. The reference to the poet who walks anywhere he desires is not fortuitous—the walk connotes the romantic tradition, and it is the idealized freedom of the romantic poet that Bishop both desires and critiques as a "minor female Wordsworth."[14]

So why not simply write war poems, or poems about talking in bars or walking through the city? Why choose to write miniaturist poetry, work that risked and suffered diminishment in conventionally gendered ways? Bishop certainly felt the pressure of norms of feminine conduct, both in terms of how her work was received and in terms of the social behavior expected of a woman of her era, education, and class.[15] As a lesbian at a time of particular intolerance, Bishop, like Frank O'Hara, made no secret of her sexuality to her circle, but did not disclose it to the general public. The history of what works Bishop published attests to the influence of social censorship: several pieces of her unpublished prose and poetry explore themes of erotic, homosexual love more explicitly than her published works.[16] Does the miniature then become a trope not only for the limits of feminine conduct, but for the closet?

While such moral pressures certainly influenced Bishop and caused her anxiety, it was more than simply social decorum or closeted fear that kept her from addressing sexuality and other "taboo" subjects in the manner of other poets of her generation, such as Sexton.[17] In her interviews, writings on her craft, and particularly in her correspondence with Robert Lowell, Bishop reveals that her use of the "illegible signature" served a critical purpose connected to her sense of the professional poet's ethical responsibilities. Bishop's correspondence with Lowell, which began in 1947 and continued until Lowell's death in 1977, provides a crucial window onto both poets' understandings of their professional role. Sharing and discussing one another's poetry in its various stages, each poet struggled to articulate what was most distinctive about each other and in turn about themselves.[18] While the correspondence records a close and nurturing friendship, mixed with their words of praise and friendship are words of criticism and self-distinction. Tellingly, it was Lowell's version of confession in *Life Studies* (1959) that brought both Bishop's anxieties and her convictions about public self-presentation to the surface.

After admiring Lowell's burst of productivity on the *Life Studies* poems and commenting favorably on his initial draft of "Skunk Hour," Bishop laments her own lack of productivity, stating that she has resumed work on a "light" poem; she adds, "Oh heavens, when does one begin to write the real poems? I certainly feel as if I never had. But of course I don't feel that way about yours—they all seem real as real—and getting more so."[19] Bishop responds to Lowell's focus on his family and personal history in *Life Studies,* signifying through the "real" his treatment of the "private." Yet in her use of the adjective "real" lies an implicit criticism of Lowell. She writes, in a continuation of the same letter: "And here I must confess . . . that I am green with envy of your kind of assurance. I feel that I could write in as much detail about my Uncle Artie, say—but what would be the significance? Nothing at all. Whereas all you have to do is put down the names! And the fact that it seems significant, illustrative, American, etc., gives you, I think, the confidence you display about tackling any idea or theme, seriously, in both writing and conversation. . . . It is hell to realize one has wasted half one's talent through timidity that probably could have been overcome if anyone in one's family had had a few grains of sense or education."[20] Bishop connects the significance of the "real" in Lowell's work to the accidents of birth and to the questionable fact that the public would consider such autobiographical detail interesting given his famous family name. On the other hand, Bishop suggests that she is restricted from such subject matter because of the insignificance of her own personal history, the likelihood that her "confessions" would be deemed trivial. Bishop's claim to "timidity" is disingenuous; she slyly suggests that Lowell's work gains public value not solely on its own merits but through the caprices of status, celebrity, and public curiosity. While we should not diminish the restraints that Bishop faced in writing a revelatory poetry, Bishop subtly valorizes her inability (lack of desire) to write "real" poems in Lowell's confessional style, which profit from the public recognition of his name. Both the slightness of her verse and production, and her concern with subjects that do not overtly dramatize the self, connote neither a lack of ability nor laziness, but the struggle that propels her work, an ethical struggle that she suggests is lacking in the work of Lowell and other confessional poets such as Anne Sexton.

In defining her work in opposition to Lowell's "real" poems, Bishop questioned and openly criticized his form of self-presentation, in particular the poet's moral role as a public figure. If the poet was to reveal private details of experience in verse, how was he to mediate this experience to a wider public? Could he dramatize, even fictionalize, personal events and experiences?[21] Lowell's own proclivities and those of other postwar poets such as Plath were toward depicting the experience of suffering, often in the context of the family, to suggest the cost of commercial and national practices on the individual.[22] While her own life was filled with suffering and loss, Bishop felt that the poet needed to do more than dramatize such experience. She wrote to Lowell in 1948: "Sometimes I wish I could have a more sensible conversation about this suffering business, anyway. I imagine we actually agree fairly well. It is just that I think it is so inevitable there's no use talking about it, and that in itself it has no value."[23] More to the point, she felt that it was the poet's responsibility not to exploit suffering, to use language with an awareness of its power to inflict as well as to expose pain.

Bishop's differences from Lowell on the subject of sincerity came to a head in 1972, when she read his manuscript of *The Dolphin*. This collection, which chronicles Lowell's affair with Lady Caroline Blackwood, contains letters from his wife Elizabeth Hardwick that he had modified.[24] Bishop called Lowell's decision to use Hardwick's letters "cruel": she wrote, "One can use one's life as material—one does, anyway—but these letters—aren't you violating a trust? IF you were given permission—IF you hadn't changed them. . . . But art just isn't worth that much."[25] Bishop felt that Lowell had violated not only his wife's trust but the trust of his public, stating, "The letters, as you have used them, present fearful problems: what's true, what isn't; how one can bear to witness such suffering and yet not know how much of it one needn't suffer with, how much has been 'made up,' and so on."[26]

Like Barbauld, Bishop connected accurate description to the ethical use of representation. Lowell's mixture of fact and fiction signified to her the exploitation of others' suffering, the misuse of his public role. On this matter she quoted Thomas Hardy, who in a 1911 letter discussed the publication of "details of a lately deceased man's life under the guise of a novel, with assurances of truth scattered in the newspapers."[27] Hardy argued, "What should certainly be protested against, in cases where there is no authorization, is the mixing of fact and fiction in unknown proportions. Infinite mischief would lie in that. If any statements in the dress of fiction are covertly hinted to be fact, all must be fact, and nothing else but fact, for obvious reasons. The power of getting lies believed about people through that channel after they are dead, by stirring in a few truths, is a horror to contemplate." Hardy, and Bishop in turn, sound a familiar concern: the sanctity and privacy of the dead, as ensured by the manner in which their names and memories are commemorated. Using fiction under the guise of fact—or blending them "in unknown proportions"—risks a reading of fictional or dramatic elements as the unblemished truth. In the same letter, Bishop wrote, "I deplore the confessional—however, when you wrote *Life Studies* perhaps it was a necessary movement, and it helped make poetry more real, fresh, and immediate. But now—ye gods—anything goes, and I am so sick of poems about the students' mothers & fathers and sex lives and so on. All that can be done—but at the same time one surely should have a feeling that one can trust the writer—not to distort, tell lies, etc."[28] If the poet decides to use a biographically grounded voice, Bishop argues, he establishes a contract of factual accuracy with the reader, a moral contract he must uphold; readers, expecting sincerity, will "read sincerely," overlooking the role of artifice, theatricality, or fiction. The "horror" Hardy alludes to is not only the slander of the dead but what this act reveals about the community of the living, a concern that plagued Wordsworth and Ted Hughes. While Hardwick had not died, her separation from Lowell rendered her vulnerable to gossip and curiosity; Bishop emphasized that Lowell would cause Hardwick needless suffering both by exposing and by changing her letters.

Bishop connects their differences regarding the need for accuracy to their handling of suffering, specifically to Lowell's exploitation of Hardwick's name. What in part rankled Bishop about Lowell's use of Hardwick's experiences for his own purposes was the permissiveness of his actions. Bishop had once written to Lowell: "I feel we must beware of the easiness of the catastrophe—the catastrophic way out of every poem."[29] "Easiness" connotes a lack of reflection about the values that enable as well as impinge upon one's authority as a poet—Bishop implied in her letters about *The Dolphin* that Lowell had neglected to consider the contours of his power, emphasizing his own self-definition at the expense of other experiences of suffering. In particular, she responded to his neglect of the gendered dimensions of his authority, a neglect she had herself experienced when Lowell used her writing as source material for his own poetry.[30]

This difference in approach to the use of autobiographical material was reflected in Bishop's and Lowell's divergent approaches to the business of poetry: different styles of production and self-marketing assumed great importance in the context of the debate over sincerity and autobiography. While Bishop published five volumes of poetry in her lifetime, Lowell published prolifically. Though at times Bishop appears intimidated that Lowell's prolific production is what is required of a successful poet, she is also critical of the values prompting such production, values that she aligns with the romanticism of the confessional poets.[31] Bishop specifically criticized the belief that writing poetry amounts to a spontaneous outpouring of feeling; spontaneity from her perspective served as an excuse for self-indulgence. Her statement that the poet must beware of the "easiness of the catastrophe" alludes to an easiness or rapidity of production that Bishop connected to the self-promotional emphasis on suffering in confessional poetry. In a 1979 letter Bishop commented that most of her students over the years seemed "to think that poetry—to read or to write—is a snap—one just has to feel—and not for very long, either," and Wehr recalls her stating that her students "should come to Brazil and see for themselves what real suffering is like" (320).[32] In the same letter, she directed this criticism at Lowell. Bishop depicts her own writing process as anything but "spontaneous," commenting that she doesn't have "sudden fits of inspiration to write poems"; rather, she observed, "once or twice most of a poem has come to me all at once, but usually I write very, very slowly" (Wehr 324). Bishop usually deemed a poem "finished" only after many drafts and often many years, and thus chose not to publish the bulk of her poetry.[33] In this sense Bishop, like Pound and the objectivists, located sincerity in techniques of making the poem: the precision and accuracy of a poem's details reflected the poet's honest craftsmanship, a craftsmanship that for Bishop articulated the poet's ethical stance.[34]

Lowell defined his own style of producing poetry against Bishop's: if she emphasized revision and the perfection of technique, Lowell, beginning with *Life Studies,* associated these habits with overprofessionalism (*Interviews,* 76–77). Instead, he emphasized an understanding of poetry as a record of a "life-in-progress," locating meaning less in the individual poem than in the volume. When Bishop's *Collected Poems* was about to be published, Lowell commented that he too planned to bring out a collected works, but noted a problem: "The books somehow seem units, hard to cut, yet full of dross. I'm afraid the time is passed, when I can do anything to the point by revision. It's not chipping off this and that, but a need for a new breath, some fountain of youth they could be boiled in, to emerge young and less blemished."[35] Bishop's drive for perfection becomes a source of backhanded praise, with Lowell using his prolific writing as a sign of his greater worth. In a 1963 letter Lowell suggests that Bishop's "slow pace must be the one that wins the race," but adds, "Still I brood about all those rich unfinished fragments, such a fortune in the bank,"[36] an image immortalized in his sonnet:

> . . . Do
> you still hang words in air, ten years imperfect,
> joke-letters, glued to cardboard posters, with gaps
> and empties for the unimagined phrase,
> unerring Muse who scorns a less casual friendship?
>
> (Lowell, *Collected Poems*, 595)

He continues to brood about the fragments in a 1967 letter, urging, "On, Dear, with those painful, very large unfinished poems!" He then adds: "I'm at the end of something," and proceeds to describe a writing frenzy that resulted in "just about a book": "Day after day, I wrote, sometimes too absorbed to even stop for lunch. . . . I look back on the last months with disgust and gratitude. Disgust because they seem so monstrous, gratitude, because I have lived through the unintelligible, have written against collapse and come out more or less healed. Oh dear, have you ever felt like a man in an unreal book?"[37] Feeling "like a man" is precisely what eludes Bishop—as well as, Lowell implies, writing like a man. Certainly Bishop was influenced by the gendered subtext to discussions of production; she commented to George Starbuck in a 1977 interview, "I know I wish I had written a great deal more. Sometimes I think if I had been born a man I probably would have written more. Dared more, or been able to spend more time at it. I've wasted a great deal of time" ("Conversation," 329).

Lowell's speed and quantity of production signified to Bishop differences in the scale of their investment in the business of poetry. In the postwar era, with the rise of institutional patronage and the increasing professionalization of poetry, Bishop felt that poetry had succumbed to a logic of gigantism that was both representational and economic. As she wrote Randall Jarrell in April 1950, "I am so sick of Poetry as Big Business I don't know what to do. What on earth is the happy medium—readers, certainly, but this recording & reading & anthologizing is getting me" (*OA*, 201–2). Bishop's use of the term "Big Business" was partially ironic, given the small income generated by sales of poetry, but it also alludes to the "huge and roaring, glaring world" in its emphasis on competition, rapid production, and self-promotion, the acquisitive values that she associated with confessional poetry and sought to counter through her use of the miniature.

Bishop's frustration stemmed in part from her frequent dependence on institutional patronage, most notably in her service as the Poetry Consultant to the Library of Congress in 1949–50; although she increasingly came to depend on teaching and poetry readings, she actively disliked these professional duties.[38] In contrast to Lowell, Bishop avoided New York in part because it was the center of the American literary and publishing worlds, and chose to live much of her life as far as possible from its influence, first in Key West and later in Brazil.[39] She wrote her friends Kit and Ilse Barker that one of the reasons she was happy to leave New York "for good" was the way in which people tied to "sell" or "push" themselves: "Everybody is so intent on using everybody else that there is no room or time for friendship any more."[40] Where Lowell seemed to thrive on publicity, Bishop often found it painful. Thus when *Time* magazine in 1962 ranked Bishop and Lowell as among the best American postwar poets (placing Lowell above Bishop), Lowell commented that it was "vulgar and often meaningless" but added, "Still in their ugly way, they did their best by us, putting us at the top of our little decadent post-war empyrean. It's funny being a poet, working in the medium that can't and shouldn't have much public. You find you want a little publicity as a by-product."[41] Bishop—with a touch of irony—conceded, "It's too bad all the poets mentioned don't have books out right now because I suppose they might sell a few hundred more."[42]

Despite her recognition of the need for publicity, and for the income generated from writing, Bishop, in contrast to Plath and Sexton, disapproved of writing with the aim of profit. In part she feared the perception that writing for money would indicate that her work was of lesser quality. She once asked Arthur Mizener to omit from his review of *North and South* a quote from her poem "Large Bad Picture": "It would be hard to say what brought them there, / commerce or contemplation" (*CP*, 12). She stated, "I am very much afraid that gives the impression that I may write for 'commercial reasons'—in which case I am a decided failure."[43] Bishop negotiated the commercial pressures of writing by emphasizing poetic labor as a form of moral labor; she remarked in "Efforts of Affection," her memoir of Marianne Moore, that Moore inspired her "to be good, to work harder, not to worry about what other people thought, never to try to publish anything until I thought I'd done my best with it, no matter how many years it took—or never to publish at all."[44] Bishop criticized Moore's moral didacticism, and was certainly more skeptical than her mentor, but embedded in a miniaturist poetics is an ethics, based on the labor involved in acts of representation, versus the easiness of expressing and marketing one's particular suffering. While she worried about the slightness of her poetic corpus due to the conflation of the "great" with the prolific and the public, Bishop also valorized the work and struggle involved in moving outward from "merely private" suffering to a geography of conflicting interests, a labor to which her underproduction—as well as her numerous drafts and her "unfinished fragments"—attests.

Juxtaposition and the Labor of Translation

Bishop's poem "The Map" provides a useful guide to her use of the miniature, in that it takes as its subject a miniaturized representation of the earth's surface. Like Barbauld's lessons on geography and history, "The Map" considers the relationship between visual, spatial mapping and the vagaries of power and politics:

> Land lies in water; it is shadowed green.
> Shadows, or are they shallows, at its edges
> showing the line of long sea-weeded ledges
> where weeds hang to the simple blue from green.
> Or does the land lean down to lift the sea from under,
> drawing it unperturbed around itself?
> Along the fine tan sandy shelf
> is the land tugging at the sea from under?   (*CP*, 3)

Throughout the poem, she questions and unsettles spatial relationships and assumptions about perspective; does land lie in water, or does it lean down to lift the sea from under? Is the green edge the shadow projected by the land, or does it represent the shallows of the sea? Later she asks, "Are they assigned, or can the countries pick their colors? / —What suits the character or the native waters best." Just as Barbauld suggests that it would be a "pleasing speculation to see how the arbitrary divisions of kingdoms and provinces vary and become obsolete," Bishop's quiet questions unsettle the relation between the map's symbols—names, colors, directions, and territorial boundaries—and assumptions about power and property. She concludes, "Topography displays no favorites; North's as near as West. / More delicate than the historians' are the map-makers' colors." Geography, Barbauld argues, is one of the eyes of history; through her poetic "map," Bishop like Barbauld suggests that representations on a map are determined by history as viewed by its victors. In her resistance to the colors of "the historians," Bishop delicately shades in an alternative history, one in which "North's as near as West."

Yet Bishop's sense of what she could accomplish as a professional poet was qualified by the limits of a miniaturist perspective, an ambivalence at the center of her poem "12 O'Clock News." Like Barbauld's poetic inventory of Dr. Priestley's study, "12 O'Clock News" considers the scene of poetic production—the writer's desk—in miniaturist fashion, and the subtext of Bishop's poem is also writing as failed warfare. Brett Millier notes that Bishop had worked with the ideas and images that would become "12 O'Clock News" since her student days at Vassar; in 1950, while at Yaddo, she completed a draft of the poem titled "Little Exercise," and she completed a substantially different version of the poem, what would become "12 O'Clock News," in the fall of 1972 (Millier, *Life*, 121, 474). Not only did the concerns of this poem preoccupy her throughout much of her career, but the poem in each of its drafts addresses her anxieties about a miniaturist writing. Thus, it's telling that she took up the poem while at Yaddo. In a retreat designed for the production of work, where she instead found herself struggling and anxious, the difficulty of writing and more generally the profession of poetry weighed heavily upon her (Millier 217–18). Her desk embodied this struggle; she would write James Merrill in 1979, "When I think about it, it seems to me I've rarely written anything of any value at the desk or in the room where I was supposed to be doing it—it's always in someone else's house, or in a bar, or standing up in the kitchen in the middle of the night."[45]

In the final draft of "12 O'Clock News," Bishop addresses both the limits and the possibilities of a miniaturist writing as an engagement with the "huge and roaring, glaring world," thematizing her ambivalence by offering divergent perspectives on the poet's desk. As it first appeared in the *New Yorker* (1973) and later in *Geography III* (1976), "12 O'Clock News" is a prose poem consisting of two columns. In the left-hand column, the poem lists objects on a desk: a lamp, a typewriter, envelopes, a bottle of ink, a pile of manuscripts, a typed sheet, an ashtray, an eraser. The right-hand column consists of prose paragraphs that correspond to each desk item; these items are described from the perspective of a miniaturized narrator who appears to be a roving reporter touring a vast, war-torn landscape. As Bishop observed, this version of the poem was written soon after the end of the Vietnam War (Starbuck, "Conversation," 320). Certainly one of the issues the poem engages is representations of the Vietnam War; more generally, Bishop explores how war breeds a particular understanding of writing as a battleground. The poem's two-column structure dramatizes the question of whether a miniaturist poetry can elude this dynamic, or whether Bishop's text, like Priestley's, is destined to become one of Cadmus's "half-formed men."

In providing the reader with a "key" to understanding the items described by the speaker, Bishop offers a potential satire of the speaker's distorted perspective, a perspective she aligns with the exaggerations of war journalism. The key reveals the speaker's "factual" reports as the self-interested news of the aggressor. For instance, in describing what Bishop identifies in the left-hand column as an ink bottle, the speaker states: "We have also received reports of a mysterious, oddly shaped black structure, at an undisclosed distance to the east. . . . The natural resources of the country being far from completely known to us, there is the possibility that this may be, or may contain, some powerful and terrifying 'secret weapon.' On the other hand, given what we do know, or have learned from anthropologists and sociologists about this people, it may well be nothing more than a numen, or a great altar recently erected to one of their gods, to which, in their present state of superstition and helplessness, they attribute magical powers, and may even regard as a 'savior,' one last hope from their grave difficulties" (*CP*, 174–75). Similarly, the speaker mistakes an ashtray for a "nest of soldiers" in "hideously contorted positions, all dead"; he argues that they are wearing the camouflage for "winter warfare" on the plains, a "fact" that "gives further proof, if proof were necessary, either of the childishness and hopeless impracticality of this inscrutable people, our opponents, or of the sad corruption of their leaders" (*CP*, 175). By indicating with the key to the desk items the speaker's mistaken impression of the landscape, the poem undercuts his assumption that this "small, backward country" is primitive, childish, and of lesser value than his own. Bishop implies that the way in which the speaker marshals "science" (anthropology) to confirm the accuracy of his perspective—an accuracy she has put into question—reveals that the "superior vantage point" of the West is an index of power and self-interest rather than a measure of the intrinsic truth or value of its perspective. In this reading the two columns juxtapose the scale and identity of the desk objects so as to diminish the claims of colonialism, gigantism, and progress.

As in Barbauld's "Written on a Marble," miniaturization exposes the representational and economic interests of imperial aggression, allowing the poet to occupy the "superiour vantage point" and to align her sympathies with the "natives" who are misrepresented by the newscaster and his national interests. Bishop satirizes reporting based on competition, attack, and one-upmanship, valorizing instead the slightness, struggle, and even anonymity of literary productions that attempt to generate sympathy for other perspectives. Her labor into the night, though not overtly "productive" in the language and economy of postwar American culture, signifies the struggle involved in such representation, versus the easiness of expressing and marketing one's particular suffering. Addressing the themes of nationalism and empire through the description of her desktop, she shows that a miniaturist perspective does not limit her, but rather decenters the visual "map" provided by "objective" communications such as the nightly news.

On the other hand, Bishop expresses ambivalence about a miniaturist writing, exposing the complicity of the miniature within an economy and culture that value the gigantic. This ambivalence qualifies her purported detachment from the newscaster-speaker. James Merrill perceived this strain in "12 O'Clock News"; he wrote to Bishop, "How I love the array on *your* worktable. It's simply uncanny what you do with tone in that poem—the newscaster's idiom grows into the saddest, truest analogue of that strange, remote 'involvement' even I have felt, those few nights I've ever been sober and lonely enough to work late. That snow-covered peak—'White is their color, and behold my head!' *This* may be the saddest poem you've ever written."[46] Merrill suggests that Bishop alludes to herself in the section of the poem that transforms cigarettes into soldiers in winter camouflage: "These uniforms were designed to be used in guerrilla warfare on the country's one snow-covered mountain peak." As the snow-covered peak, an aging Bishop may allude to a variety of personal conflicts that keep her awake at night, or may refer to her professional anxieties, exacerbated by her dependence on her writing, struggles that cause her to perform "guerrilla warfare" upon her body (perhaps an allusion to her habits of smoking and drinking).

Merrill implies that the newscaster's idiom registers the poet's involvement in the battle-torn landscape. Read from this perspective, the poem invites the reader to take up the scale and visual angle of the speaker-reporter, to become immersed in the nightmarish battle scene. Enlargements of scale do not satirize the speaker's perspective, but instead bode forth hidden or latent anxieties about the poet's "news" in the world of the gigantic, anxieties that emerge late at night. The speaker is estranged from her instruments of writing, and the magnified descriptions of the desk objects provide darkly humorous truths about "Poetry as Big Business": "It gives very little light." The speaker comments: "In this small, backward country, one of the most backward left in the world today, communications are crude and 'industrialization' and its products almost nonexistent." The natives wield ink as their "powerful and terrifying 'secret weapon'" (*CP*, 174). The poet appears as a relic of some earlier century or primitive nation, powerless to tackle the pressures of the world of the gigantic, but equally powerless to avoid them. The nighttime setting, cigarette butts, and a typewritten page depicted as a cemetery attest to the failure of the battle.

More pointedly, Bishop may confront her economic reliance on the forces of gigantism whose values she found objectionable. Her description of the typewriter keys indicate the costs of the poetic profession: "What endless labor those small, peculiarly shaped terraces represent! And yet, on them the welfare of this tiny principality depends." The speaker must perform "endless labor" to ensure her survival—labor necessitated by the disproportionate value placed on the gigantic, labor that will reach only a tiny audience compared to the nightly news. The miniature in this sense is not a choice, but "knowledge of necessity." Like the speaker in "Crusoe in England," who states, "I felt a deep affection for / the smallest of my island industries," only to correct himself: "No, not exactly, since the smallest was / a miserable philosophy," Bishop's use of the miniature is at some level shaped by "a miserable philosophy," the necessity of accepting, like Crusoe, that her stance is as much imposed as chosen (*CP*, 164). Moreover, Bishop acknowledges that her tiny world resides within and is shaped by the world of the gigantic; in literal terms, Bishop's welfare as a professional poet depended on making her name in Boston and New York. In this light, the speaker's reference to the "sad corruption" of the leaders of the war-torn landscape not only refers to the perceptions of the Western media but is an ironic allusion to Bishop's own complicity, the fact that she must keep one hand in the realm of the gigantic to succeed as a professional poet. A "superior vantage point" on the Vietnam War and on Big Business is not possible, Bishop implies, for there is no position of moral innocence. This perspective may help to account for Bishop's decision to present the poem in prose, suggesting the permeable boundary between poet and newscaster, the worlds of poetry and the mainstream media.

While Bishop locates sincerity in the accuracy and precision of minute detail, a poetic craftsmanship that could resist the demands of the marketplace, in "12 O'Clock News" we see that this aesthetic and moral ideal was formed under pressure, with the poem's two-column shape enacting the conflict.[47] The challenge Bishop faced, and which she in turn presents to the reader, is how to connect the two columns on the page, the world of the miniature to the world of the gigantic. Her use of miniaturization in this poem, while a means of deflating gigantism, can also be read as an acknowledgment that her critique is double-edged, given her own ambivalent desire for and professional dependence on institutional legitimacy. Herein, perhaps, lies Merrill's sense that this is Bishop's saddest poem.[48] Bishop's juxtaposition of scale and perspective emphasizes the ethical dilemmas of placement: how to represent her desk—the choice of perspective, whether to settle in or above or upon—is a choice inseparable from the difficulty of negotiating entrenched disparities of wealth and power. Each choice entails its own epistemological assumptions.

Instead of embracing sympathy for war's victims as a solution to this ethical dilemma, Bishop follows Barbauld in emphasizing the barriers that obstruct sympathetic identification: she is skeptical of the ability of the poetry of sentiment to bridge material gaps of geography, economic class, and race. As she remarks in "In the Waiting Room," upon looking at a *National Geographic* photograph of "black, naked women with necks / wound round and round with wire,"

What similarities—
. . . .
held us all together
or made us all just one?
How—I didn't know any
word for it—how 'unlikely'. . .   (*CP*, 161)

Specifically, she disliked the didactic dimension of sentimental literature, finding that the poet ignores the material differences that distinguish vicarious suffering from actual suffering, poetic labor from other forms of labor. Bishop also found morally and politically didactic poetry boring, a point she made in her 1970 "Notes for Poetry Reviews" in a discussion of her peer Denise Levertov: "It is unfair to single out Miss Levertov as an example, since many other poets of her generation do the same thing; but when she starts a poem 'Biafra. Biafra. Biafra.' one's heart sinks, and not because of the suffering in Biafra, alas. A kind of resentment comes over one, 'Oh, I'm not *up* to feeling that much; I *can't* . . .'" She then asks, "When have politics ever made good poems? Miss Levertov has great gifts. The poems that she apparently considers frivolous, and calls 'Embroideries' for example, are much more real." Bishop's response to politically didactic poetry is not sympathy for the suffering of others, but resentment. Her statement "Oh, I'm not up to feeling that much; I can't . . ." suggests the pointlessness of the exercise, the material gap between her actual situation and that of the suffering in Biafra; even if she had wanted to feel that much, she "can't"—the distance and difference in perspective and experience create a gap that vicarious sentiment cannot bridge.

Similarly, Bishop did not object to "politics" per se; rather, she indicated that didactic poetry goes about political and moral instruction in the wrong way because it imposes its perspective, placing the reader in the position of the student of elocution who must obey moral precepts on the basis of the authority, and power, of the instructor. Instead, Bishop believed that people learn by observation and experience, and moral and political vision is rendered in her poetry as one facet of experience. In this sense Bishop implies that a poem's value is shaped by but not reducible to its ideological commitments. What didactic poetry omits in its effort to persuade and inspire social change, she notes, is the wholeness of human experience, an experience that involves feelings of pleasure as well as suffering, and which differs markedly for different persons. Bishop finds Levertov's "embroideries"—a name that connotes her own miniatures—"much more real" than Levertov's political poetry, because she deems the pleasure and play involved in writing and reading poetry essential to its moral dimensions. Levertov's "embroideries" make room for Bishop the reader—in her diversity of experiences and feelings—in a way that didactic poetry does not.

Thus, translation for Bishop signified an ideal practice of reading, a means not just of passively receiving the poem but of actively collaborating with it. While scholars interested in the social and political aspects of Bishop's poetry have tended to focus on her work that explicitly addresses themes of race, class, and gender, her translations suggest the way in which aesthetic concerns routinely figure ethical relationships in her work. Although many writers view translation as a secondary or derivative craft, one of copying versus origination, of fancy versus imagination, translation placed Bishop squarely in familiar territory, that of the miniature. Her translation of Octavio Paz's "Objetos y Apariciones" ("Objects and Apparitions") suggests how translation presented problems of "miniaturist" authorship that she explored in many of her "original" compositions. Paz dedicated his poem to Joseph Cornell, whose miniature boxes filled with objects and collages inspired the poem. Each three-line stanza of the poem explores a different facet of Cornell's work, as if Paz were walking through a museum of Cornell's boxes as he wrote. Bishop, in turn, engages Cornell through the prism of Paz. In articulating a connection between multiple artists, languages, and nations, Bishop's translation raises questions about aesthetic and social difference as mediated by language. Is translation an act of bridging perspectives and cultures, of harmonious communication, or, conversely, is it an act of misrepresentation or appropriation?

Bishop asked these questions in her unpublished "Remarks on Translation."[49] Translation, she argues, involves an accurate use of language, a use inseparable from ethical attention to cultural differences. Bad translations, she speculates, are products of "just plain carelessness—or is it egotism?" Thus, one needs to rein in the ego, and also the emotions: "R. Lowell is a good example—here—one has a feeling right or wrong—that one does know what the poem says—a feeling like that 'feminine intuition' possible. . . . Out of this feeling can come a whole cluster of emotions, intuitions, appreciations, etc—but probably not good translations." Accuracy supplants poetic imagination as the standard of value: "I believe that no one is entitled to say a translation is good—or bad— . . . unless he or she knows the language of the original fairly well. He or she may say he or she 'enjoyed it'—or 'didn't enjoy it'—but a translation—in one dimension, so to speak—CAN NOT be judged."

In its treatment of these issues, "Objects and Apparitions" is one of Bishop's signature works, and her choice to include it as one of the ten poems in *Geography III* attests to its importance. Notably, *Geography III* juxtaposes what Bishop scholars consider her most autobiographical works ("In the Waiting Room," "Crusoe in England") with her most "objective" works ("12 O'Clock News" and the Paz translation). Like "12 O'Clock News," "Objects and Apparitions" demonstrates that this is a false opposition, a fact evidenced by the title of the collection (Costello, "Impersonal Personal," 334; Hammer, "New Elizabeth Bishop," 147). Geography suggests that representations of the self always involve a question of epistemology: the self's meaning depends on the coordinates we choose, the origins we presume, and the moral assumptions that guide these acts of placement.

Bishop's translation obscures origins in that it is essentially a translation of a translation. More specifically, Paz's ekphrastic poem translates into language another aesthetic medium, Cornell's boxes, which are themselves translations (loosely speaking) of found objects: "Minimal, incoherent fragments: / the opposite of History, creator of ruins, / out of your ruins you have made creations" (*CP*, 275–76). Translation is rendered in the poem as an act of framing found objects. With the change of medium, each artist thematizes the act, context, and layers of looking: Cornell frames found objects through their arrangement and placement in his boxes; Paz takes as his object Cornell's boxes, framing them through his choice and arrangement of words; and Bishop takes as her object this "found text," opening a further window through its translation into English. Thus the "authentic" object (and origin) of "Objects and Apparitions" remains elusive, dependent upon the frame through which it is viewed.

In this light, each translation, as a further act of framing an elusive object, is equally "original": or to put it another way, this poem in its various "apparitions" does not value origins nor originality as conventionally understood in the romantic tradition. This is not to say that translation for Cornell, Paz, and Bishop is a license to ignore the particular features of another's work. Rather, reframing another's work emphasizes the collaborative nature of artistic production, and, in doing so, challenges artistic representation as a claim to ownership confirmed by the artist's name or signature: "'One has to commit a painting,' said Degas, / 'the way one commits a crime.' But you constructed / boxes where things hurry away from their names."

In contrast to the official museum, Cornell's collections are full of unnamed objects—one must guess at their purpose and past history, the context from which they were plucked, their value to the finder:

> Monuments to every moment,
> refuse of every moment, used:
> cages for infinity.

> Marbles, buttons, thimbles, dice,
> pins, stamps, and glass beads:
> tales of the time.

The selection and arrangement of objects in Cornell's boxes is purely personal, yet the "person" behind them remains opaque: his boxes hearken back to a collection that predates the modern museum, the *wunderkammer* or curiosity cabinet, shaped by the whim and secret desire of the collector. Refusing to name and classify his collections according to rational principles or human history, Cornell makes room for the marvelous, for reverie, dream, and imagination about the world beyond the box. In this way Cornell's tiny boxes unsettle assumptions about possession that stabilize bourgeois interiors, providing instead a window onto a universe that exceeds human claims to possession: "scarcely bigger than a shoebox / with room in them for night and all its lights." This is nowhere more evident than in Cornell's "hotel" boxes whose names, as Dawn Ades observes, are "evocative of the sky and navigation": Grand Hotel de l'Observatoire, Hotel de l'Etoile, Hotel des Voyageurs, Grand Hotel de l'Univers, Grand Hotel Bon Port ("Transcendental Surrealism," 34). Inviting us inside, these hotels provide us with portals to the infinite.

In their juxtaposition of interiors and exteriors, the small and the grand, Cornell's boxes elicit the play of fancy, an invitation that his soap bubble boxes make manifest. Juxtaposing a clay pipe, a wine glass, a map of the moon, and a child's head, Cornell uses extremes of scale to inspire fanciful connections; as Dawn Ades points out, "A clay pipe becomes a bubble-blowing pipe, the bubbles themselves become heavenly bodies. . . . Cornell sees the exercise of the imagination in playing as something like the first flexing of the creative powers of the human mind whether in science or art" (31, 43). Cornell's soap bubble set, which recalls Barbauld's juxtaposition of soap bubbles and hot-air balloons in "Washing Day," asks the viewer to consider the labor of imagination by participating in it. Cornell used the word "constellation" to describe the pattern of selection and association that guided his artwork, and it was his hope that the viewer would form a further point in this constellation; he commented, "Invite the spectator to 'chart' further, elicit further dreams and musings if such he might care to do" (Ades 33). Cornell's boxes elicit such play through their use of juxtaposition, structurally making room for further framings, further perspectives; in short, the boxes make room for their own translation. Cornell often literally marked his boxes as translations by including other artists' signatures.

In translation lies the potential for conversation and collaboration, for connecting unlikely objects, however discordant. We can see an instance of this in the chain of texts constituting "Objects and Apparitions." The opacity of Cornell's collections—his "illegible signature"—inspires Paz's and Bishop's translations. Paz ends his poem, however, by naming Cornell: "Joseph Cornell: en el interior de tus cajas / mis palabras se volvieron visibles un instante," which Bishop translates as "Joseph Cornell: inside your boxes / my words become visible for a moment." Paz names Cornell at the moment when the perspective of his translation threatens to subsume that of Cornell's boxes. In naming Cornell's boxes, Paz incorporates them as "found objects" within his poem, positing their materiality distinct from his rendering of them. In this way Paz frames his words, his signature, as one perspective made possible by Cornell's act of translation. Paz reveals that Cornell's "interior," like the interior of his boxes, is not a container used to possess and defend the self against the outside world, but is social, oriented toward and defined in conjunction with other perspectives. Paz's poem is ultimately "authored" by both artists; through the act of reflecting upon and translating Cornell's boxes into language, Paz's poem took shape.

In turn, Bishop's words become visible through the frame of the Paz-Cornell collaboration. Bishop's affinities with Cornell preceded her translation of Paz's poem: she had long admired Cornell, and even constructed two collage-boxes in his style.[50] Rather than indicate that the poem is a translation below the title, she chose to do so only at the end of the poem, stating "translated from the Spanish of Octavio Paz." When George Starbuck pressed her about this choice, admitting that he thought the poem was her own and was surprised to find out that it was a translation when he finished it, she answered that the placement of Paz's name was determined by how the poem looked: "Well, I thought, of course, I should put Octavio Paz's name at the beginning, and I had it that way at first, but it didn't look right. There was the title, and then the dedication line, and the author's name seemed like too many things under the title, so I decided to put it at the end"

("Conversation," 313–14). The effect of this choice is to make the phrase "my words" from the lines: "Joseph Cornell: inside your boxes / my words became visible for a moment" refer to Bishop's words, and it is no coincidence that Starbuck thought he was reading a Bishop poem. The words of the English translation are, "for a moment," her own. As soon as one finishes the poem and sees that they are also Paz's words, however, one must reconsider the poem. And yet, translation makes the poem no less her own; Bishop's signature is most legible as she wipes it away to reveal a box within a box within a box: illegibility seals the act of translation, the art of framing.

The effect is similar to that of Bishop's unpublished, ironically titled "True Confessions." The narrator attempts to visually penetrate the house where she was born: "I was born there, sort of in the middle but slightly to the left and rather inset,—a tiny, almost invisible baby. I could see it under a magnifying glass—a tiny, almost invisible baby, a small dark haired mother upstairs in a tiny toy wooden apartment house painted gray. Years later, when it was visible to the naked eye, but still not very big, I saw it from a trolley car. Someone said 'That's where you were born' and I turned around to stare and saw briefly through its gray walls a vague fierce picture of myself being born hanging on one of them and then it receded behind my shoulder and up a curve to the left, and vanished."[51] While birth is often treated in confessional narratives as a privileged moment of origin signifying who the child is (in terms of family, class, location) and who she will become, the narrator's efforts to grasp the "truth" of her birth founder on spatial and temporal blocks to her vision; all she sees are distorted representations. If the trolley car had stopped and she had seized the picture from the wall, one has the sense that the picture would depict a room with walls on which hangs another picture, in an endless series of miniaturizations. Through the miniaturization of her birth, the speaker emphasizes that she can only see and understand herself through a distorting frame, whether of the magnifying glass, painting, memory, or language. Rather than confess the "truth" of her birth and identity through conventional codes, Bishop instead uses miniaturization of scale to draw attention to the conventions of confession as themselves an epistemological grounding for truth, and the "self" as an elusive, illegible, unknowable, entity: it "vanished."

Revealing that the "truth" of the self presumes an epistemology does not lead Bishop to the conclusion that all truth is fictive: rather, her attention to epistemology emphasizes the need to clarify the ethics involved in drawing boundaries, between fact and fiction, self and other, north and south. "Objects and Apparitions" makes explicit an aim at work in much of Bishop's poetry: in contrast to Lowell's use of Hardwick's letters in *The Dolphin*,

Bishop uses "found objects" in her poetry to preserve their inscrutability, drawing attention to the frames through which they are viewed, known, and named so as to resist their appropriation. Translation is not the work of sympathy, but of juxtaposition of scale and perspective: like Barbauld, Bishop remains suspicious of the egotism and ease with which sympathy is extended or withdrawn, inviting instead the "hard work" of connecting "unlikely" things. At the top of a draft of an early unpublished poem, "The Bees," Bishop copied a passage from *Human Nature and Conduct* (1922), a work by her friend John Dewey, the pragmatist philosopher.[52] It is an apt summary of her aims in using the illegible signature: "Any observed form or object is a challenge. The case is not otherwise with ideals of justice or peace or human brotherhood, or equality, or order. They too are not things self enclosed to be known by introspection, or objects you are supposed to see from by rational insight. Like thunderbolts and tubercular disease and the rainbow they can be known only by mysterious and minute observation of consequences incumbent in action" (56).

Coda

Confessional Criticism, Professional Culture

> Hence there is no surprise in the fact that, historically, the reign of the Author has also been that of the Critic, nor again in the fact that criticism (be it new) is today undermined along with the Author.
>
> —Roland Barthes, "The Death of the Author"

> The highest, as the lowest, form of criticism is a mode of autobiography.
>
> —Oscar Wilde, *The Picture of Dorian Gray*

> What we observe here is the simultaneous emergence in legal discourse of the proprietary author and the literary work. The two concepts are bound to each other. To assert one is to imply the other, and together, like the twin suns of a binary star locked in orbit, they define the center of the modern literary system.
>
> —Mark Rose, *Authors and Owners*

To Profess, to Confess

This book has demonstrated that the rhetoric of sincerity in the lyric responds to the threat that commercial culture taints the transparency, autonomy, and authenticity of lyric expression, and simultaneously enables immersion in commercial culture through the cultivation of dramatic performance, celebrity, and self-advertisement. The inability to "know" whether an author speaks sincerely is an epistemological problem that at once generates the need for sincerity's rhetorical assurances but also results in a deep distrust. While sincerity has been persistently associated with moral idealism and naiveté or, conversely, with a debased theatricality, I've argued for the need to move beyond this polarized opposition and the problematic ways in which it has been gendered, so that we can begin to grapple with poets' complex stagings of the moral expectations of literary authorship in a commercial setting. Given the persistence of this readerly dynamic, my feminist concern with the gendering of sincerity extends beyond lyric poetry into literary criticism, and in this coda I take seriously the argument that the historical reception of the rhetoric of sincerity has been influenced by literary criticism's struggles over its own professional aims and authority (Graff, *Professing*, 184, 191–92; Robbins, *Vocations*, chap. 2). As Clifford Siskin argues, the "point . . . is that we need not just admit the discourse of the professional into our literary histories of the past two hundred years but that we recognize that the history we have held is its product" (*Work of Writing*, 117; Klancher, "English Romanticism," 82–83).

Criticism, like poetry, became a profession in the late eighteenth century, and by the end of the nineteenth century had been formalized into an academic discipline through departments of English in British and American universities (Graff, chaps. 1–2; Scholes, *Rise and Fall*, chap. 1). From its beginnings in the eighteenth century and at important junctures in its subsequent history, professional literary criticism has defined itself through its relation to, exercises upon, and judgments of poetry; the fact that poetry is privileged in literary criticism's generic self-definition is connected not only to the association of poetry with an elevated moral and aesthetic stance, but to the importance of the rhetoric of sincerity in both genres. From the openly moral tenor of late-eighteenth- and nineteenth-century literary criticism to current poststructuralist and ideological approaches, sincerity has served either as an evaluative criterion or as a thematic concern. In the past decade there has been a resurgence of interest in the concept of sincerity, evident in histories and theories of emotion; in scholarship on sentimental literature and culture; in performance studies; and in work on memoir and confession. With this scholarship in mind, I turn to a moment from our recent past: the rise in "confessional criticism"—also known as "personal criticism," "autocritography," "moi criticism" "the new subjectivism," "intimate critique," and so forth—all of which named the trend of incorporating first-person narrative and autobiographical anecdote in academic literary scholarship in the 1980s and '90s. In a related but not analogous vein, "confessional criticism" alludes to the spate of memoirs published by literary critics in the 1990s, evidence of an interest in the critic's person.[1] Sincerity has served as an issue in the writings of critics themselves since the advent of professional criticism, and yet confessional criticism provoked heated debate within the academic literary profession in the late 1980s and early 1990s, as evidenced by a 1996 PMLA *Forum* devoted to this issue, by a 1996 collection, *Confessions of the Critics,* and by scholarly articles and opinion pieces that addressed the topic. The reasons for the uses of the personal voice in criticism are as varied as the lively debates about its merits, but in the context of my concerns in this book, one feature of these debates stands out.

Those who object to personal criticism have called it anti-intellectual, self-indulgent, celebrity-seeking, exhibitionist, and even pathological. What is striking is that these objections to the uses of the personal voice in recent literary criticism echo—almost verbatim—the objections I have chronicled in this book to the uses of the rhetoric of sincerity in British romantic and postmodern American poetry. Now, however, these criticisms are directed not at poets but at critics themselves. Numerous commentators on personal criticism have singled out romanticism for originating the problem of self evident in this trend; as Elizabeth Fox-Genovese puts it, confessional critics reenact the "hubris of the Romantics."[2] The recurrent concern with romanticism as the origin of a contemporary pathology indicates a profound ambivalence about the rhetoric of sincerity in literary criticism, connected to the profession's aims, struggles, and self-justifications. That the romantic pathology is a gendered disease—those authors deemed to suffer from it are often female, or are feminized—suggests that the resurgence of the personal voice in criticism has coincided with questions of who has the authority to participate in and define the profession. At stake is the moral autonomy and expertise of a profession conflicted about criticism's affective nature and its relation to consumer culture.

Readings in the Romantic Pathology: "Me and My Shadow"

It's worth revisiting Jane Tompkins's essay "Me and My Shadow" (1987), which sparked a huge amount of debate about confessional criticism in the 1980s and '90s, because the issues it raises remain relevant to current discussions of feeling.[3] There were many good reasons for the attention the essay received: it was one of the first to articulate the stakes of personal criticism and its debt to feminism; it bluntly challenged the masculinization of high theory in the academy; and it provocatively played with the conventions of the theoretical essay. Tompkins's essay serves as a useful case study for thinking about how and why the shortcomings of confessional criticism have been positioned as a peculiarly romantic problem.

The romantics' tendency to make the individual the ground for understandings of truth and morality originated what several critics define as the modern problem of selfhood evident in Tompkins's essay. Fox-Genovese argues that romanticism is responsible for a fundamental shift in authority from "divinity to the work of art" and from "hierarchical social structures"

to the artist's powers of self-origination (*CC*, 70), while Kauffman empha-
sizes "sincerity and authenticity" as "criteria" for this expressive view of art
("Long Goodbye," 1159). Contrasting Rousseau's and St. Augustine's con-
fessions, Fox-Genovese suggests that Rousseau is self-indulgent because
his confessions lack relation to a "higher truth," an external moral frame-
work through which to make sense of self-knowledge (*CC*, 72). Similarly,
Simpson argues that the problem of subjectivity arose when it became the
"primary explanatory principle for failure and success, virtue and vice, be-
ing and nonbeing."[4]

These critics emphasize what I have called an epistemological crisis con-
cerning the self as ground for truth claims, but rather than see the rhetoric
of sincerity as emerging from and capable of commentary on this crisis,
they articulate familiar anxieties about sincerity's commercial qualities,
narrating romanticism as a "fall" into "self"-ishness and the seductions
of a market economy. Fox-Genovese argues that current literary critics, like
Rousseau, "tend to see both certainty and Truth as extensions of the self"
and thus privilege their own responses above the texts they study, falling
prey to the pleasures of consumption: "Rather than repudiating the Ro-
mantic infatuation with self, the postmoderns have taken it to its ultimate
conclusion. And, in good global capitalist form, they have waged a revolt
against art that elevates the consumer over the producer" (*CC*, 72). Simi-
larly, Kauffman sees personal criticism, which resurrects "the mirror and
lamp of Romanticism" ("Long Goodbye," 1162), as a symptom of a fall—the
erosion of a critical public sphere (signified by the eighteenth-century "es-
say") due to the rise of consumerism (signified by the "celebrity interview")
(1159). A failure of critical detachment—what Fox-Genovese calls "a self-
effacing pleasure in the craft, artistry, and, sometimes, genius of another,"
results in "a complacent exhibitionism" (*CC*, 74). This is a common com-
plaint about personal criticism, voiced even by its advocates: it sustains a
cult of celebrity and an academic star system, costing criticism both its aes-
thetic and its ethical and political aims.[5]

Many locate the problem with Tompkins's essay less in self-promotion
than in an embrace of a naive understanding of self-expression, one guided
by a belief in its therapeutic, liberating powers. In that Tompkins's critics
are attuned to gender, the gendered subtext isn't one of antifeminism, but
rather of opposition to a liberal, bourgeois feminist criticism recuperated by
the logic of consumer capitalism.[6] Simpson, for instance, draws a clear line
from romantic poetry to confessional criticism, diagnosing the self voiced
in Tompkins's essay as "the liberal-expressive self" evident "in the poetry of
Walt Whitman" and currently associated with "a certain subculture within

academic feminism" (*CC*, 86), a model of self that Kauffman deems responsible for feminism's commodification ("Long Goodbye," 1159, 1160). Both see this model of self as the key to Tompkins's "sentimental" feminism, an attempt to recover through self-expression a freedom that has been limited by patriarchy (Kauffman 1162; Simpson, in "Forum," 1167).

In assuming "a self whose prior and repressed existence is the very license for speech itself" (Simpson, in *CC*, 85), Tompkins ignores poststructuralist critiques of the liberal subject: as Simpson states, "What has been repressed finally comes out, therefore it seems to be real and authentic" (*CC*, 87; Kauffman 1164). MacLean points out that Tompkins's "therapeutic" understanding of self-expression perpetuates the belief "that it is primarily the subject and not the structure that needs help," ignoring endemic inequalities, and defusing the energy for collective political action.[7] Kauffman argues that therapeutic paradigms defuse feminism—"Society tames the feminist through the story in particular, the allure of personal testimony in general" (1158)—and takes Tompkins to task for this: "One strain of feminism that has been commodified most successfully is the therapeutic model. Tompkins chides those who see pop psychologists . . . as 'mushy' and 'sentimental' . . . but she fails to see how by endorsing them she uncritically perpetuates individualism" (1164). In this reading Tompkins contributes to an understanding of "femininity as disease," woman as a victim who needs to be "cured of her addiction to love through a strict regimen of group therapy and confession" (1165).

Poststructuralist theory emerges as a panacea to the ills of naiveté: it establishes critical distance from romantic self-expression—if not insulating the critic from commercial culture, than at least providing an understanding of how literature may reproduce or sustain capitalist ideology through ideals of individual selfhood. In short, objections to personal criticism as exemplified by the responses to "Me and My Shadow" hinge on the commercialization of the rhetoric of sincerity: confessional critics—liberal feminist ones in particular—are accused of either knowingly using sincerity conventions for the careerist, market-driven ends of fame and celebrity or, conversely, using conventions of sincerity without awareness of their status as conventions, naively contributing to a therapeutic culture of confession that promises individual freedom but simply perpetuates consumerist logics. In diagnosing and feminizing the romantic pathology, Tompkins's critics advocate a professional disinterest achieved through detachment from the personal voice: the critic's "sincerity" can best be signified through conventions of ironic detachment, chiefly through ironic critiques of sincerity.

Ironic Critique and the Death of the Author

In literary studies, theoretical debates about the "individual" are often constituted around the figure of the author, supporting Foucault's argument that the privileging of the author in literary criticism is part of a longer history of ideas marked by "individuation" ("What is an Author," in *Foucault Reader*, 101). But the privileging of the author in literary criticism and theory—even in writing that subjects the author to skeptical critique—reveals another history, that of academic literary criticism and its own investments in bourgeois formulations of authorship. Literary criticism's ironic mode—guided by distinctions between text and author, skepticism of claims to sincerity, arguments for the death of the author—is subject to the historical contradictions of professional authorship: the belief that ironic critique can escape these contradictions has resulted in a problematic understanding of sincerity, one that mistakenly opposes it to irony, thereby reinscribing the binary of feeling versus rational thought, immersion versus critical disinterest, naiveté versus sophistication. Sophistication—and the critic's professional expertise—is signified by a critique of, and claim to rise above, the question of sincerity. However, one can be as sincere about thinking as about feeling: "ironic" discourse can work to convey the sincerity of the critical stance, but because the conventions involve the repression of the question of a "personal" sincerity, they appear embedded, less visible.[8]

The representation of romanticism as pathology by Tompkins's critics has a precedent in poststructuralist criticism on the death of the author, which explicitly took aim at romantic (expressivist) discourse and assumptions about the author as an originating subject; and, in turn, by historicist discussions of the romantic ideology, which demystified idealizations of the authorial subject by exposing evasions or repressions of determining historical conditions. A particular view of romantic authorship emerged in discussions guided by "the death of the author" and was taken up in the confessional criticism debates: it is a failed model of authorship, due to its investments in an ideology of the authorial self that purports to transcend the political and economic contradictions of aesthetic production, or what McGann calls "the romantic ideology."[9] But this is a fortunate failure for many literary critics.[10] As the responses to "Me and My Shadow" indicate, a skeptical critique that exposes the complicity, failure, or disease of romantic authorship becomes a tool of critical distance in capitalist culture. In its efforts to denaturalize or unmask this ideology, the criticism of romantic authorship, like the skeptical response to the literature of sincerity evident in the nineteenth century, has a moral subtext: authorial claims to sincerity fail due to a complicity with or ignorance of how expressivist rhetoric reproduces and benefits from capitalist ideology.

Many contemporary critics have emphasized the pressing need for such critical distance, given the encroachments of corporate culture into academe, the transformation of students into consumers, and the increasing measurement of all knowledge production in scientific and economic terms.[11] I agree that these are disturbing trends and pressing problems, but attempting to recover a position of moral purity for literary criticism is tantamount to, as Jennifer Wicke puts it, "hiding our collective heads in the sand" ("I Profess," 54; see also "Celebrity Material," 772). It is worth noting that skepticism of sincerity as a critical strategy relies on conventions of irony as signifier of the critic's moral integrity in the marketplace, but doesn't escape the "romantic" problem of self that shapes professional literary criticism. Terry Eagleton points out this contradiction in a discussion of de Man:

> In recognizing that bourgeois dreams of transcendence tend to be foolish fictions, De Man is perfectly correct. What he does not acknowledge is the equally ideological character of an irony which gazes contemplatively at the whole inauthentic scene, wryly conscious of its own inescapable complicity with what it views, reduced to a truth which consists in no more than a naming of the void between its own speech-act and the empirical self. No more familiar image of the bourgeois liberal could in fact be conceived; the line from the crippled, marginalized, self-ironizing humanists of Eliot, James and Forster to the anti-humanist deconstructor is direct and unbroken. It is because De Man consistently reduces historicity to empty temporality that he displaces the *dilemmas of the liberal intellectual under late capitalism* into an irony structural to discourse as such.   (*Function of Criticism*, 100; italics mine)

Eagleton's insight suggests that the contradictions of liberal authorship extend to the act of academic literary criticism,[12] resulting in tensions between textual accounts and material practices of authorship. Arguments for the death of the author are enabled by classically liberal protections of original authorship (M. Rose, *Authors and Owners*, 138–39): critics sign their names to the essays and books in which they subject the figure of the author and the signature to skeptical critique; upon publication, these works are bound by the laws of copyright and become forms of literary property; in publishing their works, critics advance the professional careers dependent on their names. Texts such as *Roland Barthes* by Roland Barthes,[13] like much of the poetry in this study, challenges ideals of the author upheld by property law (that is, possessive individualism), but the contradiction remains. Mark Rose sums up this contradiction well: "But today the gap between copyright and literary thinking is striking. Copyright depends on drawing lines between works, on saying where one text ends and another begins. What much current literary thought emphasizes, however, is that texts permeate and enable one another, and so the notion of distinct boundaries between texts becomes difficult to sustain" (*Authors and Owners*, 3).

With its origins in the romantic era and nascent industrial capitalism, literary criticism emerges from what is variously called a liberal, middle-class, sentimental culture, and like much literature that emerged in this culture, has morally reformist, even therapeutic aims (Robbins, *Vocations*, 80; Bennett, *Outside Literature*, 180). The dilemma of the memoirist, poet, or novelist in secular, market culture is akin to that of the literary critic, who, in seeking to accommodate the contradictions of "professing" as a living, develops strategies to engage the consumerist logics assumed to compromise the moral integrity and agency of writing. If confessional critics such as Tompkins fail to recognize the ways in which the rhetoric of sincerity is complicit with bourgeois ideology, Tompkins's critics fail to recognize that irony is complicit as well: irony and sincerity are not opposed rhetorics, but have been dialectically intertwined at least since the advent of professional authorship in the eighteenth century, one set of conventions always an implicit framework for—and commentary on—the other, divergent reponses to what I have termed a crisis in reading.

What concerns me about the polarized nature of the debate is the gendered subtext to the criticism of Tompkins's essay: critical distance depends on asserting the failure, even disease, of first-person claims to sincerity, which are aligned with a therapeutic feminism. Even if we grant the legitimacy of the critiques of Tompkins's essay, the assumption that we can conflate the commercial aspects of confessional criticism with a naive, liberal feminism is troubling. This gendered subtext is most troubling because it turns out to have a longer history, which has been well told by Suzanne Clark and Tompkins, among others: it is the history of the persistent reaction against sentiment through its assocation with a feminized consumer culture, a bias evident since the emergence of professional criticism in the late eighteenth century and central to the definition of the academic literary profession since the New Criticism.

Although the professional critic emerged alongside the professional poet and novelist in the eighteenth century, "literature" only began to take shape as an autonomous academic discipline between 1875 and 1915.[14] Philologists in particular helped to create a model of disciplinary specialization and methodological rigor by the end of the nineteenth century, but, as Bruce Robbins argues, the New Critics established the model of the profession which we have inherited: "In the early and middle years of the twentieth century, there occurred a further stage of professionalization which, perhaps because it happened around a redefinition of 'literature,' came to seem final, definitive, the one true representation of professionalization as such" (*Secular Vocations*, 66). The New Critics sought to justify the study of literature as an autonomous profession through an understanding of criticism as an activity dedicated to clarifying the aesthetic nature of literature, and in this were influenced by the modernist poetics of Eliot.[15] Collectively the New Critics defined academic literary criticism as an oppositional practice: as Robbins writes, "The narrowing of literature as autonomous professional object is simultaneously the clearing of an exemplary oppositional space, a kind of anti-capitalist microcosm, which criticism sets itself the task of propagating" (78).[16] Similarly, Robert Scholes argues, "The New Criticism functioned to construct for literature a safe place outside the pressures of the marketplace and the strict demands of scientific study (and above the realm of politics and social strife as well) in a lofty sphere of Arnoldian 'disinterestedness'" (*Rise and Fall*, 27).

Not coincidentally, the New Critics defined their anticapitalist microcosm through the genre of poetry, which they conflated with the "literary" itself, formalizing the importance of a particular understanding of the poem to the profession's self-definition. Recent discussions of romantic ideology also emphasize the lyric, due to its close association with sincerity and the "liberal self." The lyric was central to an earlier moment of professionalization as well, the late eighteenth century: "Only by the end of the century did literature begin to refer solely to special kinds of deeply imaginative writing: poetry of the lyrical kind being, of course, the deepest. Specialization is thus the link between the lyric, as the most special kind of poetry, and what we now know as Literature—the grouping into a speciality of special kinds" (Siskin, *Work of Writing*, 132). From this perspective, the New Critics extended an older, "romantic" understanding of the literary profession. Although subsequent critical schools have tended to oppose New Critical premises, many share the New Critics' understanding of the profession as exercising a critical, oppositional function in the broader cultural field.

The New Critical justification for the critic's expertise, like the modernist aesthetic of impersonality on which it was based, was shaped by a deep suspicion of authorial claims to sincerity. This stemmed in part from the suspicion that romantic expressions of feeling and subjectivity had become clichés, subject to the market for popular literature; although many modernists (and their New Critical followers) associated this trend with women's writing, modernist antisentimentalism was part of a broader feminization of mass culture (Clark, *Sentimental Modernism*, 5). What this history—albeit overly schematic—allows us to see is that a particular culture of modernism, institutionalized through the New Criticism, associated romanticism in general, and authorial claims to sincerity specifically, with the debasement of a language of feeling in consumer culture, so as to secure the moral autonomy of the profession. More pointedly, the "death" of the author is a rhetoric of authorship that is decidedly "romantic," its authority defined by its critical distance from forms of representation deemed complicit with a therapeutic consumer culture. The persistent gendered subtext to skeptical assumptions about "sincere" forms of self-expression exposes this contradiction: as Suzanne Clark argues, "We are still caught in this gendered system of representation, and so we are premature if we dismiss the sentimental as an aspect of bourgeois thinking which we can escape through a purified critical logic, whether the logic is conservative, liberal, or Marxist" (15).[17]

The Theater of Convention: Sincerity and Professional Decorum

A moral distinction guides the criticism of "Me and My Shadow," a distinction between critical disinterest and a feminized commercial culture and its associated polarities. I raise up this distinction not to argue that we should celebrate any and all uses of the personal voice, but rather to emphasize that the polarities that guide the reception of personal criticism have resulted in our overlooking, simplifying, or dismissing the strategic uses and effects of sincerity conventions as critical engagements with the exigencies of professional authorship in many interesting cases. "Me and My Shadow" is a case in point.

The understanding of "Me and My Shadow" as naive is supported by Tompkins's critics but also by Tompkins, not in her use of the personal voice but in her choice, like her critics, to adopt an oppositional language that pits personal feeling versus theory. The faultiness of the opposition is evidenced by poststructuralist theorists who explore autobiography and emotion, as well as by personal critics explicitly guided by poststructuralist insights. But even in the work of those who sustain the opposition, there is something more complicated going on than an embrace or rejection of theory. The charge of naiveté is risked by anyone who uses or discusses sincerity, sentiment, emotion: it marks a writer not fluent in theoretical approaches or critical discourse, not speaking the professional idiom of academic literary criticism, not sophisticated or self-reflexive about language use. Positing all uses of sincerity conventions as a naive embrace of the "liberal expressive self" is too simple in its understanding of the language practices of writers who historically did not have access to poststructuralist thought, such as the poetess, and of those who do not ally themselves with it, like Tompkins. Recent work on emotion guided by poststructuralist insights enables a revisiting of "Me and My Shadow" that suggests the essay's connection to poetess literature and the "female complaint." Paying attention to the varied critiques of individual autonomy that guide many uses of sincerity conventions suggests less a belief in unmediated expression than a complex engagement with the failure of this promise: historically those who mobilize the personal voice have often been the very subjects denied full citizenship, civil rights, or economic power.[18]

Contra the charge of naïveté, Tompkins begins the revised version of "Me and My Shadow" with a response to a "hostile reader" who accused the first version of the essay of a "return" to the rhetoric of presence and to an "earlier, naive, untheoretical feminism" (1103). Tompkins argues that this view "is mistaken," but admits that her essay "turns its back on theory," adding that "I now tend to think that theory itself, at least as it is usually practiced, may be one of the patriarchal gestures women *and* men ought to avoid" (1103, 1104). This statement is largely responsible for the oppositions that have characterized the debates about the essay: rhetorically, it is provocative, given the dominance of poststructuralism in the American academy when the essay appeared. Yet in her blunt assertion that the unfriendly reader's point of view is "mistaken," Tompkins distinguishes turning her back on theory from returning to a rhetoric of presence. Tompkins rejects the conventions of a particular kind of academic performance associated with poststructuralism ("theory . . . as it is usually practiced") and the assumptions about authorship embedded in this performance, rather than turning her back on poststructuralist insights per se (Olson, "Jane Tompkins," 173).

The essay demonstrates an acute awareness of sincerity as a convention, drawing our attention to the authorial voice as a rhetorical performance. While those who charge Tompkins with naïveté tend to conflate the speaker of "Me and My Shadow" with the author, Tompkins's essay engages the "author function" as a problem, so as to consider the ways in which literary theory as practiced in the American research university of the late 1980s is a performance of critical authority guided by gendered conventions of professional decorum. Tompkins not only exposes the conventions of the academic essay by deliberately and provocatively violating them, but, like writers such as Sylvia Plath, stages the costs of their ritual performance. Nancy

Miller astutely describes this strategy thus: "By turning its authorial voice into spectacle, personal writing theorizes the stakes of its own performance: a personal materialism. Personal writing opens an inquiry on the cost of writing—critical writing or Theory—and its effects. The embarrassment produced in readers is a sign that it is working" (*Getting Personal*, 24). This kind of rhetorical performance engages its situation, commenting on the context of its production and anticipating its likely reception; thus the essay draws attention to the professional "theater" in which critical texts are written and received.

The essay explores how the academic literary profession regulates the conventions of the theoretical essay with regards to voice, subject matter, and style. Tompkins explains her problem with these conventions of the academic theoretical essay thus: "The pretense is in the tone and level of language, not in what it says about post-structuralism. The claim being made by the language is analogous to what Barthes calls the 'reality effect' of historical writing, whose real message is not that this or that happened but that reality exists. . . . Let's call it the 'authority effect.' I cannot describe the pretense except to talk about what it ignores: the human frailty of the speaker, his body, his emotions, his history; the moment of intercourse with the reader—acknowledgment of the other person's presence, feelings, needs" (1109). What Tompkins disavows here is the rhetoric of much theoretical analyis, "the tone and level of the language." Theory's "authority effect" (a twist on Foucault's "author effect") relies on cultivation of a rational, knowledgeable, impartial, and objective voice, what she calls the "conventions of Western rationalism," an "impersonal, technical vocabulary" (1105).

Tompkins argues that theory's "authority effect" is constituted by "what it ignores," the realm of the "personal," and that this authority is therefore gendered: "The problem is that you can't talk about your private life in the course of doing your professional work. You have to pretend that epistemology or whatever you're writing about, has nothing to do with your life, that it's more exalted, more important, because it (supposedly) *transcends* the merely personal. Well, I'm tired of the conventions that keep discussions of epistemology, or James Joyce, segregated from meditations on what is happening outside my window or inside my heart. The public/private dichotomy, which is to say, the public-private hierarchy, is a founding condition of female oppression" (1104). Many critics have emphasized that Tompkins's conflation of the personal voice with the feminine and theory with the masculine is essentialist and universalizing (Miller, *Getting Personal*, 5–7; Candace Lang, "Autocritique," in *CC*, 47). While using polarizing language, Tompkins nevertheless situates her choice of first-person narration, and the choice of "voice" more generally, in the theater of convention; she comments, "The idea that the conventions defining legitimate sources of knowledge overlapped with the conventions defining appropriate gender behavior (male) came to me as a blinding insight. . . . No wonder I felt so uncomfortable in the postures academic prose forced me to assume; it was like wearing men's jeans" (1105). The trope of clothing suggests that like fashion, the conventions of academic prose are shaped by gender and commerce.[19] Her contrasting choice of the personal voice is not conventionless, she points out, but is often *perceived* as lacking awareness of conventions, as "soft-minded, self-indulgent, and unprofessional" (1104) precisely because it violates the *normative* conventions of voice that guide academic literary criticism. To recognize that one has been wearing men's jeans does not mean that in taking them off, one expects to reveal the naked, liberated, feminine self. Rather, Tompkins emphasizes that she exchanges one set of clothes/conventions for another, moving from writing "in the professionally sanctioned way" (1105) to trying on the personal voice, which employs unfamiliar conventions: "It isn't a practiced performance, it hasn't got a surface" (1107). Lacking surface doesn't mean that Tompkins has found "depth," but that the genre, and theater, in which such a performance could be practiced, critiqued, and rewarded is different from that of most late 1980s criticism and theory.

While Tompkins signals her reliance on the conventions of sincere feeling, like Charlotte Smith and Sylvia Plath, she simultaneously conveys a desire to access a "real" experience beyond convention, and the essay as an effort to merge the two becomes a staging of contradiction. Tompkins states that conventions of professional decorum have caused her to feel that she writes in two distinct voices: "One is the voice of a critic who wants to correct a mistake in the essay's view of epistemology. The other is the voice of a person who wants to write about her feelings" (1104). This division of voice carries over into genre: "One writes for professional journals, the other in diaries, late at night. One . . . likes to win arguments, see her name in print, and give graduate students hardheaded advice. The other has hardly ever been heard from. . . . Her works exist chiefly in notebooks and manila folders labeled 'Journal' and 'Private'" (1104). As a professional critic, she uses conventions of voice that signal her compliance with an expected performance, while in her diaries she uses conventions of voice distinct from its professional enactments. In this sense the voice of the journal signifies a desire for expression apart from a professional, commercial stage. Indeed, in an interview Tompkins suggests that the university has become overprofessionalized: "Academe . . . needs to do more than make a student marketable. It needs to educate 'the whole human being'—mind, body, and spirit." The contradictions of the endeavor to "merge" the voices and genres are clear: while Tompkins assails the professionalization of theory and the academy, "Me and My Shadow" allows her to "see her name in print," and has arguably enhanced Tompkins's success, suggesting that the institution is more flexible than the essay itself allows.[20] But her title alludes to the gap that Plath, too, dwells on: "Me" remains connected to, but distinct from, "My Shadow," much like author and textual persona, professional critic and diarist. "Me" tellingly positions the critic as object rather than subject.

But this performance of contradiction has a critical edge. Although Tompkins confesses "I've been hiding a part of myself for a long time" (1107), this isn't simply a therapeutic confession of hidden depths that yield an inner truth or liberated self; rather, this is confession à la Rousseau and Plath, an exposure of society's shame-making mechanisms, a reflection on the institutional structures that produce the very ideology by which private is separated from public, diary from academic essay, sin from moral conduct. So perhaps Tompkins hasn't strayed so far from epistemology, after all. To undertake this confessional performance—to expose and violate conventions of professional decorum—is to potentially gain a measure of success and celebrity, but also to risk shame and embarrassment: "to break with the convention is to risk not being heard at all" (1105). Tompkins confesses, in parentheses, "I have wanted to do this for a long time but have felt too embarrassed." But she also connects the embarrassment that ensues from speaking "personally in a professional context" to being "conditioned to feel that way" (1104).

Keeping in mind the theatrical tradition of the poetess, we can see that Tompkins uses deliberate and dramatic overstatement to provoke her reader, and that provocation is a crucial part of this essay's work.[21] In a manner reminiscent of Lady Lazarus, Tompkins theatrically flouts the conventions of the academic essay through her style and through her engagement with taboo subjects. The most notorious example of this is her repeated references to needing to go to the bathroom: "thinking about going to the bathroom. But not going yet" (1107). Equally taboo is Tompkins's reference to a biographical circumstance that she positions as an open secret: "What I am breaking away from is both my conformity to the conventions of a male professional practice and my intellectual dependence on my husband. How can I talk about such things in public? How can I *not*" (1109). And finally, Tompkins's explicit discussion of the anger that fuels her work belies any expectation of critical objectivity or disinterest. In this manner, Tompkins puts her finger on what is most likely to embarrass her audience.

Sentimental Performance

Here I want to return to Nancy Miller's astute comment on a personal writ-
ing that "theorizes the stakes of its own performance": "The embarrass-
ment produced in readers is a sign that it is working." (24). From this per-
spective, the embarrassment of the reader is a symptom of the ingrained
codes of professional conduct that have been violated, a testament to the
ways in which shame subtly enforces habit. One of the essay's aims, in
breaking taboos, is to use embarrassment to reveal the unspoken rules that
distinguish taboo from authorized content; like "Lady Lazarus," the essay
challenges its readers to consider how they sustain these distinctions. And
certainly, we could explain much of the hostile response to Tompkins's es-
say in this way, as a defensive effort to discipline the author who has threat-
ened the profession's unspoken rules by locating the embarrassment in
Tompkins's person rather than in the habits and values of the institution
she challenges.

But there is a more specific cause of readerly embarrassment in Tomp-
kins's performance, one connected to the threat her essay poses to the idea
of the author and authority guiding what she calls "theory." Anita Sokolsky,
for instance, astutely observes that sincerity has come to be understood as
"a desire to be equal to oneself, a refusal to acknowledge the slippage of
meaning generated in the act of representation" ("Resistance to Sentimen-
tality," 83). Conversely, we might infer the poststructuralist understanding
of irony as a desire to be unequal to oneself, through an acknowledgment
of the slippage of meaning generated in the act of representation. Tomp-
kins's "Me and My Shadow" departs from the poststructuralist under-
standing of sincerity as described by Sokolsky, for it reveals a slippage of
meaning not simply within the sincere text but also between the text and its
contexts, between author-function and author.

Nancy Miller zeroes in on the key agent of this slippage in the essay: it
is emotion, and specifically, anger. Tompkins states: "Now it's time to talk
about something that's central to everything I've been saying so far, al-
though it doesn't show, as we used to say about the slips we used to wear. . . .
Anger is what fuels my engagement with feminist issues; an absolute fury
that has never been tapped, relatively speaking. . . . I hate men for the way
they treat women, and pretending that women aren't there is one of the
ways I hate most" (1113–14). Tompkins concludes: "So for a while I can't talk
about epistemology . . . I have to deal with the trashing of emotion, and
with my anger against it. This one time I've taken off the straitjacket, and it
feels so good" (1115). Miller suggests that Tompkins's confession of anger
produces the reading of the essay as excessive: "By going/not going to the

bathroom in public, Tompkins crosses the line into the dangerous zones of feminine excess. But this intentional calling attention to herself, the deliberate flipside of the inadvertent display of dingy underwear, while to many unfortunate—a lapse in taste—may not be what unfriendly readers finally find most distressing about the essay. It is, I think, less the slip, than the anger; the *slipping of anger* into the folds of the argument: this anger is not merely a rhetorical trope: it's not supposed to show, but it does" (23, italics mine). What has slipped in this admission of anger is the purported separation between the author and her textual personification: "This anger is not merely a rhetorical trope." Anger is, and isn't, a rhetorical trope, and this ambiguity is precisely what confounds critics who address the literature of sincerity. Claims to sincerity are textual, mediated, conventional, theatrical, and yet also promise something more, a hinge to the "real" author's experiences and feelings. The "Jane Tompkins" of "Me and My Shadow" is both a textual performance, a "fiction," and—as the essay reminds us—a person. How do we talk about such texts?

As de Man remarks in an essay on Rousseau, confessional rhetoric is notable for its "double epistemological perspective: it functions as a verifiable referential cognition, but it also functions as a statement whose reliability cannot be verified by empirical means" (*Allegories of Reading*, 281). De Man's fascination with confession is that this most referential of discourses "cannot be verified"—it slips, resulting in "excuse," and more generally, in an understanding of language as difference. Another way to read this epistemological "slip," however, involves addressing the rhetoric of sincerity's claim to represent the "real." Tompkins's essay embarrasses the profession—or at the very least points to an epistemological crisis in reading (how do we talk about such texts?)—because it insists that there are material authors who write, biographical circumstances and emotions that "slip" into scholarship. The slip of emotion threatens to exceed the text itself, exposing poststructuralist theory's investments in the integrity of textual division, or rather, of keeping the divisions of subjectivity within texts. One charge of Tompkins's performance lies in the essay's acknowledgment of the slippage between textual performances and the professional contexts, and conflicts, that qualify the integrity of such performances.

Adela Pinch defines this slippage as the sentimental condition: "Sentimentality involves moments when the issue of whether feeling is authorized by literature or by life becomes a problem" (*Strange Fits*, 69). This problem involves the reader. Emotion becomes "sentimental"—and "sincere" or "theatrical"—not simply at the moment when the writer represents feeling, and thus engages convention, but also at the moment of reception, when the reader or listener interprets convention: sincerity is a product not simply of textuality but of how textual conventions are circulated and read (Howard, "What is Sentimentality?" 66, 69). As Julie Ellison argues, "To call something sentimental is to place oneself in the chain of sentimental relations" (*Cato's Tears*, 184). Tompkins implies that sincerity's impossibility is not just a textual but also a contextual condition that her essay addresses and anticipates, a condition shaped by its institutional context and by readerly suspicions and expectations. Making reception part of the picture asks us to challenge the idea that the representation of feeling is inherently liberatory or conversely, inherently doomed to fail as a means of engaging trenchant social problems. Jacqueline Rose writes, "It is often assumed, especially on the left, that emotions on display are politically demeaning and should be put to cultural or political work somewhere else. . . . Or else, more simply, they are a front" ("Cult of Celebrity," in *Sleep*, 206). "Sincere" texts can just as often be used to ground progressive responses as reactionary ones.

On the one hand, we can read Tompkins's essay as enacting the "self-circumscription" of the female complaint as Berlant describes it, in that the essay "implicitly marks the conditions and probability of its failure to persuade the addressed subject. Often a last-ditch employment, the complaint is a performative plea that implicitly holds no hope for change in the conditions of the author's misery—apart from whatever response the complaint itself might elicit from the audience" ("Female Complaint," 243). Anger in the essay can be read as anticipation of failure: just as Plath's Lady Lazarus famously directs her anger at "the peanut-crunching crowd" that has come to watch her strip-tease, so the Tompkins of "Me and My Shadow" directs her avowal of anger at her complacent or "hostile" readers, readers who are likely to dismiss discussions of feeling as "sentimental."[22] And we can read failure in the fact that the complexities of "Me and My Shadow" remain largely ignored by a reception that seeks to put Tompkins in her place, to police the conventions of professional conduct that the essay challenges. In this sense, anger has indeed circulated, but has rebounded upon Tompkins's person, reducing critique to the female complaint and rigidifying the distinction between theory and personal criticism, critical analysis and feeling.[23]

On the other hand, we might read the essay as an internal critique of the female complaint. Like poetess writing, the essay professes a desire for a "real" form of expression that serves to expose the contradictions of academic literary authorship in the late 1980s. Rather than read the avowal of anger as an assertion of the liberated self, we could just as easily read it as symptom of the impossibility of this "therapeutic" outcome. While the "straitjacket" comment that concludes the essay certainly contributes to a reading of the essay as therapeutic ("This one time I've taken off the strait-jacket, and it feels so good"), this statement may also reveal that Tompkins, like her critics, has fallen back on the way that sentimental culture tends to talk about feeling, which is to moralize it as a reponse to professionaliza-tion (feeling is "good" in the essay's moral economy, an alternative to the overprofessionalization of theory; or "bad"—feeling as co-optation—in that of its skeptical critics). Asserting that feeling can perform "moral" work is not equivalent to its privatization, however. Keeping in mind Rousseauian confession, Tompkins represents anger not to internalize or dissipate it, but to make it public, reveal the "individual" as index of larger institutional or political forces. Indeed, Tompkins explicitly rejects therapy as a solution: "My therapist meant that if I worked out some of my problems—as she un-derstood them, on a psychological level—my feminist rage would subside. Maybe it would, but that wouldn't touch the issue of female oppression" (1115).

From this perspective, the essay suggests that if institutional contexts help distinguish the professional from the personal, reason from feeling, objectivity from subjectivity, than the institution needs to be addressed. Tompkins's description of Messer-Davidow's work perhaps applies to her own as well: "What she offered was not an intellectual performance calcu-lated to draw attention to the quality of her mind, but a sustained effort of practical courage that changed the situation we were in. . . . Analysis that is not an end in itself but pressure brought to bear on a situation" (1113). We might read "Me and My Shadow" as a complaint that challenges its status as a privatizing and inherently conservative mode; the circulation of anger may in fact put pressure on the situation, exceeding "the intractability of the (phallocentric) conditions of the complaint's production."[24] More point-edly, "Me and My Shadow" is a frequent touchstone in subsequent debates; it has exerted pressure on the profession, resulting in debate as well as an increasing use of and attention to this mode. As her critics have pointed out, Tompkins doesn't discuss who gets to feel, how factors such as race and class shape cultures of feeling (see Pfister, *Inventing the Psychological*, 25). In this respect, her essay isn't personal enough. And yet, her essay helps open the field for these concerns to enter criticism. More generally, Tompkins's essay reveals conflicts about the affective nature of literary criticism that are endemic to the profession (Bledstein, *Culture of Professionalism*, 88), leaving us with more questions than solutions. As the scholarship on emotion in-dicates, they remain relevant questions.

Professional Authorship and the Slip of Genre

Some of the anxiety generated by Tompkins's essay stems from her blurring of genre: her critics argue that she tries to collapse literary criticism into literature, analysis into expressions of subjective sensibility.[25] Tompkins's generic provocation raises the question, Into what kinds of institutional and textual spaces has the personal voice "conventionally" slipped? Nancy Miller observes that personal writing "tends to occur in another literary genre, occasional writing: writing for sessions at the MLA sponsored by the Commission on the Status of Women, at Women's Studies conferences, in feminist anthologies, newsletters etc." ("But Enough about Me," 15). On the other hand, Jane Gallop notes that personal narratives have always been part of the "edge" of academic scholarship in the form of "prefaces, acknowledgments, dedications, footnotes." Academic readers testify to being fascinated by these slips in spite of the "death of the author."[26]

These slips have become increasingly central to the text itself. One has only to survey the field of contemporary literature to realize that claims to sincerity have taken center stage, and not just in literary criticism: memoirs, autobiographies, and confessions top the bestseller lists. Metanarrative in both fictional and nonfictional texts renders conventions of sincerity—and reflections on professional authorship—central to textual form and content.[27] The preface to Dave Eggers's *A Heartbreaking Work of Staggering Genius* is a good example of this trend. The use of sincerity conventions seems to have blurred boundaries between genres: all literature threatens to become "confessional," organized around the centrality of the figure of the author. Karl Kroeber comments, "Poetry has long been diminished to personal lyricism, and most novels are now told in the first person. So why shouldn't our sixty-watt leading lights melt down criticism into self-advertisement?" (in "Forum," 1163).

Conventions of sincerity seem to have simultaneously defined and eroded the distinctions between genres: even as sincerity is a rhetoric historically allied with the most "literary" genres such as poetry, it also appears to be a rhetoric of generic "breakdown," the figure of the author taking center stage not just in the lyric but in the memoir and novel. But the perception of "generic breakdown" is an inheritance of the romantics, and as Stuart Curran argues, a myth: "We have inherited the myth of a radical generic breakdown in European Romanticism that in fact never happened, but that with its own logic of cultural determinism has essentially distorted our perceptions of both Romantic literature and culture" (*Poetic Form*, 5). The efforts of the romantic poets to ground authority in the author's sensibility contributed to this myth: the contours of the poet's feelings ostensibly define the parameters of text and genre, a connection evident in Wordsworth's description of poetry as the "spontaneous overflow of powerful feelings" and apparent in the development of "free verse." A particular understanding of sincerity—as an expressive, liberatory, idealizing rhetoric—perpetuates this myth, and yet romantic and postmodern poets themselves interrogate this ideal.

In coming up with more complex accounts of sincerity as a rhetoric, we in turn need to come up with more complex understandings of genre. Approaching lyric as it is shaped by the commercial practices of professional authorship asks us to reconceive our understanding of generic traditions, not simply as a study of literary conventions, tropes, textual influence and indebtedness, but also as a study of cultural institutions, theaters in which we stage dramas of character, decorum, and trust; feeling, agency, and power. Finally, as my discussion of personal criticism suggests, sincerity is a rhetoric that stages, and responds to, the contradictions of professional authorship in many genres. My generic provocation in this book has involved showing the critical engagements of poetry not as epistemologically less knowing but as akin to those of literary criticism. To attribute the rhetoric of sincerity with generic breakdown, to pathologize it, to feminize it, to demarcate it as either "naive" or "cunning," is an attempt to deny that the category of the "literary" engages in, and is defined by, commercial culture. Our generic productions are at least in part professional performances, and the contradictions that ensue—in our practices both as authors and as readers—should be part of the story.

Notes

Introduction

1. Atlas, "Literary Memoir"; Abst and Mustazza, *Coming After Oprah;* Sontag and Graham, eds., *After Confession.*

2. Middlebrook, *Anne Sexton,* 286–87, 303–6, 319, 330.

3. Sexton, "To Elizabeth Bishop," October 21, 1965. Special Collections, Vassar College Libraries.

4. Middleton, *Anne Sexton,* 187, 272, 319–20, 332; Maxine Kumin, introduction to *Sexton: Complete Poems,* xx–xxi.

5. On Robinson's life and career, see Byrne, *Perdita.*

6. St. Augustine, *Confessions,* 208; de Man, *Allegories of Reading,* 278–301.

7. Barker Benfield in *Culture of Sensibility* connects an emphasis on individual feeling to the rise of consumer culture; see also Campbell, *Romantic Ethic.*

8. See Catherine Gallagher, "Blindness and Hindsight," in Hamacher, *Responses,* 205–6.

9. Gilmore, "Policing Truth"; Felski, "On Confession"; Foucault, *History of Sexuality,* vol. 1. Like Gilmore and Felski, I see the tradition of confession as an important context for autobiographical modes of self-representation, particularly in women's writing.

10. Quinney's *Poetics of Disappointment* argues that "the history of romantic and postromantic poetry is not a history of ambitious self-assertion but a collective testimony of chagrin over the broken promises of the self" (xii).

11. Foucault, "What Is an Author?" in *Foucault Reader,* 110. See Prins's discussion of "Anthropomorphic (mis)reading" in *Victorian Sappho,* 19, and Costello, "Elizabeth Bishop's Personal Impersonal."

12. On confessional poets' reworkings of romantic tropes, see Langbaum, *Poetry of Experience;* Trilling, *Sincerity and Authenticity;* Davie, "On Sincerity"; Rosenthal, *New Poets;* Alvarez, "Beyond the Gentility Principle," in *Beyond All This Fiddle.*

13. Forbes, introduction to *Sincerity's Shadow;* Davie, "On Sincerity"; Guilhamet, *Sincere Ideal.*

14. British romantic scholarship has clarified how critics have been influenced by the "romantic ideology," falling sway to romantic writers' own self-representations;

how romantic conceptions of subjectivity have influenced the uses of representative history; and how understandings of literary historical periodization depend on a logic of breakage or rupture that is romantic in origin. See McGann's *Romantic Ideology;* Ross, "Breaking the Period"; Chandler, "Representative Men," in Johnston, *Romantic Revolutions.* Scholarship on postmodern American poetry has challenged understandings of confessional poetry as a simple reaction against modernist impersonality; has assimilated poststructuralist insights; and has addressed midcentury contexts from the cold war to legal debates over privacy. See Longenbach, *Modern Poetry;* Nelson, *Pursuing Privacy;* Ramazani, *Poetry of Mourning;* J. Rose, *Haunting;* Travisano, *Midcentury Quartet;* Blake, "Public Dreams"; Hammer, "Plath's Lives"; Middlebrook, "What Was Confessional Poetry?"

15. Rosenthal, who coined the term "confessional poetry" in a 1959 review of *Life Studies,* commented that "it was a term both helpful and too limited" (*New Poets,* 25). Travisano sums up the problems with the confessional paradigm in *Midcentury Quartet,* 44. The term retains literary historical and cultural significance, insofar as a "confessional culture" has overdetermined the reading of lyric poetry, resulting in some common poetic tactics. I agree with Travisano that we need new paradigms, or at least new understandings of confession: a focus on the rhetoric of sincerity can help us to see that the problems we associate with "confession" are endemic to the culture of sensibility, and are shared by poets left out of the "confessional" paradigm (in this study, Bishop, O'Hara, Barbauld).

16. Clark, *Sentimental Modernism;* Ellison, *Cato's Tears;* J. Rose, *Sleep;* Berlant, "Poor Eliza!"

17. Recent scholarship positions the modernist resistance to commercial culture either as an ideology that belied actual practices or as a belated academic construction. See Rainey, *Institutions of Modernism;* Scandura and Thurston, *Modernism, Inc.;* Dettmar and Watt, *Marketing Modernisms;* Willison, Gould, and Chernaik, *Modernist Writers;* Wexler, *Who Paid for Modernism?;* Wicke, *Advertising Fictions.*

18. Ngai, *Ugly Feelings;* Nelson, *Women, the New York School, and Other True Abstractions* (forthcoming).

19. Voksuil, *Acting Naturally;* Prins, *Victorian Sappho;* Lootens, *Lost Saints;* Richards, *Lyric Mediums;* Haltunnen, *Confidence Men.*

20. Vendler, *Soul Says,* 138. On modernist poets' continuities with romanticism, see Christ, *Victorian and Modern Poetics;* Langbaum, *Poetry of Experience.*

21. See my discussion in chap. 6, n. 34.

22. Favor, *Authentic Blackness;* Chinitz, "Literacy and Authenticity." On the importance of thinking about race in terms of a performance of sincerity rather than through static evaluations of racial authenticity, see Jackson, *Real Black,* 12–18.

23. Prins and Jackson, "Lyrical Studies"; Kinnahan, *Lyric Interventions;* Orr, "Postconfessional Lyric."

24. I call sincerity a rhetoric in Booth's sense, i.e., how specific conventions circulate and make themselves understood under particular historical circumstances (*Rhetoric of Irony,* xiii).

25. On the history of sincerity as an antitheatrical rhetoric indebted to Puritan-

ism, see Agnew, *Worlds Apart*, 112, 139; Guilhamet, *Sincere Ideal*, chaps. 1–3; Halttunen, *Confidence Men*. On the antitheatrical prejudice, see Barish, *Antitheatrical Prejudice;* Puchner, *Stage Fright;* Wikander, *Fangs of Malice;* Voskuil, *Acting Naturally*.

26. In addition to Alvarez, Langbaum, Trilling, Davie, and Rosenthal, see Read, *Cult of Sincerity* (1968); Peyre, *Literature and Sincerity* (1963); Perkins, *Wordsworth and the Poetry of Sincerity* (1969). After the late 1960s there is a noticeable decline in the use of the concept of sincerity, which Wang describes thus: "The secular humanist, archetypal, and phenomenological concerns of the '50's generation thus give way to a '70's and '80's stress on linguistic indeterminacy, historical aporias, ideological critiques, and identity politics" (*Fantastic Modernity*, 5–7).

27. Barthes, "Death of the Author," in *Image-Music-Text*.

28. De Man, *Rhetoric of Romanticism*, 67–81; *Allegories of Reading*, 278–301.

29. Prins, *Victorian Sappho*, 19–20; Prins and Jackson, "Lyrical Studies"; J. Rose, *Haunting;* Pinch, *Strange Fits*, 8; Howard, "What is Sentimentality?"; Terada, *Feeling in Theory*, 18, 21, 37–38.

30. Siskin argues that professionals are precisely those who intrude into private life, converting knowledge of the "depths" of the self into professional expertise (*Work of Writing*, 106).

31. Studies of authorship locate this shift in the mid- to late eighteenth century. See Foucault, "What Is an Author?"; Woodmansee and Jaszi, *Construction*, 7; Siskin, *Work of Writing*, 12; M. Rose, *Authors and Owners;* Gallagher, *Nobody's Story*, xiii, xviii; Sheavyn, *Literary Profession*, 11.

32. Charvat usefully defines professional writing thus: "that it provides a living for the author, like any other job; that it is a main and prolonged, rather than intermittent or sporadic, resource for the writer; that it is produced with the hope of extended sale in the open market, like any article of commerce; and that it is written with reference to buyers' tastes and reading habits" (*Profession of Authorship*, 3).

33. Albisette, "Professionals and Professionalization," 57; West, *American Authors*, 8–9.

34. Colby, "Authorship and the Book Trade"; Cross, *Common Writer;* West, *American Authors*. On creative writing programs, see Alpaugh, "Professionalization of Poetry."

35. Foucault, "What Is an Author?" 108; Barthes, *Image-Music-Text*, 126.

36. Scholars credit the Statute of Anne (1710) with beginning the shift in understandings of literary property. Prior to this statute, authors' economic rights were not protected by law; as Mark Rose argues, "Parliament's concern was not with authors' economic rights, but with their potential vulnerability to prosecution merely for having held offending ideas" (214). Following Pope's 1741 lawsuit against Curll, the Statute of Anne (1710) began to be used to provide an early form of copyright protection for authors. The case of Donaldson vs. Beckett in 1774 clarified authors' rights of property in their work. Feather argues that this case defined copyright as "a form of property created by the author at the moment of composition" (25). This decision clarified that copyright was created by the author; that copyright did not exist in perpetuity but for a limited period of time; and that the the the author

had the first right to benefit from his work and would regain copyright absolutely when the time limits prescribed by the Statue of Anne expired (25). The Statute of Anne allowed for fourteen years of protection to the holder of the right of copy; this term of protection was subsequently extended. Charvat connects professional authorship in America to the copyright law of 1790 and argues that the profession became distinct later than in England, in the 1820s (*Profession of Authorship*, 6, 30). The 1790 law allowed for fourteen years of protection, renewable for fourteen more. See Woodmansee and Jaszi, *Construction*, 5–8; Mark Rose, "The Author in Court: Pope v. Curll 1741," in *Construction*, 211–29; Feather, "Publishers and the Pirates"; Kaplan, *Unhurried View of Copyright*, 25.

37. Woodmansee and Jaszi, *Construction*, 7; M. Rose, *Authors and Owners*, 121.

38. Scholars trace this notion of literary property to the tradition of possessive individualism developed by Locke and Hobbes. See Rosemary J. Coombe, "Author/izing the Celebrity: Public Rights, Postmodern Politics, and Unauthorized Genders," in Woodmansee and Jaszi, *Construction*, 101–32 (esp. 105); M. Rose, *Authors and Owners*, 85.

39. See Grosheide, "Paradigms in Copyright Law," and Strowel, "Droit d'Auteur and Copyright: Between History and Nature," in Sherman and Strowel, *Authors and Origins*.

40. Under current copyright law in the United States, works created after January 1, 1978, are under copyright protection for the life of the author plus fifty years; for works published before 1978, copyright protection lasts for seventy-five years from publication or one hundred years since creation. Great Britain ensures copyright protection for the life of the author plus fifty years. See "Copyright Basics."

41. Griffin, *Literary Patronage*, 10; Rizzo, "Patron as Poet Maker," 241; Ezell, *Social Authorship*, 8–9, 11.

42. See Griffin, *Literary Patronage*, 4, 248, 287–88; Raymond Williams, *Sociology of Culture*, 38–44, 46, 55; Benedict, *Public Money*.

43. Griffin, *Literary Patronage*, 11; Sheavyn, *Profession*, 33–5.

44. Mark Rose points out that men and some women "had been living by their pens since the sixteenth century," but notes that by the mid-eighteenth century "they were a large and growing, if not yet entirely respectable, class. That was possible only because the products of their pens commanded a market price, and that in turn was possible only because the commodity was protected against unfair competition" ("Author in Court," 209).

45. Donoghue, *Fame Machine*, 1–2; Agnew, *Worlds Apart*, 30, 39, 40–43, 56.

46. Richards, *Lyric Mediums*; see also Peter Middleton, "Contemporary Poetry Reading" (262–99), Lorenzo Thomas, "Neon Griot" (300–323), and Ron Silliman, "Who Speaks: Ventriloquism and the Self in the Poetry Reading" (360–78), in Bernstein, *Close Listening*.

47. Charvat, *Profession of Authorship*, 292–93; Siskin, *Work of Writing*, 108.

48. Peter Middleton (see n. 46, above) argues that "audience and poet collaborate in the performance of the poem," creating what he calls an "intersubjective network"

(291); "the author is the subjective crossroads for the enormously complex transactions of institutional legitimation in the contemporary world" (269).

49. Sennett, *Fall of Public Man;* Adorno, "Lyric and Society," 44; Jameson, *Postmodernism;* Batten, *Orphaned Imagination,* 2–3. See Hotelling-Zona on the feminist breakthrough narrative.

50. Agnew argues that "the characteristic forms of theatricality and of the theatrical perspective that we have seen accompanying the spread of a 'free' market in Anglo-American society can best be understood as a recurrent response, at once accommodative and critical, to the threat and promise of an embryonic market culture" (*Worlds Apart,* 202).

Part I. The Poet in the Street

1. See Langan, *Romantic Vagrancy;* J. Robinson, *Walk;* Wallace, *Walking;* A. Bennett, "Devious Feet"; Jarvis, *Pedestrian Travel;* Gilbert, *Walks in the World.*

2. Wordworth and Coleridge, *Lyrical Ballads,* 246. I quote from the 1800 Preface, hereafter cited in the text as *PLB.*

3. I sum up McGann's approach in *Romantic Ideology* and Levinson's in *Wordsworth's Great Period Poems.* See also Wallace, *Walking,* 173.

4. Schoenfield, *Professional Wordsworth;* Gill, *William Wordsworth;* Gooch, *City Poet.*

5. Priscilla Parkhurst Ferguson, "The Flaneur On and Off the Streets of Paris," in Tester, *Flaneur,* 22–42; 27.

6. On the French origins of flanerie, see Parkhurst Ferguson, "Flaneur," 22–26; Rosalind Williams, *Dream Worlds,* 116; Baudelaire, "Painter of Modern Life," in *Selected Writings,* 420. On eighteenth-century precursors to the flaneur, see Pascoe, *Romantic Theatricality,* 132–33; Moers, *Dandy.*

7. Rosalind Williams, *Dream Worlds,* 116; Parkhurst Ferguson, "Flaneur," 23.

8. See Buck-Morss, *Dialectics,* 188–89, 195–96; Chambers, "Flaneur as Hero," 147.

9. Glebber discusses flanerie as a semiotic "reading of the street" in *Taking a Walk,* 11.

Chapter 1. William Wordsworth

1. Poems that explicitly address the city include the Westminster Bridge sonnet, "To Joanna," and "The Reverie of Poor Susan."

2. See Friedman, "History"; King, "Panoramas," 32; Kramer, "Gender and Sexuality"; Jacobus, *Romanticism,* 206–36; Simpson, *Figurings.*

3. Wordsworth, "Essay, Supplementary to the Preface" (1815), in *Selected Prose,* 411. Hereafter cited in the text as *ESP.*

4. Wordsworth, "Essay upon Epitaphs, III," in *Selected Prose,* 361. Hereafter cited in the text as *EE* followed by the essay number.

5. I cite from the 1805 *Prelude.*

6. *Oxford English Dictionary,* 2nd ed. (1996), s.v. "Type," def. 5a and 7a. Subsequent references to *OED* are to this edition and appear in the text.

7. See Schwarzbach, "Review Essay"; Raymond Williams, *Country and City,* 142–52.

8. Lavater's essays were translated into English between 1789 and 1798. See A. Bennett, "Devious Feet," 147–48; Graham, "Character Description" and "Lavater's Physiognomy"; Cowling, *Artist as Anthropologist,* 121–81.

9. See Valverde, "Love of Finery"; Jacobus, *Romanticism,* 210.

10. Epstein Nord, "City as Theater," 164–65, and *Walking the Victorian Streets.*

11. Briggs, *Social History,* 203–23, and *Modern England,* 20–36.

12. Klancher, *Reading Audiences,* chap. 3.

13. See, e.g., Burney, *Monthly Review,* June 1799 (in *Lyrical Ballads,* 324) and Jeffrey's comments in the *Edinburgh Review* (qtd. in Gill, *Life,* 268).

14. Wilson, "Invisible Flaneur"; Walkowitz, *Dreadful Delight,* 21.

15. Andrew Bennett argues that "the social," denied by Wordsworth, blocks his rural walks ("Devious Feet," 150). Book 7 reverses this pattern.

16. Bolton demonstrates Wordsworth's failed effort to protect himself from the threat Mary Robinson embodies.

17. Langan argues that the "random encounter" that structures Wordsworth's walk poems emphasizes the "exigency of this formal constraint," implying "the subjection of literary composition to precisely those forces—historical, economic, social . . . —that it wishes to subordinate to absolute freedom of expression" (*Romantic Vagrancy,* 24).

18. "Wordsworth's Autobiographical Poem," *Gentleman's Magazine* 34 (1850), rpt. in *Prelude,* 552–53.

19. Pascoe points out that Wordsworth in *PLB* anticipates method acting (*Romantic Theatricality,* 219–20).

20. See Bolton, "Romancing"; Jacobus, *Romanticism,* 189, 223, 226.

21. Wordsworth to Beaumont, May 1, 1805; Wordsworth to Talfourd, April ll, 1839, in *Prelude,* 534, 538.

22. Wordsworth Jr. to Watson, June 14, 1850, in *Prelude,* 539. Siskin argues that "Wordsworth's strange decision" for posthumous publication of *The Prelude* provided him with "expert control . . . over the commodification process itself" (*Work of Writing,* 112).

23. Wordsworth to Sir George Beaumont, June 3, 1805, in *Prelude,* 534; Wordsworth to Sharp, April 29, 1804, in *Prelude,* 532; preface to "The Excursion," in *Prelude,* 535.

24. Early critics largely accept *The Prelude* as a "regular versified autobiography" even when "a veil of fiction has been dropt over the real facts" ("The Prelude," *Eclectic Review* 28 [1850]: 550–62, rpt. in *Prelude,* 547–50; see 548). Critics praised the poet's sincerity and his artlessness ("The Prelude," *Tait's Edinburgh Magazine* 17 [1850]: 27–39, rpt. in *Prelude,* 550–52; see 551). The *British Quarterly Review* points out that "in leaving instructions that it should be published, the author virtually gave it

the sanction of his maturer approbation"; see "The Prelude," *British Quarterly Review* 12 (1850), rpt. in *Prelude,* 555.

25. Eilenberg persuasively connects epitaph and copyright; see "Mortal Pages," 356, 363, 368.

26. Scodel, *English Poetic Epitaph,* 386; Ferguson, *Counter-Spirit,* 159.

27. Byrd observes that in the Westminster Bridge sonnet, Wordsworth presents London as a corpse when he states, "And all that mighty heart is lying still!" (*London Transformed,* 122).

28. Klancher argues that Wordsworth initially attempts to transform the consumption of literature by an urban class addicted to popular culture into a form of reception defined by "an active, engaged response," but by 1815 had conceded "to the middle-class culture of commodity exchange its priority and enabling necessity" (*Reading Audiences,* 143, 148).

29. "The Prelude," *British Quarterly Review* 12 (1850), rpt. in *Prelude,* 555–56.

30. Urry, *Consuming Places,* 201. Pascoe underscores the theatricality of Wordsworth's Lake District walks (*Romantic Theatricality,* 200), and Gill notes that Rydal Mount was a "must on the modern equivalent of the grand tour" (*Life,* 385).

31. Wordsworth, *Guide,* 148, 150–51.

Chapter 2. Frank O'Hara

1. O'Hara, "Meditations in an Emergency," *Collected Poems,* 197. Hereafter cited in text as *CP*.

2. Zygmunt Bauman, "Desert Spectacular," in Tester, *Flaneur,* 138–57; see 155–56.

3. Andrew Ross, "Death of Lady Day," in Elledge, *To Be True to a City,* 382. Elledge text hereafter cited as *TBTC*.

4. Susan Sontag, "Notes on Camp," in *Against Interpretation,* 275–92; Dollimore, *Sexual Dissidence,* 311.

5. Jameson, *Postmodernism,* 4–5; Huyssen, *Great Divide,* 4. See in contrast Rifkin, *Career Moves,* 16; Rainey, *Institutions of Modernism.*

6. See Davidson, "From Margin to Mainstream"; Benedict, *Public Money;* Guilbaut, *New York;* Altshuler, *Avant-Garde,* 218–19.

7. Waldo Rasmussen, "Frank O'Hara in the Museum," in Berkson and LeSueur, *Homage,* 84–90.

8. Gooch, *City Poet,* 207–8, 257–59, 294–96.

9. Gertrude Stein, qtd. in Grace Glueck, "Gertrude Stein's Art Collection Is Sought for Modern Museum," *New York Times,* October 14, 1968, p. 55.

10. Gooch, *City Poet,* 194–95, 423–25; Chauncey, *Gay New York,* 9.

11. O'Hara, "Here in New York We Are Having A Lot of Trouble With the World's Fair" (*CP,* 480–81). O'Hara and Ginsberg protested the "horrible cleanup" of the gay city before the 1964 World's Fair (Gooch, *City Poet,* 424–25).

12. On the "urban pastoral" in the 1950s, see Gray, "Semiotic Shepherds"; Diggory, "Ginsberg's Urban Pastoral."

13. Whitman, *Leaves of Grass*, 325. Hereafter cited in text as *LG*.

14. See Sharpe, *Unreal Cities*, 80–81.

15. O'Hara, back cover of *Lunch Poems*. Hereafter cited in text as *LP*.

16. Gooch, *City Poet*, 196–97. Stuart Byron, "Frank O'Hara: Poetic Queertalk," in *TBTC*, 64–69; see 68.

17. Kenneth Koch, "A Note on Frank O'Hara in the Early Fifties," in Berkson and LeSueur, *Homage*, 26–27; see 26.

18. Perloff, *Poet among Painters*, 116. Hereafter cited in text as *PP*.

19. Perloff, "Aesthetics of Attention," in *TBTC*, 159. Hereafter cited in text as *AA*.

20. See Costello's discussion of sincerity and Moore's "Poetry" in *Marianne Moore*, 18–26.

21. These poems to Bill Berkson, written at O'Hara's desk at MOMA, mimic the memo while allowing him to subtly resist the demands of his professional role. See *CP*, 551; *AA*, 169.

22. O'Hara commented, "Through habits of thought, feeling and judgment, a poet looks at things a little more peculiarly, if not entirely more peculiarly, than others" (*Standing Still*, 32).

23. See Yingling, "Homosexuality," 139, in Erkkila and Grossman, *Breaking Bounds*; Sharpe, *Unreal Cities*, 78–80.

24. See Sussman, *On the Passage*, 4, 9, 127, 144. Debord's drawings of *derivés* amount to sketches of what he calls "psychogeography."

25. LeSueur writes that O'Hara had in mind his lover Vincent Warren (*Digressions*, 223–32).

26. May, *Homeward Bound*, 167, 180, 181; Ross, "Lady Day," 389; Felski, *Gender of Modernity*, 65.

27. Sharpe observes this in Whitman (*Unreal Cities*, 91).

28. On these practices in Whitman, see Buinicki, "Walt Whitman," 263–65; Sharpe, *Unreal Cities*, 88–97.

29. Lowney argues that the web of specificity in O'Hara's poetry functions as a process of "double coding," a gay vernacular. See also Byron, "Poetic Queertalk," 66.

30. The censorship trial of Ginsberg's *Howl* in 1956 suggests what gay poets faced pre-Stonewall. See Miles, *Howl*; Byron, "Poetic Queertalk," 64–69.

31. O'Hara states that "the point is really more to establish one's own measure and breath in poetry . . . rather than fitting your ideas into an established order. . . . What really makes me happy is when something just falls into place as if it were a conversation" (*Standing Still*, 17, 21).

32. For a similar view of Whitman, see Mulcaire, "Publishing Intimacy," 472, 489; Buinicki, "Walt Whitman," 271.

33. As Lehman says of Ashbery: "The poem is the performance of an experience rather than a commentary on experience" (*Last Avant-Garde*, 105).

34. Andrew Ross and Rudy Kikel both emphasize that O'Hara practiced a "code of personal politics" (Ross, "Lady Day," 388, 390) that allowed him to resist "everyday conditions of oppression" before collective gay liberation (Kikel, "The Gay Frank O'Hara," in *TBTC*, 334–49; see 348). Thus, while Lehman (*Last Avant-Garde*, 306–

314) sees the antiprogrammatic, pleasure-seeking, and humorous nature of the poetry as incompatible with political commitment, O'Hara's "commitment" to "self-realization" (308) articulates what we might call a moral politics.

35. Perloff notes the irony that, "largely ignored by the Establishment during his lifetime," O'Hara's *Collected Poems* was published by Knopf and won the National Book Award in 1971 ("Poetry Chronicle: 1970–71," in *TBTC*, 59).

36. See the reviews by Pearl K. Bell and Herbert A. Leibowitz in *TBTC*.

37. See Perloff, *AA*, 176, and *PP*, 130–31; Lowney, "Post-Anti-Esthetic," 261; Gilbert, *Walks*, 9.

38. *Collected Poems* (1971) was supplanted by *Selected Poems* (1974) to provide the reader with a selection of O'Hara's greatest hits, indicating that readers—clinging to the romantic notion of the poem as a spot of time—felt overwhelmed by the collected works. See the reviews by Gerald Burns and Peter Schjeldahl in *TBTC*.

39. Kenneth Koch, "All the Imagination Can Hold," in *TBTC*, 31–37; see 37.

Part II. Modern Mourning

1. Fergus and Thaddeus, "Women, Publishers, and Money"; Ross, *Contours*, chap. 6; Siskin, *Work of Writing*, 133, 222–24; Turner, *Living by the Pen*, 77; Moran, *Star Authors*, 48–49.

2. Ross, *Contours*, 304. Women were believed to be "naturally more sincere than man"; see Halttunen, *Confidence Men*, 57.

3. With the exception of Lootens (*Privatizing the Poetess*, forthcoming) and Boym, who discuss the poetess in the twentieth century, the scholarship is located in eighteenth- and nineteenth-century studies. See Armstrong and Blain, *Women's Poetry*; Boym, *Death in Quotation Marks*; Brown, "Victorian Poetess"; Linley, "Dying to Be a Poetess"; Lootens, *Lost Saints*; Prins, *Victorian Sappho*; Pascoe, *Romantic Theatricality*; Richards, *Lyric Mediums*; Ross, *Contours*.

4. Wolff, *Feminine Sentences*, 58; Pascoe, *Romantic Theatricality*, 131–32; Walkowitz, *Dreadful Delight*, 41, 46; Epstein Nord, *Streetwalking*.

5. On connections between writing, prostitution, and acting, see Fergus and Thaddeus, "Women, Publishers," 191; Turner, *Living by the Pen*, 77; Pascoe, *Romantic Theatricality*, 131, 137.

6. Pollak and Noble, "Emily Dickinson, 1830–1886," in Pollak, *Historical Guide*, 13–66; on Dickinson's posthumous reception, see Morse, "Bibliographical Essay," in Pollak, *Historical Guide*, 255–74.

7. On the generic status of the poetess's performance of womanhood, see Lootens, *Lost Saints*, 11, 69–70; Jackson and Prins, "Lyrical Studies," 523, 529; Prins, *Victorian Sappho*, 14, 184–85.

8. Jackson and Prins argue that "through the figure of the poetess, they perform lyrical reflections on the conventions of subjectivity attributed to persons and poems, and thus imagine the unbearable possibility of lyric outside the terms, or boundaries, of subjectivity" ("Lyrical Studies," 523).

9. Voskuil shows that the Victorian concept of "natural acting" indicated an

understanding of theatricality and authenticity not as opposed but as necessarily intertwined concepts (*Acting Naturally*, 2–3, 11–13).

10. Many raise this problem in reference to Letitia Landon. See Lootens, "Receiving the Legend," 248–49; Prins, *Victorian Sappho*, 197; Pascoe, *Romantic Theatricality*, 237–40.

11. Mark Rose states: "Property, originality, personality: the construction of the discourse of literary property depended on a chain of deferrals. . . . The attempt to anchor the notion of literary property in personality suggests the need to find a transcendent signifier, a category beyond the economic to warrant and ground the circulation of literary commodities" (*Authors and Owners*, 128).

12. Quinney, *Poetics of Disappointment*, xii, 13. I am also indebted to Prins's argument that the poetess performs the "death of the author" (*Victorian Sappho*, 184) and to Moran's connection between the death of the author and the rise of literary celebrity (*Star Authors*, 61).

13. Poe, "Philosophy of Composition," in *Selected Writings*, 458. Bronfen, *Over Her Dead Body*, 60; Richards, *Lyric Mediums*; Brown, "Victorian Poetess," 183.

14. Like Batten, I see melancholia as a product of and response to the "systemic problems of a free-market economy" but diverge in arguing that it is complicit with this economy (*Orphaned Imagination*, 1, 19). I build on Schiesari's argument that melancholia is a gendered discourse, "coterminous with the historic rise and demise of 'the subject,'" a "perpetual mourning for the barred status imposed on [women]" (*Gendering*, 2, 17).

15. Their performances have much in common with the dramatic monologue, which turns on "the tension between sympathy and moral judgment" (Langbaum, *Poetry of Experience*, 306, 93, 79).

16. See Travisano, *Midcentury Quartet*; Nelson, *Pursuing Privacy*; Costello, "Impersonal Personal"; J. Rose, *Haunting*; Kinnahan, *Lyric Interventions*.

17. While I agree with Ramazani that many of the attributes Schenck ascribes to the female elegy can be found in the male elegy (*Poetry of Mourning*, 263, 298), I think she is correct to point out a "female funeral aesthetic" that spans centuries, one that calls for a more complex reading of "consolation" in eighteenth- and nineteenth-century elegiac poetry.

Chapter 3. Charlotte Smith

1. On Smith's biography, see Mrs. Dorset, "Charlotte Smith," in Scott, *Biographical Memoirs*, 20–58; Hilbish, *Charlotte Smith*.

2. Stanton, "Literary Business," 376. All information on Smith's finances comes from Stanton.

3. On Smith's theatricality, see Pascoe, *Romantic Theatricality*, 16–18; Pinch, *Strange Fits*, 51–71; Zimmerman, *Romanticism*, 48–51, 54–55; Pratt, "Smith's Melancholia."

4. Smith, qtd. in E. Schor, *Bearing the Dead*, 35. My discussion is indebted to Schor's argument that the dead are a "gold standard" because the sympathy they pro-

duce bridges the Christian notions of virtue and the values of a property-based commercial society (4–5, 20, 37–38).

5. Hollander, *Vision and Resonance*, 200; E. Schor, *Bearing the Dead*, 55–57; Curran, *Poetic Form*, 30; Sacks, *English Elegy*, 133.

6. "Il Penseroso" provided a textbook for the poetess role; see in particular lines 31–44. On elegy's feminine qualities see Rothstein, *Restoration*, 143; E. Schor, *Bearing the Dead*, 23.

7. Zimmerman, "Charlotte Smith's Letters," 59, 60; *Romanticism*, chap. 2. I am indebted to Zimmerman's insightful discussion of how Smith creates sympathy through the prefaces and notes to the *Elegiac Sonnets*.

8. Pascoe compares actress Sarah Siddons and the poetess in *Romantic Theatricality*, 12–32.

9. Smith, *Poems*, 6. Hereafter cited in text as *Poems*.

10. Pratt has also drawn attention to this passage ("Smith's Melancholia," 573–74).

11. In total, her prose earned £2660, versus £930 from poetry and £650 from children's books (Stanton, "Literary Business," 392). Smith produced a novel almost every year from 1787 to 1798 (Hilbish, *Charlotte Smith*, 581–86).

12. For differing views of this problem see Pinch, *Strange Fits*, 67; Pratt, "Smith's Melancholia," 577, 563–64. I see Smith exposing the impossibility of authentic experience due to her need to perform sincerity, with melancholia the affective dimension of this conflict; in contrast to Pratt, I argue that Smith articulates a desire for a realm of "real" experience beyond theater, signified through death as utopian ideal.

13. Hunt, *Figure in the Landscape*, 176–77; Sacks, *English Elegy*, 133–34; Todd, *Sensibility*, 50–53; Scodel, *Epitaph*, 329; E. Schor, *Bearing the Dead*, 40, 57; Curran, *Poetic Form*, 30.

14. Curran, *Poetic Form*, 37; Hilbish, *Charlotte Smith*, 246–48; E. Schor, *Bearing the Dead*, 57–58; D. Robinson, "Reviving the Sonnet," 109–16.

15. Curran describes Smith thus: "a disembodied sensibility at the mercy of an alien universe and without discernible exit from its condition" ("I Altered," 20), which "testifies to an alternative Romanticism that seeks not to transcend or to absorb nature but to contemplate and honor its irreducible alterity" (*Poems*, xxviii).

16. I follow Berlant and Chambers (*Melancholy*, 33–34) in reading "unexpressed anger" and "repressed violence" in the complaint. Schiesari implies the connection between the melancholic's plaint and the female complaint (*Gendering*, 55) and both Schiesari (51) and Berlant ("Female Complaint," 242–43) have suggested the importance of a "witnessing" of personal suffering to the female (com)plaint. Pinch (*Strange Fits*, 70–71) and Prins (*Victorian Sappho*, 226) connect the poetess tradition and the female complaint.

17. For a more extensive reception history, see Hilbish, *Charlotte Smith*, 249–57, 266–74; Zimmermann, *Romanticism*.

18. Seward to Theophilus Swift, July 9, 1789, *Letters*, 287. Seward accused Smith of plagiarism, and Smith acknowledged sources of phrases after the second edition of her sonnets.

19. In the preface to *Elegiac Sonnets,* vol. 2, Smith attacks "certain critics" who have reproved her "for bringing forward 'with querulous egotism,' the mention of myself," and who have charged her with "feigning sorrow"; she responds that she is "unhappily exempt" from this suspicion (*Poems,* 8, 11). In sonnets 26, 34, and 73, and in the preface to the sixth edition, Smith defends herself against the charge of feigning sorrow.

20. On Dickinson's posthumous publication and reception, see Morse, "Bibliographical Essay," in Pollak, *Historical Guide.*

21. Dickinson wrote, "When I state myself, as the Representative of the Verse—it does not mean—me—but a supposed person" (qtd. in Grabher, "Dickinson's Lyrical Self," in Grabher et al., *Emily Dickinson Handbook,* 226). See also Weisbuch, "Nobody's Business: Dickinson's Dissolving Audience," in Weisbuch and Orzeck, *Dickinson and Audience.*

22. Scott expresses the same view in 1843, but expresses sympathy for Smith's financial constraints. See *Biographical Memoirs,* 2:68.

23. Dorset writes that Smith "incurred equal censure" from "introducing politics in one of her works," which was "sinning against good taste in a female writer" (in Scott, *Biographical Memoirs,* 56–57).

24. Zimmerman's discussion of St. Cyres brought this review to my attention (*Romanticism,* 54).

25. Even Pinch falls back on moralizing evaluations of sentiment as it is absorbed into commercial logics; she argues, "Once Smith insists that the poems, with their canniness about the otherness of feelings, are really expressions of her own misery, the sonnets in fact begin to become—in Seward's words—'hackneyed scraps of dismality'" (*Strange Fits,* 68).

Chapter 4. Sylvia Plath

1. Plath, *Unabridged Journals,* 447–48. Hereafter cited in the text as *J.*

2. While Plath had not literally "lost" her mother, Freud states that melancholia may be a response to "a loss of a more ideal kind" (*Psychological Theory,* 166).

3. Plath states in her journal entry of May 20, 1959, that, in reference to her mother, "I have dissipated her image and she becomes all editors and publishers and critics and the World" (*J,* 484).

4. Plath's letters and journals refer to her literary successes in terms of paying back a financial and moral debt to her mother figures; Plath felt that she needed to live up to the ideals and ambitions of those who had sacrificed for her success (*Letters Home,* 75–80, 98, 145, 161; hereafter cited in text as *LH; J,* 435, 437). Her anger, she wrote, is directed at "my mother and all the mothers I have known who have wanted me to be what I have not felt like really being from my heart and at the society which seems to want us to be what we do not want to be" (*J,* 437).

5. On Plath's reading of Freud and her use of melancholia as a strategy of engagement with expectations of sincerity, her "mother figures," and the marketplace,

see Rosenbaum, *Confessional Commerce*. Britzolakis has subsequently developed a similar argument in *Theatre of Mourning*.

6. On Plath's theatricality, see Ramazani, *Poetry of Mourning;* J. Rose, *Haunting* and *Sleep;* Hammer, "Plath's Lives"; Britzolakis, *Theatre of Mourning;* Nelson, *Pursuing Privacy.*

7. Ted Hughes's foreword prefaces the abridged version of the journals (*Journals of Sylvia Plath,* xi, xii).

8. Juhasz, *Naked and Fiery Forms,* 3; Ostriker, *Stealing the Language,* 78, 83; J. Rose, *Haunting,* 155.

9. Stevenson, *Bitter Fame,* 17–58; May, *Homeward Bound.*

10. *LH,* 342; *J,* 422–23, 433–38, 438, 445, 450–51, 474, 517; Middlebrook, *Her Husband,* 117–20.

11. Plath, *Johnny Panic,* 62–64; J. Rose, *Haunting,* 4, 172, 184.

12. She calls this form of identity through public recognition a "murderous self," stating "its biggest weapon is and has been the image of myself as a perfect success: in writing, teaching and living. As soon as I sniff nonsuccess in the form of rejections . . . I accuse myself of being a hypocrite, posing as better then I am" (*J,* 176).

13. Plath, *Collected Poems,* 301. Hereafter cited in the text as *CP.*

14. On this struggle see Rich, *Blood, Bread, and Poetry;* Breslin, *From Modern to Contemporary.*

15. Plath as a "method actress"—a professional who uses "real" feeling to infuse a proscribed role with authenticity—is relevant. Braudy connects method acting and confessional poetry ("No Body's Perfect," 278).

16. On Plath's filmic techniques, see Britzolakis, *Theater,* 142–44.

17. Jacqueline Rose argues that the biographical approach has resulted in readings that privatize and depoliticize Plath, rendering her either an innocent victim or pathological case study. See *Haunting* and *Sleep;* Lant, "Big Strip Tease," 661; Britzolakis, *Theater,* 7–8; Bryant, "Imax Authorship."

18. Others who have challenged this "breakthrough" narrative include Hammer, "Plath's Lives"; Longenbach, *Modern Poetry;* Hotelling-Zona, *Feminist Poetics;* Nelson, *Pursuing Privacy,* 35.

19. Middlebrook identifies rage as the inspiration for Plath's late poems (*Her Husband,* 186).

20. Foucault, *History of Sexuality,* 58–63. On connections between Foucault and the female confessional poets, see Nelson, *Pursuing Privacy,* 77, 91.

21. Publication information comes from Tabor, *Sylvia Plath.* See Middlebrook's discussion of poetry sales in *Anne Sexton,* 187.

22. My argument is indebted to Jacqueline Rose's treatment of Plath's reception in *Haunting.*

23. "A Poet's Epitaph," *Observer,* February 17, 1963. Alvarez published several of Plath's poems in the *Observer* from 1960 to 1963, reviewed *The Colossus* in 1960, and in the fall of 1962 heard and discussed with Plath many of the *Ariel* poems. Alvarez reviewed most of Plath's works posthumously published in Britain.

24. Alvarez, "Memoir." The full memoir was also published as the prologue to Alvarez's study of suicide, *The Savage God* (1971).

25. Alvarez, "Beyond the Gentility Principle," in *Beyond All This Fiddle*, 41; first printed as the introduction to *The New Poetry* in 1962.

26. Alvarez's sympathetic identification with Plath stemmed from his own depression; Plath talked with him of suicide because she knew he "was also a member of the club" ("Memoir," 194).

27. See Hughes, *Birthday Letters*, 196.

28. Churchwell, "Secrets and Lies," 143. On *Birthday Letters*, see J. Rose, *Sleep*, 63–68; Bundtzen, "Mourning Eurydice"; Katrovas, "Fame Envy."

29. Middlebrook discusses the royalties from Plath's works in *Her Husband*, 257–58. In 1987, for instance, the annual earnings of the Plath estate were around $150,000.

30. Hughes, *Winter Pollen*, 163–69. Hughes admits that "for her family, I follow her principle and try to manage the writing in ways that will earn as much income as possible" (163).

Part III. The Illegible Signature

1. Bishop, "To Marianne Moore," September 11, 1940, in *One Art*, 94–95.

2. Bishop, *Poe and the Juke-Box*, 113.

3. On the property value of the name and its connection to literary celebrity, see M. Rose, *Authors and Owners*, 114–29; Moran, *Star Authors*, 41, 52, 66–67; Coombe, "Author/izing the Celebrity," in Woodmansee and Jaszi, *Construction*; Marshall, *Celebrity and Power*, 7–19.

4. Marshall, *Celebrity and Power*, 5–9, 58; Moran, *Star Authors*, 7.

5. As described by recent critics, the sentimental writer represents society's victims and their suffering, but to conservative ends, maintaining rather than subverting the status quo, ignoring the privileges that enable the sentimental gaze, and profiting from the market for others' pain. See, e.g., Berlant, "Female Complaint"; Douglas, *Feminization of American Culture*.

6. See McCarthy's discussion of this bias in his introduction to Barbauld, *Selected Poetry and Prose*, 28–29. McCarthy claims that Barbauld should be considered "a founder of British Romanticism" (11).

7. Romantic literature is distinguished from its Augustan precursors and its Victorian and modernist predecessors through assumptions about its claims to sincere antitheatricality: hence the distinctions between the romantic lyric, the Victorian dramatic monologue, and modernist masks and personae.

8. I follow Travisano in arguing for alternative paradigms that can encompass the complex connections between a "reticent" poet such as Bishop and a "self-revelatory" poet such as Lowell.

9. The use of the miniature is widespread in the literature of sentiment. Burns and Blake use the miniature to question hegemonic perspectives in ways similar to

Barbauld and Bishop. Hawthorne and Melville, Sexton and Plath, frequently make use of the miniature.

10. Fancy was not an exclusively female domain, though its use by male romantic poets such as Wordsworth and Keats often indicated the gendered economy of inspiration at work. See Ross, *Contours*, 155–86; Julie Ellison, "The Politics of Fancy in the Age of Sensibility," in Shiner Wilson and Haefner, *Re-Visioning Romanticism*, 228–55; and Ellison, "'Nice Arts.'"

11. This section is indebted to Stewart's work on the miniature in *On Longing* and to N. Schor, *Reading in Detail*.

Chapter 5. Anna Laetitia Barbauld

1. Cited in Rodgers, *Georgian Chronicle*, 57. See also McCarthy and Kraft's introduction to *Poems*, xxix.

2. "Letter I," from "On the Uses of History," in Barbauld, *Legacy*, 21.

3. Information on publication history comes from McCarthy and Kraft's introduction and "Sources of the Poems" (*Poems*, xxxi, xxxv-xxxvii, 356–63).

4. *Poems* (1773) contained thirty-three poems, and Barbauld published twenty-two additional poems during her lifetime. Lucy Aikin published fifty-two poems in the collected *Works* (1825). The 1993 collection includes twenty-four further poems, and McCarthy and Kraft speculate that many other poems have been lost (xxxv).

5. Carol Shiner Wilson, "Lost Needles, Tangled Threads: Stitchery, Domesticity, and the Artistic Enterprise in Barbauld, Edgeworth, Taylor, and Lamb," in Shiner Wilson and Haefner, *Re-Visioning Romanticism*, 167–90; quote on 181. William McCarthy argues that recent commentators have found Barbauld and her poetry "disappointingly unfeminist": see "We Hoped the Woman Was Going to Appear: Repression, Desire, and Gender in Anna Letitia Barbauld's Early Poems," in Feldman and Kelley, *Romantic Women Writers*, 114–15.

6. McCarthy, "We Hoped"; Isobel Armstrong, "Gush of the Feminine: How Can We Read Women's Poetry of the Romantic Period?" in Feldman and Kelley, *Romantic Women Writers*, 13–32, see 25; Marlon Ross, "Configurations of Feminine Reform: The Woman Writer and the Tradition of Dissent," in Shiner Wilson and Haefner, *Re-Visioning Romanticism*, 91–110, see 92, 94.

7. McCarthy and Kraft date the poem 1771, and it was published in the 1825 *Works*; however, given the discussion of flames and violence in the poem, and the references to Priestley's books and scientific instruments (Priestley's library and laboratory were burned in the Birmingham riots of 1792), one wonders whether the poem was written after the riots.

8. The Corporation and Test Acts required that anyone who held office in any corporation, or who was elected to public or to military office, take the sacrament according to the rites of the Church of England; these acts effectively barred dissenters from holding political office. Some dissenters, by pledging "occasional conformity," were elected to public office, but at the cost of their religious beliefs. Dissenters were

also barred from the universities, hence the institution of academies such as War-rington. The Corporation and Test Acts were not repealed until 1828. Most dis-senters were not holders of landed property, the most effective guarantee of political representation. See Colley, *Britons*, 61.

9. The Birmingham riots occurred on July 14–17, 1791. The homes of several Birmingham dissenters, including Priestley, were sacked and burned by a "church and king mob." The riot was ostensibly instigated by a public dinner held in Bir-mingham to celebrate Bastille Day; Thompson suggests that several Tory magis-trates and clergy were involved in organizing the riots. Priestley himself printed ev-idence in support of this theory. Thompson, *English Working Class*, 80–81, 85; R. B. Rose, "Priestley Riots of 1791."

10. Pope, *Poems*, lines 53–60. Citations are to the *Dunciad Variorum*.

11. Marlon Ross, "Authority and Authenticity: Scribbling Authors and the Genius of Print in Eighteenth-Century England," in Woodmansee and Jaszi, *Construction*, 231–57, see 244–45.

12. Many professional men in market towns such as Birmingham practiced their profession at home; thus, the house itself was divided into areas that were "public" and "private" (Davidoff and Hall, *Family Fortunes*, 366).

13. On Barbauld's use of personification, see Mandell, "Those Limbs Dis-jointed," 30.

14. Moore, "'Ladies . . . Taking the Pen in Hand,'" 392.

15. Ozouf, "Revolutionary Calendar." Davidoff and Hall argue that many dis-senters originally supported the revolution, allying their own desire for civil liberties with those of the French. Anglicans feared this alliance, and viewed Presbyterian principles as by definition republican. Following the Birmingham riots of 1791, many dissenters retreated into social and political conservatism (*Family Fortunes*, 96–97).

16. Barbauld's letters at this time indicate her fear of persecution (Rodgers, *Georgian Chronicle*, 211).

17. Ezell notes studies of name disguise in 1674 and 1690 ("Reading Pseudo-nyms," 14), though Ralph Thomas considers his work "the first of the kind . . . in the English language" (ix).

18. Halkett and Laing's *Dictionary* in four volumes was originally published by William Paterson of Edinburgh in 1882, 1883, 1885, and 1888. See also William Cush-ing, *Initials and Pseudonyms* (1886) and *A Dictionary of Revealed Authorship* (1889).

19. Gallagher, *Nobody's Story*; Jacobus, *Romanticism*, 206–36; Pascoe, *Romantic Theatricality*, 163–83, 213.

20. Gallagher, *Nobody's Story*, 155–56; M. Rose, "Author in Court," in Wood-mansee and Jaszi, *Construction*.

21. Amanda Vickery, "Women and the World of Goods: A Lancashire Consumer and Her Possessions, 1751–81," in Brewer and Porter, *Consumption*, 286–87.

22. Simon Schaffer discusses the importance of good marketing and political networking to the success of Priestley's *History of Electricity* in "The Consuming

Flame: Electrical Showmen and Tory Mystics in the World of Goods," in Brewer and Porter, *Consumption*, 489–526, see 513.

23. Barbauld, "Letter III," from "On the Uses of History," in *Legacy*, 50.

24. Barbauld, *Sins of Government*, in *Works*, 1:381–412; *National Penitence* (Brown edition).

25. Barbauld wrote a variety of puzzle poems, including "Enigma," "Logogriph," and at least six "riddle" poems.

26. On Barbauld's interest in ballooning, see *Poems*, 298; Kraft, "Barbauld's 'Washing-Day,'" 33.

27. Stafford, *Voyage into Substance*, figs. 100, 155.

Chapter 6. Elizabeth Bishop

1. Bishop, "Gallery Note for Wesley Wehr," March 1967, Special Collections, Vassar College Libraries. On his memories of Bishop's poetry workshops, see Wehr, "Elizabeth Bishop: Conversations and Class Notes."

2. Bishop, *Complete Poems*, 176. Subsequent references are cited in the text as *CP*.

3. On the Bishop reception, see Travisano, "Elizabeth Bishop Phenomenon," in Dickie and Travisano, *Gendered Modernisms;* Hammer, "New Elizabeth Bishop"; Morris, *Becoming Canonical*, 104–31.

4. Lowell, *Collected Prose*, 78; Morris, *Becoming Canonical*, 107–14; see the early reviews by Williams and Jarrell in Schwartz and Estess, *Elizabeth Bishop*.

5. "To Robert Lowell," August 14, 1947 (*One Art*, 146–48). *One Art* is abbreviated hereafter as *OA*.

6. "To Robert Lowell," July 11, 1951 (*OA*, 221–22). "To Robert Lowell," April 22, 1960 (*OA*, 381–85).

7. "To Robert Lowell," June 7, 1956 (*OA*, 318–20). See also "To Ferris Greenslet," January 22, 1945 (*OA*, 125–26).

8. See "To Dr. Anny Baumann," December 2, 1947 (*OA*, 150–51). "To Marianne Moore," September 11, 1940 (*OA*, 94–95). "To Marianne Moore," August 29, 1946 (*OA*, 139–41). "To Austin Olney," (*OA*, 293–94). "To Paul Brooks," August 2, 1954 (*OA*, 296).

9. Starbuck, "Conversation," 324, 322.

10. "To Ilse Barker," February 6, 1965. Cited in Victoria Harrison, "Recording a Life: Elizabeth Bishop's Letters to Ilse and Kit Barker," in Lombardi, *Geography of Gender*, 215–32; 227. Hereafter cited as *Geography*.

11. Cited in Joanne Feit Diehl, "Bishop's Sexual Poetics," in *Geography*, 17–45; 19.

12. "Notes for Poetry Reviews," 1970, Special Collections, Vassar College Libraries.

13. Bishop, "To Robert Lowell," July 27, 1960 (*OA*, 386–88).

14. On Bishop's response to romantic egotism, see Merrin, *Enabling Humility;* Blasing, "Gender to Genre"; Robert Pinsky, "The Idiom of a Self: Elizabeth Bishop

and Wordsworth," in Schwartz and Estess, *Elizabeth Bishop*, 49–60; Willard Spiegelman, "Elizabeth Bishop's 'Natural Heroism,'" in Schwartz and Estess 154–71.

15. Travisano, "Elizabeth Bishop Phenomenon," 225.

16. See Lorrie Goldensohn, "The Body's Roses: Race, Sex, and Gender in Elizabeth Bishop's Representations of the Self," in *Geography*, 70–90, and Bishop, *Poe and the Juke-Box*.

17. For a similar understanding of Bishop's criticisms of confession, see Marilyn May Lombardi, "Closet of Breath: Elizabeth Bishop, Her Body and Her Art," in *Geography*, 46–69; Hammer, "New Elizabeth Bishop."

18. On Bishop's and Lowell's friendship, correspondence, and mutual influence, see Kalstone, *Becoming*; Travisano, *Midcentury Quartet*.

19. "To Robert Lowell," December 11, 1957 (*OA*, 346–49).

20. "To Robert Lowell," December 14, 1957 (*OA*, 349–53).

21. For recent perspectives on these questions, see Sontag and Graham, *After Confession*.

22. Rosenthal, *New Poets*; Breslin, *Psycho-Political Muse*, 42–43.

23. "To Robert Lowell," September 8, 1948 (*OA*, 170–71).

24. Kalstone, *Becoming*, 239–44. Lowell did follow some of Bishop's suggestions for revising *The Dolphin* (245).

25. "To Robert Lowell," March 21, 1972 (*OA*, 561–64).

26. Bishop's objections to Lowell's use of Hardwick's letters echoes their 1940s discussion of Williams's use of letters in *Paterson*.

27. Qtd. in "To Robert Lowell," March 21, 1972 (*OA*, 561–62).

28. "To Robert Lowell," March 21, 1972 (*OA*, 561–64). "To Randall Jarrell," February 25, 1965 (*OA*, 431–34).

29. Cited in Kalstone, *Becoming*, 228.

30. Mariani (*Lost Puritan*, 422–23) observes that Adrienne Rich also objected to Lowell's exploitation of gender difference in her review of *The Dolphin*. See the Bishop-Lowell correspondence regarding Lowell's adaptation of a Bishop letter in *Notebook*, his use of Bishop's story "In the Village" in his sonnet "The Scream," and his narration of a shared experience in "Water."

31. Bishop criticizes Sexton's "romanticism" as "egocentric—simply that," though she refrains from criticizing Lowell in this manner, an irony that Kalstone discusses (*Becoming*, 209).

32. "To Dr. Anny Baumann," November 14 and 15, 1967 (*OA*, 639).

33. "One Art" required seventeen drafts. See Brett C. Millier, "Elusive Mastery: The Drafts of Elizabeth Bishop's One Art," in *Geography*, 233–43.

34. Pound saw "technique as the test of a man's sincerity" ("Retrospect," 9) and also wrote, "One 'moves' the reader only by clarity. In depicting the motions of the 'human heart' the durability of the writing depends on the exactitude. It is the thing that is true and stays true that keeps fresh for the new reader" ("How to Read," 22). On how Pound's location of sincerity in techniques of clear and exact presentation influence Zukofsky and Reznikoff, see Sharp, "Sincerity and Objectification"; Al-

tieri, "Transformations of Objectivism"; Cayley, "Ch'eng, or Sincerity." Costello notes a similar understanding of sincerity in Moore (*Marianne Moore*, 2–4, 26).

35. "To Elizabeth Bishop," March 23, 1967, Special Collections, Vassar College Libraries.

36. "To Elizabeth Bishop," August 12, 1963, in *Letters of Robert Lowell*, 434.

37. "To Elizabeth Bishop," January 23, 1967, Special Collections, Vassar College Libraries.

38. See Roman, *Cold War View*. "To May Swenson," February 5, 1956 (*OA*, 315–16).

39. Barbara Page, "Off-Beat Claves, Oblique Realities: The Key West Notebooks of Elizabeth Bishop," in *Geography*, 196–211.

40. "To Ilse and Kit Barker," October 8, 1953 (*OA*, 273–74).

41. "To Elizabeth Bishop," March 10, 1962, in *Letters of Robert Lowell*, 397. "Poetry in English: 1945–62" appeared in the March 9, 1962, issue of *Time*.

42. "To Robert Lowell," April 4, 1962 (*OA*, 406).

43. "To Arthur Mizener," January 14, 1947 (*OA*, 144).

44. "Efforts of Affection," *Collected Prose*, 137; Wehr, "Conversations," 323.

45. "To James Merrill," January 23, 1979. Cited in Kalstone, *Becoming*, 115.

46. "To Elizabeth Bishop," November 30, 1972, Special Collections, Vassar College Libraries.

47. I share Hotelling-Zona's understanding of Bishop's "ambivalence" (*Feminist Poetics*, 65).

48. Merrill cites lines from the first stanza of "The Forerunners" by Bishop's favorite poet, George Herbert: "The Harbingers are come. See, see their mark; / White is their colour, and behold my head. / But must they have my brain? must they dispark / Those sparkling notions, which therein were bred?" (*Poetical Works*, 186).

49. "Remarks on Translation," Special Collections, Vassar College Libraries.

50. Bishop, *Exchanging Hats*, 51. On Bishop's uses of surrealism, see Mullen, "Bishop's Surrealist Inheritance."

51. "True Confessions," in Bishop, *Poe and the Juke-Box*, 192.

52. "The Bees," Special Collections, Vassar College Libraries.

Coda

1. Begley, "I's Have It"; Atlas, "Literary Memoir"; Miller, *Getting Personal* and "But Enough about Me"; Veeser, introduction to *Confessions of the Critics;* "Forum: The Inevitability of the Personal"; Gerra, "Autobiographical Turn."

2. Elizabeth Fox-Genovese, "Confession Versus Criticism, or What's the Critic Got to Do With It?" in *Confessions of the Critics*, 68–75; 74. Hereafter cited in the text as *CC*.

3. Originally published in *New Literary History* in 1987 as a response to Ellen Messer-Davidow's "Philosophical Bases of Feminist Literary Criticisms," "Me and My Shadow" was republished in expanded form in Kauffman, *Gender and Theory*, with a reply by MacLean. The version I cite is in Warhol and Price Herndl, *Feminisms*.

4. David Simpson, "Speaking Personally: The Culture of Autobiographical Criticism," in *CC*, 83.

5. Advocates of personal criticism distinguish a useful personal criticism from an excessive, self-indulgent variant. See Diane Freedman, "Autobiographical Literary Criticism as the New Belletrism," in *CC*, 3–16, esp. 12; Rachel Brownstein, "Interrupted Reading: Personal Criticism in the Present Time," in *CC*, 29–39, esp. 36; Jane Gallop, in "Forum," 1150; Ruth Perry, in "Forum," 1166; George T. Wright, in "Forum," 1160; Mary Ann Caws, in "Forum," 1160; Norman Friedman, in "Forum," 1165; Miller, *Getting Personal*, 25.

6. Kauffman makes a similar point in her introduction to *Gender and Theory*, 2–3.

7. MacLean, "Citing the Subject," in Kauffman, *Gender and Theory*, 152.

8. I am indebted to Marlon Ross for this formulation.

9. McGann, *Romantic Ideology*, 13; Catherine Gallagher, "Marxism and the New Historicism," in Veeser, *New Historicism*, 37–48, esp. 47; Gerald Graff, "Co-Optation," in Veeser, *New Historicism*, 168–81, esp. 172.

10. Cole makes a similar point in "Evading Politics."

11. Scholes comments: "This gap, between the values of the humanities and those of the powerful worlds of business and public life, has only increased. . . . And our inability to deal with it has been a contributing cause to our present state of confusion" (*Rise and Fall*, 18).

12. Ellison's treatment of "liberal guilt" as "an embarassed position no one wants to occupy" is relevant (*Cato's Tears*, 172).

13. See Berryman, "Critical Mirrors."

14. On the establishment of "English literature" during the Victorian era in English universities, see Eagleton, *Function of Criticism*, 65–67, 77–78, and Graff, *Professing*, 55–59.

15. On Eliot and the New Critics' desire for an autonomous profession, see Robbins, *Secular Vocations*, 64–67; Graff, *Professing*, 147–48, 153–59, 195, 198, 204–6; Clark, *Sentimental Modernism*, 34–37.

16. See Graff, "Co-Optation," 171, and *Professing*, 176–77.

17. Clark observes, "The position against the sentimental still operates almost like an unconscious in critical writing" (*Sentimental Modernism*, 5). She locates the mechanism of repression in modernism: "Modernism rejected the sentimental, because modernism was sentimental"; although it transferred sentiment from "an interior of persons to the interior of a text," in doing so it simply rendered "its own genealogy unconscious" (6, 7). Similarly, June Howard argues that sentimentality "is condemned so vehemently in part because its critics feel implicated in it" ("What Is Sentimentality?" 69).

18. As many in the *PMLA* Forum observe, personal criticism, with its roots in the feminist critique of objectivity, has had a particular appeal to ethnic, racial, and sexual minorities. As Arthur Ramirez succinctly puts it, for minority writers, "Necessity drives the personal" ("Forum," 1148).

19. Tompkins discusses the university as "an extension of a very competitive, success-, status-, and money-oriented world," in Olson, "Jane Tompkins," 175.

20. See Schneider, "Jane Tompkins's Message to Academe," A9.

21. Miller writes that the essay "is a manifesto, and as such its prose is marked by the rhetorical traits that characterize polemical writing" (*Getting Personal,* 4).

22. Tompkins anticipates the tenor, if not the content, of the "police action that academic intellectuals wage ceaselessly against feeling, against women, against what is personal" (1115).

23. Terry Caesar argues that the personal voice is read as excessive, as too personal, if it's not institutionally empowered: "So the experience is assigned to perhaps the most basic of the venerable typologies of the personal: the complaint" ("Forum," 1168).

24. Berlant argues that complaints "have operated as 'safety valves' for surplus female rage and desire, rendering comfort to the women who enact the sentimental will to-not-know" ("Female Complaint," 245).

25. Simpson reads the trend of confessional criticism as an effort to "reabsorb literary criticism back into literature" ("Forum," 1167).

26. On this contradiction see Gallop, in "Forum," 1149, 1150; Angelika Bammer, in "Forum," 1151; Stephanie Sandler, in "Forum," 1162.

27. Lasch argues, "The popularity of the confessional mode testifies, of course, to the new narcissism that runs all through American culture," but adds, "Poets and novelists today, far from glorifying the self, chronicle its disintegration" (*Culture of Narcissism,* 17, 30).

Bibliography

Abrams, M. H. *The Mirror and the Lamp: Romantic Theory and the Critical Tradition.* New York: Oxford Univ. Press, 1953.

Abst, Vicki, and Leonard Mustazza. *Coming after Oprah: Cultural Fallout in the Age of the T.V. Talk Show.* Bowling Green: Bowling Green State Univ. Press, 1997.

Ades, Dawn. "The Transcendental Surrealism of Joseph Cornell." In *Joseph Cornell,* ed. Kynaston McShine, 15–39. New York: Museum of Modern Art, 1980.

Adorno, Theodor. "Lyric and Society." In *Notes to Literature.* Vol. 1, 37–54. New York: Columbia Univ. Press, 1991.

Agnew, Jean-Christophe. *Worlds Apart: The Market and the Theater in Anglo-American Thought, 1550–1750.* New York: Cambridge Univ. Press, 1986.

Albisette, James C. "Professionals and Professionalization." In *Encyclopedia of European Social History, From 1350 to 2000.* Vol. 3, ed. Peter N. Stearns, 57–65. New York: Charles Scribner's Sons, 2001.

Alexander, Paul, ed. *Ariel Ascending: Writings about Sylvia Plath.* New York: Harper & Row, 1985.

Alpaugh, David. "The Professionalization of Poetry, Part I." *Poets & Writers* (January/February 2003): 17–22.

Alpers, Svetlana. *The Art of Describing: Dutch Art in the Seventeenth Century.* Chicago: Univ. of Chicago Press, 1983.

Altieri, Charles. "The Transformations of Objectivism: An Afterword." In *The Objectivist Nexus: Essays in Cultural Poetics,* ed. Rachel Blau Du Plessis and Peter Quartermain, 25–36. Tuscaloosa: Univ. of Alabama Press, 1999.

Altshuler, Bruce. *The Avant-Garde in Exhibition: New Art in the Twentieth Century.* New York: Harry N. Abrams, 1994.

Alvarez, Alfred. *Beyond All This Fiddle: Essays, 1955–1967.* London: Allen Lane, 1968.

———. "Sylvia Plath: A Memoir." In Alexander, *Ariel Ascending,* 185–213.

———, ed. *The New Poetry.* Harmondsworth, UK: Penguin, 1962.

Arac, Jonathan. "Romanticism, the Self, and the City: The Secret Agent in Literary History." *Boundary 2* 9, no. 1 (1980): 75–90.

Armstrong, Isobel. "Caterpillar on the Skin." *Times Literary Supplement,* July 12, 1996.

———, and Virginia Blain, eds. *Women's Poetry, Late Romantic to Late Victorian: Gender and Genre, 1830–1900*. New York: St. Martin's Press, 1999.

Atlas, James. "The Age of the Literary Memoir Is Now." *New York Times Magazine*, May 12, 1996, 25–26.

Augustine, Saint. *Confessions*. Trans. R. S. Pine-Coffin. New York: Penguin Books, 1961.

Baillie, Joanna. *Fugitive Verses*. London, 1840.

Barbauld, Anna Laetitia, ed. *The British Novelists; with an Essay and Prefaces, Biographical and Critical*. Vol. 36. London, 1810.

———. *A Legacy for Young Ladies, Consisting of Miscellaneous Pieces, in Prose and Verse*. Providence, RI: Brown/NEH Women Writer's Project, 1993.

———. *The Poems of Anna Laetitia Barbauld*. Ed. William McCarthy and Elizabeth Kraft. Athens: Univ. of Georgia Press, 1994.

———. *Reasons for National Penitence*. London, 1794; Providence, RI: Brown/NEH Women Writer's Project, 1993.

———. *Selected Poetry and Prose*. Ed. William McCarthy and Elizabeth Kraft. Peterborough, Ontario: Broadview Press, 2002.

———. *The Works, with a Memoir by Lucy Aikin*. Ed. Lucy Aikin. 2 vols. London: Longman, 1825.

Barish, Jonas. *The Antitheatrical Prejudice*. Berkeley: Univ. of California Press, 1981.

Barker Benfield, G. J. *The Culture of Sensibility: Sex and Society in Eighteenth-Century Britain*. Chicago: Univ. of Chicago Press, 1992.

Barthes, Roland. *Image-Music-Text: Roland Barthes*. Ed. Stephen Heath. New York: Hill & Wang, 1977.

Batten, Guinn. *The Orphaned Imagination: Melancholy and Commodity Culture in English Romanticism*. Durham, NC: Duke Univ. Press, 1998.

Baudelaire, Charles. *Charles Baudelaire: Selected Writings on Art and Literature*. Trans. P. E. Charvet. London: Penguin, 1972.

Bauer, Dale M., and Philip Gould, eds. *The Cambridge Companion to Nineteenth-Century American Women's Writing*. Cambridge: Cambridge Univ. Press, 2001.

Begley, Adam. "The I's Have It: Duke's Moi Critics Expose Themselves." *Lingua Franca* (March/April 1994): 54–59.

Benedict, Stephen, ed. *Public Money and the Muse: Essays on Government Funding for the Arts*. New York: W. W. Norton, 1991.

Benjamin, Walter. *Illuminations: Essays and Reflections*. Ed. Hannah Arendt. Trans. Harry Zohn. New York: Schocken Books, 1968.

———. *The Origin of German Tragic Drama*. Trans. John Osborne. 1977; New York: Verso, 1994.

Bennett, Andrew J. "Devious Feet: Wordsworth and the Scandal of Narrative Form." *ELH* 59 (1992): 145–73.

Bennett, Paula. *Poets in the Public Sphere: The Emancipatory Project of American Women's Poetry, 1800–1900*. Princeton, NJ: Princeton Univ. Press, 2003.

Bennett, Tony. *Outside Literature*. New York: Routledge, 1990.

Berkson, Bill, ed. *In Memory of My Feelings*. New York: Museum of Modern Art, 1967.

———, and Joe LeSueur, eds. *Homage to Frank O'Hara*. Bolinas, CA: Big Sky, 1988.

Berlant, Lauren. "The Female Complaint." *Social Text* 19/20 (Fall 1998): 237–59.

———. "Poor Eliza." *American Literature* 70, no. 3 (September 1998): 635–68.

Bernstein, Charles, ed. *Close Listening: Poetry and the Performed Word*. Oxford: Oxford Univ. Press, 1998.

Berryman, Charles. "Critical Mirrors: Theories of Autobiography." *Mosaic* 32, no. 1 (March 1999): 71–84.

Bishop, Elizabeth. *The Collected Prose*. Ed. Robert Giroux. New York: Farrar, Straus and Giroux, 1984.

———. *The Complete Poems, 1927–1979*. New York: Farrar, Straus and Giroux, 1979.

———. *Edgar Allen Poe and the Juke-Box: Uncollected Poems, Drafts and Fragments*. Ed. Alice Quinn. New York: Farrar, Straus & Giroux, 2006.

———. *Exchanging Hats, Paintings*. Ed. William Benton. New York: Farrar, Straus & Giroux, 1996.

———. *One Art: Letters*. Ed. Robert Giroux. New York: Farrar, Straus & Giroux, 1994.

Blake, David Haven. "Public Dreams: Berryman, Celebrity, and the Culture of Confession." *American Literary History* 13, no. 4 (2001): 716–36.

Blasing, Mutlu Konuk. *American Poetry: The Rhetoric of Its Forms*. New Haven, CT: Yale Univ. Press, 1987.

———. "From Gender to Genre and Back: Elizabeth Bishop and 'The Moose.'" *American Literary History* 6, no. 2 (1994): 265–86.

Bledstein, Burton. *The Culture of Professionalism: The Middle Class and the Development of Higher Education in America*. New York: W. W. Norton, 1976.

Bolton, Betsy. "Romancing the Stone: 'Perdita' Robinson in Wordsworth's London." *ELH* 64, no. 3 (1997): 727–59.

Boone, Joseph. "Queer Sites in Modernism: Harlem/The Left Bank/Greenwich Village." In *The Geography of Identity*, ed. Patricia Yaeger, 243–72. Ann Arbor: Univ. of Michigan Press, 1996.

Booth, Wayne C. *A Rhetoric of Irony*. Chicago: Univ. of Chicago Press, 1974.

Bourdieu, Pierre. *The Rules of Art: Genesis and Structure of the Literary Field*. Trans. Susan Emanuel. Stanford: Stanford Univ. Press, 1996.

Boym, Svetlana. *Death in Quotation Marks: Cultural Myths of the Modern Poet*. Cambridge, MA: Harvard Univ. Press, 1991.

Braudy, Leo. *The Frenzy of Renown: Fame and Its History*. 1986; New York: Vintage Books, 1997.

———. "'No Body's Perfect': Method Acting and 50s Culture." In *The Movies: Texts, Receptions, Exposures*, ed. Laurence Goldstein and Ira Konigsberg. Ann Arbor: Univ. of Michigan Press, 1996.

Breslin, James. *From Modern to Contemporary: American Poetry, 1945–1965*. Chicago: Univ. of Chicago Press, 1984.

Breslin, Paul. *The Psycho-Political Muse: American Poetry since the Fifties*. Chicago: Univ. of Chicago Press, 1987.

Brewer, John, and Roy Porter, eds. *Consumption and the World of Goods*. New York: Routledge, 1993.

Briggs, Asa. *The Making of Modern England, 1783–1867*. New York: Harper & Row, 1959.

———. *A Social History of England*. London: Weidenfeld and Nicolson, 1994.

Bronfen, Elisabeth. *Over Her Dead Body: Death, Femininity and the Aesthetic*. New York: Routledge, 1992.

Brown, Susan. "The Victorian Poetess." In *The Cambridge Companion to Victorian Poetry*, ed. Joseph Bristow, 180–202. New York: Cambridge Univ. Press, 2000.

Britzolakis, Christina. *Sylvia Plath and the Theatre of Mourning*. New York: Oxford Univ. Press, 1999.

Bryant, Marsha. "IMAX Authorship: Teaching Plath and Her Unabridged Journals." *Pedagogy* 4, no. 2 (2004): 241–61.

Buck-Morss, Susan. *The Dialectics of Seeing: Walter Benjamin and the Arcades Project*. Cambridge, MA: MIT Press, 1989.

Buinicki, Martin, "Walt Whitman and the Question of Copyright." *American Literary History* 15, no. 2 (Summer 2003): 248–75.

Bundtzen, Lynda K. "Mourning Eurydice: Ted Hughes as Orpheus in Birthday Letters." *Journal of Modern Literature* 23, nos. 3–4 (2000): 455–69.

Burke, Edmund. *A Philosophical Enquiry into the Origin of our Ideas of the Sublime and Beautiful*. Ed. Adam Phillips. New York: Oxford Univ. Press, 1990.

Butler, Marilyn. *Romantics, Rebels and Reactionaries: English Literature and Its Background, 1760–1830*. New York: Oxford Univ. Press, 1981.

Byrd, Max. *London Transformed: Images of the City in the Eighteenth Century*. New Haven, CT: Yale Univ. Press, 1978.

Byrne, Paula. *Perdita: The Literary, Theatrical, Scandalous Life of Mary Robinson*. New York: Random House, 2004.

Campbell, Colin. *The Romantic Ethic and the Spirit of Modern Consumerism*. London: Basil Blackwell, 1987.

Cayley, John, "Ch'Eng, or Sincerity." *Paideuma* 13, no. 2 (Fall 1984): 201–10.

Certeau, Michel de. *The Practice of Everyday Life*. Trans. Steven Rendall. Berkeley: Univ. of California Press, 1984.

Chambers, Ross. "The Flaneur as Hero (on Baudelaire)." *Australian Journal of French Studies* 28, no. 2 (1991): 142–53.

———. *The Writing of Melancholy: Modes of Opposition in Early French Modernism*. Trans. Mary Seidman Trouille. Chicago: Univ. of Chicago Press, 1993.

Chandler, James. "Representative Men, Spirits of the Age, and other Romantic Types." In *Romantic Revolutions: Criticism and Theory*, ed. Kenneth R. Johnston, 104–32. Bloomington: Indiana Univ. Press, 1990.

Charvat, William. *The Profession of Authorship in America, 1800–1870: The Papers of William Charvat*. Ed. Matthew J. Bruccoli. Columbus: Ohio State Univ. Press, 1968.

Chauncey, George. *Gay New York: Gender, Urban Culture, and the Making of the Gay Male World 1890–1940*. New York: Basic Books, 1994.

Chinitz, David. "Literacy and Authenticity: The Blues Poems of Langston Hughes." *Callaloo* 19, no. 1 (1996): 177–92.

Christ, Carol. *Victorian and Modern Poetics.* Chicago: Univ. of Chicago Press, 1984.

Churchwell, Sarah. "Secrets and Lies: Plath, Privacy, Publication and Ted Hughes's Birthday Letters." *Contemporary Literature* 42, no. 1 (2001): 102–48.

Clark, Suzanne. *Sentimental Modernism: Women Writers and the Revolution of the Word.* Bloomington: Indiana Univ. Press, 1991.

Colby, Robert A. "Authorship and the Book Trade." *Victorian Periodicals and Victorian Society.* Ed. J. Donn Vann. Toronto: Univ. of Toronto Press, 1994.

Cole, Steven E. "Evading Politics: The Poverty of Historicizing Romanticism." *Studies in Romanticism* 34, no. 1 (Spring 1995): 29–49.

Colley, Linda. *Britons: Forging the Nation, 1707–1837.* New Haven, CT: Yale Univ. Press, 1992.

Costello, Bonnie. "Elizabeth Bishop's Impersonal Personal." *American Literary History* 15, no. 2 (2003): 334–66.

———. *Marianne Moore: Imaginary Possessions.* Cambridge, MA: Harvard Univ. Press, 1981.

Cowling, Mary. *The Artist as Anthropologist: The Representation of Type and Character in Victorian Art.* Cambridge: Cambridge Univ. Press, 1989.

Cowper, William. *The Life and Letters of William Cowper, Esq.* Ed. William Hayley. London, 1809.

Cross, Nigel. *The Common Writer: Life in Nineteenth-Century Grub Street.* Cambridge: Cambridge Univ. Press, 1985.

Curran, Stuart. "The I Altered." In *Romanticism and Feminism,* ed. Anne Mellor, 185–207. Bloomington: Indiana Univ. Press, 1988.

———. *Poetic Form and British Romanticism.* Oxford: Oxford Univ. Press, 1986.

Cushman, Stephen. *Fictions of Form in American Poetry.* Princeton, NJ: Princeton Univ. Press, 1993.

Davidoff, Leonore, and Catherine Hall. *Family Fortunes: Men and Women of the English Middle Class, 1780–1950.* Chicago: Univ. of Chicago Press, 1987.

Davidson, Cathy N., and Jessamyn Hatcher, eds. "No More Separate Spheres!" *American Literature* 70, no. 3 (September 1998); rpt. as *No More Separate Spheres!* Durham, NC: Duke Univ. Press, 2002.

Davidson, Michael. "From Margin to Mainstream: Postwar Poetry and the Politics of Containment." *American Literary History* 10, no. 2 (1998): 266–90.

Davie, Donald. "On Sincerity: From Wordsworth to Ginsberg." *Encounter* 31, no. 4 (October 1968): 61–66.

de Man, Paul. *Allegories of Reading: Figural Language in Rousseau, Nietzsche, Rilke, and Proust.* New Haven, CT: Yale Univ. Press, 1979.

———. *The Rhetoric of Romanticism.* New York: Columbia Univ. Press, 1984.

Dettmar, Kevin, and Stephen Watt, eds. *Marketing Modernisms: Self-Promotion, Canonization, and Rereading.* Ann Arbor: Univ. of Michigan Press, 1996.

Dewey, John. *Human Nature and Conduct: An Introduction to Social Psychology.* New York: Henry Holt, 1922.

Dickie, Margaret. "Race and Class in Elizabeth Bishop's Poetry." *Yearbook of English Studies* 24 (1994): 44–58.

———, and Thomas Travisano, eds. *Gendered Modernisms: American Women Poets and Their Readers.* Philadelphia: Univ. of Pennsylvania Press, 1996.

Diggory, Terence. "Allen Ginsberg's Urban Pastoral." *College Literature* 27, no. 1 (Winter 2000): 103–20.

———, ed. *The Scene of My Selves: New Work on New York School Poetry.* Orono, ME: National Poetry Foundation, 2001.

Dollimore, Jonathan. *Sexual Dissidence: Augustine to Wilde, Freud to Foucault.* Oxford: Clarendon Press, 1991.

Donoghue, Frank. *The Fame Machine: Book Reviewing and Eighteenth-Century Literary Careers.* Stanford: Stanford Univ. Press, 1996.

Doolittle, Hilda. (H.D.) *Selected Poems.* Ed. Louis L. Martz. New York: New Directions, 1988.

Douglas, Ann. *The Feminization of American Culture.* New York: Alfred A. Knopf, 1977.

Dyce, Alexander. *Specimens of British Poetesses.* London: T. Rodd, 1825.

Eagleton, Terry. *The Function of Criticism: From the Spectator to Post-Structuralism.* London: Verso, 1984.

Eilenberg, Susan. "Mortal Pages: Wordsworth and the Reform of Copyright." *ELH* 56, no. 2 (1989): 351–74.

Elledge, Jim, ed. *Frank O'Hara: To Be True to a City.* Ann Arbor: Univ. of Michigan Press, 1990.

———. "The Lack of Gender in Frank O'Hara's Love Poems to Vincent Warren." In *Fictions of Masculinity: Crossing Cultures, Crossing Sexualities,* ed. Peter Murphy, 226–37. New York: New York Univ. Press, 1994.

Ellison, Julie. *Cato's Tears and the Making of Anglo-American Emotion.* Chicago: Univ. of Chicago Press, 1999.

———. "'Nice Arts' and 'Potent Enginery': The Gendered Economy of Wordsworth's Fancy." *Centennial Review* 33 (1989): 441–67.

Ellmann, Maud. *The Poetics of Impersonality: T. S. Eliot and Ezra Pound.* Brighton, UK: Harvester Press, 1987.

Epstein Nord, Deborah. "The City as Theater: From Georgian to Early Victorian London." *Victorian Studies* 31, no. 2 (1988): 159–88.

———. *Walking the Victorian Streets: Women, Representation, and the City.* Ithaca, NY: Cornell Univ. Press, 1995.

Ezell, Margaret J. M. "Reading Pseudonyms in Seventeenth-Century English Coterie Literature." *Essays in Literature* 21, no. 1 (1994): 13–25.

———. *Social Authorship and the Advent of Print.* Baltimore, MD: Johns Hopkins Univ. Press, 1999.

Fabricant, Carole. "The Literature of Domestic Tourism and the Public Consumption of Private Property." In *The New Eighteenth Century: Theory, Politics, English Literature,* ed. Felicity Nussbaum and Laura Brown, 254–75. New York: Methuen, 1987.

Favor, J. Martin. *Authentic Blackness: The Folk in the New Negro Renaissance.* Durham, NC: Duke Univ. Press, 1999.

Feather, John. "The Publishers and the Pirates: British Copyright Law in Theory and Practice, 1710–1775." *Publishing History: The Social, Economic and Literary History of Book, Newspaper and Magazine Publishing* 22 (1987): 5–32.

Feldman, Paula R., and Theresa M. Kelley, eds. *Romantic Women Writers: Voices and Counter-Voices.* Hanover, NH: Univ. Press of New England, 1995.

Felski, Rita. *The Gender of Modernity.* Cambridge, MA: Harvard Univ. Press, 1995.

———. "On Confession." In *Women, Autobiography, Theory: A Reader,* ed. Sidonie Smith and Julia Watson, 83–95. Madison: Univ. of Wisconsin Press, 1998.

Fergus, Jan, and Janice Farrar Thaddeus. "Women, Publishers, and Money, 1790–1820." *Studies in Eighteenth-Century Culture* 17 (1987): 191–207.

Ferguson, Frances. *Wordsworth: Language as Counter-Spirit.* New Haven, CT: Yale Univ. Press, 1977.

Forbes, Deborah. *Sincerity's Shadow.* Cambridge, MA: Harvard Univ. Press, 2004.

"Forum: The Inevitability of the Personal." *PMLA* 3, no. 5 (October 1996): 1146–69.

Foucault, Michel. *The Foucault Reader.* Ed. Paul Rabinow. New York: Pantheon Books, 1984.

———. *The History of Sexuality: Volume 1, An Introduction.* Trans. Robert Hurley. New York: Vintage, 1990.

Freud, Sigmund. *General Psychological Theory.* Ed. Philip Rieff. New York: Collier Books, 1963.

Friedman, Geraldine. "History in the Background of Wordsworth's Blind Beggar." *ELH* 56 (1989): 125–48.

Gallagher, Catherine. *Nobody's Story: The Vanishing Acts of Women Writers in the Marketplace, 1670–1820.* Berkeley: Univ. of California Press, 1995.

Gallop, Jane. *Thinking Through the Body.* New York: Columbia Univ. Press, 1988.

Gerra, Michael. "The Autobiographical Turn." *Transition* 68 (Winter 1995): 143–53.

Gilbert, Roger. *Walks in the World: Representation and Experience in Modern American Poetry.* Princeton, NJ: Princeton Univ. Press, 1991.

Gill, Stephen. *William Wordsworth: A Life.* New York: Oxford Univ. Press, 1989.

Gilmore, Leigh. "Policing Truth: Confession, Gender, and Autobiographical Authority." In *Autobiography and Postmodernism,* ed. Kathleen Ashley, Leigh Gilmore, and Gerald Peters, 54–78. Amherst: Univ. of Massachusetts Press, 1994.

Gilmore, Michael. *American Romanticism and the Marketplace.* Chicago: Univ. of Chicago Press, 1985.

Glebber, Anke. *The Art of Taking a Walk: Flanerie, Literature, and Film in Weimar Culture.* Princeton, NJ: Princeton Univ. Press, 1999.

Gooch, Brad. *City Poet: The Life and Times of Frank O'Hara.* New York: Alfred A. Knopf, 1993.

Grabher, Gudrun, Roland Hagenbuchle, and Cristanne Miller, eds. *The Emily Dickinson Handbook.* Amherst: Univ. of Massachusetts Press, 1998.

Graff, Gerald. *Professing Literature: An Institutional History.* Chicago: Univ. of Chicago Press, 1987.

Graham, John. "Character Description and Meaning in the Romantic Novel." *Studies in Romanticism* 5, no. 4 (1966): 208–18.

———. "Lavater's Physiognomy in England." *Journal of the History of Ideas* 23 (1961): 561–72.

Gray, Thomas. *The Complete Poems of Thomas Gray.* Ed. James Reeves. London: Heinemann, 1973.

Gray, Timothy G. "Semiotic Shepherds: Gary Snyder, Frank O'Hara, and the Embodiment of an Urban Pastoral." *Contemporary Literature* 39, no. 4 (Winter 1998): 523–60.

Griffin, Dustin. *Literary Patronage in England, 1650–1800.* Cambridge: Cambridge Univ. Press, 1996.

Guilbaut, Serge. *How New York Stole the Idea of Modern Art: Abstract Expressionism, Freedom, and the Cold War.* Trans. Arthur Goldhammer. Chicago: Univ. of Chicago Press, 1983.

Guilhamet, Leon. *The Sincere Ideal: Studies on Sincerity in Eighteenth-Century English Literature.* Montreal: McGill-Queen's Univ. Press, 1974.

Hall, Catherine. *White, Male and Middle Class: Explorations in Feminism and History.* Cambridge, UK: Polity Press, 1992.

———, and Leonore Davidoff. *Family Fortunes: Men and Women of the English Middle Class, 1780–1850.* Chicago: Univ. of Chicago Press, 1987.

Halttunen, Karen. *Confidence Man and Painted Women: A Study of Middle-Class Culture in America, 1830–1870.* New Haven, CT: Yale Univ. Press, 1982.

Hamacher, Werner, Neil Hertz, and Thomas Keenan, eds. *Responses: On Paul de Man's Wartime Journalism.* Lincoln: Univ. of Nebraska Press, 1989.

Hammer, Langdon. "The New Elizabeth Bishop." *Yale Review* 82, no. 1 (1995): 135–49.

———. "Plath's Lives: Poetry, Professionalism, and the Culture of the School." *Representations* 75 (Summer 2001): 61–88.

Harvey, David. *The Condition of Postmodernity: An Enquiry into the Origins of Cultural Change.* Cambridge: Blackwell Publishers, 1990.

Haskell, Thomas L. "Professionalism versus Capitalism: R. H. Tawney, Emile Durkheim, and C. S. Peirce on the Disinterestedness of Professional Communities." In *The Authority of Experts: Studies in History and Theory,* ed. Thomas L. Haskell, 180–225. Bloomington: Indiana Univ. Press, 1984.

Herbert, George. *The Poetical Works of George Herbert.* Ed. George Gilfillan. Edinburgh, UK: James Nichol, 1853.

Hilbish, Florence May Anna. *Charlotte Smith, Poet and Novelist.* PhD diss., Univ. of Pennsylvania, 1941.

Hiller, Mary Ruth. "The Identification of Authors: The Great Victorian Enigma." In *Victorian Periodicals: A Guide to Research,* ed. J. Don Vann and Rosemary T. Van Arsdel, 123–48. New York: MLA, 1978.

Hollander, John. *Vision and Resonance: Two Senses of Poetic Form.* New Haven, CT: Yale Univ. Press, 1975.

Homberger, Eric. "The Uncollected Plath." In *Sylvia Plath: The Critical Heritage,* ed. Linda Wagner-Martin, 187–91. New York: Routledge, 1988.

Hotelling-Zona, Kirstin. *The Feminist Poetics of Self-Restraint: Marianne Moore, Elizabeth Bishop, and May Swenson.* Ann Arbor: Univ. of Michigan Press, 2002.

Howard, June. "What Is Sentimentality?" *American Literary History* 11, no. 1 (Spring 1999): 63–81.

Hughes, Langston. *Selected Poems.* New York: Vintage, 1990.

Hughes, Ted. *Birthday Letters.* New York: Farrar, Straus & Giroux, 1998.

———. *Winter Pollen: Occasional Prose.* Ed. William Scammell. Boston: Faber & Faber, 1994.

Hunt, John Dixon. *The Figure in the Landscape: Poetry, Painting, and Gardening during the Eighteenth Century.* Baltimore, MD: Johns Hopkins Press, 1976.

Hunt Jr., Bishop C. "Wordsworth and Charlotte Smith." *Wordsworth Circle* 1, no. 3 (1970): 85–103.

Hurd, Richard. *Moral and Political Dialogues.* Vol. 1. London, 1765.

Huyssen, Andreas. *After the Great Divide: Modernism, Mass Culture, Postmodernism.* Bloomington: Indiana Univ. Press, 1986.

Jackson Jr., John L. *Real Black: Adventures in Racial Sincerity.* Chicago: Univ. of Chicago Press, 2005.

Jacobs, Edward. "Anonymous Signatures: Circulating Libraries, Conventionality, and the Production of Gothic Romances." *ELH* 62 (1995): 620.

Jacobus, Mary. *Romanticism, Writing, and Sexual Difference: Essays on the Prelude.* Oxford: Clarendon Press, 1989.

Jameson, Fredric. *Postmodernism, or, the Cultural Logic of Late Capitalism.* Durham, NC: Duke Univ. Press, 1991.

Jarvis, Robin. *Romantic Writing and Pedestrian Travel.* MacMillan Press/St. Martin's Press, 1997.

Juhasz, Suzanne. *Naked and Fiery Forms: Modern American Poetry by Women: A New Tradition.* New York: Harper & Row, 1976.

Kalstone, David. *Becoming a Poet: Elizabeth Bishop with Marianne Moore and Robert Lowell.* Ed. Robert Hemenway. New York: Farrar, Straus & Giroux, 1989.

Kaplan, Benjamin. *An Unhurried View of Copyright.* New York: Columbia Univ. Press, 1967.

Katrovas, Richard. "Fame Envy." *Poetry* 34, no. 4 (Winter 2000): 124–30.

Kauffman, Linda, ed. *Gender and Theory: Dialogues on Feminist Criticism.* New York: Basil Blackwell, 1989.

———. "The Long Goodbye: Against Personal Testimony, or an Infant Grifter Grows Up." In Warhol and Price Herndl, *Feminisms,* 1155–71.

Kavanagh, Julia. *Collection of British Authors.* Vol. 622. London, 1863.

King, Ross. "Wordsworth, Panoramas, and the Prospect of London." *Studies in Romanticism* 32 (1993): 57–73.

Kinnahan, Linda. *Lyric Interventions: Feminism, Experimental Poetry, and Contemporary Discourse.* Iowa City: Univ. Of Iowa Press, 2004.

Klancher, Jon. *The Making of English Reading Audiences, 1790–1832*. Madison: Univ. of Wisconsin Press, 1987.

Koch, Kenneth. *On the Great Atlantic Rainway: Selected Poems, 1950–1988*. New York: Alfred A. Knopf, 1994.

Kraft, Elizabeth. "Anna Letitia Barbauld's 'Washing-Day' and the Montgolfier Balloon." *Literature and History* 4, no. 2 (1995): 25–41.

Kramer, Lawrence. "Gender and Sexuality in *The Prelude:* The Question of Book Seven." *ELH* 54 (1987): 619–37.

Kuist, James M., ed. *The Nichols File of The Gentleman's Magazine: Attributions of Authorship and Other Documentation in Editorial Papers at the Folger Library*. Madison: Univ. of Wisconsin Press, 1982.

Kunzel, Regina. "Pulp Fictions and Problem Girls: Reading and Rewriting Single Pregnancy in the Postwar United States." *American Historical Review* 100, no. 5 (1995): 1465–87.

Labbé, Jacqueline M. "Selling One's Sorrows: Charlotte Smith, Mary Robinson, and the Marketing of Poetry." *Wordsworth Circle* 25, no. 2 (Spring 1994): 68–71.

Langan, Celeste. *Romantic Vagrancy: Wordsworth and the Simulation of Freedom*. Cambridge: Cambridge Univ. Press, 1995.

Langbaum, Robert. *The Poetry of Experience: The Dramatic Monologue in Modern Literary Tradition*. New York: W. W. Norton, 1957.

Lant, Kathleen. "The Big Strip Tease: Female Bodies and Male Power in the Poetry of Sylvia Plath." *Contemporary Literature* 34, no. 4 (1993): 620–69.

Larkin, Phillip. *Collected Poems*. Ed. Anthony Thwaite. Boston: Faber & Faber, 1988.

Lehan, Richard. *The City in Literature: An Intellectual and Cultural History*. Berkeley: Univ. of California Press, 1998.

Lehman, David. *The Last Avant Garde: The Making of the New York School of Poets*. New York: Doubleday, 1998.

LeSueur, Joe. *Digressions on Some Poems by Frank O'Hara*. New York: Farrar, Straus & Giroux, 2003.

Levinson, Marjorie. *Wordsworth's Great Period Poems: Four Essays*. Cambridge: Cambridge Univ. Press, 1986.

Lindenberger, Herbert. *On Wordsworth's Prelude*. Princeton, NJ: Princeton Univ. Press, 1963.

Linley, Margaret. "Dying to Be a Poetess: The Conundrum of Christina Rossetti." In *The Culture of Christina Rossetti: Female Poetics and Victorian Contexts*, ed. Mary Arseneau, Antony H. Harrison, and Lorraine Janzen Kooistra, 285–314. Athens: Ohio Univ. Press, 1999.

Lofft, Capel, ed. *Laura, or An Anthology of Sonnets and Elegiac Quatuorzains*. 5 vols. London, 1814.

Lombardi, Marilyn May, ed. *Elizabeth Bishop: The Geography of Gender*. Charlottesville: Univ. Press of Virginia, 1993.

Longenbach, James. *Modern Poetry after Modernism*. Oxford: Oxford Univ. Press, 1997.

Lootens, Tricia. *Lost Saints: Silence, Gender, and Victorian Literary Canonization*. Charlottesville: Univ. Press of Virginia, 1996.

———. "Receiving the Legend, Rethinking the Writer: Letitia Landon and the Poetess Tradition." In *Romanticism and Women Poets: Opening the Doors of Reception*, ed. Harriet Kramer Linkin and Stephen C. Behrendt, 242–59. Lexington: Univ. Press of Kentucky, 1999.

Lowell, Robert. *Collected Poems*. Ed. Frank Bidart and David Gewanter. New York: Farrar, Straus & Giroux, 2003.

———. *Collected Prose*. Ed. Robert Giroux. New York: Farrar, Straus & Giroux, 1987.

———. *Interviews and Memoirs*. Ed. Jeffrey Meyers. Ann Arbor: Univ. of Michigan Press, 1988.

———. *The Letters of Robert Lowell*. Ed. Saskia Hamilton. New York: Farrar, Straus & Giroux, 2005.

Lowney, John. "The Post-Anti-Esthetic Poetics of Frank O'Hara." *Contemporary Literature* 32, no. 2 (1991): 244–64.

Loy, Mina. *The Lost Lunar Baedeker*. Ed. Roger Conover. New York: Farrar, Straus & Giroux, 1996.

Malcolm, Janet. *The Silent Woman: Sylvia Plath and Ted Hughes*. New York: Alfred A. Knopf, 1994.

Mandell, Laura. "'Those Limbs Disjointed of Gigantic Power': Barbauld's Personifications and the MisAttribution of Political Agency." *Studies in Romanticism* 37 (Spring 1998): 27–41.

Mariani, Paul. *Lost Puritan: A Life of Robert Lowell*. New York: W. W. Norton, 1994.

Marshall, P. David. *Celebrity and Power: Fame in Contemporary Culture*. Minneapolis: Univ. of Minnesota Press, 1997.

Martin, John. "Inventing Sincerity, Refashioning Prudence: The Discovery of the Individual in Renaissance Europe." *American Historical Review* (December 1997): 1308–42.

May, Elaine Tyler. *Homeward Bound: American Families in the Cold War Era*. New York: HarperCollins, 1988.

Mays, Kelly. "The Disease of Reading and Victorian Periodicals." In *Literature in the Marketplace: Nineteenth-Century British Publishing and Reading Practices*, ed. John O. Jordan and Robert L. Patten, 165–94. Cambridge: Cambridge Univ. Press, 1995.

McClatchy, J. D. *Anne Sexton: The Artist and Her Critics*. Bloomington: Indiana Univ. Press, 1978.

McGann, Jerome. *The Poetics of Sensibility: A Revolution in Literary Style*. New York: Clarendon Press, 1996.

———. *The Romantic Ideology: A Critical Investigation*. Chicago: Univ. of Chicago Press, 1983.

McGillis, Rod. "That Great Writer in the English Language." *Children's Literature Association Quarterly* 13, no. 4 (1988): 162–64.

Mellor, Anne K. "Making an Exhibition of Her Self: Mary 'Perdita' Robinson and

Nineteenth-Century Scripts of Female Sexuality." *Nineteenth-Century Contexts* 22 (2000): 271–304.

———. *Romanticism and Gender.* New York: Routledge, 1993.

Merrin, Jeredith. *An Enabling Humility: Marianne Moore, Elizabeth Bishop, and the Uses of Tradition.* New Brunswick, NJ: Rutgers Univ. Press, 1990.

Middlebrook, Diane. *Anne Sexton: A Biography.* New York: Vintage Books, 1992.

———. *Her Husband: Hughes and Plath, A Marriage.* New York: Viking Penguin, 2003.

———. "What Was Confessional Poetry?" In *The Columbia History of American Poetry,* ed. Jay Parini and Brett C. Millier, 632–49. New York: Columbia Univ. Press, 1993.

Miles, Barry, ed. *Howl* by Allen Ginsberg. New York: Harper & Row, 1986.

Miller, Nancy. "But Enough about Me, What Do You Think of My Memoir?" *Yale Journal of Criticism* 13, no. 2 (2000): 421–36.

———. *Getting Personal: Feminist Occasions and Other Autobiographical Acts.* New York: Routledge, 1991.

Millier, Brett C. *Elizabeth Bishop: Life and the Memory of It.* Berkeley: Univ. of California Press, 1993.

Milton, John. *L'Allegro and Il Penseroso.* New Rochelle, NY: Elsten Press, 1903.

Moers, Ellen. *The Dandy, Brummell to Beerbohm.* 1960; Lincoln: Univ. of Nebraska Press, 1978.

Moore, Catherine. "'Ladies . . . Taking the Pen in Hand': Mrs. Barbauld's Criticism of Eighteenth-Century Women Novelists." In *Fetter'd or Free? British Women Novelists, 1670–1815,* ed. Mary Anne Schofield and Cecilia Macheski, 383–97. Athens: Ohio Univ. Press, 1986.

Moran, Joe. *Star Authors: Literary Celebrity in America.* London: Pluto Press, 2000.

Morris, Timothy. *Becoming Canonical in American Poetry.* Urbana: Univ. of Illinois Press, 1995.

Mulcaire, Terry. "Publishing Intimacy in Leaves of Grass." *ELH* 60, no. 2 (1993): 471–501.

Mullen, Richard. "Elizabeth Bishop's Surrealist Inheritance." *American Literature* 54, no. 1 (March 1982): 63–80.

Nelson, Deborah. *Pursuing Privacy in Cold War America.* New York: Columbia Univ. Press, 2002.

O'Hara, Frank. *The Collected Poems of Frank O'Hara.* Ed. Donald Allen. Berkeley: Univ. of California Press, 1995.

———. *Lunch Poems.* San Francisco: City Lights Books, 1964.

———. *Poems Retrieved.* Ed. Donald Allen. Bolinas, CA: Grey Fox Press, 1977.

———. *Standing Still and Walking in New York.* Ed. Donald Allen. Bolinas, CA: Grey Fox Press, 1975.

Olson, Gary A., ed. "Jane Tompkins and the Politics of Writing, Scholarship, and Pedagogy." In *Philosophy, Rhetoric, Literary Criticism: (Inter)views,* 161–89. Carbondale: Southern Illinois Univ. Press, 1994.

Orr, Gregory. "The Postconfessional Lyric." In *The Columbia History of American Poetry*, ed. Jay Parini, 650–73. New York: Columbia Univ. Press, 1993.

Ostriker, Alicia Suskin. *Stealing the Language: The Emergence of Women's Poetry in America*. Boston: Beacon Press, 1986.

Ozouf, Mona. "Revolutionary Calendar." In *A Critical Dictionary of the French Revolution*, ed. Francois Furet and Mona Ozouf, trans. Arthur Goldhammer, 538–47. Cambridge, MA: Harvard Univ. Press, 1989.

Parker, Alice C. *The Exploration of the Secret Smile: The Language of Art and of Homosexuality in Frank O'Hara's Poetry*. New York: Peter Lang, 1989.

Pascoe, Judith. *Romantic Theatricality: Gender, Poetry, and Spectatorship*. Ithaca, NY: Cornell Univ. Press, 1997.

Perkins, David. *Wordsworth and the Poetry of Sincerity*. Cambridge, MA: Harvard Univ. Press, 1964.

Perloff, Marjorie. *Frank O'Hara: Poet among Painters*. New York: George Braziller, 1977.

———. *The Poetic Art of Robert Lowell*. Ithaca, NY: Cornell Univ. Press, 1973.

Peyre, Henri. *Literature and Sincerity*. New Haven, CT: Yale Univ. Press, 1963.

Pfister, Joel, and Nancy Schnog, eds. *Inventing the Psychological: Toward a Cultural History of Emotional Life in America*. New Haven, CT: Yale Univ. Press, 1997.

Phillips, Elizabeth. *Emily Dickinson: Personae and Performance*. University Park: Penn State Univ. Press, 1988.

Pike, Burton. *The Image of the City in Modern Literature*. Princeton, NJ: Princeton Univ. Press, 1981.

Pinch, Adela. *Strange Fits of Passion: Epistemologies of Emotion, Hume to Austen*. Stanford: Stanford Univ. Press, 1996.

Plath, Sylvia. *The Collected Poems*. Ed. Ted Hughes. New York: Harper & Row, 1981.

———. *Johnny Panic and the Bible of Dreams: Short Stories, Prose and Diary Excerpts*. New York: Harper & Row, 1979.

———. *The Journals of Sylvia Plath*. Ed. Ted Hughes and Frances McCullough. New York: Dial Press, 1982.

———. *Letters Home: Correspondence, 1950–63*. Ed. Aurelia Schober Plath. Boston: Faber & Faber, 1977.

———. *The Unabridged Journals of Sylvia Plath, 1950–1962*. Ed. Karen V. Kukil. New York: Random House, 2000.

Plumb, J. H. "The New World of Children in Eighteenth-Century England." In *The Birth of a Consumer Society: The Commercialization of Eighteenth-Century England*, ed. Neil McKendrick, John Brewer, and J. H. Plumb, 286–315. Bloomington: Indiana Univ. Press, 1982.

Poe, Edgar Allan. *Selected Writings of Edgar Allan Poe*. Ed. Edward H. Davidson. Boston: Houghton Mifflin, 1956.

Pollak, Vivian R., ed. *A Historical Guide to Emily Dickinson*. New York: Oxford Univ. Press, 2004.

Poovey, Mary. *The Proper Lady and the Woman Writer: Ideology as Style in the Works* of Mary Wollstonecraft, Mary Shelley, and Jane Austen. Chicago: Univ. of Chicago Press, 1984.

Pope, Alexander. The Poems of Alexander Pope. Ed. John Butt. New Haven, CT: Yale Univ. Press, 1963.

Pound, Ezra. Literary Essays. Ed. T. S. Eliot. New York: New Directions, 1935.

Pratt, Kathryn. "Charlotte Smith's Melancholia on the Page and Stage." SEL 41, no. 4 (Summer 2001): 563–81.

Prins, Yopie. Victorian Sappho. Princeton, NJ: Princeton Univ. Press, 1999.

———, and Virginia Jackson. "Lyrical Studies." Victorian Literature and Culture (1999): 521–30.

Puchner, Martin. Stage Fright. Baltimore, MD: Johns Hopkins Univ. Press, 2003.

Quinney, Laura. The Poetics of Disappointment: Wordsworth to Ashbery. Charlottesville: Univ. Press of Virginia, 1999.

Rainey, Lawrence. Institutions of Modernism: Literary Elites and Public Culture. New Haven, CT: Yale Univ. Press, 1998.

Ramazani, Jahan. Poetry of Mourning: The Modern Elegy from Hardy to Heaney. Chicago: Univ. of Chicago Press, 1994.

Ratliff, Ben. "Performance Anxiety: Hiding on Stage." New York Times, sec. E4, January 5, 1999.

Raycroft, Brent. "From Charlotte Smith to Nehemiah Higginbottom: Revising the Genealogy of the Early Romantic Sonnet." European Romantic Review 9, no. 3 (Summer 1998): 363–92.

Read, Herbert. The Cult of Sincerity. New York: Horizon Press, 1968.

Rich, Adrienne. Blood, Bread, and Poetry: Selected Prose, 1979–1985. New York: W. W. Norton, 1986.

Richards, Eliza. Lyric Mediums: Gender and the Poetics of Reception in Poe's Circle. Cambridge: Cambridge Univ. Press, 2004.

Rifkin, Libbie. Career Moves: Olson, Creeley, Zukofsky, Berrigan, and the American Avant-Garde. Madison: Univ. of Wisconsin Press, 2000.

Robbins, Bruce. Secular Vocations: Intellectuals, Professionalism, Culture. New York: Verso, 1993.

Robinson, Daniel. "Reviving the Sonnet: Women Romantic Poets and the Sonnet Claim." European Romantic Review 6, no. 1 (Summer 1995): 98–127.

Robinson, Jeffrey C. The Walk: Notes on a Romantic Image. Norman: Univ. of Oklahoma Press, 1989.

Robinson, Mary. Mary Robinson: Selected Poems. Ed. Judith Pascoe. Peterborough, Ontario: Broadview Press, 2000.

Rodgers, Betsy. Georgian Chronicle: Mrs. Barbauld and Her Family. London: Methuen, 1958.

Roman, Camille. Elizabeth Bishop's World War II–Cold War View. New York: Palgrave, 2001.

Rose, Jacqueline. The Haunting of Sylvia Plath. Cambridge, MA: Harvard Univ. Press, 1992; London: Virago Press, 1991.

————. *On Not Being Able to Sleep: Psychoanalysis and the Modern World.* Princeton, NJ: Princeton Univ. Press, 2003.

Rose, Mark. *Authors and Owners: The Invention of Copyright.* Cambridge, MA: Harvard Univ. Press, 1993.

Rose, R. B. "The Priestley Riots of 1791." *Past and Present* (Nov. 1960): 68–88.

Rosenbaum, Susan. *Confessional Commerce: The Marketing of Sincerity in British Romantic and American Postwar Poetry.* Ann Arbor, MI: University Microfilms, 1997.

————. "Elizabeth Bishop and the Miniature Museum." *Journal of Modern Literature* 28, no. 2 (2005): 61–99.

Rosenthal, M. L. *The New Poets: American and British Poetry since World War II.* New York: Oxford Univ. Press, 1967.

Ross, Marlon. "Breaking the Period: Romanticism, Historical Representation, and the Prospect of Genre." *ANQ* 6 (April/July 1993): 121–31.

————. *The Contours of Masculine Desire: Romanticism and the Rise of Women's Poetry.* New York: Oxford Univ. Press, 1989.

Rothstein, Eric. *Restoration and Eighteenth-Century Poetry, 1660–1780.* Boston: Routledge & Kegan Paul, 1981.

Rousseau, Jean-Jacques. *The Confessions.* Trans. J. M. Cohen. New York: Penguin Books, 1953.

Rzepka, Charles. *Sacramental Commodities: Gift, Text, and the Sublime in De Quincey.* Amherst: Univ. of Massachusetts Press, 1995.

Sacks, Peter. *The English Elegy: Studies in the Genre from Spenser to Yeats.* Baltimore, MD: Johns Hopkins Univ. Press, 1985.

Scandura, Jani. "Deadly Professions: Dracula, Undertakers, and the Embalmed Corpse." *Victorian Studies* 40, no. 1 (Autumn 1996): 1–30.

————, and Michael Thurston, eds. *Modernism, Inc.* New York: New York Univ. Press, 2001.

Schenk, Celeste. "Feminism and Deconstruction: Re-Constructing the Elegy." *Tulsa Studies in Women's Literature* 5 (1986): 13–28.

Schiesari, Juliana. *The Gendering of Melancholia: Feminism, Psychoanalysis, and the Symbolics of Loss in Renaissance Literature.* Ithaca, NY: Cornell Univ. Press, 1992.

Schneider, Alison. "Jane Tompkins's Message to Academe: Nurture the Individual, Not Just the Intellect." *Chronicle of Higher Education,* sec. A8–A10, July 10, 1998.

Schoenfield, Mark. *The Professional Wordsworth: Law, Labor, and the Poet's Contract.* Athens: Univ. of Georgia Press, 1996.

Scholes, Robert. *The Rise and Fall of English.* New Haven, CT: Yale Univ. Press, 1998.

Schor, Esther. *Bearing the Dead: The British Culture of Mourning From the Enlightenment to Victoria.* Princeton, NJ: Princeton Univ. Press, 1994.

Schor, Naomi. *Reading in Detail: Aesthetics and the Feminine.* New York: Routledge, 1987.

Schwartz, Lloyd, and Sybil P. Estess, eds. *Elizabeth Bishop and Her Art.* Ann Arbor: Univ. of Michigan Press, 1983.

Schwarzbach, F. S. "Review Essay: London and Literature in the Eighteenth Century." *Eighteenth-Century Life* 7, no. 3 (1982): 100–112.

Scodel, Joshua. *The English Poetic Epitaph: Commemoration and Conflict from Jonson to Wordsworth.* Ithaca, NY: Cornell Univ. Press, 1991.

Scott, Sir Walter, ed. *Biographical Memoirs of Eminent Novelists, And other Distinguished Persons.* Vol. 2. Edinburgh, 1843.

Sennett, Richard. *The Fall of Public Man.* New York: Knopf, 1977.

Seward, Anna. *Letters of Anna Seward: Written between the Years 1784 and 1807.* Edinburgh, 1811.

Sexton, Anne. *The Complete Poems.* Boston: Houghton Mifflin, 1981.

———. *No Evil Star: Selected Essays, Interviews, and Prose.* Ed. Steven E. Colburn. Ann Arbor: Univ. of Michigan Press, 1985.

Sharp, Tom. "Sincerity and Objectification." *Sagetrieb* 1, no. 2 (Fall 1982): 255–66.

Sharpe, William. *Unreal Cities: Urban Figuration in Wordsworth, Baudelaire, Whitman, Eliot, and Williams.* Baltimore, MD: Johns Hopkins Univ. Press, 1990.

Shattock, Joanne. *Politics and Reviewers: The Edinburgh and the Quarterly in the Early Victorian Age.* Leicester: Leicester Univ. Press, 1989.

Sheavyn, Phoebe. *The Literary Profession in the Elizabethan Age.* Manchester: Manchester Univ. Press, 1909.

Sherman, Brad, and Alain Strowel, eds. *Of Authors and Origins: Essays on Copyright Law.* Oxford: Clarendon Press, 1994.

Shevelow, Kathryn. *Women and Print Culture: The Construction of Femininity in the Early Periodical.* New York: Routledge, 1989.

Siebers, Tobin. *The Ethics of Criticism.* Ithaca, NY: Cornell Univ. Press, 1988.

Simpson, David. "What Bothered Charles Lamb about Poor Susan?" *SEL* 26, no. 4 (1986): 589–612.

———. *Wordsworth and the Figurings of the Real.* London: Macmillan, 1982.

Siskin, Clifford. *The Work of Writing: Literature and Social Change in Britain, 1700–1830.* Baltimore, MD: Johns Hopkins Univ. Press, 1998.

Smith, Barbara Herrnstein. *Poetic Closure: A Study of How Poems End.* Chicago: Univ. of Chicago Press, 1968.

Smith, Charlotte. *The Poems of Charlotte Smith.* Ed. Stuart Curran. New York: Oxford Univ. Press, 1993.

Sokolsky, Anita. "The Resistance to Sentimentality: Yeats, de Man, and the Aesthetic Education." *Yale Journal of Criticism* 1, no. 1 (Fall 1987): 67–86.

Sontag, Kate, and David Graham, eds. *After Confession: Poetry as Autobiography.* St. Paul, MN: Graywolf Press, 2001.

Sontag, Susan. *Against Interpretation.* New York: Dell, 1978.

Spender, Dale, ed. *Living by the Pen: Early British Women Writers.* New York: Teachers College Press, 1992.

St. Cyres, Viscount. "The Sorrows of Mrs. Charlotte Smith." *Cornhill Magazine* 15 (1903): 686–96.

Stafford, Barbara. *Voyage into Substance: Art, Science, Nature, and the Illustrated Travel Account, 1760–1840.* Cambridge, MA: MIT Press, 1984.

Staniszewski, Mary Ann. *The Power of Display: A History of Exhibition Installations at the Museum of Modern Art.* Cambridge, MA: MIT Press, 1998.

Stanton, Judith. "Charlotte Smith's Literary Business: Income, Patronage, and Indigence." In *The Age of Johnson: A Scholarly Annual,* ed. Paul J. Korshin, 375–401. New York: AMS Press, Inc.

Starbuck, George. "The Work! A Conversation with Elizabeth Bishop." In Schwartz and Estess, *Elizabeth Bishop,* 312–33.

Stevenson, Anne. *Bitter Fame: A Life of Sylvia Plath.* London: Viking Press, 1989.

Stewart, Susan. *On Longing: Narratives of the Miniature, the Gigantic, the Souvenir, the Collection.* Durham, NC: Duke Univ. Press, 1993.

Sussman, Elisabeth, ed. *On the Passage of a Few People through a Rather Brief Moment in Time: The Situationist International, 1957–72.* Cambridge, MA: MIT Press, 1989.

Tabor, Stephen, ed. *Sylvia Plath: An Analytical Bibliography.* London: Mansell Publishing, 1987.

Tebbel, John. *Between Covers: The Rise and Transformation of Book Publishing in America.* New York: Oxford Univ. Press, 1987.

———. *A History of Book Publishing in the United States: Volume IV, The Great Change 1940–80.* New York: R. R. Bowker, 1981.

Terada, Rei. *Feeling in Theory: Emotion after the "Death of the Subject."* Cambridge, MA: Harvard Univ. Press, 2001.

Tester, Keith, ed. *The Flaneur.* New York: Routledge, 1994.

Thompson, E. P. *Customs in Common.* New York: New Press, 1993.

———. *The Making of the English Working Class.* New York: Vintage Books, 1966.

Todd, Janet. *Sensibility: An Introduction.* New York: Methuen, 1986.

Travisano, Thomas. *Midcentury Quartet: Bishop, Lowell, Jarrell, Berryman, and the Making of a Postmodern Aesthetic.* Charlottesville: Univ. Press of Virginia, 1999.

Trilling, Lionel. *Sincerity and Authenticity.* New York: Harcourt Brace Jovanovich, 1972.

Turner, Cheryl. *Living by the Pen: Women Writers in the Eighteenth Century.* New York: Routledge, 1992.

Urry, John. *Consuming Places.* London: Routledge, 1995.

U.S. Copyright Office. *Copyright Basics,* http://www.copyright.gov/circs/circ1.html. Accessed February 14, 2006.

Valverde, Mariana. "The Love of Finery: Fashion and the Fallen Woman in Nineteenth Century Social Discourse." *Victorian Studies* 32, no. 2 (1989): 168–88.

Veeser, H. Aram, ed. *Confessions of the Critics.* New York, London: Routledge, 1996.

———, ed. *The New Historicism.* New York: Routledge, 1989.

Vendler, Helen. *Soul Says: On Recent Poetry.* Cambridge, MA: Harvard Univ. Press, 1995.

Voskuil, Lynn. *Acting Naturally: Victorian Theatricality and Authenticity.* Charlottesville: University of Virginia Press, 2004.

Walkowitz, Judith. *City of Dreadful Delight: Narratives of Sexual Danger in Late-Victorian London.* Chicago: Univ. of Chicago Press, 1992.

Wallace, Anne D. "Farming on Foot: Tracking Georgic in Clare and Wordsworth." *Texas Studies in Literature and Language* 34, no. 4 (1992): 509–40.

———. *Walking, Literature, and English Culture: The Origins and Uses of the Peripatetic in the Nineteenth Century.* Oxford: Clarendon Press, 1993.

Wang, Orrin N. C. *Fantastic Modernity: Dialectical Readings in Romanticism and Theory.* Baltimore, MD: Johns Hopkins Press, 1996.

Warhol, Robyn R., and Diane Price Herndl, eds. *Feminisms: An Anthology of Literary Theory and Criticism.* Rutgers: Rutgers Univ. Press, 1997.

Watson, Steven. *Strange Bedfellows: The First American Avant-Garde.* New York: Abbeville Press, 1991.

Wehr, Wesley. "Elizabeth Bishop: Conversations and Class Notes." *Antioch Review* 39, no. 3 (1981): 319–28.

Weisbuch, Robert, and Martin Orzeck. *Dickinson and Audience.* Ann Arbor: Univ. of Michigan Press, 1996.

West, James L. W., III. *American Authors and the Literary Marketplace since 1900.* Philadelphia: Univ. of Pennsylvania Press, 1988.

Wexler, Joyce. *Who Paid for Modernism? Art, Money, and the Fiction of Conrad, Joyce, and Lawrence.* Fayetteville: Univ. of Arkansas Press, 1997.

Whitman, Walt. *Leaves of Grass.* Ed. Michael Moon. New York: Norton, 2002.

Wicke, Jennifer. *Advertising Fictions: Literature, Advertisement, and Social Reading.* New York: Columbia Univ. Press, 1988.

———. "Celebrity Material: Materialist Feminism and the Culture of Celebrity." *South Atlantic Quarterly* 93, no. 4 (1994): 150–58.

———. "I Profess: Another View of Professionalization." *Profession* (2001): 52–57.

———. "Joyce and Consumer Culture." In *James Joyce,* ed. Derek Attridge, 234–53. Cambridge: Cambridge Univ. Press, 2004.

Wikander, Matthew H. *Fangs of Malice: Hypocrisy, Sincerity, and Acting.* Iowa City: Univ. of Iowa Press, 2002.

Williams, Raymond. *The Country and the City.* Oxford: Oxford Univ. Press, 1973.

———. *The Sociology of Culture.* Chicago: Univ. of Chicago Press, 1981.

Williams, Rosalind. *Dream Worlds: Mass Consumption in Late Nineteenth-Century France.* Berkeley and Los Angeles: Univ. of California Press, 1982.

Willison, Ian, Warwick Gould, and Warren Chernaik, eds. *Modernist Writers and the Marketplace.* New York: St. Martin's Press, 1996.

Wilson, Carol Shiner, and Joel Haefner, eds. *Re-Visioning Romanticism: British Women Writers, 1776–1837.* Philadelphia: Univ. of Pennsylvania Press, 1994.

Wilson, Elizabeth. "The Invisible Flaneur." *New Left Review* 191 (1992): 90–110.

Wolff, Janet. *Feminine Sentences: Essays on Women and Culture.* Oxford: Polity Press, 1990.

Wolfson, Susan. *Formal Charges: The Shaping of Poetry in British Romanticism.* Stanford: Stanford Univ. Press, 1997.

Woodmansee, Martha. *The Author, Art, and the Market: Rereading the History of Aesthetics.* New York: Columbia Univ. Press, 1996.

————, and Peter Jaszi, eds. *The Construction of Authorship: Textual Appropriation in Law and Literature.* Durham, NC: Duke Univ. Press, 1994.

Woolf, Virginia. *A Room of One's Own.* 1929; New York: Harcourt Brace, 1981.

Wordsworth, William. *Guide to the Lakes.* Ed. Ernest de Selincourt. Oxford: Oxford Univ. Press, 1991.

————, and S. T. Coleridge. *Lyrical Ballads: The Text of the 1798 Edition with the Additional 1800 Poems and the Prefaces.* Ed. R. L. Brett and A. R. Jones. New York: Routledge, 1991.

————. *Poetical Works.* Ed. Thomas Hutchinson and Ernest de Selincourt. Oxford: Oxford Univ. Press, 1989.

————. *The Prelude 1799, 1805, 1850.* Ed. Jonathan Wordsworth, M. H. Abrams, and Stephen Gill. New York: W. W. Norton, 1979.

————. *Selected Prose.* Ed. John O. Hayden. New York: Penguin Books, 1988.

Yingling, Tom. "Homosexuality and Utopian Discourse in American Poetry." In *Breaking Bounds: Whitman and American Cultural Studies,* ed. Betsy Erkkila and Jay Grossman, 135–46. New York: Oxford Univ. Press, 1996.

Zeiger, Melissa F. *Beyond Consolation: Death, Sexuality, and the Changing Shapes of Elegy.* Ithaca, NY: Cornell Univ. Press, 1997.

Zimmerman, Sarah. "Charlotte Smith's Letters and the Practice of Self-Presentation." *Princeton University Library Chronicle* (53) 1991: 50–77.

————. *Romanticism, Lyricism, and History.* Albany: SUNY Press, 1999.

Index